THE LAWIERS LOGIKE, exemplifying the *præcepts of Logike by* the practise of the common Lawe,

by

Abraham Fraunce.

With a New Introduction and Table of Contents

by

Steve Sheppard

Enfield Distinguished Professor of Law,
University of Arkansas School of Law

THE LAWBOOK EXCHANGE, LTD.
Clark, New Jersey

ISBN 978-1-61619-249-5

Lawbook Exchange edition 2013

The quality of this reprint is equivalent to the quality of the original work.
Folio 21 is misnumbered as 17.
Folio 23 is misnumbered as 19.
The Nineteenth Chapter (Book One) is miswritten as The Eighteenth Chapter (65a)

THE LAWBOOK EXCHANGE, LTD.
33 Terminal Avenue
Clark, New Jersey 07066-1321

Please see our website for a selection of our other publications and fine facsimile reprints of classic works of legal history:
www.lawbookexchange.com

Library of Congress Cataloging-in-Publication Data

Fraunce, Abraham, active 1587-1633, author.
The lawiers logike, exemplifying the praecepts of logike by the practice of the common lawe / by Abraham Fraunce ; with a new introduction by Steve Sheppard, Enfield Distinguished Professor of Law, University of Arkansas School of Law. -- Lawbook Exchange edition
pages cm
Includes bibliographical references.
ISBN 978-1-61619-249-5 (hardcover : alk. paper) -- ISBN 1-61619-249-6 (hardcover : alk. paper)
1. Common law--Early works to 1800. 2. Logic--Early works to 1800. I. Sheppard, Steve, 1963- author. Abraham Fraunce : legal analysis and legal scholarship. II. Title. III. Title: Lawyer's logic.
K588.F73 2013
160.24'34--dc23 2013040758

Printed in the United States of America on acid-free paper

Introduction

Abraham Fraunce, Legal Analysis, and Legal Scholarship

Steve Sheppard[1]

Four centuries after Abraham Fraunce published *The Lawiers Logike* his work informs three fields of American law — the study of legal analysis and argument, the intersection of law with other disciplines, and the moral justification of law itself. As a matter of legal history, the work is now largely unknown, but its influence in the early modern law may have been greater than it might seem. As a forerunner of later arguments about the structure and meaning of law, its significance has yet to be fully considered.

Lawiers Logike was a sustained application to the law and to legal arguments of what was then the state of the art of logical forms. It was the first printed work in English that deliberately integrated the formal tools of logical analysis into legal argument. Fraunce saw this endeavor as controversial, or at least contrary to the expectations of lawyers of his time. He believed lawyers had failed to alter the disorganized and unmethodical common law owing to prejudices against academic scholars. At length he railed against the pettyfogging "tenurist," who argued that law and logic could never stand together and who preferred the circuitous arguments of tradition to the clearer arguments of orderly arranged

---

[1] Enfield Distinguished Professor of Law, University of Arkansas School of Law. I offer many thanks to Sir John Baker for his thoughts on several matters in this essay. Also, Katherine Ferran deserves praise for her valuable assistance in locating materials.

invention leading to judgment.[2] Thus, in this book Fraunce offers a technique of identifying such inventions, ordering them, and critiquing them to avoid the risk of fallacy when seeking judgment.

In this conflict between parochial tradition and more powerful analytic tools, the book is rather like the arguments that have recurrently attended interdisciplinary legal studies in the United States. American law professors of the twentieth century argued at length over the meetness and utility of the "Law And" movement, by which the law, its institutions and agents, and its influence in society are analyzed and critiqued from the perspective of other academic disciplines. Thus, obviously related fields such as economics and the social sciences, and less clearly applicable perspectives such as biology, may be used either analytically or metaphorically to describe and criticize the operation of laws.[3]

Fraunce and the Sidneys

Abraham Fraunce was born in Shrewsbury, in Shropshire, England, probably in 1559. From an early age and throughout his life, Fraunce's fortunes were tied to those of the great families of the age.

Shrewsbury — and indeed the county of Shropshire, the English borderlands with Wales, and most of Wales itself — was at that time greatly under the influence of Sir Henry Sidney. The interrelated Sidneys, Dudleys, and Herberts (or Pembrokes) formed one of the great dynasties of sixteenth century Britain, and they not only influenced Fraunce's life but served as a polestar near which later scholars have recurrently found the orbiting Fraunce. Thus at least some familiarity with these rather illustrious kin helps to understand Fraunce and his role in English letters.

---

[2] See Fraunce's Introduction, To the Learned Lawyers of England, below.

[3] On the "Law and" movement generally, see Edward L. Rubin, *Law And and the Methodology of Law,* 1997 Wis. L. Rev. 521 (1997), in Steve Sheppard, *The History of Legal Education in the United States: Commentaries and Primary Sources (*Lawbook Exchange, 2005).

In 1559, Sir Henry Sidney had only by five years succeeded his father, Sir William Sidney, a soldier and powerful courtier in the reign of Henry VIII who would tutor Prince Edward (later Edward VI). Sir Henry was appointed in 1560 to be Lord President of the Council of the Marches, the law court with jurisdiction over Wales and most of the western counties of England. The court's seat was Ludlow Castle, about twenty-five miles from Shrewsbury, and Henry settled there, though he was often in London or Ireland, until his death (in 1586). Sir Henry married Mary Dudley, the daughter of the Duke of Northumberland, lady-in-waiting to Elizabeth the queen, and sister of Elizabeth's great courtier, Sir Robert Dudley. Henry and Mary had seven children, of whom two matter here: Philip and Mary.

Philip Sidney was born at the Sidney ancestal home, Pennshurst Place, in Kent, in 1554. As a child, his face was scarred for life by the same smallpox that afflicted his mother and the Queen, whom she had nursed. Philip attended Shewsbury School, entering in October 1564 and staying for several years, before brief stays at Eton; Christ Church, Oxford; and perhaps Cambridge (though he seems not to have matriculated there). He was enrolled as a student in Gray's Inn, aged twelve, though he was not called to the bar. Rather than staying for degrees or credentials, he left for Europe, at first on a visit to the diplomatic mission to France — which found him in Paris during the Bartholomew's Day Massacre — and then on a Grand Tour. Over the next decade, he was at times a courtier, a diplomat, and a soldier, dying in the war against Spain in the Netherlands in 1586, at the age of thirty-one.

Throughout his life, Sidney was a patron of writers and artists. An accomplished poet in his own right, he sponsored the writings of his friend Edmund Spenser, among others. His own works were disseminated first in manuscript but printed posthumously, some under the guidance of his childhood friend Fulke Greville and some under that of his sister Mary. In the Elizabethan court, he was counted among the greatest of noble humanists, a dashing image heightened by his tragic death.

Mary Sidney was born in 1561 and received an education like Philip's — a Protestant, humanist exposure, rich in languages and music. Like her mother, she was a lady in Elizabeth's court, but in 1577 she was married at the age of fifteen to the older and much wealthier Henry Herbert, second Earl of Pembroke, thus becoming Mary, Countess of Pembroke. It was Henry's third marriage, having been earlier married to Lady Catherine Grey (sister of Lady Jane Gray) and then to Elizabeth's close friend Lady Catherine Talbot, who died. Henry was close to the Sidneys personally and politically, and the year after Sir Henry Sidney died, Henry, Earl of Pembroke, succeeded him as Lord President of the Council of Marches, a post he held until his death in 1601.

Mary had considerable influence as Countess of Pembroke. She managed many of the Pembroke estates, spending much of her time at Wilton House in Salisbury and at Barnards Castle in London, though she also traveled to her estate Ivychurch, in Kent, among others. She controlled immense wealth and property, which she managed well.

Mary's influence was directed much less to politics and much more to letters. As an author and patron, her interest in music, science, and the arts was a considerable force in the Elizabethan Age. Her own translations of Petrarch and of current French works of drama and philosophy were well received. She published a play based on Roman history, and wrote in blank verse, being one of the first English writers to do either (quite likely influencing Shakespeare's works). Her translations of psalms into English were praised by John Donne. But her greater influence came through her informed and apparently enthusiastic encouragement of a wide circle of poets, musicians, scientists, and authors, including Edmund Spenser, William Shakespeare, Ben Jonson, Michael Drayton, and others. Christopher Marlowe sought her attentions (though it is unclear he received them.) She supported Walter Raleigh's half-brother, Adrian Gilbert, who ran her chemistry laboratory and gardens at Wilton House. She and her husband were patrons of the Earl of Pembroke's Men, a company of players affiliated with William Shakespeare; famously, Shakespeare dedicated his first folio to William and Philip, two of the Pembroke sons. She died in 1621.

Constructing the Life of Abraham Fraunce

Scholars have written several brief histories of Fraunce's life, and his writings have received intermittent attention, mainly by scholars of sixteenth century letters.[4] Yet a curious view of him arises from this effort, perhaps resulting from the frustratingly spotty survival of older English records and the more careful collection of records that affect the famous and the noble. There are just enough threads from which a whole cloth cannot be well woven.

Still, much can be pieced together. The Fraunce family, sometimes spelled "France" or "ffraunce," was a family of artisans in western England, near the Welsh border. In the last century, no one has found an extant record of Abraham's birth. His father may have been Thomas Fraunce, a respected Shrewsbury glover who was the Churchwarden of the Abbey Church of the Holy Cross in 1550 and 1553.[5] Though he is often noted as born in 1559, this is based solely on a presumed commencement of his schooling, though the exact date on which he started is not known. He might have been born earlier than supposed.

In all events, Abraham certainly attended Shrewsbury School, then the largest school in the kingdom and, thanks to its location near Ludlow, the school of Philip Sidney. Fraunce's name is on the register as of January 1571,[6] though he likely entered the school earlier, perhaps as early as 1567. He was the child of a burgess (or, freeman) of the town, whose sons were charged four pence for

---

[4] The most useful remains G.C. Moore Smith, Introduction, in Abraham Fraunce, *Victoria: A Latin Comedy Edited from the Pennshurst Manuscript* (A. Uystpruyst, 1906). William Barker's entry in the *Oxford Dictionary of National Biography* (2004) is the more recent and nicely explains the literature relating to Fraunce's death.

[5] This is a quite reasonable conjecture by G.C. Moore Smith, following the records of the *Transactions of the Shropshire Archeological Society,* which, he notes, record several local branches of the Fraunce family in the sixteenth century. See G.C. Moore Smith, Introduction, in Fraunce, *Victoria, op, cit.* Despite digital archives, the records of births and baptisms in Shropshire available today bear little more information than Smith transcribed a century ago.

[6] Abraham Fraunce and Thomas Fraunce were both listed as students on January 11, 1571, each being battelled four pence. *Shrewsbury School Registrum Scholarium 1562–1635* 36 (E. Calvert, ed.) (1902), reprinted in G.C. Moore Smith, Introduction, in Fraunce, *Victoria, op, cit.*, at xv.

tuition.[7] The curriculum included recitation of poetry and the performance of plays, among the study of classics and the courses more common among grammar schools of the age.

The Shrewsbury headmaster, Thomas Ashton, had been a student of St. John's College, Cambridge, and then a fellow there.[8] It is likely that Ashland's influence led to Fraunce's matriculating at St. John's in 1575, first as a pensioner and then as a Lady Margaret scholar.[9] Yet these funds were slight, and Fraunce was later said to have been also supported by funds from Philip Sidney (or through him from his father, Sir Henry).[10]

Writers have long supposed Fraunce met and earned the support of Sidney as a fellow Shrewsbury student. But it is much more likely that Ashton, or his successor as headmaster Thomas Lawrence, or another party arranged such support, even had it come from the Sidney purse. There are many reasons to doubt Philip's direct subsidy of Fraunce as a student. Sidney was probably four or five years older than Fraunce. Sidney might have met him in school but would have been quite apart in study if he had. (Though they could have met in dramatic roles, this, too, is unlikely). Fraunce was not sent to Christ Church, Oxford, the college selected for Sidney, but to St. John's, Cambridge, the college of Ashton, with close links to the school. In all events, the

---

[7] Id.

[8] Ashton is sometimes said to have been a fellow of Trinity. There are two Cantabrian Ashtons to choose from, but it seems likely that Smith was right to argue for the Shrewsbury Ashston being from St. John's. Martin Speight's evidence is quite strong in the entry for Ashton in the *Oxford Dictionary of National Biography* (Oxford, 2004).

[9] Ashton endowed two fellowships at St. John's and increased the links between the Shrewsbury School and the college. Though Ashton left Shrewsbury to enter the employ of Walter Deveroux, later Earl of Essex, he continued to influence school affairs until his death in 1578. See James. B. Oldham, *Headmasters of Shrewsbury School, 1552–1908* (Wildey, 1937).

[10] The only evidence of financial support of Fraunce by Philip Sidney comes from Sidney's brother-in-law, Henry Lord Pembroke, in a much later letter to Burghley, in 1590, when Pembroke must have been relating a story told him by Mary his wife about Fraunce: "he was bred up by my brother Sr Phillip Sidney longe in Cambridge ..." Letter of Pembroke to Burghley, Aug. 25, 1590, Harleian Manuscripts 6995, at folio 35. Quoted in G.C. Moore Smith, Introduction, in Fraunce, *Victoria, op, cit.*, at xxxiv.

potential is not overwhelming for the noble young Sidney to have grown so fond of the burgess's son as to pay for his expenses as a youthful patron.[11] Most tellingly, as noted below, Fraunce dates his meeting with Sidney to 1580, long after they each had left Shrewsbury.

In any event, by 1575 Fraunce was surely in St. John's College, where his preparation in Shrewsbury, which emphasized drama, stood him in good stead. In 1578 and 1579 Fraunce acted in several Cambridge plays, including *Hymenaeus*, which he might have written. Fraunce was made B.A. in 1580 and elected a fellow of the college.

During his years at St. John's, Fraunce not only practiced drama and poetry but also engaged in the arguments over philosophy and rhetoric then fueled by the French thinkers Peter Ramus and Omar Talon. Cambridge, particularly St. John's College, was then the English center of Ramist debate, about the very nature of argument and language.[12]

Around the time of his fellowship, Fraunce became friends with Philip Sidney. Either in discussion or correspondence, Fraunce discussed his interest in logic and rhetoric, informed by the Ramist arguments of St. John's and apparently interesting Sidney, who encouraged Fraunce to further develop this interest.

In the opening paragraph to his introduction to this book, Fraunce notes he had been working on it for seven years (thus dating its inception to 1580 or 1581). He credits his meeting and his discourse with Sidney for much of its inspiration and at least some of its development:

---

[11] Smith quotes an earlier "mere assertion" in the *Dictionary of National Biography* and then relies on the letter of Henry, Earl of Pembroke, quoted above. But to make this work, Smith has Fraunce entering the school before 1568, when Philip Sidney left it, though we've yet no evidence of Fraunce being there before January 1571. To do so, Fraunce would either have to have been nine when he entered or born earlier than is usually thought.

[12] See Steven J. Reid, *Andrew Melville and Scottish Ramism: A Re-Interpretation*, In *Ramus, Pedagogy, and the Liberal Arts: Ramism in Britain and the Wider World* (Steven J. Reid, Emma Annette Wilson, eds.) (Ashgate, 1988).

> I first began, (when I first came in presence of that right noble and most renowned knight sir Philip Sidney) with a general discourse concerning the right use of Logic, and a contracted comparison between this of Ramus and that of Aristotle. These small and trifling beginnings drew both him to a greater liking of, and my self to a further travailing in, the easy explications of Ramus, his Logic.[13]

However Fraunce's communications proceeded with Sidney and his friends, it resulted in at least three manuscripts, apparently initiated while at college:

– The *Shepheardes Logike*, an early draft of a portion of the later *The Lawiers Logike*, was dedicated to the poet Edward Dyer and (rather famously for later scholars) included quotations from the yet unpublished *Shepheardes Calender* of Edmund Spenser.

– The *Arcadian Rhetorike,* based on Talon's method, which he would not publish until 1588 and then dedicate to Mary, Countess of Pembroke. Again relying on manuscript works of Spenser, this quoted from *Faerie Queene*, Book 2, acknowledging Spenser as the quotations' author, at a time Spenser was still not popularly identified with his writings.[14]

– *Victoria*, a comedy in Latin, based on Luigi Pasqualigo's *Il Fedele* (1576).[15] Fraunce dedicated *Victoria* to Philip Sidney in a short but elaborate Latin inscription that suggests friendly admiration more than distant appeal.

---

[13] Abraham Fraunce, Introduction, in *The Lawiers Logike*, f.1. (1588), below.
[14] See Katherine Koller, *Abraham Fraunce and Edmund Spenser*, 7 ELH 108 (1940).
[15] This remained in manuscript until the twentieth century, when G.C. Moore Smith edited and published it. See Fraunce, *Victoria, op, cit.*

In 1583, Fraunce took his M.A., left Cambridge, and began the study of law, enrolling on June 5, 1583, at Gray's Inn.[16] Five years later, the Pension Book of Gray's Inn records Abraham Fraunce being called to the bar, on February 8, 1588, with six other admittees. Fourteen senior members of the Inn were recorded present at that induction, including Christopher Yelverton and Francis Bacon.[17]

His writings during his years as a law student indicate his continuing interest in letters, as well as his involvement with the Sidneys. In 1587, he published his translation of the English poet Thomas Watson's *Amyntas* (1585), which Fraunce dedicated to Mary, Countess of Pembroke, in a symbolic sharing of her grief at the death of her brother, Philip, who had recently died.[18] In 1588, he published his book on insignia,[19] then dedicated to Robert Sidney, Philip's younger brother, who had been with him at his death in the Netherlands (and who would soon be created the new Earl of Leicester). In the same year, he published *The Lawiers Logike, Exemplifying the Praecepts of Logike by the Practise of the Common Lawe*, which had two printings in the same year.[20] The book was dedicated to Philip Sidney's brother-in-law, Henry, Earl of Pembroke, who had by then become President of the Court of the Marches of Wales, the court before which the young lawyer had already or would soon appear. As noted, the *Logike* was written

---

[16] *Gray's Inn Admission Register: 1521–1887* 63 (folio 37) (Joseph Foster, ed) (Hansard, 1889).

[17] *Pension Book of Gray's Inn (Records of the Honorable Society) 1569–1669* (8 Feb. 1588, 30 Eliz.) 78 (Reginald J. Fletcher, ed.) (Chiswick Press, 1901).

[18] *The Lamentations of Amuntas for the Death of Phillis; Paraphrastically Translated out of Latine into English Hexameteres* (1587). Fraunce failed to acknowledge in that edition the original authorship of Watson, though Fraunce later did so. Watson did not seem to have long begrudged him a greater audience for the translation than the original received.

[19] Abraham Fraunce, *Insignia Armorum, Emblematum, Hieroglyphonicorum et Symbolorum* (1588). The book is an extended discussion in Ramist form of what we might now think of as semiotics. It is quite likely that Fraunce wrote the book earlier, including Sir Philip's device and motto and dedications that make more sense if Philip were alive when they were written. Smith notes that the dedication to Robert did not notice his knighthood, which also suggests it was written prior to Philip's death, as both occurred in 1586.

[20] The editions are S.T.C. 11344 and 11345.

years before, and the manuscripts suggest that it was written as a gift to Philip Sidney in 1582 or, perhaps, 1585.[21]

Fraunce thus appears to have returned home to practice law, which in Shropshire was primarily before the Court of the Marches (or, the Council of the Marches).[22] The court's seat was at Ludlow, but few detailed records of the court from that period seem to have survived. Yet he did continue his poetry, writing three long pastorals in dedication to Mary Countess of Pembroke, published in 1591 and 1592.[23]

This raft of publication following the end of Fraunce's law studies might suggest that he relied more on letters than on law practice for income, and indeed he seems to have been the butt of at least one joke among his lettered friends on this account. In *Colin Clouts Come Home Again* (1595), Edmund Spenser alludes to Fraunce, calling him after his translation but noting his meager earnings at the bar:

---

[21] Smith describes the several Latin and English mss at xxvi–xxvii. They are British Library Additional MSS. 34, 361 and Bodleian MS Rawlinson MSS D. 345 I. *The Shephearde's Logike* is one of three logic treatises in Fraunce's hand, all of which are in some way incorporated into this book.

[22] See Sir Edward Coke, Fourth Institute of the Laws of England 242 (1644).

[23] All three books celebrate Mary, Countess of Pembroke. The first was *The Countesse of Pembrokes Yvychurch, Conteining the Affectionate Life, and Unfortunate Death of Phillis and Amyntas: That in a Pastorall; this in a Funerall: Both in English Hexameters* (1591), a volume based in part on a new editing of Fraunce's earlier *Amintas*, now with an acknowledgement to Watson but include the Countess Mary as a character; the volume also includes Fraunce's translation of Virgil's *The Lamentation of Corydon for the Love of Alexis*, as well as Fraunce's translation of *Heliodorus his Auethopicall History.* Next was *The Countesse of Pembrokes Emanuel. Conteining the Natiuity, Passion, Buriall and Resurrection of Christ: Togeather with Certaine Psalmes of Dauid: All in English Hexameters* (1591). The last is a reconstruction of Ovid's Metamorphoses, *The Third Part of the Countesse of Pembrokes Yvychurch. Entituled, Amintas Dale, Wherein Are the Most Conceited Tales of the Pagan Gods in English Hexameters, Together with Their Auncient Descriptions and Philosophicall Explications (*1592).

The business of hexametrical verse was later condemned but still honored by poets in Fraunce's time and later. Alexander Pope commended him. See Letter of Alexander Pope to Joseph Spence, November 1730, in Joseph Spence, 1 *Anecdotes* 181 (Osborn, ed.) (1966).

And there is Corydon, though meanly waged
Yet ablest wit of most I know this day.[24]

Still, there must have been some law. The Court of the Marches indirectly provides our best record of Fraunce's short life as a lawyer, though that record is scant. In August 1590, its president, Henry Herbert, Earl of Pembroke, wrote Queen Elizabeth's great councilor, William Cecil, Lord Burghley, noting that the post of Queen's Solicitor in the court had been vacant since the death of John Amyas and seeking appointment of Fraunce to the post.[25]

Herbert wrote,

> Since the death of Mr. Amias, her Majestie's Solicitor at the Counsel in the Marches, no man is appointed to that service. There is in that Court one Abraham ffraunce, a pleader at the bar: he was bred up by my brother Sir Philip Sidney long in Cambridge: continued afterwards in Grays Inn until he was called to the bar. I conceave him in each respect a man sufficient for that service: if it will therefore please your Lordship at my hearty request to commend him to her Majestie, I shall think myself much pleasured herein."[26]

Burghley apparently had not acted a month later when Herbert wrote again, repeating that he doubted not that Fraunce would be sufficient for the service.

Herbert waited until April to learn that Burghley had presented the Queen with forms for the appointment of Fraunce to the

---

[24] The identification of Fraunce with Corydon in this later work of Spenser's is argued at length by Edmond Malone. See Edmond Malone, in 2 *Plays and Poems of William Shakespeare* 239–245 (1821). The poem was likely written in 1591; it was dedicated on December 27, to Sir Walter Raleigh. See Edmund Spenser, *The Yale Edition of the Shorter Poems of Edmund Spenser* 517 (William Oram, ed.) (Yale, 1989).

[25] Amyas presented a bleak description of his office to the Council via Walsingham in August 1586. See 1 Calendar of State Papers, Domestic, Eliz. 1 346 (HMSO 1865).

[26] Letter of Pembroke to Burghley, Aug. 25, 1590, Harleian Manuscripts 6995, at folio 35. Quoted in G.C. Moore Smith, Introduction, in Fraunce, *Victoria, op. cit.*, at xxxiv. (Spelling here modernized and abbreviations and contractions enlarged).

office.[27] Indeed Burghley had chosen the moment to give her two forms of the letters patent, one to hold the office for a term of life and to have deputies, the other to hold the office only for a period of good behavior (*quam diu se bene gesserit*) and to have no deputies. She naturally chose the form that more limited the office, as Burghley surely intended.[28] Yet his note does not indicate her endorsement of the patent, and there is no record of it. Rather, the next appointment to the post was of a different lawyer, Thomas Medlycote, in October 1591. There is no known record of why Fraunce's appointment was not completed.

Fraunce was thought by Smith and others to have entered the service of the Earl of Bridgewater and to live another four decades.[29] This mistake was apparently the result of a confusion of Abraham Fraunce with the playwright Abraham Darcie, and it was only dispelled in the 1970's.[30]

It is not clear from any known direct surviving evidence, precisely when Fraunce died. The only evidence of Fraunce living past 1591 is the entry of his last book into the Register of the Company of Stationers, *The Third Part of the Counteess of Pembrokes Yvychurch* being listed in 1592. However, the functioning of the licenses and printing was less a matter of the author and much more a matter for the printer. Indeed, the delay between the listing of the first and second parts in 1591 and the listing of the third in 1592 might have been the result of presses and

---

[27] Letter of Pembroke to Burghley, Sept. 11, 1590, Lansdowne Manuscripts 63, at folio 77. Quoted in G.C. Moore Smith, Introduction, in Fraunce, *Victoria, op, cit.*, at xxxiv.

[28] Letter of Burghley to Pembroke, April 28, 1591, Harleian Manuscripts 6995, at folio 51. Quoted in G.C. Moore Smith, Introduction, in Fraunce, *Victoria, op, cit.*, at xxxiv.

[29] S.L. Lee's entry in the *Dictionary of National Biography* Fraunce entry listed Fraunce's death as in 1633. See 20 Dictionary of National Biography 229 (1889).

[30] V. Skrekowicz, Abraham Fraunce and Abraham Darcie, 31 The Library, Fifth Series 239 (1976). Skrekowicz concludes that Fraunce likely died in 1592, though he mentions no evidence of a record or action by which to pick this year. Skrekowicz attributed the long-standing mistake in Fraunce's death to an error by the antiquarian Joseph Hunter, whose notes to Darcie's Chorus Vatum were cited in the *DNB* entry by S.L. Lee.

type of Thomas Orwin, Fraunce's printer, being seized in 1591 and not returned until later that year.[31]

This lack of evidence for the date of Fraunce's death has provoked some wonderfully inventive speculation regarding his post-mortem years and those preceding his demise. Noted above is the long-held belief that he decamped from the orbit of Countess of Pembroke to serve her cousin, Bridgewater. More convoluted is the tale of a critic of English literature who speculates that Fraunce lost his position owing to a fall from favor with the Countess of Pembroke, by allowing an unscrupulous middleman to see the manuscript of Philip Sidney's *Astrophil and Stella* and thus to publish it without authorization.[32]

Yet a far simpler answer is that Fraunce died. It seems likely to have been in 1591, or in 1592 following an illness. Thus he did not take up the post that Pembroke sought and Burghley advanced, and the patent, if it had been issued would have been destroyed. It need not have been after his book was struck: news of the death of a lawyer in the Welsh borders might not have reached a London printer until after one of his books was printed and sold (particularly a printer distracted by other affairs). Nor would Fraunce's death then have been of such notice as to require public comment in London or more record in Shrewsbury than the many that have not survived of other figures.[33] The most compelling evidence of his death is, though, that Fraunce disappeared in 1591: there was but one more publication (soon thereafter), and there were no more mentions of him by the Pembrokes or, practically anyone else, with one exception.

---

[31] See Mr. C.R. Rivington's Paper on the Records of the Stationer's Company, 1881–1893, in 5 *A Transcript of the Registers Stationers' Company* li (Edward Arber, ed.) (1894). There are other reasons for curiosity, as well as delay in this printing. The seller for whom Orwin printed the *Third Part of Yvychurch* was not William Ponsonby, as had been the case for the earlier two parts (1591). Rather the seller was now Thomas Woodcocke.

[32] See Roger Kuin, *Chamber Music Elizabethan Sonnet-Sequences and the Pleasure of Criticism* 174–192 (Toronto 1998).

[33] Though Shropshire did not have a significant outbreak of plague in 1590, it had suffered a similar contagion in 1584. J. F. D. Shrewsbury, *A History of Bubonic Plague in the British Isles* 236 (Cambridge University Press, 1970). Disease and sudden death remained a common occurrence.

Fraunce's death apparently was marked by the poet Thomas Lodge, who in 1593 dedicated a work to Mary Sidney, Countess of Shrewsbury, that alluded to Fraunce and the poet Thomas Watson, the author in Latin of the *Amintas* Fraunce had translated. In the poetic metaphor of mourning for them, "in their Swan-like songs *Amintas* wept."[34]

Before ending this discussion of Fraunce's life and the vast portions of it draped still from later view, we might consider his possible relationship with another contemporary whom later conjecture has included among his companions, the playwright William Shakespeare. The contacts between Fraunce and Pembroke and between Shakespeare and Pembroke, as well as those between Fraunce and Mary Sidney and Shakespeare and Mary Sidney give rise to a tantalizing opportunity for Fraunce and Shakespeare to have known one another, perhaps introduced by the Countess herself.[35] Fraunce, after all, had been trained in acting as a child and remained, as all men of letters, interested in drama. Such a meeting, if it occurred, might have been during Shakespeare's vaunted lost years from 1585 to 1592, which might well have been spent in the west country, perhaps in Pembroke's circle just when Pembroke himself was taking an interest in Fraunce. There seems to be no evidence of such a meeting.[36] Perhaps, and more likely, Shakespeare learned of Fraunce's *Lawiers Logike* from other members of the Sidney circle. Again, there is no direct evidence, though booksellers have long believed there was a connection,

---

[34] Thomas Lodge, *Phillis*, in 2 *The Complete Works of Thomas Lodge 5* (Edmund W. Grosse, ed.) (Russell & Russell, 1963). The link of this poem to Fraunce was asserted in Michael G. Brennan, The Date of the Death of Abraham Fraunce, 5 The Library, Sixth Series 391 (1983).

[35] These second-degree relationships explain why Edward Malone developed such an extensive biography of Fraunce in his Georgian study of Shakespeare: he was explaining references that might relate to Shakespeare and his contemporaries in Sidney's Colin Clout, in which Corydon, as noted is like Fraunce. Edward Malone, *The Life of William Shakespeare*, in 2 *The Plays and Poems of William Shakespeare* 240 (1821). Yet even the thorough Malone described no direct connection between the bard and the lawyer.

[36] Odds are, though, that the surest way to find such evidence is to print a statement it does not exist. If you know of any, please contact me at sheppard@stmarytx.edu.

perhaps even that Shakespeare learned his law from Fraunce's book.[37] Perhaps.

Fraunce's Logic

Sixteenth-century England witnessed significant arguments over the nature of truth and authority, bound as those concepts are with the problems of religion and knowledge at the heart of the Reformation. Though not as well remembered now as the arguments over the nature and language of the Bible, one arena of Reformation contests was the very nature of knowledge itself. This argument took many forms, often in physical experimentation in what would be thought later as the natural sciences. But as common were arguments over the use and significance of logic and rhetoric, tools for the evaluation and for the expression of truth.

The scholastic model of the 1570s was based on later-discovered classical sources, especially the works of Aristotle, Cicero, and Quintilian, as applied and criticized by scholars since the middle ages. The dominant text of this approach in England, indeed the first book in English to explore these ideas at length, was Thomas Wilson's *Rule of Reason*, published in 1551,[38] which was based largely on Aristotle's writings. Wilson followed the usual distinction between rhetoric, which was really a matter of style in communication, from logic, which was the basis for determining truth.

Logic consisted of invention, or the methods for stating an argument, and judgment, or the methods of resolving an argument. Wilson wrote his book in two major sections, the first being on judgment, the second on invention. Judgment and invention both incorporated statements that could satisfy the Aristotelian tests of scientific reliability: statements based on definition, genus, species,

---

[37] See W. Harold Maxwell & Leslie F. Maxwell, compilers, 1 *Sweet and Maxwell's Legal Bibliography of the British Commonwealth of Nations*, 238 (1955–1957) (Of *Lawiers Logike*, "From this work Shakespeare is supposed to have acquired some of his legal knowledge.").

[38] Thomas Wilson, *The Rule of Reason: Conteyning the Arte of of Logique, Set Forth in Englishe* (Richard Grafton, 1551).

property, accident, or (and this was a medieval addition based on definition) differences were scientifically true. These informed ten predic-aments, or categories of proposition, that were based in part on Aristotle's categories: substance, quantity, quality, relation, manner of doing, suffering, when, where, location, and appearance. Each of these predicaments imply certain maxims, or truisms, that would test the logical sufficiency of a statement or designate some essential conditions or corollaries. The remainder of judgment consisted of definition (and division), proposition, and argument. Turning then to invention, he first considered the problem known since Aristotle, as the place, which is in fact the foundation or grounding of an argument. Wilson listed two groups of places, one group of inward (or intrinsic) arguments and one outward (or extrinsic) places. An argument can be broken into constituent statements and compared by considering the places that affected the argument, and if they agreed, the argument was sound.[39]

Though Wilson's synthesis of scholastic learning was the leading edge in English thought in 1551, by Fraunce's day, three decades later at Cambridge, Wilson's model was under pressure from reforms argued by two Frenchmen: Peter Ramus and Omer Talon.[40] Ramus was a charismatic teacher and prolific writer who had converted to Protestantism and was killed in the St. Bartholomew's Day Massacre of the Huguenots. This martyrdom gave Ramist arguments about authority and truth all the more receptive an audience in the Protestant England of Elizabeth. With his less-known collaborator Talon, Ramus argued for a new division between rhetoric and logic, and for a clearer and more practical approach, especially to logic, in which he emphasized the role of judgment and the need for combining the arts in their

---

[39] Wilson's book can be difficult going for a modern reader unfamiliar with Cicero and Aristotle. Howell's exposition is very useful as a guide. See W. S. Howell, *Logic and Rhetoric in England, 1500–1700,* chapter one (Princeton University Press, 1956).

[40] Ramism was certainly not the only threat to Wilson's neo-scholastic synthesis. Perhaps even great danger lurked in the oversimplified summary published by Dudley Fenner, whose *The Artes of Logike and Rethorike Plainelie Set Foorth in the English Tounge, Easie to Be Learned and Practised* was trivial by comparison, for which reason the 1584 text received an expanded printing in 1588.

application. Thus, Ramus's logic still considered the role of invention and judgment, but with considerable variation from the traditional modes presented in Wilson.

Fraunce himself explains he was exposed to Ramus at Cambridge, where his works were then hotly debated and available in both Latin and English.[41] Though in the *Lawiers Logike*, Fraunce clearly and routinely followed Ramist forms of category and argument, at places Fraunce employs variation that echoes not just Wilson but a long scholastic tradition debated in his still-recent college days.[42] More, Fraunce was happy to expand on Ramus, following fairly well Ramus's categories but expanding upon them. Among other developments, his descriptions in chapter four of fallacy, or fallacians, as forms of Sophistry might be the first English writings that describe false definition, false etymology, false testimony, and false analogy.[43]

Fraunce made his categories and principles for reasoning within each category. He then selected models to illustrate his principles, both when they are satisfied and when they are not. These models were quotations, with lengths varying from a snippet to pages on pages. Building his *Lawiers Logike* on the foundations of his more general, *Shepherd's Logike*, he interspersed his

---

[41] Ramus was published in England, in both English and Latin editions, in 1574. See the *Logike of the Moste Excellent Philosopher P. Ramus Martyr, Newly Translated, and in Diuers Places Corrected, after the Mynde of the Author. Per M. Roll. Makylmenaeum Scotum, Rogatu Viri Honestissimi, M. Aegidii Hamlin* (Thomas Vantroullier, 1574).

[42] Authors Fraunce expounds as sources of logical thought are Homer, Plato, Diogenes Laertius, Demosthenes, Parmenides, the Stoics, the Pyrrhonians (or skeptics), Aristotle, Cicero (Tully), Quintilian, and books of the Bible, as well as Pierre de la Ramée (Petrus Ramus), Fredericus Berhusius, Philip Melancthon, Omer Talon, François Hotman (Hottoman), Johannes Piscator, Johannes Sturm (Sturmius), and Simon Thelwall, among others.

[43] On its novelty, see Ralph S. Pomeroy, *The Ramist as Fallacy-Hunter: Abraham Fraunce and* The Lawiers Logike, 40 Renn. Q. 224 (1987). Charles Hamblin collected the arguments about "fallacians" throughout Fraunce's argument and developed them into something of a coherent theory of fallacy. See C.L. Hamblin, *Fallacies* 142 (Vale Press, 1970).

illustrations from poetry and prose[44] with often quite technical illustrations from law treatises and case reports.[45]

To the modern reader, the jolting selection of quotes, usually taken quite out of context, and presented in sometimes rapid-fire succession, can be jarring. This is especially true of the excerpts and quotations from judicial opinions and legal arguments. The modern reverence for the text as a source of law had yet to arise, and the arguments presented were selected solely to present the logical relationship of concepts therein, *not* as one would today, to assess particularly the arguments in issue presented by a counsel or judge. Indeed, often the quotations selected are quite peripheral to the main arguments of the case, sheer dicta in the contemporary sense. Coupled to this are the acontextual lines from poems, which either presumed the reader's familiarity with them or for which such context remained just immaterial. For some of these, the risk was low. A sixteenth-century reader quite likely knew, for example, that Piers was in the great poem of Piers Plowman. Yet the reader would not nearly have been so likely to realize Edmund Spenser had recycled and retaskes this character in his *Shepheardes Calendar*, from which Fraunce plucked also Colin Clout, Perigot, and Willy (usually placing them in the months in which they occur in Spenser's poem). When Fraunce first played out the dialectic possibilities of their roles, in the *Shepheardes Logike* Spenser's *Shepheardes Calendar* had yet to be published.[46]

---

[44] Poetry and prose came not only from the Wilton Circle, notably the Countess of Pembroke, Edmund Spenser, and the near-sainted Sir Philip Sidney, but also from classical authors, particularly Virgil but also Martial and Philo, exercises in the vein of Quintilian, and lines from then-contemporary poets such as Torquato Tasso and Guillaume de Salluste du Bartas.

[45] Legal sources included not only civilian authors but also common-law books, such as Bracton, Glanville, Littleton's *Tenures*, Crompton's *Authority and Jurisdiction*, Staunford's *Please of the Crown*, Lambarde's *Archaionomia*, Fitzherbert's *Natura Brevia*, and *The Book of Entries*. Reports came from assize rolls and yearbooks as well as the occasional statute, but Fraunce prominently quoted from recent reporters, particularly (and sometimes at extraordinary length) from Edmund Plowden's *Commentaries*.

[46] Spenser's poem was published in 1579. It would have been quite well known (among the literati) before the publication of the *Lawiers Logike*. That, however,

Yet for Fraunce, the assessment of the whole argument depended on exactly this sort of clinical assessment of each part. His essential claim was that every element of an argument could be assessed for its logical relationship and context. A reader would not have needed to know the merits, of even the identity, of an author to assess a text's authority: the authority was apparent in the content and technique of the assertions in the text.

This is the heart of Ramist inductivism: certain axioms can determine the accuracy of a statement. If one can understand all of these axioms, one can discern the truth or falsity of most arguments. More, one can craft a clear and truthful argument.

Thus, Fraunce sought to apply these seemingly quite powerful tools to the law. His methods may strike the contemporary lawyer in some places as naive, as when certain assumptions are made about the nature of a man or woman in a given circumstance, but in others quite sophisticated, as when looking at the problem of multiple causes for a given action. Yet overall, whether Fraunce's tools were used to assess an idea for its truth or falsity, or to expound an idea in a clear and accurate manner, the tools would have led to greater clarity and to greater accuracy than arguments made vaguely from authority alone.

What Was Fraunce's Influence on the Law?

At first blush, Fraunce's efforts to influence his colleagues at the bar seems to have been a prodigious effort, ending in defeat. The tenurists won, and the young scholar was largely overlooked by the lawyers. He simply does not seem to have been read. Certainly, he is little quoted. There are references, certainly, but they are few and infrequent. The logic book is quoted in a discussion of coroner's duties in 1760,[47] but there are not many legal claims on the book in the two centuries earlier.

---

does not appear to have been as important to Fraunce as that he liked the poem as a source of illustration of true arguments.

[47] Edward Unfreville, *Lex Coronatoria, The Office and the Duty of Coroners* (1761), quoted in Ralph Griffiths, Review, 23 Monthly Review 442, 450 (1760).

Still, the book did get around, and like many primers and exercise manuals, its influence on the law would not have been confined to its quotation or citation by lawyers. Circumstantial textual evidence suggests that book might have influenced at least three leaders of the bar who never thought to cite it.

Francis Bacon, who knew Fraunce and was present when he was called to the bar, seems to likely to have been familiar with the book.[48] Indeed Bacon must have seen the copy dedicated to the lawyers of Gray's Inn, where he, in 1588, was a leading member.

Sir Edward Coke was recurrently fascinated by law as reason and law as logic. It would seem quite odd that he was unfamiliar with the book, and indeed, many elements of Coke's taxonomic and graphical presentations in the *First Institute* resonate, at least, with the graphical analysis employed by Fraunce, particularly in his depiction of the elements of estates and descents in property.[49]

Sir John Doddridge, a contemporary of Coke and Bacon and a justice on the Court of Kings Bench, in 1631 wrote a manual for law students, *The English Lawyer*.[50] Fully two hundred of its two hundred and seventy pages are concerned with instruction on logic and syllogistic reasoning, quoting many of the same classical sources as Fraunce and presenting similar illustrations, yet never managing to cite him.

Though Fraunce's book did not go through but two printings,[51] it was of sufficient significance to travel to North America. Thomas

---

[48] Dan Coquillette notes that Bacon's *Collection of Some Principal Rules and Maximes of the Common Law*, written about 1596, is in the tradition of Fraunce's *Logike*. Daniel R. Coquillette, *Francis Bacon* 35–36 (Stanford University Press, 1992).

[49] As an editor of three volumes of Coke's writings, I cannot, however avoid the caveat that there might be a reference buried in the flurries of citations that I have yet to see. Further, Hassall's publication of Coke's library handlist suggests Coke did not have a copy of Fraunce in his rather extensive private library. See *A Catalogue of the Library of Sir Edward Coke* (W.O, Hassall, ed.) (Yale University Press, 1950).

[50] Sir John Dodderidge, *The English Lawyer: Describing a Method for the Managing of the Lawes of the Land* (1631).

[51] Both printings were in 1588 by William How. They are in the STC as numbers 11344 and 11345. They are apparently from the same plates.

Jefferson owned a copy, which went with his library to the Library of Congress in 1830.[52]

Fraunce's enduring significance to the law is probably symbolic. Careful modern scholars have seen his work as a step along a continuum in the intellectual development of English law, a moment in which genuine academic skills were used to enhance the lawyer's understanding of the law itself.[53] This injection of skills into the law from philosophy and rhetoric not only presaged linguistic analysis but also anticipated the arguments of justice based on the sufficiency of a legal process. It would become as important for the law to prove that how it worked was just as would matter for the law to prove that its effects were just. These were arguments that could not be proved from the sources of law alone: some tools external to the law would be required. Fraunce's comparison of logical truth to the law was only the first step.

Post Script: On the Word "Tenurist"

In his opening letter to the Members of the Bar, Fraunce uses the marvelous word, "tenurist" to demean a pettyfogging legal traditionalist. This is a rare word, used just once earlier and just once later in printed texts, at least among those I've searched.

Fraunce did not invent the term. It seems first to have been used by Thomas Elyot in *The Governour*, in 1531. Elyot used the term as one of abuse, though not for the tenurists' refusal to listen to reason or reform the law but rather for the tenurist's corruption of the once-pure Roman law.[54] Fraunce and Dodderidge would later use it, similarly, though more broadly, derisively.[55]

---

[52] See *Catalogue of the Library of Congress* 241 (Library of Congress, 1830).

[53] See Mark Walters, *Legal Humanism and Law as Integrity*, 67 Camb. L.J. 352 (2008). See also Dan Coquillette's discussion, noted here above.

[54]

> What hath beene in this kinde brought in upon the pure and cleare fountaines of the Digests of the Civill Lawes – which being compiled out of sundry most excellent sentences, drawne out of the workes and passages of the ancient Romane lawyers, doe retaine the same purity and conformity of a cleane and neat stile, as though all had beene

The OED burnishes its hard-earned reputation for comprehensiveness for collecting such a rare term, as it does. Yet its deadpan definition, "one who deals with or treats of tenures" quite misses the point. The term is derogatory. Like pettifogger, tenurist should not be used without intending harsh judgment.[56]

> penned by one man ; and yet are in a manner defiled by the Feudary Tenurist writers of the middle age in their Glosses and commentaries ...

Thomas Elyot, 1 *The Governour* (Henry Herbert Stephen Croft, ed.) 146 (Keegan, Croft, 1871).

[55] See Fraunce's Introduction, below. See also, Sir John Doddridge, *The English Lawyer* 53 (1631).

[56] While quoting Fraunce and Dodderidge as their source, the *OED* editors define the term merely as "tenurist n. Obs. one who deals with or treats of tenures." *Oxford English Dictionary*, q.v. (3d ed.) (Oxford University Press, 2010).

Further Reading

The Life of Abraham Fraunce

M. G. Brennan, *The Date of the Death of Abraham Fraunce*, 5 The Library, 6th ser., 392 (1983)

G. C. Moore Smith, Introduction, in Abraham Fraunce, *Victoria: A Latin Drama*, In 14 *Materialen zur Kunde des älteren Englischen Dramas* (W. Bang, ed.) (Louvain, 1906)

Charles Henry Cooper and Thompson Cooper, *Athenae Cantabrigienses* (3 vols.) (1858–1913); repr. (1967)

John Venn and John A. Venn, *Alumni Cantabrigienses: a Biographical List of All Known Students, Graduates, and Holders of Office at the University of Cambridge, from the Earliest Times to 1900* (1922–1954); repr. in 2 vols. (1974–1978)

Influence of Abraham Fraunce

D. S. Bland, *Rhetoric and the Law Student in Sixteenth-Century England*, 57 Stud. Philol. 57 (1957).

Peter Goodrich, *Visualizing Law in the Digital Age Devising Law: On the Philosophy of Legal Emblems*, 57 N.Y.L. Sch. L. Rev. 133 (2012)

Pamela N. Gray and Scott Mann, *The Fraunce (1588) Model of Case-Based Reasoning*, In *ICAIL '03 Proceedings of the 9th International Conference on Artificial Intelligence and Law* 89 (2003)

Charles L. Hamblin, *Fallacies* (Methuen, 1970)

W. S. Howell, *Logic and Rhetoric in England, 1500–1700* (Princeton University Press, 1956)

Ralph S. Pomeroy, *The Ramist as Fallacy-Hunter: Abraham Fraunce and* The Lawiers Logike, 40 Renn. Q. 224 (1987)

R.J. Schoeck, *Rhetoric and Law in Sixteenth-Century England*, in 50 Stud. Philol. 110 (1953)

Mark Walters, *Legal Humanism and Law as Integrity*, 67 Camb. L.J. 352 (2008)

A Few Works on the Sidneys and Spenser

Margaret P. Hannay, *Philip's Phoenix Mary Sidney, Countess of Pembroke* (Oxford University Press, 1990)

Mary Sidney Herbert, *The Collected Works of Mary Sidney Herbert, Countess of Pembroke* (2 vols.) (Margaret P. Hannay, Noel J. Kinnamon & Michael G. Brennan, eds.) (Oxford University Press, 1998)

Kathrine Koller, *Abraham Fraunce and Edmund Spenser*, 7 ELH 108 (1940)

Steven W. May, *Marlowe, Spenser, Sidney and—Abraham Fraunce?* 62 Rev. of English Studies, N. S. 30 (2011)

Harry Morris, *Richard Barnfield, "Amyntas," and the Sidney Circle*, 74 PMLA 318 (1959); but see contra Walter F. Staton, Jr. and Harry Morris, *Thomas Watson and Abraham Fraunce*, 76 PMLA 150 (1961)

Peter Ramus and Legal Ramism

Huntington Cairns, *Leibniz's Theory of Law*, 60 Harv. L. Rev. 200 (1946)

Peter Goodrich, *Ars Bablativa: Ramism, Rhetoric, and the Genealogy of English Jurisprudence, in Legal Hermeneutics: History, Theory, and Practice* (Gregory Leyh ed.) (University of California Press 1992)

Peter Goodrich, *Languages of Law: From Logics of Memory to Nomadic Masks* (Weidenfeld & Nicolson 1990)

Bernard J. Hibbitts, *Making Sense of Metaphors: Visuality, Aurality, and the Reconfiguration of American Legal Discourse*, 16 Cardozo L. Rev. 229 (1994)

George A. Kennedy, *Classical Rhetoric & Its Christian & Secular Tradition from Ancient to Modern Times* (2d ed., U.N.C. Press 1999)

Louis A. Knafla, *Ramism and the English Renaissance, in Science, Technology, and Culture in Historical Perspective* (Louis A. Knafla et al. eds.) (University of Calgary Press, 1976)

Louis A. Knafla, *The Influence of Continental Humanists and Jurists on English Common Law in the Renaissance, in Acta Conventus Neo-Latini Bononiensis: Proceedings of the Fourth International Congress of Neo-Latin Studies* (R.J. Schoeck ed.) (SUNY Binghamton Press, 1985)

James J. Murphy, *Rhetoric in the Middle Ages: A History of Rhetorical Theory from Saint Augustine to the Renaissance* (University of California Press 1974)

Norman E. Nelson, *Peter Ramus and the Confusion of Logic, Rhetoric, and Poetry, in 2 Contributions in Modern Philology* (University of Michigan Press, 1947)

Walter Ong, *Ramus: Method and the Decay of Dialogue* (Harvard University Press, 1983)

Richard J. Ross, *The Commoning of the Common Law: The Renaissance Debate over Printing English Law, 1520–1640*, 146 U. Pa. L. Rev. 323 (1998).

David J. Seipp, *The Structure of English Common Law in the Seventeenth Century*, in Legal History in the Making: Proceedings of the Ninth British Legal History Conference Glasgow 1989 (W.M. Gordon & T.D. Fergus eds.)(University of Glasgow, 1991)

Ramus, Pedagogy, and the Liberal Arts: Ramism in Britain and the Wider World (E.A. Wilson and S.J. Reid, eds.) (Ashgate, 2011)

Table of Contents[1]

[1]Note: spelling is modernized throughout.

THE LAWIERS LOgike, exemplifying the *præcepts of Logike by* the practise of the common Lawe,

by

Abraham Fraunce.

AT LONDON,
Imprinted by William
How, for Thomas Gubbin, and T. Newman.

1588.

To the Right honorable, Henry Earle of *Pembrooke, Lord Herbert of Cardyffe,* Marmyon, and S. Quynten, Lorde Præsident of the principality of Wales, and the Marches of *the same, Knight of the most noble order of* the Garter, and Lord Liuetenant of Wales, of the Marches, and of the counties of Wyltes and Sommerset.

IF Lawes by reason framed were, and grounded on the same;
If Logike also reason bee, and thereof had this name;
I see no reason, why that Law and Logike should not bee
The nearest and the dearest freends, and therfore best agree.
As for the fonde conceyt of such which neuer knew them both,
Better beleeue some mens bare worde, than their suspected oth.
I say no more then what I saw, I saw that which I sought,
I sought for Logike in our Law, and found it as I thought.
If all that I haue sought and found your Honor doe content,
(Let scribes and pety penmen talke) I thinck my time well spent,
And labour herein well imployd: Acceptance is my meede,
I craue no more, I haue no lesse, if you vouchsafe to reede.

Your Honors

most vnfainedly affectionate

Abraham Fraunce.

TO THE LEARNED *Lawyers of England, especially the Gentlemen of Grays Inne.*

THere bee almost seauen yeares now ouergone mee, since first I began to be a medler with these Logicall meditations: And whilest I haue said and vnsaid, doone and vndoone, and now doone all a new, mee thinkes these seauen yeares haue quickly ouergone mee. I first began, (when I first came in presence of that right noble and most renowmed knight sir Philip Sydney) with a generall discourse concerning the right vse of Logike, and a contracted comparison betweene this of Ramus and that of Aristotle. These small and trifling beginnings drewe both him to a greater liking of, and my selfe to a further trauayling in, the easie explication of Ramus his Logike.

Sixe tymes in thease seauen yeares haue I perused the whole, & by a more diligent ouerseeing corrected some ouersights: thrise at S. Iohns colledge in Cambridge, thrise at Grays Inne, since I came to London. This last alteration hath chaunged the name of the Booke, & this new name of the Booke proceeded from the chaunge of my profession. For hauing resolutely determined to

¶. acquaint

acquaint my ſelfe with our Engliſh laws & conſtitutiõs, I thought good to make tryall, whether my eight yeares labour at Cambridge, would any thing profit mee at an Inne of Court, wheather Law were without Logike, or Logike not able to helpe a Lawyer. VVhich when I prooued, I then perceaued, the practiſe of Law to bee the vſe of Logike, and the methode of Logike to lighten the Lawe. So that after application of Logike to Lawe, and examination of Lawe by Logike, I made playne the precepts of the one by the practiſe of the other, and called my booke, The Lawyers Logike; not as though Logike were tyed onely vnto Law, but for that our Law is moſt fit to expreſſe the præcepts of Logike. Yet, becauſe many loue Logike, that neuer learne Lawe, I haue reteyned thoſe ould examples of the new Shepheards Kalender, which I firſt gathered, and therevnto added theaſe alſo out of our Law bookes, which I lately collected.

I doubt not, but that ſome welwillers, and many malitiouſly diſpoſed cauyllers will as much reprehend this ſtraunge coniunction of Lawe and Logike, as they did meruayle at my ſodayne departure from Philoſophy to Lawe. To thoſe that meane well, and ſpeake according to their meaning, I wiſh no woorſe vſe of Logike than may be had in Lawe. For the reſt, which make proclamations without authoritie, and exclamations with greater indignation, than diſcretion, I leaue them to their ſtandiſh, and pray for their good ſucceſſe, that after the tearme of ſeauen yeares fully compleate and ended, they may bee in their blewe veluet night-caps ſolempnly called to the Barre for their extraordinary skill in making of obligations.

Tully, at the earneſt requeſt of Trebatius, a towardly

Lawyer

Lawyer of Rome, hath eloquently put downe the first part of Logike in his Topikes, to the præcepts whereof hee applyeth Law-like examples, for the better instruction of Trebatius and helpe of other Lawyers. Seruius Sulpitius, as the same Tully reporteth, became the most excellent Lawyer in all Rome, and that onely by the helpe and direction of Logike: insomuch that he onely, by thease meanes, was said to haue the art & knowledge of the Lawe, whereas the rest had nothing but the practise of the same, by continuall beating of their braynes about endles controuersies. Hee knew what was Law, & what was the reason of Law; they like good Catholikes and modest minded men, beleeued as the Church beleeued, but why the church beleeued so, it neuer came within the compasse of their cogitation.

But all this notwithstanding, it cannot bee, sayde one great Tenurist, that a good Scholler should euer prooue good Lawyer. God forbid, good sir, you offer your selfe tootoomuch iniury: for wee, countreymen, take your woorship for a greate wise learned man, and I doubt not but that your selfe are well perswaded of your woondrous knowledge in the Lawe, and yet you say, that Lawe and Logike can neuer stande togeather. Tis great pity, God wot, that thease two excellent qualities can neuer bee reconciled. Alas; what should ayle them, if it like your good Maystership? Mary, quoth hee, thease finē Vniuersity men haue beene trained vp in such easie, elegant, conceipted, nice, and delicate learning, that they can better make new-found verses of Amyntas death, and popular discourses of Ensignes, Armory, Emblemes, Hieroglyphikes, and Italian Impreses, than apply their heads to the study of the Law, which is hard, harsh, vnpleasant, vnsauory, rude and barbarous. VVell said good Iohn a style.

Dij te, Damasippe, deæque
Verum ob iudicium, donent tonsore; sed vnde
Tam benè nos nosti ?

For my selfe, I must needes confesse I was an Vniuersitie man eight yeares togeather, and for euery day of these eight yeares, I do not repent that I was an Vniuersitie man. But for that delicacie of studie whereof you dreame, because it seemeth somewhat straunge, a worde or two, before wee go further. Surely sir, by your patience be it spoken, it seemeth you came abruptly from a countrey schoole to an Inne of court, or els riding poast towards London, you chaunged horse at the Vniuersitie, and comming thither late in the euening, and riding away early in the morning, saw nothing but by candell light. It was incident to my nature (as I thinke) to bee caried away with as delicate and pleasant a kinde of learning, as any of my time in Cambridge. VVhich (notwithstanding an inestimable delectation that drowned the paines of studie) did yet so racke my raunging head, and bring low my crased body, that I felt at last when it was too late, the perpetuall vexation of Spirite, and continuall consumption of body, incident to euery scholler.

And if the most easie conceipts in Vniuersities be so hard, the most delicate studies so full of toyle, how troublesome then and painefull the foundation of arts, the framing of an English tongue to vnknowen languages, must in any case bee, I leaue to be iudged of them, who can discerne betweene a superficiall apparance and true substance, betweene the brauery of a Midsommers Comencement,

mencement, and the ſeauen yeares paynes of a Maiſter of arts.

Now for the ſtudy of the law, which, by theſe lawmens report, is ſo hard, ſo vnſauory, ſo rude, and ſo barbarous, ſhee may well pronounce of her profeſſors, as Horace of his gueſtes.

Tres mihi conuiuæ propè diſſentire videntur,
Poſcentes vario multum diuerſa palato.
Quid dem? quid non dem? renuis tu, quod iubet alter,
Quod petis, id certè eſt inuiſum acidumque duobus.

For the hardenes and difficulty, I ſay nomore, but τὰ καλὰ χάλεπα: and if Philoſophy be harde, and law be harde, *Iam ſumus ergò pares*. In deede the want of teachers and good diſcipline which is in Vniuerſities, makes law ſeeme harde, and Philoſophy very eaſie, which, if either we had, or they had not, no doubt, law would ſooner be learned in ſeauen yeares, then ſeauen arts in one & twenty. But the law is vnſauory, ſaith an other: But the fault is in your corrupt taſt, ſay I, not in the nature of the thing, which vnto the wiſeſt is moſt acceptable, vnleſſe you play the part of Philoxenus, and vnder pretence of abhorring the loathſome ſauour of the law, intend the deuouring of all profites proceeding from the law, whiche ſeemeth indeede to be the ſcope you ayme at. You would loue the law but *ſine riuali*: you would raigne, but alone: *Hinc illæ lachrymæ*. For otherwiſe I can hardly thinke ſo hardly of you, as to meaſure your diſcretion by the vnprobable aſſertion cõpriſed in your two laſt Epithetes, wherein you diſgrace the law with rudeneſſe and barbariſme. For, as for that Hotchpot French, ſtufft vp with ſuch variety of borowed words, wherein our law is written, if this be all the Dunſicaltie you talke of, you are farre more nyce then any Vniuersitie man of mine acquaintance. I know by experience, there is no word so outworne, no speach so vast and gaping in Brytton, Bracton, Glanuyll, Lytleton, Parkins, and the rest of our Law autors and reporters of the law, as is in Bricot, Burley, Bonauenture, Duns, Durand, D'orbell, Aquinas, Andreas, Albertus, and a farre more infinite number of those Moonkish cloysterers deuoured of Schollers, than bee of thease others perused by Lawyers. And yet, notwithstanding all their Perseities, Formalities, Quiddities, Hæcceities, Albedinities, Animalities, Substantialities, and such like, hee that would not gather gould out of Aquinas dregges, as Virgill did out of Ennius, I shall thinke him as wise, as some seelly Pettyfogger, who rather than hee would trouble his conscience with Feetayle and Feesimple, will lyue like a simple foole, and neuer take fee.

VVhether it bee malice therefore and enuy, or ignorance and simplicitie, that causeth you to wrangle and chatte so vndiscreatly, you may see how you doo erre by the one, and are deceaued by the other. For neyther are Vniuersity men so daynty, as to loose their dinner because the Cooke had not on his holiday apron, neither is the Law more vnsweete, than other learning vnsauory, whatsoeuer you cast out to the contrary.

But the Law is in vaste volumes confusedly scattered and vtterly vndigested: so was all other learning not long agoe: yet herein blame not the Law, if it bee darke, but Lawyers themselues that had no light: blame not the Lawe, I say, which was out of order, but Lawyers themselues that neuer knewe Methode: Nay, blame neyther Lawe, nor auncient Lawyers, who by reason of of the generall misery of their obscure age, could not see euery thinge, but exclayme against your selues, who in this floorishing time and blessed opportunity, will see nothing. If those auncient fathers of our Lawe had lyued now, all had beene well, but if you had beene extant then, all had beene woorse. For neyther can you doo what you should, nor will let others doo what they would for the more orderly explication of the Lawe. Such is the vntowardly disposition of this scornefull age of ours, wherein no man prayseth any more, then hee thinketh himselfe able to performe, but seeketh to cloke his owne ignoraunce by deriding other mens skill, beeing himselfe so simple in other mens iudgement, and wise in his owne conceipt, that when hee hath spoken without measure to a doosen of poynts, all is not worth a penywoorth of pinnes: for neyther himselfe can well vnderstand his vnioynted discourse, nor the hearers conceaue his vncohærent iangling.

But I feare mee, I haue mooued their patience, whom I most desire to bee patient, and to suffer without grudging Schollers to bee Lawyers, as they wish some Lawyers to become better Schollers. VVhich if it were so, then would there not bee so many vpstart *Rabulæ Forenses*, which vnder a prætence of Lawe, become altogeather lawlesse, to the continuall molestation of ignoraunt men, and generall ouercharging of the countrey, with an ouerflowing multitude of seditious cauyllers: who, when their fathers haue made some lewde bargayne in the countrey, run immediatly to the Innes of Court, and hauing in seauen yeares space met with six French woordes, home they ryde lyke braue Magnificoes, and dashe their poore neighboures children quyte out

of

of countenance, with Villen in gros, Villen regardant, and Tenant per le curtesie : much like the ſwarming rable of our coyſtrell curates, which when their fathers haue either compounded with their Landlord for ſome pelting vicaredge, or payd ready money for a better parſonage, conuey themſelues to Cambridge or Oxford, where hauing once knowen the price of an Admiſsion, Salting, and Matriculation, with the intertayning of Freſhmenne in the Rhetorike ſchooles, they returne whence they came, with their mothers wit and fathers learning carefully kept togeather, that when they haue wearied menne with reading ſkarce true Engliſh on the Sonday, all the weeke after they may plague poore boyes with falſe Latine in a belfraye. Or elſe, if the ould Parſon be not yet dead, they ſtaye a little longer, and vnder a preciſe cloake of Diuinitie, (notwithſtanding they bee Arch-aſſes in all humanitie) creepe in among Batchlers of artes with croſſe caps on their groſſe pates, and ſheepes ſkinnes caſt ouer their lubberlike ſhoulders, whereof they are more prowde then euer was any foole of his bell and bauble : then come they home to ring their belles, to the vtter diſgrace of the Vniuerſities, the perpetuall plague of the Countrey, and euerlaſting ſhame of the corrupted Clergie.

Yet I heare ſay, that ſome great lawyers haue had litle learning, and ſome good churchmen haue beene no great clearkes : VVherevnto I anſwere, that it were but follie to contemne ordinarie meanes, becauſe ſome men haue extraordinarie gyftes, and if thoſe rare qualities of nature had beene directed by precepts of art, I thinke they had proued much more excellent.

But to returne thither from whence I came, and to make

make an ende with that wherewith I began, thus much I dare bee bould to affirme, notwithstanding the præiudicate cõnceipt of twenty Ciuilians, and as many common Lawyers to the contrary, that if the Ciuyll law bee elegant and delectable, the Common lawe is neyther barbarous nor vnsauory. For the volumes, theyrs bee farre greater, and much more infinite. For the style, it is more easily determined that both bee bad, then which is better: and yet both Bartolus his Latine, and Brytton his French, in some mens iudgement is therefore sufficiently elegant, because it is fully significant. For the matter, all is Lawe, although not all one Lawe: and hee that lyketh the one, let him leaue the other, or ioyne them both togeather, if his leysure bee so good, and his ability correspondent.

It is not my meaning to disgrace the one, or aduance the other in comparison wise, by superlatiue woordes, and hyperbolicall amplifications: I haue yenough if I haue this graunted, that our Common lawe is as easie, as short, as elegant, and as delightsome as is the Cyuill, which euery man extolleth, and I am well content, as long as I see these twoo thinges in credite with other men, wherevnto I haue already betaken my selfe. For, as for Fortescues comparing of them both togeather and præferring of ours, it maketh all with mee, yet I vrge not all: albeit I thinke, as by office hee was a Iudge in Court of conscience, so in this Treatise hee dealt not *summo iure*, with the Cyuilians, but reasonably and with ἐπιείκεια.

But the Cyuill lawe will some man say, is both in it selfe more constant and philosophicall, and also by Iustinian more methodically, and by later wryters more

¶¶. eloquent-

eloquently put downe.

I sayde before my meaning was not to enter into any needles discourse of comparison betweene thease twoo lawes, yet because thease bee obiections of latter tyme, I must præsume a lyttle further. And first, for the constancy and philosophicall foundation of the Romayne Lawe, which Iustinian calleth the Cyuill law κατ᾽ἐξοχήν, (as Homer is called the Poet) the name, Cyuill, beeing common to the seueral lawes of any peculiar kingdome: no doubt, this obiection was made by them, that heard somewhat at the Vniuersity of the Cyuill lawe, but neuer read any thing of our Common lawe. They haue *Plebiscita*, *Senatus consulta*, *Principum placita*, *Magistratuum edicta*, *Responsa prudentum*: VVee haue ruled Cases, Maximaes and Principles, Customes and Vsages both generall and speciall; and lastly, continuall reformation of newe abuses by Statutes and Actes of Parlament. Now let any one skilfull in both, iudge of the reason and certeinty of eyther, and remember withall, what Aristotle sayth of the imperfection of all Lawes, least hee impute that as a speciall blemishe to our Lawe, which is a generall want incident to the nature of euerie Lawe.

There is no Law-maker so prouident, as that hee can in particularity foresee, and, as it were, by some propheticall spyrite fore-tell and præuent the infinite variety of future inconueniences, by application of so many peculiar prouisoes, and speciall constitutions, but must of necessity leaue his Lawe generall, referring the addition, detraction, or mitigation of woordes, vnto the conscience and discretion of the

learned.

learned and vnderstanding Iudge. Thus much would I haue remembred, and then let that Lawe bee accused as least sufficient which is most generall, and therefore not so well able to præuent imminent myschiefes.

For, as for the methode of Iustinian, it doth not so well content the Cyuilians, but that they dayly contend with newe innouations and continuall printing of freshe methodes, to bring it vnto better order. Yet if it bee such, as some say it is, then I say, wee haue our Common lawe penned after the selfe same methode twoo hundreth yeares agoe, by that famous and learned Iudge Henry de Bracton, skilfull in both thease Lawes. And if it bee not Iustinians order that thease men fancy, but rather the late Abridgements of finer heades, let them not then with reuyling speaches discourage them, which hope to see the Common lawe of England brought to as good and easie a methode, as euer was any.

For the style of theasc late Cyuilians, whiche is somewhat more laboured and lesse vnseemely then that of their forefathers, wee maye as iustly say that there is the lyke diuersitie to bee manifestly perceaued betweene the homely speach of oure auncient Lawyers, and the finer phrase of late wryters in our Common lawe. VVoordes are lyke leaues, as Horace reporteth: leaues spring before Summer, and fall before VVinter; and the same inconstancy is in words. Let vs therefore vse that phrase whiche is most vsuall: and though in knowledge and conceipt wee contend to bee singular, yet in vttering our thoughtes, let all bee made partakers.

But loe, I see on the sodayne this extrauagant discourse abruptly cut off by the importunate exclamations of a raging and fireyfaced Aristotelean; who seeing Ramus his Logike in some estimation, maketh small accoumpt of his owne credite in vttering such impatient speaches.

Good God, what a world is this? VVhat an age doe wee now lyue in? A Sopister in tymes past was a tytle of credite, and a woord of commendation; nowe what more odious? Aristotle then the father of Philosophy; now who lesse fauoured? Ramus rules abroade, Ramus at home, and who but Ramus? Antiquity is nothing but Dunsicality, & our forefathers inuentions vnprofitable trumpery. Newfangled, youngheaded, harebrayne boyes will needes bee Maysters that neuer were Schollers; prate of methode, who neuer knew order; rayle against Aristotle assoone as they are crept out of the shell. Hereby it comes to passe that euery Cobler can cogge a Syllogisme, euery Carter crake of Propositions. Hereby is Logike prophaned, and lyeth prostitute, remooued out of her Sanctuary, robbed of her honour, left of her louers, rauyshed of straungers, and made common to all, which before was proper to Schoolemen, and only consecrated to Philosophers.

I haue heard the lyke speaches to thease before this, and I looke for no better hereafter: I neuer esteemed of those, and I litle care for thease. Yet, good mayster Quidditary, if you had beene as diligent in meditation of the cause, as you haue beene ouer earnest in admiration of the effect, the knowledge of the one would haue remoued the straungenes of the other. For, if the wisedome of the auncient *Sophi* bee nowe degenerate into the ydle

subtleties.

ſubtleties of the new-found *Sophiſtæ*, what meruayle is it, if when the thing is not aunſwering to the name, the name become odious?

Ramus doth not ſo rule, but that he can ſuffer reaſon to ouer rule him. Ould doating graybeards talke much of Baralipton, whileſt youngheaded boyes beare away Logike. They thinke much that a boy ſhould conceaue that in a weeke, which they could skarce perceaue in a yeare: but more, that their ould learning ſhould bee corrected by newe teaching, and their labour loſt with ſo little profiting.

Coblers bee men, why therefore not Logicians? and Carters haue reaſon, why therefore not Logike? *Bonum, quò communius, eo melius,* you ſay ſo your ſelues, and yet the beſt thing in Logike you make to be the woorſt, in thinking it leſſe commendable, becauſe it is more common. A ſpytefull ſpeach, and a meaning no leſſe malitious, to locke vp Logike in ſecreate corners, who, as of her ſelfe ſhee is generally good to all, ſo will ſhee particularly bee bound to none. Touching the gryefe you conceaue for the contempt of Ariſtotle, it is needles and vnneceſſary: for, where Ariſtotle deſerueth prayſe, who more commendeth him then Ramus? VVhere he hath toomuch, Ramus cutteth off, where too little, addeth, where any thing is inuerted, hee bringeth it to his owne proper place, and that according to the direction of Ariſtotle his rules. Then, whereas there can bee no Art both inuented and perfected by the ſame man, if Ariſtotle did inuent Logike, as hee perſwadeth you, hee did not perfect it, if hee did not finiſh it, there is ſome imperfection, if there bee any want, why then allow you all?

To the Learned Lawyers of England.

But alas, ſee how farre I haue ouerſhot my marke : tis more then time to make an ende of this raunging digreſsion . I ende therefore, yet with an endleſſe deſire, that no leſſe profite may bee perceaued by others in practiſing, then I had pleaſure in peruſing this laſt explication of Ramus his Logike.

Abraham Fraunce.

Faultes eſcaped.

PAg: 6, a: line, 3: after κελπκη reade, of κρισις: Pag: 12, b, line, 11: for pius, read, puis: Pag: 15. a: line, 23: for deius, read, deins: Pag: 19: b: line, laſt but two, for, or, read, ou: Pag: 26, b: line, laſt but 4: for miguarde, read mignarde: Pag: 39: a: line, laſt but 8: for eſſigne, read, aſſigne: Pag: 40: a: line, 2: for reddit reade, redit: Pag: 45: a: line, laſt but 6: for le, read, de: Pag: 48: a: line, 10: for his, read, her, and line, 11: for her, read his: Pag: 56: b: the firſt foure lines of the 13 chapter be out of their proper place a litle: Pag: 61: a: line, 21: for Brittou, 17: read, Britton 17: & elſ- where: Pag: 62: b: line, laſt but foure, for poſſuit read, poſuit: Pag: 73: a: line, laſt but one, for canſe, reade, cauſe: Pag: 86: b: line, laſt: for meus, read, mens: Pag: 99: b: line, laſt but one, for the word that is blotted out, reade, a plague, a torment: Pag: 108: a: line, 19: for n'eſt, read, eſt: Pag: 110: a: line, 13: for there, read, then: Pag: 113, a: line, laſt but two, for, and ſyllogiſme, read, and a ſyllogiſme. Pag: 113: b: line, 21: for, the, read, this. Pag: 119: a: line, laſt but two, for learnings, read, learning. Pag: 122: b: line, 8: for, appeareth: read, apeareth. Pag: 128: a: line, laſt but fiue, for, les, reade, leaſe. Pag: 129. b: line, 17: for de, read, le. Pag. 137. a: line, laſt, for 4. 4. 4. reade, 7. 7. 7.

Some other faultes there bee: but theaſe be the greateſt.

THE FIRST CHAPTER OF THE FIRST BOOKE.

What Logike is.

Logike is an Art of Reaſoning.

Annotations.

ALthough this woord, *Logike*, bée generally receaued of Engliſhmen, and vſed euen of them that know no Logike at all, yet for that it was a ſtranger at the firſt, I thinke it not impertinent to ſéeke from whence it came, and what it doth betoken: λόγος, therefore in Gréeke ſignifieth Reaſon, of λόγος, is deriued this word, λογική that is to ſay, Reaſonable, or belonging to Reaſon, which although it bée an adiectiue, and muſt haue ſome ſuch like word, as Arte, Science, or Facultie, to be adioyned vnto it as his ſubſtantiue, yet is it ſubſtantiuely taken and vſed in Latine, as alſo in our Engliſh tongue.

Sturmius and ſome others, deriue this word Logike from λόγος as λόγος betokeneth ſpéech or talke: whoſe opinion, although the other name of this Art (which is διαλεκτική, of διαλέγεσθαι, to ſpeak or talke) doe in ſome reſpect ſéeme to confirme, yet for that the whole force and vertue of Logike conſiſteth in reaſoning, not in talking: and becauſe reaſoning may be without talking, as in ſolitary meditations and deliberations with a mans ſelfe, ſome holde the firſt deriuation as moſt ſignificant.

Dialectica & Logica, ſaith *Hotoman*, dictæ ſunt a ſermone ſiue oratione, ſed illa propriè ab eo genere ſermonis, qui cùm altero interrogando & reſpondendo commiſcetur. Fictum enim verbum eſt παρὰ τὸ διαλέγεσθαι; quod eſt, verba cum altero commutare, colloqui, diſputare, ſermocinari, ſermones cædere. Nam cùm philoſophorũ conſuetudo hæc eſſet, vt de rebus ad artes ſuas pertinentibus ſæpè inter ſe commentarentur, eruditas illas collocutiones, διαλόγους, (vt Laertius in Platone ſcribit) apellarunt, earumq; habendarum artem, Dialecticam, qua de cauſa eandem Laertius eodem loco definit artem sermonis, per quam ex eorum quibuscũ sermo est interrogatione, & responsione aliquid vel confirmatur vel refellitur. Quod cùm ita sit, difficile dictu est, dialecticæ nomen non eius sermonis esse proprium, qui in dialogis habetur, cùm perpetua non continuatur oratio; sed in rebus singulis insistitur & intelligitur quid quisq; concedat aut abnuat, vt ex concessis disputatio concludatur. Et infra.

Ex quo intelligi potest, cùm & Græcorum & Latinorum consuetudine, nihil quicquam inter dialecticæ & Logicæ verbum, pręter vocis sonum intersit, videri tamen Logicæ vocabulum, ad eam disserendi rationem quæ perpetua oratione constat, & quà hodiè plurimùm vtimur, ac multò magis ad eas disputationes quæ literis mandantur, accommodatum esse. Thus farre *Hottoman.*

Some others haue sayd, that this art may bée called λογική, of the internall forme, essence, and nature thereof consisting in reason: but διαλεκτική, of the externall maner and order of working, which is commonly done by speache and talke, as that word importeth, although Ramus vse them both as one, following Plato herein, who expoundeth διαλέγεσθαι, by τῷ λόγῳ χρῆσθαι, which is to vse reason.

Diogenes Laertius in the life of Plato, writeth, that Plato was the first who called this Arte Dialectica, and Valla reporteth that Aristotle was the first that named it Logica.

λογίζεσθαι, hathe a certaine relation to accompts, wherevpon λογισμός, and συλλογισμός, as also λόγος it selfe whence both they come, are vsed for accompting and deducting of summes, and by a Metaphoricall sence are applied to Logike, but especially to Disposition the second part of Logike, where discoursing and drawing of one reason from another is put downe. But vse hath accepted them in a generall sence for the whole Arte of Logike, as wée shall sée hereafter the like in those Latine wordes, Disserere and disputare.

[Is in Art :] An Art is a Methodicall disposition of true and coherent preceptes, for the more easie perceiuing and better remembring of the same: and this Methodicall or orderly disposition of diuers preceptes is taught in Logike, as perteining essentially therevnto. So that Logike was deseruedly called the

Art

Art of Arts, the instrument of instrumentes, the hand of Philosophie, because by the helpe thereof, not onely the groundes of naturall reason are artificially put downe, but all other Arts also are made to be Arts, as wee shall hereafter shew when wee come to the place appoynted for the due explication of Methode.

It is therefore said here, that Logike is an Art, to distinguish artificiall Logike from naturall reason. Artificiall Logike is gathered out of diuers examples of naturall reason, which is not any Art of Logike, but that ingrauen gift and facultie of wit and reason shining in the perticuler discourses of seuerall men, whereby they both inuent, and orderly dispose, thereby to iudge of that they haue inuented. This as it is to no man giuen in full perfection, so diuers haue it in sundrie measure. And because the true note and token resembling nature, must bee esteemed by the most excellent nature, therefore the preceptes of artificiall Logike both first were collected out of, and alwayes must be conformable vnto those sparkes of naturall reason, not lurking in the obscure head-peeces of one or two loytering Fryers, but manifestly appearing in the monumentes and disputations of excellent autors. And then is this Logike of Art more certaine then that of nature, because of many particulers in nature, a generall and vnfallible constitution of Logike is put downe in Art. So that, Art, which first was but the scholler of nature, is now become the maystres of nature, and as it were a Glasse wherein shee seeing and viewing herselfe, may washe out those spottes and blemishes of naturall imperfection. For there is no one particuler nature so constant and absolute, but by examining and perusing her owne force, shee may bee bettered: no nature so weake and imperfit, which by the helpe of Art is not confirmed.

Hottoman in the third Chapter of his first booke hath these wordes: Estne igitur dialectica quędam naturalis, quędam artificiosa? nequaquam: sed eius initia & semina quędam in hominum mentibus natura ingenerauit, quæ cùm pręceptis ac disciplinà, tùm vsu & assiduitate excoluntur. Eademq; cùm aliarũ artiũ omniũ, tùm pręcipuè Musicæ ratio est. Nã omnibus a natura rudis quędã canẽdi facultas data est: ab arte verò, quã naturæ notatio atq; animaduersio peperit, certa ratio traditur. Nõ enim ars naturã *imitatur tantummodò, verumetiam, vt veteres docuerunt, confirmat & amplificat: causamq;, cur quidq;, vel hoc vel illo modo fieri debeat, reddit, quod pręstare natura non potest, eaq; sola re artifex ab inscio discernitur.*

Wasserleider therefore in séeking to reforme *Ramus* his Logike, bewrayeth his owne ignoraunce, for hauing first generally defined Logike to bée an Art, hée afterwardes diuideth it into naturall Logike and artificiall, as though the naturall facultie of reason were an Art of reasoning, which is contrarie to all reason, and includeth in it selfe a manifest contradiction. To conclude this poynt, there ought nothing to bée put downe in Art, whereof there is no ground in nature, for *ars imitari debet naturam*, and as that paynter is most cunning who can moste liuely expresse his face whose counterfaite hée is to drawe, so hée that teacheth Logike must set forth no idle conceiptes of extrauagant braynes, but the true vse of naturall reason and vnderstanding: which is a necessary confutation of that absurditie mayntayned by Logicians, and inuented in Cloysters, that *ficta*, yea *falsa exempla*, bée good enough to make preceptes playne, whereas *Plato* in *Theęteto* calleth examples, μάρτυρες τῷ λόγῳ *sponsores & praedes rationes, tanquam ab eis fideiussum persolueretur.* And *Aristotle* in the eight of his *Topikes* requireth such examples as *Homer* can afford, not such as the pelting Poet *Chęrilus* did inuent.

[*Of Reasoning*:] This our English word, Reasoning, is more proper and fit to expresse the nature of Logike, then either that other word, of disputing, deriued from *disputare*, or the like, as *disserere*, and *docere*, vsed of *Cicero* and *Melanchton*: although I knowe that *Beurehusius* standeth in defence of these wordes, *disserere*, and *disputare*, which *Ramus* also vseth: and I am not much to mislike them in respect of any other Latine word, yet not altogether to compare them with this our English word of reasoning. For the word, disputing, which commeth of *disputare*, it is Metaphoricall, as *Varro* reporteth, and so is *disserere*: the one being borrowed of the Winemayster, the other fet from the sower: for as the first cutteth off superfluous branches in his Wine, which is properly *disputare*, so the other disperseth his séed in diuers places, and not confusedly throweth

all

all on one heape, which is the natural signification of this word, differere. Now because the Logician cutteth of all idle and vnnecessarie curiosities, whereof there is no vse in reasoning, seuereth truth from falshood, that which followeth from that which followeth not, order from confusion, and handleth diuers arguments and axiomes in diuers places distinctly, not euerie thing in euerie place disorderly: therefore hath hee friendly presumed vpon the good nature of these two countreymen, in vsing their words of husbandrie, to expresse a more elegant conceipt, although at the first not properly, yet by continuance of time, so conueniently, as that the Metaphoricall sence is now better knowne than the naturall signification. Yet for that both these rehearsed properties of Logike, be rather particular functions of methode, than general operations of the whole art, it is plaine, that this word disputing, with his originall disputare, and that, differere, if you respect the naturall signification thereof, cannot expresse the whole nature of Logike. Although I am not ignorant, as I said before, that Ramus and his interpreter Beurhusius, applie these words to the generall vse of this art, not restraining them to those two functions belonging to methode: whose iudgement as vse alloweth, so I doo not reiect, yet by their leaue leaue their Latine words behind our English.

Melanchton vseth this word, docere: Docere, is to teach, and Logike is an art of teaching: but then marke what I meane by teaching, for you must not restraine the signification of it in such sort, as though there were no teaching, but onely in schooles among Philosophers and schoolemaisters, or in pulpits among doctors and diuines: but generally, hee teacheth, whosoeuer maketh anie other man know that, whereof before hee was ignorant, whether hee doo it by explication and illustration, or proofe and conclusion: and thus if wee take this word, docere, it is somewhat more generall than disputare, or differere, put downe by Tully and Ramus: yet not so ample, as the nature of this art, whose vertue is seene not onely in teaching others, but also in learning thy selfe, in discoursing, thinking, meditating, and framing of thine owne, as also in discussing, perusing, searching and examining what others haue either deliuered by speach, or put downe in writing: this is called Analysis, that Genesis, and in them both consisteth the whole vse of Logike.

As farre then as mans reason can reach, so farre extendeth it selfe the vse and vertue of this art of reasoning, whose most ample and almost infinite vse and power, hath neuer had in anie tong a more generall and yet proper name, than this of reasoning, as wee vse it now adaies. Men reason in schooles as Philosophers, in Westminster as Lawyers, in Court as Lords, in Countrey as worldly husbands: whatsoeuer it bee, nay whatsoeuer thou canst imagine to bee, although it bee not, neuer was, nor neuer shall bee, yet by reason it is inuented, taught, ordered, confirmed: as the description of fame in Virgil, of famine in Ouid, of Elysian fields, of Styx, of Acheron, of the golden apples, and a thousand such poeticall imaginations. And therefore Logike hath beene of a long time vntollerably abused by those miserable Sorbonists, & dunsicall Quidditaries, who thought there was no reasoning without, Arguitur quod sic: Probatur quod non: no part of Logike without Ergò and Igitur. Whereas indeede the true vse of Logike is as well apparant in simple playne, and easie explication, as in subtile, strict, and concised probation. Reade Homer, reade Demosthenes, reade Virgill, read Cicero, reade Bartas, reade Torquato Tasso, reade that most worthie ornament of our English tongue, the Countesse of Penbrookes *Arcadia*, and therein see the true effectes of natural Logike which is the ground of artificiall, farre different from this rude and barbarous kind of outworne sophistrie: which if it had anie vse at all, yet this was all, to feede the vaine humors of some curious heades in obscure schooles, whereas the Art of reasoning hath somewhat to doe in euerie thing, and nothyng is any thing without this one thing. Some Artes are appliable onely to some certayne subiect, but Logike is scientia scientiarum, as I sayd before, not tyed to one thing, but apt for anie thing, free from all, yet fit for all, framing orderly, prouing strongely, expounding playnly, perswading forcibly, any Arte, any cause, any question, any man whatsoeuer.

What then, will some man say, neede wee any other Arts, if Logike alone can suffice for all? I aunswere, Logike alone is sufficient to helpe all, yet Logike suffiseth not for all. Logike telleth how to reason, dispute, examine, proue, or disproue any thing

thing, but the thing that is to bée reasoned, disputed, examined, proued or disproued, that Logike cannot affoord, and therefore it is to bée sought for at such Arts, as professe suche thinges, so that Logike is profitable vnto all, and yet not any of them vnprofitable : but euen as they without this bée mangled and confused, so this without them is bare and naked. Logike is necessary for a diuine, yet Logike yéeldeth no diuinitie : but when a Preacher hath by continuall perusing of the sacred Scriptures furnished himselfe with store of matter, then Logike wil teach him how to teach others, & not onely that, but also how to learne himselfe, to defend, to confute, to instruct, to reprehend. Logike sheweth generally what an argument is, and how to vse an argument, but the seuerall argumentes are elsewhere to be had. For as Arithmetike teacheth to counte money, not to finde money, and Geometrie to measure ground, not to purchase grounde : so Logike can tell you howe to reason of thinges, and yet reserueth the peculier doctrine of the same thinges to the seuerall professors thereof. I doe not denie, but one and the same man may purchase ground, measure ground, and also reason of the same ground, but hée purchaseth it by one Art, measureth it by another, and reasoneth of it by a third, hée purchaseth it as a worldling, measureth it as a Geometer, reasoneth of it as a Logician : and although one man may be furnished with all these thrée properties, yet euery Art must haue her owne by the lawe of Iustice, confusion must bée auoyded, and the preceptes of euery Art distinctly put downe, although the vse of the same preceptes may be common and concurre altogether in one man, if one man bée skilfull in all these Artes.

Ramus addeth this word, well, in the ende of the definition, which me thinkes were as well left out as put in, for although it may séeme to seuer the perfection of Art from the imbecilitie of nature, yet indéede, the very name of an Art, includeth this word, well : euery Art being an habite of doing that well whereof it is an Art. Howsoeuer it bée, it appeareth, that to reason well and artificially, is the duetie and ende of Logike: for it is not essentiall vnto Logike alwayes to perswade, no more then to a Phisitian alway, to heale, but to performe those thinges which are prescribed in his Art, although the hoped euent and successe do not alwayes ensue.

The second Chapter.

Of the partes of Logike, and the seuerall kindes of Argumentes.

There bée two partes of Logike, Exposition of the nature of argumentes, and Disposition of the same. Exposition is the first part of Logike which expoundeth the diuers kindes of argumentes by their seuerall affections and mutuall relations one to another, which for that it helpeth to inuent argumentes, is called Inuention. An argument is any seuerall conceipt apt to argue that whereunto in reason it is referred.

First, an Argument is either inhærent, or set elsewhere. Inhærent is that which is inuented by consideration of the nature of the thing argued: and is either originall and first or secondary and deriued. First is that which hath his beginning of it selfe. It is agréeable or disagréeable. Agréeable is that which agréeth with the thing which it doth argue. The agréeable is either fully agréeable, or agréeable in part: fully agréeable is that, where there is a greater cohærence and affinitie betwéene the argument and the thing argued: fully agréeable is first, the cause and the thing caused.

Annotations.

The Art of Logike, as is declared already, layeth downe the right vse of naturall reason: and this that wée call shewing or declaring how to reason, is no giuing of reason to him that had it not, but an applying or directing of the minde to the view and contemplation of that, which of it selfe it might perceaue, if it were turned and framed thereunto. For, as Plato sayth, 7. de repub. the trueth of the things comprised in Arts is as naturally propounded to the viewe of the minde, as colours bée to the sight of the eye: and therefore Aristotle in his first booke of of Elenchs hath ſet downe that which common experience doth confirme, that euery common perſon or ſilly ſoule vſeth Logike in ſome part, and practiſeth of himſelfe by naturall inſtinct that which artificiall Logike doth preſcribe in her ſeuerall rules and conſtitutions. Artificiall Logike then is the polyſhing of natural wit, as diſcouering the validitie of euerie reaſon, bée it neceſſary, wherof cometh ſcience: or contingent, whence procéedeth opinion. Although I knowe there is a great controuerſie and contention among the auncient Philoſophers, concerning theſe two: whileſt ſome of them mayntayne onely Science, ſome others holde with opinion onely. Heraclitus called opinion the falling ſickneſſe, for that thereby men many times fell headlong into diuers deluſions and erronious conceiptes. So in like maner, the Stoikes held this for one of their Paradoxes, that Sapiens nihil opinatur, a wiſe man is not opinatiue, a wiſe man neuer iudgeth according to opinion. On the other ſide Anaxarchus was of this opinion, that all mans iudgment was but opinion, and that his vnderſtanding coulde perfitly vnderſtand nothing, which the Pyrrhonians taught after him, and the new Academikes: and a man may coniecture that Plato and Ariſtotle ſometimes inclyned that way; for Plato in his bóoke called Timęus, aſcribeth truth to God and Gods children, leauing nothing but truelike to mortall men, and Ariſtotle in the ſecond of his Metaphiſikes compareth mans vnderſtanding in reſpect of perfect knowledge of trueth to the dazeling eyes of a Batt in the broade day light. But yet notwithſtanding theſe forealledged places, both Plato and Ariſtotle haue elſewhere euidently declared that man is capable both of Science and certayne knowledge, as in thinges contayned in Arts: and alſo of opinion, as in infinit affaires which are dayly incident: and this was long before their tyme, elegantly put downe by the famous Poet and Logician Parmenides.

χρεὼ δέ σε πάντα πύθεσθαι,
ἡ μὲν ἀληθείαν εὐπείθεος ἀτρεκες ἦτορ,
ἡ δε βροτῶν δόξας, τῶν οὐκ ἐπι πισις ἀληθης.

Oportet verò te omnia noſſe,
Tùm veritatis ſuaſu facilis ſententiam,
Tùm verò mortalium opiniones, quarum non amplius fides vera.

C. Becauſe

Because of these two kinds of conceiptes, Aristotle woulde néedes make two Logikes, the one for Science, the other for Opinion: wherein (if so it may be sayde of so great a Philosopher) it séemeth hée was but an Opinator. For although among thinges conceaued and knowne, some bée necessary and vnfallible, some doubtfull and contingent, yet the Arte of Knowing and Reasoning of the same (I meane Logike) is only one and the same, as the sight of the eye in perceyuing all colours, bée they chaungeable or not chaungeable. And aswell might a man say there must be two arts of Grammer (if Grammer bée a distinct Art) one for courtly spéeche, an other for country talke: or two distinct arts of making of cups, one for golden cuppes, an other for cuppes of siluer, as two Logikes, one for vnfallible Argumentes, and another for Contingent. Therefore one Logike suffiseth to dispute of all thinges, necessary or contingent whatsoeuer. Yet this one Logike her selfe in respect of her preceptes is alway necessary and neuer contingent, for otherwise it were no Art, but the application of it may bée in contingent causes aswell as necessary.

[Two partes of Logike:] The Stoicall diuision of Logike into Inuention and Judgement, although both Aristotle himselfe séeme to commend it in some places, as in 8. Topi.3: Rhet: and Tully and Quintilian doo altogether obserue it, is yet reprehended of some, who thinke that Judgement is not any seuerall part of Logike, but rather an adiunct or propertie generally incident to the whole Art: because, say they, there is vse of iudgement euen in inuention. But in my fancie they might better haue founde some fault with these wordes, Judgement, and Inuention, then reprehended the distribution, which is most true, if they consider what the Stoikes did vnderstand by these wordes. For by the first part called τοπικὴ, they intend the explication of the diuers kindes, natures, affections, relations, and proprieties of seuerall argumentes, which because it helpeth inuention, is called Inuention, as I sayd before: although indéede a man shall no more finde argumentes by this first part of Logike, then hée shall get Latine wordes by Etymologie the first part of Grammer: which made me alter the wordes, as not proper, but rather borowed from the Mathematikes, where two

or

or thrée numbers being receiued or put downe, a third or fourth number proportionable is found out, which of them is called εὕρεσις, Inuention.

And by κριτική. Iudicium, Judgement, is meant nothing els, but a Disposition, ordering or placing and setling of these seuerall argumentes alreadie inuented, to the intent that a man may the better iudge of them, so that here Judgement is taken for Disposition, the effect for the cause, for Judgement ariseth of the ordering and disposing of arguments.

They might therefore haue chaunged the wordes, and kept the thing, which yet they haue not done: but brought in new diuisions of Logike, correspondent to the setling and placing of Aristotles Logicall discourses in his booke called Organon: sometimes into thrée partes, as Apodicticall, Topicall, Elenchticall, sometimes into two, by name Apodicticall and Dialecticall. Topicall, or Dialecticall they will haue to bée a seuerall kinde of Logike by probable argumentes. Apodicticall, that which disputeth by necessary conclusions, as though there were not one and the same Art, Science, and order of reasoning both by probable and necessary argumentes, as I sayde before, and the selfe same places of argumentes both in the one and in the other, as causes, effectes, subiectes, adiuncts, &c. both contingent and necessary. For, as for that third kinde of Logike, which they call Elenchticall, séeing it is no Logike at all, but rather the abuse and peruersion of Logike, I sée no cause why it shoulde be taught in Logike: yet if any man thinke that the true preceptes of Logike once knowne, will not be sufficient to descry the falsenesse of sophisticall argumentations, he may for his contentation séeke for a full discourse thereof out of some commentarie, and not ouercharge the Art it selfe with vnnecessary institutions. I graunt there is something profitable in the Elenches, as also in some other tractates of the same kind, but if wée shall put downe all in Logike, for true Logike, which doth in any respect helpe Logike, wée shall neuer make an ende of Logike.

[Exposition is the first part:] As in Grammer, Aetymologie concerneth seuerall wordes, and Syntaxis the due coherence of the same, so Exposition the first part of Logike, declareth the particular affection and nature of euery seuerall argument, and

Disposition the second part, by ordering and setling the same, causeth iudgement and vnderstanding. And as seuerall words bée in respect of Grammer, so seuered reasons in respect of Logike; and as of many words is made speech, so of diuers arguments arise axioms.

Exposition and Disposition are not two seuerall arts of Logike, as though wée should haue one Logike to expound the natures of seuerall arguments, and another to iudge of the same by Disposition, but they bée two essentiall parts of the whole, which ioyned togither make one true Logike.

The doctrine of Inuention or Exposition is generall, and not restrained onely to the finding out of a Medium, which they commonly take for the onely argument, but absolutely and vniuersally appliable to the inuenting of any thing, either true or fained whatsoeuer.

Againe, the arguments in Inuention must bée considered seuerally, singlely, and alone, then after to bée disposed and ordered by certeine precepts, thereby to iudge of the truth or falsenesse of the same: as for example.

Paris A good sheepheard.

These two singly put downe as two arguments, to wit, the subiect and the adiunct, are afterwards disposed in an axiome, to iudge of the truth thereof, as thus:

Paris is no good sheepheard.

But because this proposition is contingent and doubtfull (for the arguments bée but in part agréeable) therefore it is confirmed by another argument, that is to say, by an effect and working of Paris, I meane that which Thomalin putteth downe in Iuly, in these words.

But nothing such thylk sheepheard was
 whome *Ida* hill did beare:
That left his flocke to fetch a lasse,
 whose loue he bought too deare.

So then, héere bée thrée seuerall arguments, or two ioyned in the axiome before, and the third following in these verses of Thomalin; which third they call, Medium, or third argument, thus:

1 *Paris*: 2 A good sheepheard.
3 To leaue his flocke to fetch a lasse.

Whereof it is concluded in this wise syllogistically, by disioyning the two first arguments, the subiect and adiunct, Paris, and, The good sheepheard.

He that leaueth his flocke to fetch a lasse, is no good sheepheard:
But Paris did leaue his flocke to fetch a lasse,
Therefore Paris is no good sheepheard.

That which they call Medium, and third argument, is, as it were, an Arbiter honorarius, a determiner, a reconciler, a daies man: which if it agree with both the other arguments, maketh the conclusion affirmatiue: but negatiue, if with one onely, as in the former example of Paris, the Medium, the arbiter, the determiner, is that effect of Paris, To leaue his flocke to fetch a lasse: which because it is agreeable with the nature of Paris, but is flatly repugnant to the dutie of a good sheepheard, therefore is the conclusion negatiue, Paris is no good sheepeheard. So in Maister Ploidens reports, fol. 474. Saunders is a murderer. The Mediũ is that effect of Saunders, to minister venim to the intent to poyson: which, because it agreeth as well with the nature of murder, as the affection of Saunders, maketh the conclusion affirmatiue, thus:

He that doth minister venim to poyson any one, is a murderer:
But Saunders ministred venim to poyson one,
Therefore Saunders is a murderer.

In this order, first of single arguments wee make axioms: which axioms, if of themselues they bee perceiued and graunted, they bee straightway iudged as true or false. And this is the first part of iudgement in axioms, called axiomaticall, determining only truth and falsenes in propositions or axioms. Now if these propositions bee doubtfull, then therof be made questions, which are to bee proued by third arguments, set from the affections of the other two which were ioyned in the axiome, and lastly are to be concluded by syllogisme, the onely iudge of all coherence or consequence: as finally, Methode hath only to deale with the ordering and setling of many axioms, thereby to giue sentence of methodicall proceeding or vnorderly confusion. And therefore I see no reason why I should with the common Logicians, chop in Canons, Maximaes, and rules of consequence, as they call them, applying them to euery argument of inuention, seeing that syllogismes, and onely syllogismes are the true and onely rules of consequence and inconsequence, as I said before.

The occasion, as I thinke, of this their errour, heereof arose: because if an Enthymeme be denied, we cōmonly confirme it by some axiome, which indeed is nothing els, but the supplying of the part wanting, as either the Maior, or Minor, as they terme them, or els some prosyllogisme. And this rule, Canon or Maxima, beeing so supplied, a plaine syllogisme proceedeth, the onelie determiner of coherence. And as all the force of consequence is in syllogismes, so all the vertue of arguing is in the seuerall affection of euery argument to the thinge argued: whiche affection is truely and artificially put downe in Inuention: in such sort that from euerie definition, and precept in Inuention, such rules, maximaes, canons, axioms, consectaries, corollaries, or howsoeuer you tearme them, may easily bee deduced: and, when necessitie requireth, shall be of vs put downe distinctly in their seuerall places. For, as for most of those outworne maximaes hudled vp in schooles, they be either vnnecessarie, and may bee easily perceaued by the definitions and explications of the arguments, or els not generally true, but in part: and therefore in no wise to bee put downe in art, but rather to be reserued for Commentaries, as that, Quod efficit tale, magis est tale, &c. which cannot stand, but by a number of friuolous and sophisticall distinctions. Let him read Beurhusius, if any list to see the true canons of Ramus his Logike, compared at large with these same rules. It shal suffice at this time to vnderstand, that ẏ true maximaes, or canons of Inuention, are nothing els but certain rules concerning the seuerall force or affection of arguments: The canons of axioms, such precepts as declare the vse & force of axioms: and so, in a word, the canons of syllogisms and methode, are precepts touching the consequence and inconsequence of the one, & the perspicuitie or confusion of the other. Neither are there any rules of consequence at all, but only those of syllogisms, I haue in my text kept my selfe onely to such maximaes

both

both in Inuention and Disposition, as are put downe orderly by Ramus, and are essentially belonging to this art: yet for the satisfying of the expectation of some yong Logicians, somewhat vnacquainted with this newfound Logike, as it pleaseth some to tearme it, I will héereafter, as occasion shall serue, put downe in the annotations, some of the other stampe.

But héere may a doubt arise: For, séeing that euery axiome and rule of Inuention is a part of Judgement (because it is an axiome, and euery axiome is of iudgement) it may séeme that Inuention and Judgement be not distinct parts, but rather, as was obiected before out of Carpentar, confounded the one with the other. I answere, the rules and precepts of Inuention bée indéed axioms, and therefore consequently procéed from Judgement: but so, as you must take them to be the fruits of Judgement already shewed in ordering the axiomes and rules of Inuention: or examples of Judgement, teaching the part of Inuention: Not as though these precepts were put downe in Inuention to teach a man how to iudge, either axiomatically, syllogistically, or methodically, which onely belongeth to the second part of Logike called Judgement or Disposition: And if you so take them, then euerie axiome is not straight way a part of Judgement: but onely such rules and precepts, as teach to make, order, and frame axioms. For otherwise, euery precept of euery art, because it is an axiome, should bée taken for a part of Judgement in Logike: whereas indéed they bée but the fruites and examples of that Logicall iudgement appéering in the orderly constitution of euery art. And so in Inuention, euery rule is an axiome, euery rule doth iudge, but euery rule teacheth not how to frame an axiome, euery rule sheweth not how to iudge, which onely is the peculiar duetie of Logicall iudgement.

The art and doctrine of euery argument, is distinct, firme, constant, and immutable: yet the affection of arguments may bée altered, changed, and diuersly considered, either in the same things diuersly compared among themselues, or in one thing referred to diuers, as in those examples, put downe by Beurhusius and Talæus,

God	Created man.	So the affectiō is of the	Cause procreant to the effect.
	Preserueth man.		Cause conseruant to the effect
	Is not man.		Disparats among thēselues.
	Is not like man.		Unlikes among themselues.

Where the things be as they were, I meane, God, and Man, which are heere compared togither, yet the diuers kinds of relations and respectes, make the selfe same thinges haue diuers names and titles, according to their seuerall and diuers affections.

In like manner also it is, if one thing be referred to many, and drawne, as it were, through the places of arguments, although some arguments bee not incident to some things:

As, Man referred vnto	God, his maker,	hath ÿ affection of	Effect procreated.
	Body, his matter,		Effect materiall.
	Reason his forme,		Effect formed.
	Gods glory, his end,		Effect finall.
	Actions, his effects,		Cause.
	Body, his part,		Whole.
	World, his whole,		Part.
	Liuing creature, general,		Speciall.
	Paule, speciall,		Generall.
	Earth, subiect,		Adiunct.
	Riches, adiuncts,		Subiect.
	Tree, his disparate,		Disparate.
	Beast, contrary,		Contrary.
	Homo ab humo, the notation.		Name interpreted.
	Reasonable, liuing, Creature, definition,		The thing defined.
	Angell, equall,		Equall.
	Blub, like,		Like.

Yet the art is certeine and immutable, for, that which is a cause, can neuer bee an effect in the same respect and relation, which relation chaunging, altereth the argument, not the art.

[An Argument:] Euery thing hath his seuerall name according to his naturall proprietie, or by the imposition and fancie of man, but Logike respecting a second vse in these seuerall things, thinges, hath giuen them an artificiall and secondary name. As, fire hath this his name vsually knowne : but because it is sometimes considered of Logicians, as a cause of heate, therefore hath it his second note and name, and is called a Cause, one of the arguments, for that it argueth heate as his effect, and so in others. And by this affection wee learne whether one argument agree or disagree with another, and how it agreeth, whether as a cause with his effect (which is an absolute and full agreement) or as an adiunct with his subiect, which is but an agreement in part, and after a certeine manner, and so of the rest. So that argumentes bee nothing els, but singularum rerum affectiones extrà collocationem considerat æ, quibus ad arguendum sunt affectæ & comparatæ, sed vt Grammatica non voces, non vocum significationes, sed vocum affectiones, sic Logica non res, non rerum naturas, sed rerum inter se habitudines explicat. Itaq; omnia argumenta sunt relata : sed quia istæ relationes variæ sunt, itaq; varia sunt argumentorum genera. This affection of argumentes is by Hottoman expounded in this manner. Affectio ista est ratio quam quæq; res habet ad alterā. Græci λόγον appellant; itaque commodius rationem appellare possemus, sed vitandæ ambiguitatis causa, nomen affectionis delegimus, quo eodem *Cicero*, & in topicis, & in partitionibus hac eadem in re est vsus. Rationis autē verbū à Mathematicis sumptum est, qui λόγον definiunt duarum eiusdem generis quantitatum comparationem; interpretes proportionem Latinè nominarunt : quidam habitudinem : nonnulli habitum : qui commodius, respectum : barbari fortasse correspondentiam appellarent. Huius vis ac facultas ea est, vt declaret, quænam rei cuiusq; cum altera ratio sit, quemadmodum inuicem affectæ sint, quo modò se inter se habeant, qualis inter ipsas comparatio aut affectio sit, sitne pars an totū, genus an species, consentanea an dissentanea, &c.

[To argue :] To argue, is generall; either in inuenting onely one argument by the affection of the other, as when by the notion of the cause we seeke the effect, or els in placing them axiomatically, syllogistically, or methodically, wee argue some other thing either by explication or confirmation. The first consideration is of arguments seuerally conceaued and alone by themselues, the second as they bée placed by disposition: and therfore Piscators animaduersion in this place is to small purpose, whereas hée reprehendeth Ramus, for saying that euery seuerall thing considered alone is an argument. For he in so saying meaned not, that an argument should bée so alone, as though it had no affection or relation to any other thing, but so seuerally considered, as that in Inuention we should not intermeddle with axiomaticall, syllogisticall, or methodicall conioining and setting together of the same seuerall arguments, for that doth wholy and only belong to Disposition.

[Any seuerall conceipt:] Except those wordes which doo but bind and knit together the parts of spéech, as coniunctions, which signifie no seueral and distinct thing in nature. Except againe copious and Rhetoricall phrases, where many wordes expresse but one thing, as, A man of an excellent and heauenly wit, where the words be many, the arguments but two, that is, the subiect and the adiunct. Lastly, except full comparisons, diuisions, definitions, and descriptions, where the argument is put downe in a whole proposition. This is Beurhusius exception, although to small purpose: for Ramus saith not, all such wordes as are alone, but all such reasons, conceipts, and thinges as are alone, and by themselues conceaued seuerally, as these arguments bée which hée héere excepteth: for though there bée many wordes, yet they all expresse but one conceipt of reason, and that is this single and sole argument which wée héere talke of.

But to let that passe, hée that taketh this word Argument, onely for a proofe or confirmation, deceaueth himselfe, and bereaueth Logike of halfe hir dignitie. Indéede it is vsually taken for that thing onely which doth proue and confirme, but héere it hath a more generall signification, and betokeneth not onely confirmations, but also declarations without any syllogisme or forme of concluding, and so doth arguere in Latine signifie, declarare, ostendere, perspicuum manifestumq; facere, vt in Virgilio.

Degeneres animos timor arguit, *id est*, ostendit.

Yet neuerthelesse the same kinde of argument may commonly

monly serue both to declare and to confirme (although some there bée which onely declare) so in the end of the first Aegloge of the Shepheardes Kalender, Hobbinol vseth an argument of the cause, onely for explication sake.

Ah faithlesse *Rosalynde*, and voide of grace,
Thou art the roote of all this ruthfull woe.

And in the ninth Aegloge, Diggon Dauy vseth the same kinde of argument to the same purpose.

Their ill hauiour garres men missay,
Both of their doctrine and of their say.

And yet here the cause argueth the effect, although there bée no syllogisticall probation intended, for that the proposition of it selfe séemed to Diggon true inough. And in our lawe, In euery count, barre, replication, reioynder, &c. Argumentes of asseueration and exposition bée asmuch vsed as those of proofe and conclusion. Now for the other parte, no man doubteth but that an argument of the cause may bée very well vsed for confirmation, wherof examples are euery where apparant. Let no man therefore thinke there is no Logike, where there is no syllogisticall conclusion, for euery argument serueth not euery where onely for confirmation.

[Inhærent:] I vse this word till I méete with a better. I meane not so Inhærent, as though it should allwayes agrée with the thing argued, for many times it is flatly repugnant thereunto, but so conioyned, as that the thing argued in maner offereth the argument to the Inuention of the Logician, and this is true in disagréeable argumentes: otherwise it is in testimonies, which bée as it were borrowed from other matters, and brought to the Logician to bée framed accordingly.

Ramus diuideth an argument into artificiall and inartificiall, wherupon Piscator tooke occasion of reprehension. For I sée no reason, sayth hée, why testimonies shoulde bée called inartificiall argumentes, séeing that there is as good Arte shewed in applying them, as in finding other argumentes: and if in Art there ought to bée nothing without Art, either Inuention wanteth Art, or testimonies are not inartificiall, they answere him thus. They bée not called Inartificiall, for that they want Art, but because they argue not of themselues, but by the force of some artificiall: Which answere doth not fully satisfie mée: For the testimonie of God argueth most absolutely of it selfe, neither can wée well say, that his testimonie were not to bée beléeued, vnlesse hée were verus, bonus, iustus &c. sith wée cannot distinguishe these so from his diuine essence, but that whatsoeuer is in God, is God: and therefore it is an vnfallible argument, God spake it, therefore it is so, ipse dixit, is here sufficient, neyther néede wée séeke for any artificiall argument to confirme it, as wée doe in the testimonies of men.

I holde on the same course which Ramus doth in deuiding still by certaine steps and degrées, till I come at last to the lowest. For it were against Platoes precept and all Arte, to iumpe abruptly from the highest and most generall, to the lowest and most speciall, without passing by the subalternal.

[First:] First may bée conceiued of it selfe, without respect had to any other, as not depending on those that follow. So the cause may be knowne without any mention of a definition, but the definition can neuer bée conceiued without notice of the cause, as being made thereof: therefore the cause is first and originall, the definition secondary.

[Fully agreeable:] Scribonio & Piscatori non placet ista distinctio: nam si Logicè considerentur, æqualis & eadem est consensio: nam subiecta & adiuncta æquè non possunt alterum esse absq; altero, atq; causa & effectū: sin physicè, tùm accidentalis illa consensio est æq; in his & illis: nam faber potest non facere, quomodò puer potest non esse tinctus literis. Et nec omnis causa essentialiter conuenit cum effecto, nec omne subiectum accidentaliter cum suo adiuncto. hæc illi. Quia tamen diuersi sunt gradus dissentaneorum, ideò & consentaneorum videntur esse eodem modo. Itaq; hic nihil mutaui, hæreo.

These generall heades of argumentes haue béene diuersly tearmed of diuers Philosophers, as appeareth by Diogenes Laertius, and Aristotle. For sometimes they are called Categoremes, and the handling or discoursing of the same, Categories, both which are Gréeke wordes of like signification,

borrowed

borrowed from the place of iudgement, and applyed to phylosophicall conceipts. κατηγορεῖσθαι signifieth to say, or affirme one thing of an other, as in accusations it is vsually séene, and in arguments easily perceaued: where one thing added to an other, is affirmed of the same, or else denied. Otherwhiles the preceptes of them bée called τόποι, wherevpon, Aristotles bookes where these bée handled, are intituled τοπικὰ. τόπος is a place, and therefore Tully called them in Latine, locos, sedes, fontes, places, seates, springes or fountaynes of argumentes. Sometimes they haue more apt and easie titles, as when they bée called Principles, Elementes, Reasons, Proofes, Argumentes, Termini and Media. Of all which, I vse for the most part, this word Argument, and sometimes Reason, and Proofe, as most vsuall and significant, the rest béeing rather straunge and metaphoricall.

The third Chapter.

Of the efficient and materiall cause.

A Cause is that by whose power and force a thing is caused: therefore this first place of Inuention is the fountayne of all knowledge, and that thing onely is knowne, whose cause is vnderstoode. A cause is eyther before the thing caused, or els, in and with it. The cause before the thing caused, is eyther the efficient or the material. The efficient is a cause from the whiche a thing is: which although it cannot bée artificially deuided, yet it may bée for order, thus distinguished. First the efficient worketh eyther of it selfe and by his owne proper force, or els accidentally and by some external power. By it selfe, either naturally as the windes blowe, the fire heateth, or with aduice and voluntary deliberation as man in his seueral actions. Accidentally, eyther by necessitie, as when the efficient is by some violent compulsion constrayned to doo this or that, or by chaunce and hazard; when any thing happeneth contrary to the purpose and intent of the worker, as if a man digging for stones shoulde finde treasure, which comming to passe by some secret cause, is by vs ascribed to fortune: Secondly the cause efficient either worketh alone, which of it selfe without any help of others bringeth to passe his effect, as fire heateth, these bée αἴτια ἐνεργοῦντα καθ᾽αὑτά, or with others, which is holpē by others, these be called συναίτια or συνεργοῦντα, this is either principall, which in working ruleth the instrumental, as the Carpenter the axe, or instrumental which is vsed of the principal: and is eyther idle, and of it selfe hath no action, but is onely moued of the principal, as the Sawe of the Sawyer, or helping, as béeing moued of the principall, and yet mouing it selfe also, as all such instrumentes which haue life, as the Oxe ploweth partly by his owne motion, partly moued by the plowman. Agayne it is such as the efficient cannot worke without it, as the writer without a pen, or contrarily.

Lastly, the cause efficient either maketh or destroyeth: that which maketh causeth a thing to bée γεννητική, and doth either procreate or bring forth that which was not before, as God the worlde, king Lud the Citie of London, or preserue and kéepe that in béeing which before was procreated, as God the world, magistrates the cities. The destroying is that which causeth a thing not to bée that was, and doth eyther vtterly abolish and make that to haue no béeing whiche before was, as the floud, or in part destroy and deface, as sicknesse the body.

In Iune Hobbinoll reciteth a number of particular efficients of delight and pleasure, describing thereby the place where hée was, thus:

Loe *Collyn* heere the place whose pleasant syte
From other shades hath weand my wandring minde,
Tell mee what wants mee here to woorke delyte?
The simple ayre, the gentle warbling winde,
So calme, so coole, as no where els I finde.
The grassy ground with dainty daysies dight,
The bramble bush, where birds of euery kinde
To the waters fall their tunes attemper right.

Collyn in the first Egloge maketh loue the efficient of his weale and woe.

A thousand sithes I cursse that carefull howre,
Wherein I lou'de the neighbour towne to see,
And eke ten thousand siths I blesse the stowre
Wherein I saw so faire a sight as shee.
Yet all for naught, such sight hath bred my bayne,
Ah God, that loue should breede both ioy and payne.

In April Hobbinoll declareth the procreant causes of Elissa.

Pan may bee proud that euer he begot
such a bellibone,
And *Syrinx* reioyce that euer was her lot
to haue such an one.

And in July, Thomalyn describing that tyme of the yeere, poetically, in the ende bringeth in the doggestare as causing death.

And now the sunne hath reared vp
his fierie footed teame
Making his way betweene the cup
and golden Diademe.
The rampant Lyon hunts hee fast
with dogge of noysome breath:
Whose balefull barking bringes in haste
pynes, plagues, and dreary death.

Such examples as want in the Kalender, shall be supplied out of our law.

In May, Piers vseth conseruant causes.

But tract of time, and long prosperitie,
That nourse of vice, this of insolencie:
Lulled the sheepheards in such securitie, &c.

Maister Plowden, Folio, 262: a: Et quant a ceo, ils disoyent, que le forfeture icy auera relation al temps del original offence commence, que enforce le mort, et ceo est le metter luy en ewe, et ceo fuit fait en sa vie, et ceo act fuit felony, et l'enditement dit, et doyt dire, que il mist luy en le eawe feloniousement. Car ceo que cause mort, doyt estre dit feloniousement fayt: et pur ceo si vn percust vn auter, issintq; apres, il de ceo morust, l'enditement doyt dire, que il luy feloniousement percusse, issintque felony est attribute al acte, lequel act est fait per viue home, et en sa vie, come Browne dit. Car il dit; sir Iames Hales fuit mort, et coment aucigne il al mort? Poet est redit per surrounder, et que surrounde luy? poet estre responde, sir Iames Hales. Et quant fist il ceo? Poet estre responde, en son vie. Issint que sir Iames Hales esteant en vie causa sir Iames Hales d'estre mort, et l'act del vive home fist le mort del mort home. Heere sir Iames Hales did of himselfe voluntarily drowne himselfe.

Issint. Fol. 366. Si estrange al fine, que est de bon memory, devignie de non sane memorie, ou est imprison le tierce an apres les proclamations fait, et issint continue tanque les sinque ans soyent expire, et pius il vyent en son memorie, ou est hors del prison, il ne serra conclude: car laches ne puit estre assigne en luy que fault memory, ou libertie en son prosecution, et pur ceo ne fueront comprehende en le entent. Mes si en ceo case lestraunge al fine, en le tierce an, vst ale ouster le mere, ou vst prise baron, et issint vst continue tanque les sinque ans vssent estre passe, la ils serront lye. Car le aler oustre le mere, ou prender del baron fueront acts voluntarie: Mes infanitie del memory, et imprisonment sont encounter le volunt del partie, et issint ils disoyent, que reasonable sence doyt estre done al letter.

Fol. 9.b. 13.b. 18.b. 19. a.b. Les parols del ley de nature, del ley de ceo realme et dauter realms, et del ley de dieu auxi voile yelder et doner lieu a ascunacts et choses faits encoûter les parols de mesme le leys et ceo est lou les parols del ley sont infringe pur avoyder greinder inconveniences, ou pur necessite, ou per compulsion, ou per involuntary ignorance. Pur avoyder greinder inconveniences, come le bater del person de ascun home en ascun cases, uncore le batre et naufre de ascun home per auter, est exbien encounter le ley de nature, come encounter le ley del terre.

Mes uncore en 22. lib. ass. lou home fuit en arrage et non sane memorie, et fist grand male, et le home, et ses parents auxi luy prisseront, et luy lieront, et bateront oue verges, et est la tenus, que ils puissoyent ceo iustifier en avoydance del grand male que il puissoit faire, esteant de non sane memorie. Et uncore le ley de nature, et le ley del realme prohibite generalment ascun de bater auter:

mes

mes cest especiall case pur auoyder de greinder mischiefe, ad vn exemption et speciall priuilege. Et nous voiromus auxi (come iay dit) que necessitie en toutes leys serra bone excuse, et que touts leys done lieu al necessitie. Car il est conmon prouerb, que Necessitas non habet legem: et pur ceo, In præcipe quod reddat, le tenant excusera sa default per cretein de eaw, et vncore chescun default est abhorre en nostre ley, pur ceo que il est vn contempt del court: mes pur ceo que sans perill de mort, il ne puit veigner, le necessitie del chaunce en tiel case, entant que nul default est en luy, luy excusera.

Issint enfriender del priso est felony en le prisoner mesme per lestatute De frangentibus prisonam, vncore si le prison soit ignie, et ils que sont eins, enfreindre le prison pur le saluation de lour vies, ceo serra excuse per le ley del reason: et vncore les parols de lestatute sont encounter ceo. Issint in 14: H.7. les iurors que fueront iures sur lissue, pur fear d'un grand tempest departont dillonques et seuerot eux mesmes, et fuit la tenus que ils ne serra amercies, et que lour verdit apres fuit bone, et que ils ne fesoyent malement, et ceo fuit issint tenus pur le necessitie del chaunce: mes auterment ils serra grœuousement punye. Et issint pur saluation de ma vie, ieo puis tuer auter que assault moy. Car coment que effusion del sange, et tuer des homes est prohibite per le comen ley, vncore chescun home en son defence, ou come champion en tryall en briefe de droyt, ou tiels semblables poyent tuer autres: et ceo est pur le necessitie del saluation de son vie en son defence, et en l'auter case pur le necessitie del triall.

Issint per le commen Custome del realme, les hostelers serra charges pur les biens de lour gestes perdus, ou embeseles de lour measons: vncore si lour measons soyent enfreints per les enemyes de roy, et les biens dillonques prises, ils ne serra charge pur eux. Car per reason, ceo ne poet estre resist: et pur cest cause ceo violence infringera le violence del custome. Et auxi le ley de Dieu done lieu al necessitie. Issint que les parols del ley de dieu poient estre infringe per necessitie sans offence al dieu: et pur ceo en le viel ley, per le ley de dieu il fuit prohibite que nul comederoit le sacre pane s. panem propositionis: vncore il ap-

E.j. piert

piert que Dauid pur necessitie de fampne comede le dit pane, et il ne infringe le ley, coment que il infringe les parols del ley, come Christ mesme declare en le gospell, pur ceo que il ceo fist pur necessitie.

Issint les Apostles del Christ per necessitie del fampne auolsont les spices del frument dauters persons, et les comederent, et coment que ils infringe lexpresse parols del sacre scripture, que prohibite a prender les biens del auters sans le volunt del owners, uncore ils ne offenderont per ceo, come il apiert per le gospell. Issint que per ceux cases nous veyomous que le ley des homes et de dieu yelde et done lieu al necessitie.

Et compulsion auxi est bon excuse en nostre ley, come si home fist obligation per dures, il auoydera ceo. Issint si le brache de ascun est traie per compulsion, et le weapon en son mayne tue un auter, ceo ne serra felony: et issint en touts auters cases lou home fait chose esteant a ceo coact et compell, il ne serra pur ceo damnifie. Et auxi si home infringe les parols del ley per inuoluntary ignorance, ceo nest enfreinder del ley. Come si un infant de tender age tue un home, ceo ne serra fellony en luy, pur ceo que il nauoit discretion, ne intelligence, et pur ceo le ley impute ceo a son ignorance, lequel est a luy a ceo age per nature, et issint nul default en luy, et pur ceo il est dit Inuoluntary ignorance. Car il ne puit esse sapient ne sage, coment que il voil, mes est ignorant per compulsion, et pur ceo il serra excuse, et tiel act est proprement dit destre fait ex Ignorantia. s. lou inuoluntary ignorance est aiudge le cause del act. Issint si une home de non sane memorie tue un auter, coment que il ad enfreint les parols del ley, uncore il nad enfreint le ley, pur ceo que il nauoit ascun memory, ne intelligence, mes mere ignorance, lequel vient a luy per le main de dieu; et pur ceo est dit inuoluntary ignorance; a quel le ley impute le act destre fait, en tant que nul default est en luy, et pur ceo il serra excuse, entant que il est ignorant per compulsion, et tiel act est dit et terme desse fait ex ignorantia, s. coque inuoluntary ignorance est le cause. Et in Deuter. in principio cap. 9: Dieu prouide especiall remedy, que cesty que fist chose per tiel ignorance

norance ne serra puny pur ceo: car la il est ordeigne, que si vn laborer est al labor oue vn hatchet, et le test del hatchet eschue, et tue vn que est south luy, que tiel laborer ne serra mise al mort, mes vn especiall ville fuit ordeigne pur sanctuary pur luy, pur ceo que il ceo fist per inuoluntary ignorance. Mes lou home enfreint les parols del ley per ignorance voluntary, la il ne serra excuse: come si vn home que est yure, s. drunke, tue vn auter, ceo serra felony, et il serra pende pur ceo, et vncore il fist ceo per ignorance. Car quant il fuit yure, il nauoit intelligence ne memory: mes entant que ceo ignorāce vient a luy per son act et folly demesne, et il puit resister cest ignorance, il ne serra priuilege pur ceo, et Aristotle dit, que tiel home est digne de double punishment, pur ceo que il ad doublement offende, s. en esteant yure, en male example de auters, et en feasance del act. Et ceo act est dit et terme deste fait ignoranter, s. ou il est cause de son ignorance demesne: et issint le diuersitie perenter chose fait ex ignorantia, & ignoranter. Et issint come iay dit, lou les parols del ascun ley sont infringe pur auoyder greinder inconuenience, ou per necessitie, ou per compulsion, ou per inuoluntary ignorance, que en touts ces cases le ley nest offende. Et adonques veyoromus et examineromus nostre case. Et en nostre case le Woade fuit eiect, et le incerteintie fait pur auoyder le greinder mischæfe. Car le vie de chescun home est plus pretious que ascun biens sont, et le perder del vie del home est plus grand mischyefe que le perder del biens. Et issint en auoydance del ceo plus grand mischæfe, le eiectement, et le incerteintie fueront faits. Auxi ceo fuit per necessitie, et per le plus grand necessitie que puissoit este fait, s. per necessitie en auoydance del mort. Et le necessitie icy fuit cy grand que en les auters cases auāt dits, s. le necessity en le case de creteine de ewe, et del famine: car est pur saluation de vie en l'un case et l'auter. Et auxi l'act poet estre dit d'estre fait per compulsion: Car quant vn chose veigne a tiel point, que sil ne fait tiel act, que adonques il present ment morera, et en auoydance del present mort il ceo fait, tiel act poet bien este dit d'estre fait per compulsion, et per le plus grand compulsion que poet estre. Car il nad plus grand compulsion que compulsion del mort, s. que il morera, sil ne fist tiel chose, et issint icy l'eiectement del woade, et le incerteintie del remenant vient per compulsion. Et auxi il ne poet estre deny mes que le ignorance icy del incerteintie fuit inuoluntary, entant que l'eiectement del woad que fuit cause del ignorance, fuit per compulsion, que est inuoluntary. Et entant que le ignorance del incerteintie est deste ascribe et impute tantsolement al necessitie et compulsion, et par auoyder greinder myschyefe, queux choses per prouydence ne puissent estre preuent, ne per circumspection eschue, ne per poiar resist, adonques ieo dye, que nul default est in Fagassa &c.

Principal, instrumental. Fol. 98. Car ils disoyent, que quant plusors veignont a faire vn act, et vn solement ceo fait, et les auters sont present, abbettant luy, ou prist de luy aider en le fait, ils sont principalles a tous entents cy fortement come cesty que fait le act. Car le presence de les auters est terror a cesty que est assault, et occasion que il ne osast luy mesme defender. Car si vn viest son enemy, et 20. de ses seruantes veignant a luy assaulter, et ils touts trayeront lour espees, et luy enuyron, et vn solement luy percust, issint que il de ceo morust, ore les auters serrõt per bone reason aiudge cy grande offendours que cestuy que luy percust.

Car si les auters, nussent estre present, il peraduenture voile auer luy defende, et issint eschape. Mes le number de les auters present et preste a luy percusser auxi, serra aiudge grande terror a luy, et abatement de sa corage, et occasion a faire luy despeirer a se defender, et est occasion de sa mort. Issint que lour presence est la cause de son terror, et le terror est cause que il receiue les plagues, et les plagues sont cause de sa mort, et donques entant que ambideux les choses, s. les plagues, et le presence les auters que ne donont pas les plages, sont aiudges la cause de sa mort, il ensuit que touts eux, s. les ferriors, et les auters present sont en semblable degree, et chescun est participant del fait del auter. Et le fait, quant a cesty que est mort, et quant al punishment de ceo, (coment, que il consist de deux parties) vncore en le ley il est sans diuision. et nyent contristeant que ne soit que vn plage, done per vn solement, vncore il serra aiudge en le ley,

le

le plage de chescun, s. done per cesty que le done pur luy mesme, et done pur les auters per luy come lour minister et instrument. et est cy fortement le fait de les auters, sicome ils touts ount tenus ioyntment oue lour maynes le baston, ou le auter instrument, oue que le plage fuit done, et vssent touts ensemblement percusse l'occise.

Fol. 497. et 498. Touts les Iustices agreont en vn, que le ordinary, le Patron, et le roy, doyent agrèer a faire vn appropriation, et sont actores huius fabulæ (come le seignior Dyer le terme) cestassauoir, le ordinary inferior, ou supreme. Car il est le principal agent en ceo, eo que il ad le spirituel iurisdiction, et lact del appropriation est chose spirituel. Et lordinary dit, Appropriamus, consolidamus, & vnimus, come principal actor en le cause, come Manwood Iustice dit: eoque le chose que concerne le cure de esglise, est chose que concerne les alms des parochians, de queux, deins sa diocesse, le euesque ad charge. Et pur ceo en le appropriation le ley attribute a luy principall part. Et ceo que le ordinary del diocesse puit faire, ceo le pape que vendicat a luy supreme iurisdiction oultre touts ordinaries, vsast de faire deins le realme, come supreme ordinary, et fuist long temps suffer de ceo faire, et issint il vsast de faire visitations, corrections, dispensations, et tolerations, deins chescune diocesse de ceo realme, et tolle de les euesques deins ceo realme tout come luy plest: et ensuant cest vsage il vsast de faire appropriations sans l'euesque, quel fuit prise d'estre bone et l'euesque, que ne fuit accoumpt forsques come inferior ordinary, ne vnques counterdist ceo, mes ceo fuist vse et accept come bone. et tiel autoritie et iurisdiction que le pape vsast deins ceo realme fuit agnise per le parlyament in Anno. 25. H. 8. et auters statutes, deste en le dit roy Henry le Huyte: et de luy descendist al successors: donques le appropriation fait per le roy solement sans l'euesque, est si bone, come si l'euesque vst le fait, ou sicome il fuist prise en auncient tēps quant le pape le fist. Mes coment que le ordinary inferior, ou superior est celuy que doit faire le appropriation vncore il ne poet ceo faire sans le bon volunt del patron. Car le Patron ad en le aduouson temporal inheritance cestassauoir, fee simple, le quel le ordinary, ne en auncient temps le pape, ne puit toller de patron, ne alterer sans le bone volunt del patron. Mes en appropriations le patron est vn part, car il doit accepter ceo: et le ordinary est le agent, et il est le patient. Et son assent en submission de luy al volunt le ordinary, et en acceptance del son order, et en exeqution del ceo que est ordeigne, est declaration de son entent: et tout serra entende deste fait a son request, car le benefite est soen: et issint le ordinary, et le patron sont duo actores huius fabulæ. Et oultre eux, il y ad vn tierce, que ad parte a faire en cest action, et ceo est le roy, come roy: car il puit estre lede per cest mariage. Car le auouson est tenus de luy mediatment, ou immediatment, &c.

Fol. 79. a. Car troys choses sont ceo vn act (il entende vn act de Parlement) s. l'assent de les seigniors, de les comons, et de le roy: et l'un, ou deux sans le tierce ne fait ceo vn act. Car coment q; les seigniors et comons agrée al chose, vncore n'est act tanq; le roy ad assent auxi. Cause en compaigne.

Cause procreant. Fol. 214. Adonques icy en le principal case, le roy Henry le quart fuit fits et heyre a Iohn de Gaunt, que fuit vn des fits le roy Edward le tierce, et fuit auxi fits et heyre al Blaunch feme del dit Iohn de Gaunt, que fuit file et heyre Henry Duke de Lancaster. Issint q; le Duchy de Lancaster vient al dit Henry le quart per discēt del part sa mere.

Folio 242. b. Car del heure que tout iustice, tranquilitie, et repose est deryue del roy come del fountaine de ceo, le ley en tous ses besoignes et choses luy fauour cõme le chiefe test del ceo.

Cause conseruant. Fol. 315. b. le roy est le test del bien publique, et les subiects ses membres: et l'office le roy que le ley a luy appoynt, est, de preseruer ses subiects.

The matter is the cause of the which a thing is made.

So in August Willy sheweth what matter his cup was made of, thus:

> Then lo, *Perigot*, the pledge which I plight,
> A mazer ywrought of the maple warre.

In December Collyn in his complaint,

> Where I was woont to seeke the honny Bee

Woorking

Woorking her formall roomes in waxen frame,
The grisly toadestoole growne there might I see,
And loathed paddocks lording on the same. Againe,
And learn'de of lighter timber coats to frame,
Such as might saue my sheep & me fro shame. Againe,
To make fine cages for the Nightingale,
And baskets of bulrushe was my woont.

Maister Plowden. Fol. 15. b. Les vlnes del panne sont le mater del toge.

Annotations.

ARistotle sometimes calleth the efficient, the beginning of motion and rest, as in the first of his Metaphysikes, and second of his Physikes. And otherwhiles hee vseth this very name, Efficient, as in his Topikes and Demonstrations.

The auncient Philosophers made great discourses concerning this cause, but some very fabulous, sayth Aristotle 3. Metap. As Hesiodus and Parmenides made Loue the maker of all things; some obscure and ambiguous, as Hermotimus and Anaxagoras sayde that a certaine diuyne spirite was the author of all; so Empedocles giues all to Concord & Discord, and diuers others to other diuers things. Wherfore Aristotle compareth them to yong fresh souldiers and vnexperienced fellowes, that many times hit home, and lay on loade, without eyther art or order.

αἴτια, or αἴτιον in Greeke is a cause in English. It is somtimes taken generally for any reason or argument by common custome and vse of speech: but heere it hath a more speciall and proper signification, and conteyneth onely these foure kinds of causes following. αἴτιον and αἰτιατόν, bee very significant words to expresse the cause and that which is made of the cause: The Latinistes haue none so good, vnlesse you take that dunsicall deriuation, Causa, Causatum, which wee imitate in English to very good purpose, thus, the cause, and the thing caused: Where, as the word, Cause, comprehendeth efficient, materiall, formall, and finall cause, so, the thing caused, aunswering αἰτιατόν in Greeke, and Causatum in Latine, conteyneth the seuerall effectes of euery particuler cause, as proportionably wée may say, the ende and the thing whose end it is: the forme and the thing formed, the maker and the thing made, the matter and the thing materiate. For otherwise, although in Latine, Effectum doo stand for all foure, yet properly it onely betokeneth that which is caused by the efficient. For thus wée may distinguishe the generall vertues of the foure causes, although I knowe they all concurre togither in causing, so that the constitution of the thing caused is not set from this or that alone, but from all foure ioyntly.

Fœlix qui potuit rerum cognoscere causas, sayth Virgill. For although by effects and other argumeuts wée may haue a probable gesse and make sensible coniectures at thinges: yet no true science or knowledge is had but from the causes: By the effectes and euentes wée sée τὸ ὅτι, that thinges bée so: but by the causes wée knowe τὸ διότι, why they be so: and that is onely worthy the name of knowledge.

These diuers sortes and distinctions of efficients are greatly to bée considered in dayly affaires, as containing in them the reason of the well or ill dooing of any thing: of all punishments, rewards, excuse, compassion. &c.

Omnis procreatio & conseruatio fit natura, consilio, per se, vel per accidens: itaq; illa primo, hæc postremo in loco collocaui.

[Naturally:] So all naturall thinges bée made, marde, augmented, diminished, altered, and remooued from place to place by this operation of nature.

I sayd before that the efficient was rather distinguished then artificially deuided. For in trueth the preseruing cause is the efficient rather of the preseruation it selfe, than of the thing preserued. And the instrumentall cause, as it is an instrument, is no efficient at all, but rather a helping member or part of the efficient, sith it hath no power in it selfe to cause the thing caused. Causa sine qua non is of some referred to helping causes. Occasio est agendi tempestiuitas siue opportunitas casu oblata, quod postremum ex nominis etymologia intelligitur, reliquum ex appellationibus græcis καιρὸς, εὐκαιρία, ἀφορμή, quorum nominum extremum

notat

notat tempus vnde agens initium agendi facit, quod græcè expresſius ſonat, τὸν χρονον ἀφ' ὃ ὁρμαῖ ὁ πρακτικός. videtur occaſio eſſe cauſa per accidens, ſed diuerſa ab illis duabus a *Ramo* poſitis.

Ariſtotle in the ſecond of his Phyſikes diſtinguiſheth betwéene Fortune and Chaunce, as making Fortune properly incident to thoſe efficients onely which worke with aduiſe and deliberation, yet then vſe it not, and this is called Imprudentia, when wée doo a thing vnawares. But Chaunce hée will haue that to bée which is found in things void of ſuch deliberation. So that if a man ſhould call the ſtones that couer ſome honourable perſonage, fortunate, for that they bée ſomewhat honored, this were but an vnproper kind of ſpeaking by Ariſtotles rule.

A man goeth towards Weſtminſter to talke with his coũſeller, and miſſeth of him, héere his going was in vaine: but in going hée findeth a ringe: His going to Weſtminſter was the cauſe of the finding of the ringe, but yet ſuch a cauſe as wée call Fortune, or Haphazard. So Ouid excuſeth himſelfe for ſéeing ſomewhat more than hée ſhould, before he would.

Cur aliquid vidi? cur noxia lumina feci?
Cur imprudenti cognita culpa mihi eſt?
Inſcius *Actæon* vidit ſine veſte *Dianam*,
Præda fuit canibus non minus ille ſuis.
Scilicet in ſuperis etiam fortuna luenda eſt,
nec veniam læſo numine caſus habet.

In like maner Tully reporteth in his thirde booke de natura deorum, what good fortune befell Iaſon Phæreus, who hauing an impoſtume, as hée thought, incurable, went to fight with purpoſe to dye, but with a wound his impoſtume was opened, a thing which neyther himſelfe nor his phiſitians euer imagined: Héere then was fortune on eyther ſide, in Iaſon that was wounded, and in him that gaue him the wound: good in the firſt, bad in the ſecond. For the enemies weapon was by fortune a cauſe of Iaſons vnexpected health, whereas death was deſired of the one, and intended by the other, for he that gaue the ſtroake, thought rather to make a new wound than cure an olde diſeaſe. This is fortune with

Ariſtotle. Nowe on the other ſide, if a thrée-footed ſtoole ſhould fall from aloft, and yet in falling ſtand on his féete, this with him is chaunce, for the ſtoole fell for no ſuch ende, and it is a thing altogether ſenceleſſe. Epicurus ſaid that the world was made by the caſual concourſe and mixture of litle round indiuiſible bodies, like moates in the ſunne, whoſe ridiculous blaſphemy Tully mocketh not without deſerued cauſe, 2. de nat. deorum: for ſo, if a man ſhoulde by chaunce caſt abroad an hundred thouſand or more of characters or Printers ſtampes, hée might as well reade on the ground all ſaint Auſtins workes or Cowpers dictionary by the caſuall ſcattering of A. B. C. Theſe bée examples of chaunce with Ariſtotle, not of fortune. But it is folly to ſtand vpon this nice and friuolous diſtinction of Chaunce and Fortune, ſith in common ſpéech they be taken all as one, and ſo they bée héere to bée vnderſtoode.

In this kinde of cauſe, ignorance and vnwitting ſimplicitie haue place as I ſayd before, whereof come excuſes and ſupplications, when a man pleadeth ignorance, and therefore hopeth to finde pardon, as Tully for Ligarius, Ignoſce pater, errauit, lapſus eſt, non putauit, ſi vnquam poſthac. And againe, Erraui, temerè feci, ad clementiam tuam confugio, delicti veniam peto, vt ignoſcas oro. But indéede, this name of Fortune, Chaunce, Hap, or Hazard, was onely inuented by ſuch as knewe not the firſt cauſe, Gods prouidence: And therefore when any thing fell out contrary to theyr expectation, whereof they neyther vnderſtoode the cauſe, nor could yéeld any reaſon, they ſaid it came by chaunce, fortune and hazarde. Whereupon Fortune was made a goddeſſe of good luck: and many chriſtians vſe theſe prophane tearmes, God ſend mée good lucke, and good fortune. Whoſe idle prayers bée noted by an Ethnike Poet.

> Nullum numen abeſt, ſi ſit prudentia, ſed te
> Nos facimus, fortuna, deam, cæloq; locamus.

Ariſtotle calleth Fortune, παράλογον, ἀόριστον, ἀβέβαιον, ἀνθρωπίνῳ λογισμῷ ἄδηλον, improuidum, incertum, dubium, humano iudicio ambiguum, and yet ὡς θεῖόν τι ὂν καὶ δαιμονιώτερον, vt diuinum quiddam & beatum.

Canons

Canons incident to cauſes generally.

God onely is the firſt and principall cauſe of all thinges. All other cauſes whatſoeuer are ſecondary, and ſubiect ſo his eternall direction.

Nothing is without a cauſe.

If all the cauſes concurre, the effect will followe.

To whatſoeuer thing you aſcribe the cauſe, or deny the cauſe to ỹ ſame you attribute or deny ỹ effect or thing cauſed.

Such as the cauſe is, ſuch for the moſte part is the thing cauſed: this holdeth not in deſtroying cauſes.

Particuler Canons of the efficient.

When many efficient cauſes ioine and concurre together in any action (as the principall cauſe with other helpers and inſtrumentes) there they all ioyntly together bée onely the full and perfect efficient cauſe of that effect.

Cauſe naturall, voluntary, accidentall, violent.

God hath diſtributed to euery creature ſome naturall proprieties, vertues and operations.

If the naturall vertue, and propertie of any thing bée affirmed, the naturall effect will follow, vnleſſe that naturall facultie bée otherwiſe let or hindered, and if the effect bée, the cauſe muſt alſo haue gone before.

If will, and aduiſe, or deliberation bée, then the effect may bée.

Such as the naturall diſpoſition and will is, ſuche is the effect iudged to bée.

If the cauſe be in hazard, that is, if the cauſe bée to vs vncertaine and vnknowne, then may the effect fall out vncertainely and by hazard, or when wée looke not for it.

Alone and with others.

If the ſole cauſe worke continually, the thing cauſed is alwayes, if not, then otherwiſe: if the efficient doo neceſſarily require the helpe of others in working, then without them nothing can bée doone: if not, then otherwiſe: if it worke by inſtrumentes, then are thoſe inſtrumentes required. If the efficient worke alone, then it deſerueth the more, either prayſe or condemnation, if with others, then the leſſe, ſo Niſus 9. Aeneid. accuſeth himſelfe, and excuſeth

F. y. Euryalus,

Euryalus. Me,me,adsum qui feci,in me conuertite ferrum,
ô Rutuli,mea fraus omnis,nihil iste,nec ausus,
Nec potuit:

Procreant,conseruant.

No efficient cause, except God, can make any worke without matter. Hinc illud,

gigni,

E nihilo nihil; in nihilum nil posse reuerti. And if the matter bée, the worke may bée made.

If the procreant and conseruant cause bée, the thing may bée procreated and conserued. If the vndoing and destroiyng cause bée,then must the thing decay.

If the cause efficient bée good,the effect will bée good: and bad, if bad.

If the destroying cause bée good,ẏ thing destroyd was bad: If the thing destroyed bée bad, the cause destroying must bée good,ẏ is to say,hath doon some good,hath brought some profit.

The efficient may bée expressed by variety both of Grammaticall cases and Rhetoricall figures: as in procreant causes, God is the father and fountayne and well of all goodnes, The beginning of euery good thing is in,of,and from God.

From procreant causes the Poets do ofttentimes fetch their epithites & circumloqutions,as, Sole satus *Phaeton,&c.* Phaeton borne of the sunne.

If you put downe, or take away,that is, if you affirme or deny the cause efficient, procreant and conseruant, in tyme fit and conuenient to worke,and béeing not idle, then the effect must bée put downe, or taken away: but diuersly, according to the diuersitie of the causes themselues. For,

If such a cause bée, as that it worketh of his owne proper force, plainly and certainly, no other thing helping it, then must the effect follow certeinly.

Now let vs sée a little the vse of these Canons, in comparison of the plaine definitions and explications of proprieties put downe by Ramus. Let this serue for an example.

He that is idle, is wanton:
But *Paris* is idle,
Therefore *Paris* is wanton.

In the proposition, which is the first axiome of the three, Idlenesse, as a procreant cause, doth argue Wantonnesse, as his effect. In the second axiome which maketh the assumption, the same Wantonnesse, is an adiunct of Paris; that is, a qualitie adioyned, or incident to the nature of Paris. Nowe according to the common Logicians, in this sorte must you iudge by disposition.

Paris is idle,

Therefore he is wanton,

For the cause béeing put downe, the effect will followe. But otherwise; if you beléeue Ramus, thus:

The proposition, which was this; He that is idle is wanton, is a doubtfull and contingent axiome, and yet, for the most part, most true, by reason of the affection of such a cause to such an effect. The assumption was this, But Paris is idle, which is also a contingent axiome, and must bée confirmed by the maners and behauiours of Paris. The conclusion it selfe doth follow necessarily, by force of the forme and constitution of the syllogisme: but yet, of it selfe, it is but a contingent axiome, although the deduction of it from the premises, bée, as I sayd, necessary, by reason of the lawfull framing of the syllogisme. If therefore the proposition bée denyed, I aunswere, that it is a contingent axiome, for the most part true, and therefore you cannot iudge it altogether false. And this I confirme by the definition of the efficient cause already put downe, thus; The efficient is a cause from which a thing is, which cause if it bée, the thing caused either is, or may bée. This nowe is a new and prosyllogisticall argument, fet from the very naturall definition of the argument it selfe, that is of the cause efficient: nay rather this is that common maxime vsed of others, if the efficause bée (that is, in due time, and not hindered) the effect will follow. But héere, the variety of efficient causes is diligently to be marked, as some be alone, some with others, some accidentally, some of their owne force; as before I haue shewed. So then, by this we perceiue, that the Canon or Maxima, doth nothing concerne the consequence, but onely the confirmation of the proposition and thing it selfe. Thus much for the proposition.

Now if any man deny the assumption, it must, as I sayde before, bee proued by the life and conuersation of Paris himselfe. For in euery syllogisme, the premisses, as they terme them, that is, the proposition and the assumption, must bee proued and confirmed, eyther by axiomaticall iudgement in Logike proceeding from the seuerall affection of argumentes to the things which they argue, or els by other arts and daily affayres incident to mans life. And commonly the propositions are proued to bee eyther contingent or necessary axioms, by Logicall definitions of argumentes, and certayne rules or canons, which are, as it hath beene tolde, brought in for new and prosyllogisticall arguments for the confirmatiō of the said proposition, and not as proofes of the consequution. And if you thus apply rules, canons, and maximaes, whether proper to this Art, or those common receiued ones, you shall not doo amisse.

Lastly, concerning the conclusion of this syllogisme, if any man doo so much want good maners, as to deny it, you may iustly say, there is no reason why it should bee denied, vnlesse the constitution of the whole syllogisme bee not lawfull and artificiall.

I will heere insert a few examples gathered out of our Law bookes, for the better vnderstanding of some of these canons, & those distinctions of efficient causes put down before.

Cause principall and instrumentall.

Hitherto may bee referred, what is sayde of principall and accessaries. Stamford, lib.1, cap.44. Nota que in grand treason, yl y ad nul accessories, eins touts sont principals. Vt patet, An.3. H.7. fol.10. Issint que quecunque offence fait home accessarie en felony, mesme l'offence in grand treason fait luy principall. Mes en petit treason, ou felony, ou auters tiels crimes, accessaries poient estre.

Accessaries sont deuant l'offence perpetrate, in procuring or commaunding auter de faire vn felony, mes n ient esteant present a lè fait: issint, apres l'offence perpetrate sont ceux qui receuont vn felon attaint, bien conusants del fait que il

ad

ad fait, ou luy fauoront, ou aydont, &c. In attainder sur apparance et default, le principall doit estre attaint deuant l'accessory: et l'acquitel del principal est auxi acquitel del accessory.

Accidentall.

De Homicide per misaduenture, vide Fitz. tit. co. 3. E. 3. P. 354. & P. 302. P. 2. H. 4. P. 69. & P. 11. H. 7. f. 24.

Si homicide soit fait nient per home, eins per auter casualtie, de ceo surda Deodandum. Deodandum est ou home auient a sa mort per misaduenture d'ascun chose que chiet sur luy, ou per misaduenture dun laps que il mesme suffra, in chiant de ascun chose sans estre enchesonée per ascun auter home; cest chose quelle enchesona sa morte, serra forfet, et pris come Deodand. Vide Fitz. tit. coron. P. 403.

Concerning casuall homicide, I remember an odde historie of a certaine man who falling from the top of a house, lighted on an other mans necke, and crushing him to death, preserued himselfe. The sonne of the dead man, procuring the reuenge of his fathers death, caused him that fell to bée had before the Judge: Where hée no lesse pretily then reasonably, offered him this faire play: gett thée vp, quoth hée, to the top of the same house: I will stand where thy father did: and if by falling vpon mée thou bruse mée to death, and saue thy selfe, I promise thée, my sonne shal neuer séeke to reuenge my death.

Necessitie, Fortune, &c.

Stamford: lib. 1. cap. 5. Homicide fait de necessitie ineuitable pur auancer iustice, est Justifiable. Car le vicount, Baylie, ou ascun auter, qui ad garrant darrester home endite de felony peut bien Justifier le tuer de luy, sil ne voile suffrir luy mesme estre arrest, eins estoit al defens tielment, que l'officer ne peut faire l'arrest sans luy tuer. et en tiel case l'officer serra discharge sans attender le grace le roy. s. sans, acquerer pardon, vt patet 22. lib. Ass. p. 55. et tit: coro in Fitz: P. 22. E. 3. P. 2. 61.

Item si plusors veignont a comburer ma meason, moy esteant la dedeins, et inuironnont la meason, mes ils ne ceo comburont: et ieo saetta hors, et occida vn de eux, ceo nest felony, vt patet 26. lib. ass. p. 23. Mesme ley est sils veignont a ma meason pur moy robber, et mon garcon qui est ove moy in la meason, tua vn de eux. Fits: tit: coro: 3. E.3. Itiner. North: P. 330. per Louth.

Mes coment necessitie serra interprete in homicide seipsum defendendo. Vide Fitz. tit. coro: P. 266. an 43. lib. ass. P. 31. & 3. E.3. P. 284. P. 286. P. 287. & P. 297.

Item, 21. H. 7. 39. Per Tremayle Iustice, seruant poit occider home in sauant le vie son maistre, sil ne poit auterment eschaper.

That this hath béene practised in England continually, it may appeare by the discourse of Bracton, who wrote in king Henry the thirds time, in this manner.

Est enim inter alia crimina, crimen quod ex parte tangit ipsum regem cuius pax infringitur, et ex parte priuatam personam, quæ nequiter & contra pacem regis occiditur. Vnde primò videndum est de homicidio, quid sit & vnde dicatur, quæ eius species, & qua pœna homicidæ punientur.

Est enim homicidium, hominis occisio ab homine facta. Si autem à boue, cane, vel alia re: non dicitur propriè homicidiū.

Dicitur propriè homicidium, ab homine, & cædo, quasi hominis cędium.

Species homicidij sunt multæ. Nam aliud spirituale, aliud corporale: de spirituali verò ad præsens non est dicendum.

Sed corporale est quo homo occiditur corporaliter: & hoc dupliciter committitur; lingua, & facto. Lingua tribus modis: s. præcepto, consilio, defensione vel tuitione. Facto quatuor modis; s. iustitia, vt cum iudex vel iusticiarius reum iustè damnatum occidit. Istud autem homicidium, si fit ex liuore, vel delectatione effundendi humani sanguinis, licet ille iustè occidatur, iudex tamen peccat mortaliter, propter intentionē corruptam. Si verò hoc fiat ex amore iustitiæ, nec peccat iudex ipsum condemnando ad mortem, & præcipiendo ministro vt occidat eum; nec ministe r si iussus à iudice occidat condemnatum. Et peccat vterq; si hoc fecerint iuris ordine non seruato.

Necessitate: quo casu distinguendum est vtrum necessitas illa fuit ineuitabilis, an non: Si autem euitabilis, & eam euadere potuisset occisor absq; occisione, tunc erit reus homicidij.

Si

Si autem ineuitabilis, quia occidit hominem sine odij meditatione, in metu & dolore animi, se & sua deliberando, cum aliter euadere non potuisset, non tenetur homicidij.

Casu, sicut per infortunium, cum quis proijcit lapidem ad auem, vel animal, & alius transiens ex insperato percutitur, & moritur. Vel siquis arborem inciderit, & per occasum arboris aliquis opprimatur, & huiusmodi. Sed hic distinguendum est, vtrum quis dederit operam rei licitæ an illicitæ, vt si lapidem proijciebat quis versus locum per quem consueuerunt homines transitum facere: vel dum insequitur quis equum, vel bouem, & aliquis à boue vel equo percussus fuerit, & huiusmodi, hic imputatur ei. Si verò licitæ rei operam dabat, vt si magister causa disciplinæ discipulum verberauit, vel dum quis deponebat fœnum de curru, vel arborem incidebat, & huiusmodi, & adhibuit diligentiam quam potuit, f. respiciendo, & proclamando, nec nimis tardè aut dimisse, sed tempore congruo & ita clamose, vt si aliquis ibi fuisset, vel illuc venisset, potuisset aufugere, aut sibi præcauere, non imputabitur ei. Idem iuris est de magistro non excedendo modum verberandi discipulum.

Voluntate, vt siquis ex certa scientia, & in assultu præmeditato, ira vel odio, vel causa lucri, nequiter & in felonia, contra pacem domini regis, aliquem interfecerit. Et fit aliquando huiusmodi homicidium pluribus astantibus & videntibus, aliquando verò clanculum & nemine vidente, ità vt sciri non possit, quis sit occisor: huiusmodi homicidium dici poterit murdrnm, secundum quod inferius dicetur.

Pœna verò homicidij duplex est, spiritualis videlicet & corporalis: spiritualis tollitur per pœnitentiam. Et occidit quis alium dupliciter: quandoq; lingua, quandoq; facto. Lingua, vt si quis dissuadendo, retrahit aliquem à proposito volentem alium liberare à morte. Et sic aliquandò indirectè facit quis homicidium. Pœna verò homicidij commissi facto variatur. Nam pro homicidio iustitiæ iusta & recta intentione facto, non est aliqua pœna insligenda.

Si sit aliquis qui mulierem pregnantem percusserit, vel ei venenum dederit, per quod fecerit abortiuum, si puerperium iam formatum vel animatum fuerit, & maximè si anima-

G, tum

tum, facit homicidium (Mes contrarium tenetur. Fitz. cor. P. 263. & 146. Car a faire homicide, il est requisite, que le chose occise soit in rerum natura.) Possunt & multi culpabiles esse homicidij sicut & vnus, vt si plures rixati fuerint inter se in aliquo conflictu, & aliquis sit interfectus inter tales, nec apparet à quo, vel à cuius vulnere; omnes dici possunt homicidæ, & illi qui percusserunt, & tenuerunt malo animo percussum dum percussus fuerit. Item & illi qui voluntate occidendi venerunt, licet non percusserint. Item & illi qui non occiderunt, nec voluntatē occidendi habuerunt, sed venerunt ad præstandum auxilium & consilium occisoribus &c. Item & ille qui præcepit percutere & occidere, quia cum non sint immunes à culpa, immunes esse non debent à poena.

I haue written the whole discourse, for that there is herein conteined the practise of most of these precepts concerning efficient causes.

Hereunto may bee added also, our Essoynes de malo lecti, del creteine del ewe, &c. as standing all vpon the same grounds of violent and compulsiue causes, and therefore in themselues reasonable excuses of absence.

Ceux parols, Heyres, tantsolement font l'estate d'enheritance en touts feofmēts et grāūts. Litleton pag. 1. for the sole cause. So agayne Littleton, fol. 166. a. Home ne voyt unques que cest paroll, Defendemus, fuit en ascun fine, mes tantsolement cest paroll, Warrantizabimus. Perque semble que cest paroll et verbe, Warrantizo, fait la Garrrantie, et est la cause del Garrantie, et null auter verbe en nostre ley.

For the destroying cause, Vide 47. E. 3. fol. vltimo, Nota, que diuorce poet estre per cinq; voyes, s. Causa professionis, præcontractus, cōsanguinitatis, affinitatis, frigiditatis. Et nota, que apres diuorce causa professionis le feme serra endowe, et le heyre inherite: mes en auters cases el ne serra endowe, ne le heyre inherite. Here diuorce is a dissolution of matrimony, and the constitution of the one is the destruction of the other.

For instrumentall causes, see 21. E. 4. 76. per Brigges: Qui fait per auter, fait per Luymesme; Come de seruant &c.

et

et Fayrfax, la. 44. b. For voluntary aduiſe and deliberation, 41. E. 3. 30. per Finche. Si deux ſont vouche per lour fayt demeſne, et al ſequatur ſub ſuo periculo l'un vient, et l'auter fayt defaut; et le tenant ſurmit que ceſtuy que fiſt defaut n'ad rien de fayre en value, il auera l'entiere garrantie vers ceſtuy que appiere, car fuit ſon folly de ioynder en garrantie oue ceſtuy que rien ad. Sic ſi feme ſole ad title d'entre en terres, et priſt baron, que ſuffer diſcent et ne entra, la feme ſerra barre del entry apres le mort ſon baron: car ſerra dit ſa folly de prendre tiel baron, que n'entra en temps. Héere the frée choyſe, will, and election taketh away all occaſion of excuſe.

Materiall cauſe.

The materiall cauſes, as alſo all other arguments Logicall, are not to bée tied onely to ſenſible or bodily matters: but generally to bée applyed to any whatſoeuer, bée it ſubiect to ſence, or conceiued by reaſon. As, a man conceiueth in his mind or memory the Art of Logike or any other ſcience, the matter whereof is their ſeuerall rules and preceptes, the forme, the due diſpoſition of the ſame: and yet nether firſt nor laſt is ſubiect to ſence, but onely vnderſtoode by reaſon, and imprinted in the inward power of mans ſoule. The old honeſt philoſophers haue had many odde conceiptes and fantaſticall imaginations touching this cauſe, as appeareth by Ariſtotle in the firſt of his Metaphyſickes. For Thales thought the water was the materiall cauſe of all thinges, as the Miſticall fellowes and Pagan diuines thought ẏ Ocean, Thetis, and Stix to bée. Anaximenes ſayde it was the ayre, Heraclitus, the fire, Heſiodus the confuſion of the worlde, Pythagoras numbers, Plato litle and great, all whiche and others alſo are but derided of Ariſtotle, as though they had thus ſpoken of the Logicall materiall cauſe, which ſhould bée generall to all thinges, and not rather of the material ground of naturall thinges.

Canons.

If the thing bée made, then the matter muſt néedes bée. If the matter bée, the thing materiate may bée: if not, then it cannot bée, in ſecondary cauſes.

The matter sheweth the excellency or goodnesse of the thinges made thereof: for if the matter bée good, the thing made is good: if better, better: therefore in deliberation and consultation of dyet, of building, of weapons, of garments and such like, as also in praysing or dispraising of any thing made, there is an especiall consideration and regard had of the matter.

Theloall his definition of a writte containeth both the materiall cause and others also. Un briefe est un formal letter ou epistre del roy, escript en le langue latyne, en perchemyne, selée ouesq; son seale, direct al ascun iudge, officer, minister, ou auter subiect, al suyte del roy mesme, ou al playnte et suyte d'auter subiect, commaundant ou autorisant ascun chose conteigne en mesme la letter de estre fait pur la cause briefement en celle letter expresse, que est d'estre discusse en ascun court le roy per la ley.

The fourth Chapter.

Of the formall and finall cause.

The cause before the thing caused, is as I haue already taught. Now followeth the cause in and with the thing caused, which is eyther the forme, or the end.

The forme is a cause by the which a thing is that which it is, and therefore by the forme thinges bée distinguished.

The forme is euer ingrauen, as it were, in and together with the thing formed, as the reasonable soule in man, and with man the selfe same instant.

The forme is eyther internall, or externall: Internall which is not perceiued by sence. Externall, which is subiect to sence. Externall is eyther naturall, which is ingrauen in euery thing naturally: or Artificiall, which Art hath framed and performed.

The naturall and internall formes of thinges bée hardly either knowen and understoode, or expressed and made plaine.

The artificiall and externall, is much more easily both

conceiued

conceiued in reason, and expressed by worde: and of such there bee many.

In August, Willy describeth the forme of his cup which hee layd against Perigots spotted lambe.

Then loe, Perigot, the pledge which I plight,
A Mazer ywrought of the maple warre,
Wherein is enchased many a faire sight
Of Beares, and Tygers that maken fierce warre.
And ouer them spread a goodly wilde Vyne
Entrayled with a wanton yuy twyne.
There by is a lambe in the Wolues iawes:
But see how fast runneth the shepheardes swayne
To saue the innocent from the beastes pawes,
And here with a sheepehooke hath him slayne.
Tell me, such a cup hast thou euer seene?
Well mought it beseeme any haruest queene.

In February, Cuddy describeth the girdle hee gaue Phillis by the forme.

I wan thee with a girdle of gelt,
Embost with buegle about the belt.

And in the same Egloge hee layeth downe the accidentall and externall forme, together with some effectes of his bullocke.

Seest how bragge yond bullocke beares
So smirke, so smooth his pricked eares?
His hornes bene as broade as raynebowe bent,
His dewlap as lythe as lasse of kent.
See how hee venteth into the winde.
Weenst of loue is not his minde?

Maister Plowden: Fol. 15. b. vt supra in le materiall cause: Car le shaping et fesance del toge, est forme del toge.

The ende is a cause for the which, or for whose sake the thing is. Palinode in the fift Aegloge,

Good is not good, but if it bee spend:
God giueth good for none other end.

Thenot in the second Aegloge.

It chaunced after vpon a day
Th'usbandman selfe to come that way.

Of custome for to suruey his ground,
And his trees of state in compasse round.

The ende of goodes, is to bée spent: the end of the husbandmans going abroad, was to view his ground.

Maister Plowden: Fol. 18. a. Et pur ceo le scope et fine de chescun matter est deste consider principalment en toutes choses: et si le scope et fine del dit estatute est satisfie, donques tout le matter et lentent del matter est accomply. Et icy le substance et fine del dit estatute, et lentent del feasors de ceo fuit, que le roy auera le subsidie, et ceo solement fuit le scope et summe del dit estatute, et del intent del feasors de ceo. et si lagréement icy est sufficient a doner le subsidie, et de faire le roy deste en suertie de ceo, adonques il ensuist que lestatute et l'entent del feasors de ceo est performe et satisfie. Et que ceo issint est, ieo ay prove deuant; car lagréement garrant et autorize le roy del weyer la lygade per son collector, a quel temps que plerra luy, et quant ceo est fait, le roy ad title de action, et essint est en suertie.

Fol. 59. a. Et issint chescun vener sur le terre ne'st entre. Car fuit dit que Littleton en son lyeur tyent le ley destre, que contynuall clayme doyt estre fayt sur le terre, s'il osast vener la. et en tiel case, sil vient sur le terre, et fayt clayme, et depart mayntenant, ceo ne serra en son disaduantage adiudg vn entre; car il auera assise del primer disseisin, et recouera damages del primer iour del assise, car son entent fuit de faire claime, et nyent de prendre profit, ou de expeller le tenant tout oustcrment, et de custodier le possession: et issint lintent del vener sur le terre est destre respect.

Annotations.

The formall and materiall cause bée essentiall partes of the thing caused: the end and the efficient are not so.

The forme is alwaies made by the efficient, the matter is commonly prepared, not alwayes made by it, as the quill is the matter whereof a pen is made, here the maker of the pen, doth but order, polish, and prepare the quill, but hée altogether maketh the forme and fashion of the pen. And although forma bée effectum efficientis, yet it is causa formati.

Dicitur

Dicitur forma à formando, differentia verò quia differre facit: vna enim eademq; res est, etsi diuersa nomina: and according to these two names, hath Aristotle in the first of his Topiks assigned it two properties; The one for giuing essence and knowledge of the same essence, the other for causing difference: And in respect of the former, it is sometimes called, τὸ τί ἦν εἶναι, quod quid erat esse, as 1. post. Sometimes λόγος τῆς οὐσίας, ratio essentiæ, 1. de ortu animal: sometimes οὐσία τοῦ πράγματος, essentia rei, 1. Philo: sometimes λόγος εἰδικὸς καὶ οὐσιώδης, ratio specifica & essentialis, 4. Phil: sometimes εἰδοποιὸς, συμπληρωτικὸς, συστατικὸς, specifica, completiua, constitutiua, as in Porphyry: and sometimes μορφὴ καὶ λόγος, forma & ratio: sometimes εἶδος καὶ παράδειγμα, species & exemplar, 5. Phil. In consideration of the latter propriety, it is commonly called διαφορά, differentia, for that especially by the forme things differ one from another; so the formall cause of man is his reasonable soule, for this maketh man, to bee man, and to differ from all other thinges that bee not man. So euery naturall thing hath his peculiar forme, as a lyon, a horse, a tree, &c. the heauen, the earth, the sea, &c. So euery artificiall thing also, as a house, a shippe, &c. So things incorporall, as vertue, vice, &c. So in a word, whatsoeuer is, by the formall cause it is that which it is, and is different from all other things that it is not.

Onely the forme among all other causes is ὁμόγονος, simul congenita, extant at the same instant with the thing formed: so that there is a most necessary and reciprocall consequence betweene the forme and the thing formed. But now, as the vnderstanding of the formall cause causeth surest knowledge, so hardly can wee vnderstand what the formall cause is; which peraduenture made Democritus thinke that truth lay hidden in the bottome, and plunged in the deepe. Indeede wee generally conceaue and gather, that euery particular thing hath his peculiar forme, but what is the peculiar forme of euery particular thing, that we know not; or if peraduenture wee gesse at them now and then, yet hardly can wee expresse our conceits with laboursome and tedious circumlocutions. So that, for the most part things bee not knowne,

And if they bée in part perceiued, then haue wée no names for the thinges. Here therefore the auntient philosophers were wonderfully troubled, as Aristotle reporteth 2.Meta. Pythagoras would haue his numbers to bée ŷ cause of things, and that euery thing was an image or resemblance of numbers: and Plato altered their wordes a little, saying that Idæa was the forme, and that thinges formed were communications and participations of Idæas: of whome Aristotle concludeth thus, that they valdè simpliciter & imperitè egerunt, & hée sæmed but nugari,& poeticas metaphoras loqui.

Canons.

If you remoue the forme, it is impossible for the thing formed to consist.

Such is euery thing, as the forme permitteth it to bée.

The forme is the fountayne of actions.

The forme of euery thing is the especial part of ŷ thinge, and the alteration of the forme chaungeth the thing formed, and maketh it an other thing: but héere wée must distinguish betwéene the vniuersall chaunging of the forme, and the particuler alteration thereof. For if a house bée vtterly defaced, though it bée reedified of the selfe same timber and stone, yet it is not the same house, but if it bée but a litle decayed and so repayred in part, it remayneth the same house still, though in continuance of time, euery stick and stone bée altered by often repayring of it.

The formall cause is generall, as all other partes of Logike. For the declaration whereof I will purposely note out some examples of the formall cause in actions and exercises aswell as thinges corporall.

Formalitie in pleading is now partly abridged by the statutes of 32.H.8.ca.20.18. Elis.ca.14. and 27. Elis. but how much it was estéemed heretofore, sée 14.H.8. 27. per Brooke Iustice. Car vn forme couyent d'estre tenus et vse, ou auterment touts choses serra en confuse et sans order. Car en trespasse couyent doner colour (et vncore le sentence n'est le meilleur en le veritie del matter) pur ceo; est formalitie. Et a vne plée en l'affirmatiue couyent prendre auerment: et si

soit

soit en le negatiue, couyent concluder al negatiue, et ceo n'est forsq; formalitie : et formalitie est le pluis chiefe chose en nostre ley.

And the booke of Entries standeth all vpon formall precidents of declarations, barres, replications, reioynders, surreioynders, rebutters, issues, verdites, iudgements, executions, processe, continuances, essoynes &c.

Brytton, whose booke was published in Edward the first both time and name. Fol 42. describeth the order and forme of battayle, but somewhat discrepant from the forme described, 17. E. 3. and 19. H. 4.

In 11. H. 6. 7. the ioyning of battayle in a writ of right is solemnply set downe, betweene sir Piers Colts and the Earle of Northumberland for the maner of Capenhow.

See 14. E. 4. 8. the forme of punishment called Fort et dure, pronounced in Newgate by Iustice Needham. vide 8. H. 4. 2.

Finall cause.

Ramus in his French Logike placeth the end first, sith, according to Aristotle in the second of his Physikes, the ende is first in conceipt and consideration, though last in execution. But in the last edition of his Latine Logike hee setteth it in the last place, respecting rather finem rei, then efficientis scopum & intentionem, which last resolution of his I follow at this present, yet not so resolutely, but that I can bee content to heare their aduise, who bid vs take heede that we confound not the finall cause with the thing caused : which wee shall the better doo, say they, if wee consider exactly the order and due coherence of the foure causes in the absolute constitution of a thing caused. For first, the finall cause, the end, purpose, intent, drift, marke, or scope, as it were of the whole action, is propounded to the efficient, and so vrgeth and moueth him to prepare the matter, and apply the forme thereunto for the full accomplishing of the enterprise : which beeing once performed, the efficient cause now ceaseth, as hauing obteined that it sought for. And this beeing thus atchieued, is not the finall cause, but the thing caused. As for example, I purpose to sweate, and therefore I daunce: heere

D. the

the sweating is not the finall cause, but the intent and purpose which I had to sweate, is the cause that moued mée to daunce, and so caused mée to sweate, which sweating is the thing caused: and although in vulgar spéech, the vse of a thing and the end of the same thing bée confounded, yet by art and reason they should bée distinguished, the one a cause, the other a thing caused. If any man obiect, that if wée say the end is onely the purpose of the efficient, then this place will bée restrained to such things onely, as vse reason, and can purpose, where all Logike must bée generall, and applyable as well to Non ens, as to Ens, to that which is not, as that which is: they aunswere, that wée néede not take this word, purpose or deliberation so strictly, as to apply it onely to reasonable creatures, but generally say, that euery thing worketh for some end and purpose, whether it bée by natures instinct, or voluntary consultation. Or if this séeme more philosophicall then religious, wée may say, that in all artificiall thinges, and such naturall things as haue no deliberation, that which wée call the ende, is but the thing caused by them, and the cause finall is the purpose of God in naturall thinges, and the intent of the artificer in things that bée artificiall.

Et finis mouet efficientem, & cogitatio de fine: finis vt obiectum, cogitatio de fine, vt adiunctum agenti inhærens, sayth Piscator. Some others make the finall cause to bée nothing but a part of the efficient, and no distinct cause it selfe, sith it onely moueth the efficient to forward the operation.

The end is chiefe, or subordinate: chiefe, which the efficient desireth for it selfe, as the couetous man Riches, and it is either vniuersall, to the which all thinges in the world generally be referred, as Gods glory; or speciall, wherunto euery thing in his kinde is referred, as the house is the ende of the builder, for hée séeketh no further. Subordinate is that which is not for it selfe desired, but referred to the chiefe end.

Canons.

If the ende bée, then the thing must also be whose ende it is: and if the ende cease to bée, then the thing whose ende it was, can no longer bée.

Euery

Euery thing is referred to his ende.

The end doth eyther allow or disallow euery mans action; Or thus, that is good, whose end was good, and contrarily: Sic *Aristotle* 3. Rhet. *Laco*, cum rationem de *Ephoratu* in iudicio redderet, rogatus, an ipse alios iure periisse existimaret, assensus est: Ille verò, nonne hæc tu cum illis decreuisti? & ille assensus est: nonne igitur & tu (inquit) peribis? Minimè verò, inquit: illi enim pecuniis acceptis hęc commiserunt, ego verò nequaquam, sed ex sententia.

The end is more to bée desired, than those things that bée referred to the end. He that séeketh the ende, séeketh also those things that bée referred to the same end.

All the arguments that common Rhetoricians fetch from Honestum and Vtile, are for the most part deriued from the end or finall cause, sith for the cause of these two, most things are enterprised. In like maner, the gesses and coniectures of Iudges are fet from the end, as, hée was most like to worke the mischiefe, who might haue any end or profit in practising of the same.

Whose vse is good, that is good, but not contrarily, the thing is bad, because it is abused.

The end doth not alwaies follow the efficient cause, eyther because the efficient could not accomplish the thing alone, or els because hée would not.. Theloall. lib. 7. cap. 2. Le finall intent del chescun que pursuyte briefe, est, ou a recouerer seisin ou possession de terre ou tenement, ou d'auer chose dont home peut auer heritage, ou franktenement, ou ferme; ou d'auer remedy et recõpence pur iniury et damage a luy auenue per le act, ou non feasance d'un auter, ou pur le non performance des contracts et obligations ou auters parts et causes que sont come contracts.

Home vient pur auower son atturney, cest presence ne sera dit apparance, car son intent, ne fuit d'apperer al briefe &c. 8. H. 7. 8.

Abuses of causes.

Sophistry, as I haue said elswhere, is no Logike: & therefore least I should iniury the art by ioyning sophisticall fallacians with Logicall institutions, I haue rather reserued them to these annotations, then thrusted them in among the precepts. Some vse, I confesse, there may bée had of them (although I know, that who so throughly perceaneth the truth of this art, néedes to séeke no other meanes to auoyde these deceipts, sith Rectū est index sui, & obliqui.) But if wée shall put downe euery thing in Logike, which hath any litle shew of profite therevnto; Grammer will be good Logike, because it helpeth vs to vtter ŷ which wée haue Logically conceaued.

The word, Sophista, was at the first, a title of commendation, and onely applyed vnto him that was a Philosopher or teacher of wisedome. But now it is become odious, as Tyrannus, and such like. Sophistry therefore is the abuse of Logike, deceiuing the simple with a glorious shew of counterfeit reasons, commonly called Fallacians.

Fallacians bée eyther in the word, or in the reason. Fallacians in the word bée of two sorts, some in a simple word, some in the coniunction of wordes. In a simple word bée thrée. The first is when vnusuall and vpstart wordes bée foisted in, as hée putteth his felicitie in circumpugnable goods, circumpugnabilibus bonis, meaning Riches, because men fight about them. Le seignieur des Accords in his Bigarrures, pag. 198. hath many of this making, although somewhat more tollerable, because of the ridiculous application. Ils font (saith hée, speaking of some French Carminificators) de petitelettes descriptionettes qui sōt fort agreabletets aux oreillettes delicateletes, principallettement des mignardelettes damoisellettes, Come

Ma nymphe follastrelette,
Ma follastre nymphelette. And after
Ie vous vens une goutette,
Vne goute clairelette:
Vne claire goutelette,
Qui vient d'une fontenette,
Miguarde fontenelette,
Fontaine mignardelette. &c.

And page 65. of another sputatilicall goose, he saith thus.

Un certayne predicant qui veuloit Pindariser en chaire, et choisir des mots courtisans, pour applaudir a quelques

damoiselles

damoiselles fraischemēt reuenues de la cour, auoit coustume de inuenter des mots, et entre auters, il appelloit la destinée, Fatū in latyn, fat in Francois, sur quoy vn gentil personage rencontra ce distique

Frere Iehan Chassepoi, tu te romps trop la teste
De nous prescher le fat escrit par *Ciceron*:
Ne t'eschauffe pas tant, va, tu n'es qu'vne beste,
Pour bien monstrer le fat, oste ton Chapperon.

The like absurditie would it bée for a man of our age, to affectate such wordes as were quite worne out at héeles and elbowes long before the natiuitie of Geffrey Chawcer.

The second is, when doubtfull and ambiguous words bée vsed, as in those verses of Martiall, where, tuus, is eyther thine by gargayne, or by inuention.

Carmina Paulus emit; recitat sua carmina Paulus:
nam quod emis possis dicere iure tuum. And that,
All the maydes in Camberwell
may daunce in an egge shell. Of a little village by London, where Camberwell may be taken for the Well in the towne, or ẏ towne it selfe. So that, Ware and Wadesmill bée worth al London. Where Ware is either ẏ towne Ware, or els merchandize. So lastly, the Mayre of Earith, is the best Mayre next to the Mayre of London. Where the towne, God knowes, is a poore thing, and the mayre thereof a séely fellow, in respect of the Mayres of diuers other cities, yet it is the very next to London, because there is none betwéene.

Accords pag. 96. vne ieune damoiselle interrogée en quelle espece d'oyseau elle desireroit veoir son amy, si nous estions aux temps des Metamorphoses, elle dit, qu'elle le voudroit veoir en Phaisant: vrayement vous aues raison, dit dame Jaquette caquillon, il ne scauroit estre plus agreable qu'en le faisant. Heare not the word written, but the voyce and sound caused the ambiguitie.

The third and last is, when store of Metaphorical words is the cause of a ridiculous obscuritie, as if a man meaning to bée brief, should promise that hée would gallop ouer al the rest of his text. Wherefore Arist. reprehended Plato for that his spéeche was obscure and ambiguous by reason of Metaphors.

When any of these thrée fallacians bée vsed, wée may say with him in Tully, Sputa quid sit, scio: Tilica, nescio. Wée may desire him to speake better English.

In the coupling or coniunction of wordes bée two: the first is Amphiboly, when the sentence may bée turned both the wayes, so that a man shall be vncertayne what waye to take, for this is the signification of the gréeke worde Amphiboly, and this fallacian commeth not from the diuers signification of any one word, but from the ambiguous construction of many wordes, as that olde sophister the Deuill deluded Pyrrhus by giuing him such an intricate answere.

Aio te, *Aeacida*, Romanos vincere posse.
I now foretell the thing to thee
which after shalbe knowne;
That thou, king *Pyrrhus*, once shalt see,
the Romaines ouerthrowne.

Where this word, ouerthrowne, may eyther bée the nominatiue case and appliable to king Pyrrhus; or the accusatiue, and attributed to the Romaynes. The like is that giuen to Cræsus.

Cræsus Halyn penetrans magnam peruertet opum vim.

Where hée hoping to haue destroyed Cyrus and the Persian power, ouerturned his own estate, as Herodotus reporteth. Such an one was that also giuen to the countesse of Flaunders concerning the battell betwéene her sonne Ferrande and king Philip, Que le roy seroit abatu, foulle aux pieds des cheuaux sans sepulture, et Ferrand receu a Paris en grand pompe et triomphe apres la victorie. Where the king, although troden downe, yet dyed not, but ouercame, and triumphed at Paris ouer Ferrande, who was then taken prisoner contrary to the expectation of the Countesse. Cardan de Martin Abbot of Assello, had this verse ouer his gate.

Porta patens esto nulli. Claudaris honesto.

Where, by the error of the Paynter, the poynt béeing made after, nulli, caused the Pope which roade that way, to displace Martyn, and preferre another to his roome, who reteyned the verse, but altered the poynt, & put it immediately after esto, thus. Porta patens esto. Nulli claudaris honesto.

Where-

Whereupon these verses went together.

Porta patens esto. Nulli claudaris honesto.
Ob solum punctum caruit *Martinus Asello.*

The verse of it selfe is very ambiguous, if the poynt bée altogether omitted, Porta patens esto nulli claudaris honesto.

The seconde is in the vnorderly expounding of the words, as

No sicknes can bee health:
Dido is sicke,
Therefore she cannot be whole.

For if you turne the words into good order of exposition, the falsenes of the proposition will easily appeare, thus, No sicke body can be whole.

Thus much of such fallacians as bée in the words eyther seuered or conioined: which indéed are rather Grammaticall and Rhetoricall than belonging to Logike: Those that are in the reason be more Logicall: whereof some belong to Inuention, some to Disposition.

Fallacians of Inuention are eyther common to all the places, or peculiar to some certaine places.

Common to all bée two. The first is called, Petitio principij, the requesting of the thing in controuersie: when, to proue any thing, wée séeke to haue, eyther the same in effect graunted vs, or some other thing as donbtfull. Petitio principij then, is eyther when the same thing is proued by it selfe, as, The soule is immortall, because it neuer dyeth: Or when a doubtfull thing is confirmed by that which is as doubtfull, as

The earth mooueth,
Because the heauen standeth still.

The second is, Superfluitie: eyther when wée cast in things impertinent: or els in vnnecessary repetitions of the same things.

For the first, that may serue for an example, which Tully hath in his second booke of Diuination: as if a physitian should commaund his patient to take such a beast, as is bred of the ground, walketh on grasse, carrieth her cottage, and wanteth bloud, whereas hée might with lesse labour, and to better purpose haue willed him take a Snaile, which hee calleth

Terrigenam,herbigradam,domiportam,sanguine cassam.

To this example you may adde that of Martiall,as more conuenient. lib.6.

Non de vi,neq; cæde, nec veneno,
Sed lis est mihi de tribus capellis:
Vicini queror has abesse furto,
Hoc iudex sibi postulat probari.
Tu Cannas, Mithridaticumq; bellum,
Et periuria Punici furoris,
Et Syllas,Mariosq; Mutiosq;
Magna voce sonas, manuq; tota.
Iam dic Posthume, de tribus capellis.

Much like as if a preacher in expounding a text of charitie, should talk out his houre-glasse,in discoursing of Bell the Dragon of Babylon. To such fellowes wee may say,turne to your text, or Iam dic Posthume de tribus capellis.

For the second, which is vnnecessary repetition of the same thing, this shall suffice, that when I haue generally put downe the nature of an argument,it were sophisticall to repeate the same in euery particuler, as, when I haue once sayd generally, that an argument is that which is affected to argue, what neede I in the particuler discourse of a cause to say, a cause is that which is affected to argue.

Now let vs come to the particuler fallacians of seuerall places. And first for the causes. It is sophisticall to argue from that which is no cause: as if it were a cause. So Sinon the false captife fayneth a cause why the wodden horse was builded.

Hanc pro Palladio moniti,pro numine læso,
Effigiem statuêre, nefas quæ triste piaret.

It is, and allwayes hath beene a common practise among lewd men, to pretend counterfaite causes to cloake their malitious intent, and disgrace other mens good meaninges. The true cause therefore must bee carefully distinguished rom the shadow ouercast: Arist. 2: Rh. à non causa quasi ausa, quippe prop terca q simul,aut post eam euenerit: quod enim

enim post illam est, æquè ac propter illam accipiunt, maximeq; qui in republica versantur, vt *Demades*, *Demosthenis* politiam causam calamitatum omnium extitisse, quia post eam bellum est excitatum.

Also in efficient causes, the diuers kindes of working must bée diligently considered, as, what causes can worke alone, what require the helpe of others, what worke necessarily, what voluntarily, and so forth.

The fift Chapter.

Of the thinge caused.

THe thing caused is that which is made by the force of all the causes, which usually, although not so properly, is called the effect.

Howsoeuer any thing bée altered, moued or changed, the motion, and the thing moued, or chaunged, belong to this place, and are called effects, or thinges caused: as also, sayinges and writinges, thoughtes and all cogitations, although neither vttered nor accomplished.

Matter of praysing and dispraysing commonly is fet from this place. So in February, Thenot telleth how the Briar made a pitifull complaint to the husbandman, dispraising the Oake, and exclaiming against it, by reason of his iniurious dealing: which hée at large putteth downe to incense the husbandman against the Oake.

How fals it then that this faded oke,
Whose body Is seare, whose braunches broke,
Whose naked armes stretch vnto the fire,
Vnto such tyranny doth aspire?
Hindring with his shade my louely light,
And robbing me of the sweet suns sight?
So beate his olde boughs my tender side,
That oft the bloud springeth from wounds wide.
Vntimely my flowers forced to fall,
That bene the honour of your coronall.
And oft he lets the cankred wormes light

Vpon my braunch to woorke me more spight.
And oft his hoary lockes downe doth cast.
Wherewith my fresh flowers bene defaste.
For this, and many more such outrage,
Crauing your goodhyhead to asswage
The rancorous rigour of his might,
Nought aske I but onely to holde my right.

In May Piers prooueth the sheepheards to bee euill, by their effects, thus:

Those faytors little regarden their charge,
While they, letting their sheepe run at large,
Passen their tyme that should be sparely spent,
In lustyheade and wanton meryment.
Thylke same bene sheepheards for the deuils sted,
That playen whiles their flocks be vnfed.

In the same Aegloge Palinode setteth foorth the effectes of youth agreeable to the pleasantnes of the time.

Youths folke now flocken in euery where
To gather May buskets and smelling brere.
And home they hasten, the posts to dight,
And all the kirke pillers ere day light,
With hawthorne buds and sweet Eglantine,
And gyrlonds of roses, and Sops in wine.

In July, Thomalin prayseth Christ the great sheepheard, by his effectes.

O blessed sheepe, ô sheepheard great,
that bought his flocke so deare,
And them did saue with bloudy sweat
from Wolues that would them teare.

In the eight Aegloge Piers rehearseth the effects of loue, in these wordes.

Ah fone, for loue does teach him climbe so hye,
And lifts him vp out of the lothsome myre.
Snch immortall myrrour as he doth admire,
Would raise ones mynde aboue the starry skye,
And cause a captiue courage to aspire,
For lofty Loue doth loath a lowly eye.

Colyn

Colyn in December repeateth the pastimes and effectes of his youth in these verses.

Whylom in youth, when flowrd my ioyfull spring,
Lyke swallow swift I wandred here and there.
For heate of headlesse lust me so did sting,
That I of doubted danger had no feare.
I went the wastfull woods, and forrest wyde,
Withouten dread of wolues to bene espyde.

I woont to raunge among the mazy thicket,
And gathered nuts to make me Christmas game,
And ioyed oft to chase the trembling pricket,
Or hunt the hartles hare till she were tame.
What wreaked I of wintry ages waste?
Thoe deemed I my spring would euer laste.

How often haue I skaled the craggy oke,
All to dislodge the rauen of her nest?
How haue I wearyed with many a stroke
The stately wallnut tree? the whyle the rest
Vnder the tree fell all for nuts at strife,
For ylike to me was libertie and life.

And so after, in the same pitifull lamentation, the effectes of his sommer and winter bée set downe.

But in March, Thomalins long tale of Cupide, hath almost nothing els, but a rehearsall of his owne doinges and Cupids. The narration is this.

It was vpon a holyday
When sheepheards groomes han leaue to play,
I cast to go a shooting:
Long wandring vp and downe the land
With bow and bolts in eyther hand
for byrdes in bushes tooting.
At length within an yuy tod,
There shrowded was the little god,
I heard a busie bustling.
I bent my bolt against the bush
Listning if any thing would rush,
But then heard no more rustling.

Thoe peeping cloſe into the thicke,
Might ſee the moouing of ſome quicke,
Whoſe ſhape appeared not.
But were it fayry, feend, or ſnake,
My courage earnd it to awake,
And manfully thereat ſhot.
With that ſproong foorth a naked ſwayne,
With ſpotted wings, like peacocks trayne,
And laughing lope to a tree :
His golden quiuer at his backe,
And ſiluer bow which was but ſlacke,
Which lightly he bent at mee :
That ſeeing I, leueld agayne,
And ſhot at him with might and mayne
As thicke as it had hayled :
So long I ſhot that all was ſpent,
The pumy ſtones at laſt I hent
And threw, but nought auailed.
He was ſo wymble and ſo wight,
From bough to bough he ſtepped light,
And oft the pumyes latched.
Therewith affrayd I ran away,
But he that earſt ſeemd but to play,
A ſhaft in earneſt ſnatched :
And hit mee running in the heele ;
For then I little ſmart did feele,
But ſoone it ſore increaſed ;
And now it rankleth more and more,
And inwardly it feſtreth ſore,
Ne wot I how to ceaſe it.

Maiſter Plowden : Fol. 163. a. Et certes, les Cloyſterers communement en feaſant lour leaſes et faits, auoyent vn forme, lequel ils cy preciſement voile tener, et purſuer, que ils voillent, marrer tout, pluiſtoſt que alterer lour cuſtome : et iſſint purceoq; ils ne voilent encliner lour forme al ley, mes voilent auer le ley a incliner a lour vſage, ils deſtroyeront le force de pluſours fayts.

Annotations

Annotations.

This argument of the thing caused conteyneth not onely déedes and workes, but also thoughtes, and wordes, counsayles and deliberations, and all motions whatsoeuer. Parmenio the father, and Philotas the sonne, were both put to death for suspicion of treason against Alexander: Where, their cogitation and compassing of their Soueraignes death, were such effectes as were plagued by death. For like occasion also were Lentulus, Cethegus and other complices of Catyline brought to confusion.

Yet when sayinges, writinges, counsayles, and deliberations bée brought in as testimonies, then are they argumentes borrowed, assumpta aliunde.

Canons.

Wée commend men by their causes and adiuncts, as for their noble auncestors, great possessions, &c. but especially by reason of their effectes, as for that they did this or this &c.

Nam genus, & proauos & quæ non fecimus ipsi,
Vix ea nostra voco.

And as for Riches, perinde sunt, as hée that vseth them: good, if hée apply them well: bad, if otherwise.

If the thing caused bée, then the cause eyther is or was, but not alwayes contrarily.

Such as the thing caused is, such commonly is the cause.

That which is attributed, or not attributed to the thing caused, must bée applyed or not applyed to the cause.

Fit. Cor. 22. E. 3. p. 26. Thorpe recita coment vn gaoler vient al gaole oue vn lanterne en sa maine a veier ses prisoners, queux auoyent debruse lour fers, et estoyēt touts prestes d'auer occise luy, et batoyent et naufroyent luy malement: mes il auoyt vn hatchet en sa maine, oue quelle il occist trois de eux, et puis eschapa, et fuit aiudge per tout le counsell, que il auoyt bien fayt.

Stanford: lib. 1. ca. 9. Nota, que en auncient temps la volunt fuit cy materiall, que il fuit repute pur le fait. Fit. Cor. 15. E. 3. P. 383. ou vn compassant le mort d'auter, luy naufra cy gréuousement, que il luy lessa giser pur mort, et puis s'en-sua, et l'auter reuiua, et non obstant, fuit aiudge felony, eo q; quant sa volunt apiert ey ouertment de luy auer tue, voluntas reputabitur pro facto et oue ceo accorda Bracton qui dit, In maleficijs spectatur voluntas & non exitus, & nihil interest vtrum quis occidat, an causam mortis praebeat. Mes le ley n'est issint a cestiour. Car il doyt morir en fayt, auant que il serra aiudge felony. Et si home ferist auter oue intent de luy bater, mes nemy a luy tuer, uncore sil morust de tiel bater, il est felony en luy que ferist: perq; a cest iour, home peut conuerter le dit text de Bracton, et dire, q Exitus in maleficijs spectatur, & non voluntas duntaxat.

Elenchs.

Martiall useth this argument sophistically in his first booke.

> Extemporalis factus est meus Rhetor,
> Calphurnium non scripsit, & salutauit.

As though this were an affect of an extemporall Rhetor, to salute a man by name without premeditation. But here hys meaning was to bée merry, in taunting the man for his ill memory, who could skarce remember his familiar friendes name, unlesse hée had written it before, and learned it without booke.

The sixt Chapter.

Of the whole, part, generall, speciall.

Hitherto of the first diuision of argumentes fully agréeable, in the cause and the thinge caused. Now followeth the second. Secondly therefore the argument fully agréeable is eyther the whole and his part, or els the generall and his speciall.

The whole is that which conteyneth partes: the part is that which is conteyned of ẏ whole. The whole is integrall, or uniuersall: The whole integral is that which hath his essence or béeing of the partes, as Logike hath two partes, exposition of argumentes, and disposition of the same, and of these two parts the whole essence and nature of Logike consisteth. So a messuage is made of two partes, del terre et structure.

structure. And héere the part is called a member, and is that which giueth essence to the whole, as Exposition and Disposition in respect of Logike, terre and structure in respect of a messuage.

The whole vniuersall, called the general, is such a whole as giueth the essence or béeing to his specials; as, an Inherent argument, is the generall, conteyning originall arguments, and those ÿ are secondary as his specials. For here an inherent argument is a whole essence, which dooth equally perteyne to originall arguments, and such as are secondary.

The speciall is a part of the generall, as arguments first and secondary are specials of an Inherent argument, as being parts put vnder it indifferently and equally or alike.

The general is eyther most generall or subalternall, the speciall is either most speciall or subalternall, that is, put vnder.

The chiefe or moste generall is that which hath no generall aboue, As in Logicall Inuention, an argument, is the most generall, comprising both Inherent and borrowed argumentes vnder it.

The generall and speciall subalternall, or vnder another, are those which may bée in diuers respects both generals and specials.: generals, in respect of their inferiors; specials, in respect of their superiors, as, a cause, is a speciall in respect of an argument fully agréeable: but it is a generall in respect of the materiall or formall cause.

The most speciall is that, which cannot be deuided into specials, as this or that singuler materiall or formall cause conteining none other vnder it.

Generals are certayne resemblances of causes in themselues comprehended; as specials are of effects. Speciall examples referred to their generals, belong to this place.

Annotations.

Hottoman. Totum & partes vtrum prius an posterius sunt, anne simul? primum distinctio adhibenda est, vt aliud sit totum naturale, veluti arbor, fundus, auis, equus: aliud artificiosum, veluti domus, nauis, currus. si naturale totum est, ve-

 risimum

rissimum est quod *Aristoteles* libro de natura octauo scribit prius esse, & naturæ,& temporis, & rationis ordine, id quod perfectum est, eo quod est inchoatum. sin autem artificiosum est, tum eiusdem *Aristotelis* monitu, altera distinctio adhibenda est, vtrum subtiliter & artis ratione, an populariter ex sermonis consuetudine disseratur. Nam quia subtili ratione ea demum pars verè propriéq; dicitur,quæ suo munere fungitur, fungi autem suo munere, nisi suo toti inhærens, non potest, certè totum & pars naturæ ac temporis ordine simul sint necesse est. Nam vbi est domus, ibi necesse est esse tectum, & vbi tectum reuera tegens, ibi necesse est esse domum: vbi currus, ibi rota; & vbi rota reuera, & actu voluëns est, ibi currus: sin autem populariter loquamur, & homonymia, id est, communione nominis abutamur, tùm verò pars dicetur esse prior, totum verò posterius, vt area, quam iuris consulti potissimam domus partem appellant, priòr est ædificio; & fundus priòr vitibus, aut arboribus, aut fructibus.

Canons of the part.

If you put downe or affirme all the essentiall partes, you must also put downe the integrall it selfe. But if you put downe one, or some of the parts onely, you cannot therefore put downe the whole; for the partes, not seuered, but all ioyntly, make vp the nature of the whole.

If you deny or take any one essentiall parte away, the whole is also gone.

Of the Integrall.

Prohibitus à toto,prohibitus est à qualibet parte.

He that hath the whole, hath also the principall or essentiall partes.

Although yée put downe all the parts, yet vnlesse they bée conioyned,the whole will not necessarily follow.

If you deny the whole, all the partes are not therefore straightway denyed, vnlesse you meane, that the whole béeing gone, the remnant is not properly to bée called a parte, Vt non est tectum,nisi tegat,&c.

7. H. 7. 8. a. b. 20 acres fueront agrée d'estre touts temps parcel del manor, Ergò sil deuy seisie del manor, il deuy seisie des.20.acres.

That

That which agréeth with the whole Integrall, must also agrée with the parts conioyned, but not seuered.

If the whole bée not attributed to any thing, it will not follow, that therfore no part should bée applied vnto it.

The whole Integrall cannot bée affirmed of any one of his parts: for a part is not the whole: but all the parts together make the essence of the whole. But the generall may bée affirmed on one speciall, for that the whole nature and essence of the generall is in euery one of the specials, so that the speciall is the same thing indéede with the generall, (although not in such ample maner) or rather a patterne and resemblance of the generall. Yet, as the speciall conteyneth in it somewhat more than the generall (I meane, his proper formall cause moreouer and besides that hée had of his generall) so the generall comprehendeth vnder it more than one speciall; as béeing therefore common and indifferently applyable to many, because it is abstract from all, and not determinately bound to any. Wherevpon they say in schooles, Genus abstrahit ab vtroq;, vt posit esse vtrumq;, and conteyneth vnder it, not in it, repugnant specials, according to Porphyry. Yet, notwithstanding all this, you may affirme the Integrall on his parte in a simple axiome, so that this worde, Part, bée added therevnto, as, Inuention is a part of Logike, the body is a part of man.

21. H. 7. 21. per Fineux, & Tremayle Iustices, le person auera trespas de arbres coupes et emportes en le cimitorie, et d'entry et infreindre del eglise, car l'eglise, le cimitorie, et les dismes sont le Rectorie.

In assise, le pl. dit, que le terre est tenus d'un tiel, come de son manor de D. que est auncient demesne: le def. in maner confesse ceo, et tamen il prist general auerment, que parcell del mesme le manor, le quel il ad conus d'estre auncient demesne, serra francke fée, sans monstre coment per matter speciall; que n'est reason, car chescun chose serra intende del mesme le nature, come le chose est, dont il est parcell. Sic hic le manor de D. est conus d'estre auncient demesne, & sic per consequens serra intende, que tout ceo que est tenus del dit manor, serra del mesme le nature prima facie. 3. H. 6. 47. a.

The first Booke.

Generall. Speciall.

Litleton. pag. 80. Si soit rent, il serra rent seruice, charge ou seck, mes n'est, &c. Ergo. Et pag. 90. Chescun que ad francktenement, ad vel fee, vel tayle, vel pur vie, vel auter vie : mes n'est issint icy. Ergo.

21.E.4.79. Si essoine gist pur corporation, tum vel hoc vel illud, &c. sed nec l'essoyne de mal vener gist pur ceo, nec de malo lecti: car ceux excuse defaut, et ils ne poient appearer in person; et ils touts ne serront sicke ensmble : nec de seruitio, nec de vltra mare, nec de terra sancta, car ils ne serrōt intendes d'estre touts in tiel case, Ergo nul essoin gist pur corporation.

The generall is nothing els, but a multitude or vniuersality of thinges like in essence, or one like essence in many thinges.

Hottoman, γένος ἐστὶ (vt *Zeno* apud *Laertium* definit) πλειόνων ἐννοημάτων σύλληψις. Itaq; plures cognati qui sanguinis eiusdem communione inter se cohærent, quam ab vno eodēq; capite duxērunt, idcirco à Græcis appellantur ὁμογενεῖς vel συγγενεῖς, cum alij, qui gentis ac stirpis alterius sint, ἑτερογενεῖς vel ἀλλότριοι, alieni & extranei nominentur. So that this word, Genus; is Metaphoricall.

The higher you ascend, the more generall thinges bée: the more generall thinges bée, the fewer particuler proprieties are they tyed vnto: and therefore the moste generall doth agrée to most particulers. But, the lower you descend, the more is alwayes in particularitie comprehended in the words, so that they can not bée applied to so many.

The generall precepts put downe in all Artes, were first inuented by the induction of many particulers and specials.

The generall béeing affirmed vniuersally, euery one of his specials must also necessarily bée affirmed. But if the generall bée but indefinitely, simply, or vndeterminately put downe; some one of his specials must indéede bée put downe also, and that necessarily, but no certayne one aboue the rest, but onely contingently, as If there bée any driggle draggle in Shrewsbury shée must bée eyther Jenny Dymmocke, or some other : this is necssarily true : but it is but contingent

to

to say, that if there bée any, it must néedes bée shée: for there may be many others also.

Generi per speciem derogatur. Nam qui de vna aliqua specie loquitur, is cæteras sub eodem genere contentas species non dissimulanter excludit, sic legatum speciale detrahit generali.

Denie the generall, howsoeuer you list, and all his specials bée denyed.

Whatsoeuer is attributed to the vniuersall nature of the generall, must bée giuen to the speciale. But there may bée many thinges applyed to the indefinite nature of the generall, which cannot bée ascribed to any of his particulers, vnlesse the thing bée common both to the generall and speciall.

Of the speciall.

The speciall doth onely conclude affirmatiuely, vnlesse all the specials bée denied togither.

If you put downe one, more, or all the specials, you also put downe the generall, for that the nature and essence of the generall is in euery of the specials. If you deny one onely speciall, you deny the whole generall in his moste ample and largest vniuersalitie: but not as hée is indefinite. But if you deny euery speciall, then the generall is taken away, howsoeuer you meane it.

Whatsoeuer agreeth with the specials, agreeth also with the generall: if so bée that the thing applyed bée common, and not peculierly proper to one speciall alone, as apud Tribalos patrem immolare est laudabile, ergo ἁπλῶς. *Hottoman.*

Quod vni speciei non conuenit, non continuò generi indefinito non conuenit, vt, si homo est animal, quod non est animal id non est homo: sed non, siquid non sit homo, id continuò sequitur, non esse animal. Nam etsi contrariorum contraria sunt consequentia, tamen differentiæ causa hic est in negatione posita, quæ cum priuatio sit, affirmatione, quæ habitus est, semper est deterior neq; parē cum illa vim habet.

Species eiusdem generis sunt simul natura: est tamen aliqua differentia ordinis, vt in arte speciem hanc illi preponas.

The Grecians call the most speciall, ἄτομον, Indiuiduum, quod diuidi in partes corporatas sine interitu non potest. Nam ſi totum in partes diſtrahatur, nulla pars erit totum, neq; totius nomine appellari poterit. **There was neuer any Logician before** Ramus **that durſt abſolutely pronounce an** Indiuiduũ, **as** Socrates, **to bée a ſpeciall, or a man to bée a generall: yet I could neuer ſée eyther good reaſon, or reaſonable experience to the contrary.** Neq; enim audiendum eſt quod dici videtur à *Porphyrio*, & nonnullis pręterea in *Ariſtotelea* bibliotheca locis, indiuidua non differre forma eſſentiali, ſed proprietate accidentiũ, vt mas, & fæmina: quæ accidentia in *Hermaphrodito* miſcentur. Nam tum detractis (quod omnino ſaltem cogitatione fieri poteſt) accidentibus, omnes homines eſſent vnicus & ſingularis homo: imò neq; deus, neq; dæmon, neq; homo, neq; vlla prorſus eſſentia eſſet (quod eſt ab *Ariſtotele* nominatim improbatum, cum idealem hominem eiuſmodi derideat) ſed accidentia ſola. *Talæus*.

Hottoman. Plato ea demùm eſſe verè ac propriè dicebat, quæ à ſenſibus remota, tantùm ratione & animo perciperentur, propterea quod ſemper vniuſmodi eſſent, neq; ortũ neq; interitum haberent: cum indiuidua infinita, fluxa, & caduca eſſent, orirenturq; & occiderent, nec diutiùs vno & eodem ~~ſtatu~~ eſſent. *Ariſtoteles* verò nullas putabat eſſe extrinſecus ſubſtantias, ſed intellectam plurimorum inter ſe differentium ſimilitudinem, vel genus, vel ſpeciem appellabat. Primus *Ariſtoteles*, ait *Cicero*, ſpecies labefactauit, quas mirificè *Plato* fuerat amplexatus, vt in ijs diuinum quiddam eſſe diceret. Ac de vtriſq; iſtiuſmodi ſubſtantijs idem *Cicero* in lib. de vniuerſitate ex *Platonis Timæo* ita ſcribit.

Quid eſt quod ſemper ſit (hęc idæa eſt) neq; vllum habet ortum. Et quod gignatur (hoc indiuiduum eſt) nec vnquam ſit. Quorum alterum intelligentia & ratione comprehenditur, quod vnum ſemper atq; idem eſt: alterum quod affert opinionem per ſenſus, rationis expers, quod totum opinabile eſt, id gignitur & interit, nec vnquàm eſſe verè poteſt?

Vtrius igitur illorum probabilior ſententia videtur? Non eſt humilitatis noſtræ tantam inter ſummos omnium philoſophos controuerſiam diſceptare. Magis tamen aliquantò ad notionum noſtrarũ rationem accommodata *Platonis* ſententia videtur: quippè cum ſatis conſtet, non omnes notiones ex oblata

lata extrinsecus indiuiduorum corporum impulsione existere, sed quasdam per se constare; neq; vel aliundè originem habere, vel alio quàm suo ac proprio fundamento niti. Quo in genere sunt intellectæ res omnes, vt quantitates & qualitates, veluti longitudo, latitudo, & altitudo. Item iustitia, temperantia, eloquentia: Item morbus, valetudo, imbecillitas: quæ si in subiecto aliquo insunt, per se tamen, & tanquam auulsæ & abstractæ considerantur. Infra.

Videsnè quam sutores & calceolarij formam calceorum appellant? Nimirùm lignum oblongum, calcei instar, proportione aptum, atq; incisum. At ijdem formam calcei aliam in mente atq; intelligentia impressam atq; insignitam habent: quæ vna verè proprieq;, tum Idea, tum forma, & est, & dici debet. Ad quam, tanquam pictores ad exemplar, suam picturam; ità illi opus suum dirigunt. Forma igitur calcei lignea subiectum est: species in mente insita, auulsa atq; abstracta est.

In an other place more plainly.

Iubent enim (s. *Plato* & *Aristoteles*) poni Calliam procul ad nos longo interuallo venientem. Ea species extrinsecus oblata sensibus continuò generis vniuersi notitiam in animo informat. Primùm enim corpus esse intelligimus, mox, vbi propiùs accessit, animal: tùm hominem: ad extremum, Calliam. Sic, qui in statione sunt, & procul aliquem venientem intuentur, primum corpus esse animaduertunt; secundò, ex cursu animal esse iudicant: tertiò, equitem: quartò, ex colore, amicum vel hostem: postremò, Titium, vel Sempronium. Atq; hi sunt nimirùm notionum & intelligentiarum gradus.

So much I haue borrowed of Hottoman, concerning generall Idæas: too little for Quidditaries: yenough for our purpose. Hee that desireth more shalbe sure to finde too much, if hee doe but once shew himselfe willing to entertaine those euerlasting praters de vniuersalibus.

Morrell in July, to enforce the generall commendation of hils, bringeth in speciall examples, as saint Michaels mount, S. Brigets Bower, Mount Oliuet, Parnassus, Ida: &c.

Before I goe further, it were expedient to yeeld some reason why I seuer the generall, speciall, whole and parte from the tractate of diuision, where Ramus placed them. For

 Genus

Genus sayth Taleus, significat causam speciei, & species ideò significat effectum generis. itaq; originem suam è primis argumentis ostendunt, quotiesq; genus explicatur à speciebus causa arguitur ex effectis; quoties contra species arguitur è genere, effectus arguitur è causis. Alia tamen est hîc inuentionis via, quàm illic. Causa enim & effecta subtilius illic explicantur, hic comprehenduntur. Which yet can hardly make mée beléeue that they bée argumentes made of the first, as they should bée, if they were secondary argumentes: For I call that secondary which is made of some originall, as diuision and definition is. For as for Coniugates and notation although I giue them leaue for a time to soiourne among the annotations, yet I dare not admit them into the text.

[The generall] hęc definitio generis & speciei aduersas superioris & huius topici differentias ostendit: illic integrum sumit essentiam è membris: hîc genus essentiam speciebus tribuit: illic membra constituunt totum, hîc species constituuntur à genere.

Theloall. Et sunt quædam breuia formata super certis casibus de cursu, & de communi consilio totius regni concessa & approbata, quæ quidem nullatenus mutari possunt absq; consensu & voluntate eorum: il intende original briefs. Sunt etiam breuia ex ijs sequentia, dicuntur Iudicialia, & sæpius variantur secundũ varietatem placitorum &c. hæc ex *Bracton*.

Done est vne nosme generall plus que n'est feofment. Car done est generall a touts choses moebles et nyent moebles, et feffment est riens forsq; de soyle. Britton 87. a.

Generale crimen falsi plura sub se continet crimina specialia, quemadmodum de falsis chartis, de falsis mensuris, de falsa moneta &c. *Glanuil.*

Essoniũ est
- de malo veniendi
  - vltra mare
    - de seruitio regis.
    - terra sancta.
  - citra mare
- malo lecti

Bracton. 339.

21. H. 7. 16. Frowike. Si ieo voyle prescriber, que ieo et touts ceux &c. ont vse de temps &c. a distreyner touts les tenantes a terme de vie, ou d'ans del manor de D. pur vn haroit

soit apres le mort de chescun tenant &c. ceo est bon prescription: car il est in le generalitie; issintq; comentq; vn ou deux, ou trois des tenures soyent determines, vncore auters poyent demurrer, issint la poet il estre vn contynuance de les tenants, comentq; diuers morreront &c.

In 4.H.6.30. There is an argument vsed from the denial of all the specials to take away the generall. Recordare, le def. fist conusance come bayly A.B. file et heire P. le pl. dit, que A.B. est bastard &c. et sur ceo le def. pria ayd de A.B. et per Bab et Cott: il auera ayd: mes contra per Strang et Martin. car par luy, il doyt auer pria l'ayde in le conclusion de son conusance: et in ple personell home auera ayd puis plée plede et nemy deuant; mes in ple reall home auera ayd deuant ple pleade. Et n'ad mes deux maners de entries de ayd: l'un est de ayd deuant ple pleade, s. q defendens vel tenens petit auxilium de A. sine quo ipse non potest respondere, et si soit puis ple plede, le entry est, quod def. petit auxilium de B. ad manutenendum exitum. Et in cest case il ne poet estre ad manutenendum exitum, car nul issue est ioyne: et il ne poet estre, sine quo non potest respondere, car il ad respondé al action, et in le conclusion del ceo ne ad prie ayde et ideo il est passa l'aduãtage del ceo et ne sont plusors entries del ayd, mes ceux deux.

Elenchs of the whole.

A double Elench lurketh in this place, one of composition an other of diuision: for composition thus. Humfrey Crowther is a good fidler, therefore hée is good: and this fallacian is from the whole, because those two thinges so ioyned togither séeme to make vp the whole, whereupon afterward the part may bée concluded, as though in this example, Humfrey Crowther were a whole integrall thing, made and consisting of these two partes, goodnesse and fidlery. Some other call this à dicto secundum quid, ad dictum simpliciter, when wée apply that absolutely and generally which was spoken but in part and in respect, as héere Humfrey is called good, not generally, for his good conditions, but particulerly in respect of his gitterne. Issint in 9.H.7.19.a. Cestuy que est heyre al pere et mere, est heyre al pere, mes l'issue del baron et sa second feme donées in speciall tayle, est heyre al pere et mere, ergo il est heyre generallment al pere et simpliciter, non sequitur, car le pere poet auer fits per le primer feme. Vauisor. expone Maiorem & apparebit fallacia, Cestuy que est heyre al pere et mere coniunctim, est heyre al pere diuisim; ore ceo est false. Vide. L.5.E.4.43. Leas fuit fait per abbe et couent, ergo per abbe sole, nul reason. q. an serra intende mesme le leas.

Now on the other side, Diuision is a fallacian, as it were from the partes, when thinges are seuerally propounded and ioyntly concluded, as

Antony Now-Now is good, and a singer, therefore
Antony Now-Now, is a good singer.

For indéede these two thinges seuerally put downe are not essentiall partes of Antony Now-Now, but onely accidentall qualities: whereas if they had béene his essentiall partes the argument would haue followed, as here

A man is a liuing and sensible creature, and also
reasonable, therefore
A man is a reasonable liuing creature.

And so in composition, thus,

A man is a sensible creature endued with reason, therefore
A man is sensible; or therefore A man is reasonable.

Elenchs of the part.

First when you inferre the whole, some of the partes wanting. Isabell Greenesleeues hath a fayre hand, a good leg, a quick eye, therefore shée is a proper fayre woman: it followeth not, for shée is splayfooted, crookbacked: tunnebellied, sawtoothed &c. The like is that of Catullus.

Quintia formosa est multis, mihi candida, longa,
recta est: hæc ego sic singula confiteor.
Totum illud, Formosa, nego. Nam nulla venustas,
nulla in tam magno corpore mica salis.

So elswhere of Formianus his trull.

Salue nec minimo puella naso,
Nec bello pede, nec nigris ocellis,
Nec longis digitis, nec ore sicco,
Nec sanè nimis elegante lingua,

Decoctoris

Decoctoris amica Formiani:
Ten' prouincia narrat esse bellam?
Tecum *Lesbia* nostra comparatur?
O sęclum insipiens & infacetum.

Vide 44. E. 3. 13. a. b. Vbi Wickingham & Persay disputant, vtrum le playnt d'un molyn in assise abatera, eoque fuit troue, que parcell del molyn fuit sur auter terre, issint il n'auoit entier molyn. Et sic come vn sophister petit plus quã oportuit.

Home esteant seisie en fée de certeine terres in vn ville, et in deux hamlets del mesme le ville, deuisa touts ses terres esteants in le ville, et in vne de les hamlettes per nosme et deuy; riens del terre in l'auter hamlet passera: car son entent appere per l'expressing d'un des hamlets. Mes Browne ex rigore Logices fuit è contra, per vn argument à toto, car le ville conteigne les hamlets, Ergo &c. mes le ley fauour deuises, quia sont faits quant homes gisont in extremis, sans reason ou erudite counsell pur le pluis part, 9. Eliz. 27. Dyer. Mes certes auterment, le deuisor plaide but the sophister. Come in trespas vers I. del parish del Aluale in com. S. yeoman; le def. dd. iudgement del briefe, car in le parishe del Aluale est vn ville appelle Wilton, et le def. iour del briefe purchase fuit demurrant en Wilton, sans ceo que il demurra in le parish del Aluale; cest, sans ceo, est repugnant al matter deuant; car s'il demurra in le ville, et le ville est in le parish, donq; il demurra in le parish, L. 5. E. 4. 20. a. Issint in l'auter case, il dona touts ses terres in le ville, et ambideux les hamlets sont in le ville, Ergò il dona touts ses terres que sont in les hamlets.

Secondly, this place is abused, when the whole is diuided into such partes as bée not his owne: as when Rhetorike is diuided into Inuention, Disposition, &c. For both these bée the parts of Logike, not of Rhetorike, as they are commonly taken: but of Elenchs in diuision more in the tractate of Diuision.

Elenchs of Generall and Speciall.

If a man, when hée knoweth one or two specials, thinketh that hée knoweth the generall; hée is much deceyued:

but more, if when hee hath gotten a generall notion of any Art, hee thinketh himselfe a sufficient artificer. For it is one thing to haue a generall and superficiall sight in an arte, but another matter, to bee able to practise those general precepts in euery particularitie.

In 26. H. 8. 6. a. Shelley abuseth this argument: Si ieo ay le manor de grand Dirtleby, ieo ay le manor del Dirtleby. Et le case fuit, que fine fuit leuy del manor de D. et in mesme le county fueront deux D, grand et petite, et null sans addition, hîc Shelley dit, que passa per le fine pur le reason auāt dit: mes Fitz. denia ceo, car ne fuit ascun tiel manor, mes per feffment le manor intendus passeroit per le liuery. Shelley fuit deceaue in ceo que il prist grand D et petit D, d'estre specials, et D, sans addition d'estre le generall: et issint re-uera, si ieo ay grand D, ieo ay D, come, ceo que est, homo est animal: mes in veritie, grand D et petite D, sont indiuidua, s. singuler lieues conues per tiels nosmes sans ascun general those que conteigne ambideux.

Issint 7. H. 6. 39. Hals arguit eodem modo, Vous ne dedits, mes que il y ad D maior, & D minor deins le county, Ergò il yad D, argumentum ab inferiore ad suum superius, issint est proue, que il yad tiel ville. But by his fauour it followeth not, because there is vpper Dale and nether Dale, therfore there must be a third Dale, without addition at all, that is neyther vpper Dale nor neather Dale, but distinct from them both. For, if in one county there bee two manors, the one called grand Higham, the other petite Higham, the true generall to these two singular manors, is, this word, Manor; and so it will follow well. Is. hath the manor of grand Higham, Ergò Is. hath a manor: but the manor of Higham is no such generall as should include the manors of grand Higham and petite Higham. Vide L. 5. E. 4. 47. Mesme le error, que Combe conteigne longe Combe et short Combe.

The

The seuenth Chapter.

Of the Subiect.

Thus muche shall suffise for the argument fully agréeable: now it followeth to speake of that which is agréeable but in part and after a certeine maner, as is the subiect and the adiunct.

The subiect is that whereunto some thing is adioyned. The subiect receiueth the adiunct, eyther in it, as the minde learning, the place the thing placed: or to it: & this is either affected by the thing adioyned, as the body receiueth garments to it, and is of them affected: or els it doth affect the thing adioyned, as a sicke man receyueth vnto him the physitian, and doth affect him, by occupying and busiyng his heade and minde in inuenting remedies for him.

Thenot in Febzuary.

You thinken to be Lords of the yeare,
But oft when you count you freed from feare,
Comes the breame winter with chamfred browes,
Full of wrinckles and frosty furrowes.

Where the browes be the subiect of wrinckles and furrows.

In Aprill, Hobbinoll beginneth his song, in prayse of Elysa, with the subiect of the place, in these verses.

Yee daintie nimphes that in this blessed brooke
doe bathe your brest:
Forsake your watry bowres, and hither looke
at my request.
And eke you Virgins that on *Parnasse* dwell,
Whence floweth *Helicon* the learned well.
Helpe me to blaze
Her worthy prayse.
Which in her sex doth all excell.

Where the Brooke is the subiect to their bodies, and Parnassus Mount, to the Well, Hellicon.

In Aprill by Hobbinoll, Elysa is described by her garmentes and place.

See where she sits vpon the grassy greene
 ô seemely sight,
Yclad in skarlet a mayden queene
 and Ermynes white.
Vpon her head a cremosin coronet,
With damaske Roses and Daffadyllies set,
 Bayleaues betweene
 And Primeroses greene
Embellishe the sweete Violet.

Where Elysa is the subiect to these particulers, and the grassy gréene the subiect to Elysa.

Maister Plowden : Fol. 217. b. Et enfancy, que est grand disabilitie, est repugnant all estate del roy; et coment que enfancy est in le naturall corps, uncore quant le corps politike del roy est conioyne a ceo, et un corps fayt de eux ambideux, tout le corps auera les properties, qualities, et degrées del corps politique, que est le greinder et le pluis digne. en que il nad my, ne poet estre, ascun enfancy.

Fol. 237. a. Le roy auoyt en luy troys choses, s. poyar, Iustice, et Mercy, poyar a faire, Iustice a enforcer luy de faire : et Mercy a stayer luy de faire.

Fol. 500. b. Et quant al quart point, si usurpation poet estre eu sur person en personée, touts les Iustices agréont en unque il ne poet, eo que leglise ad incumbent, et est pleine. Car cesty a que le appropriation est fait, est incumbent, et cy perfect, sicome auter incumbent serroyt, que vient eins per presentment, institution, et induction. Et adonques ne poyent esse deux encumbents d'un mesme eglise a une mesme temps. Car destre incumbent est l'office d'un corps, et si un incumbent est, et auter est present, admitte, institute, et inducte, tout ceo est voide, sicome une est officer dune office pur vie, come seneschall del manner, ou tiels : patent fait a auter de mesme l'office presentment, est voyde, et le primer person auera action de trespas vers cesty que est darreynement admitte; et issint person en personée auera action de trespas vers un auter que est present, institute, et induct al eglise approprie a luy, sil intromitte oue le glebe et dismes.

Fol. 280. a. Si home ust morust intestate le propertie de

ses biens vient per le comen ley, al ordinary, entant que le mort nauoit appoint eux a ascun. Car sicome francktenement per le course del comen ley serra en ascun, et ne serra en suspence, issint per le comen ley, le propertie del biens serra en ascun, et ne serra en suspence. Et quant home ad propertie en biens, le property ne poet estre pluis longement que il viue, et apres sa mort les biens sont a vn auter. come le auncient verse est, da tua dum tua sunt, quia post mortem tua non sunt: adonques entant que ne point estre soiens apres sa mort, et il nad appoint eux a ascun auter, mes ad relinque eux al monde, le ley done le propertie de eux al ordinary, et a luy (pur ceo que auoyt cure de sa alme en sa vie) le ley done les biens a disposer apres sa mort.

Lieu. Fol. 149. b. Et issint religious persons serront entende touts foits a demurrer a lour meason, et ne poyent estre entende destre ailours.

Fol. 37. b. Et en ceo realme sont diuers autorities, et nul poet exceder ses limits et bounds, et pur ceo si le marshall teigne plée de chose fait hors del vierge, ou le Admirall de chose fait en corps le countie, ceo serra voide, car lour autoritie sextend al lieu certeine, et deins certeine precinct, et nemy aylours. Et si cesty que prist sanctuary, va hors, chescun poet luy prender car il nest priuiledge de hors, et issint touts foits le precinct del libertie ne poet estre excede, et icy le vicounte nad a faire forsq, en Loundres, et donques quant le prisoner vient hors del libertie del Loundres, a mesme cesty instant il est discharge.

Fol. 396. a. Mes icy, syr Thomas White et les compagnions ne fueront iustices auterment ne as auters cases, que a ceux, queux le commission le roy essigne. et sils sont assigne a faire vne chose, et ils sont auter, cest auter est sans autoritie. Come si vn est eslie arbitrator a faire arbiterment sur vne chose, et il fait arbiterment sur auter chose, tiel arbiterment est voyd tout nest. Issint icy, ceo que sir Thomas White et ses compagnions fieront fuit coram non iudice, et merement voyde.

Fol. 15. a. b. Et pur ceo ieo entende ceo come vn principle, quant il est agrée perenter ascuns que vn principall chose serra fait ou esse, et devant que ceo poet estre fait ou esse, il yad un auter chose primes deste fait, et n'est certeinement agrée, que faire le dit auter chose, que le ley appoynt cesty que ad le pluis science et skyll, a faire le dit auter chose, come le brasier a weyer et mettre en sew les bells, le taylour a shaper un toge, le collector a weyer chose pur que le subsidie serra paye al roy.

Vide Fol. 320.b. Le proper subiect del courts le roy, come Escheqer, common bancke, Banck le roy, en l'information pur mynes, l'analysis du quel est annexe al fine de cest lyuer,

Annotations.

A [Subiect:] Not onely, οὐσία, or ὑπόστασις, an essence, or substance, as the common Logicians vsually take it, but also whatsoeuer can bée imagined or fayned to haue any thing adioyned vnto it, in it, or about it: so one quality may bée the subiect to another, as in this axiome, Vertue is commendable, where commendation is adioyned to vertue, being the subiect thereof.

That subiect wherein the adiunct is exercised and (as it were) vsed, is called an obiect, or matter subiect, as colours bée the obiect of séeing, sounds of hearing, souldiers bée busied in fighting, plowmen in plowing, &c. as in those verses, &c.

Nauita de ventis, de tauris narrat arator,
Enumerat miles vulnera, pastor oues.

Which béeing turned, tutch those that intermedle with matters of other mens professions.

Nauita de tauris, de ventis narrat arator,
Enumerat pastor vulnera, miles oues.

The verses bée made by Propertius, and by Ronsard translated into French, thus,

Des vents parle le marinier,
Le labourer de ses toreaux,
Ses playes compte le guerrier,
Et leurs brebis les pastoreaux.

Claudian hath the like.

Omnia quæ sensu voluuntur vota diurno,
Pectore sopito reddit amica quies.

Venator

Venator defessa thoro cum membra reponit,
Mens tamen ad syluas & sua lustra reddit.
Furto gaudet amans, permutat nauita merces,
Et vigil elapsas quærit auarus opes.
Iudicibus lites, aurigæ somnia currus,
Vanaq; sollicitis meta cauetur equis.
Me quoq; Musarum studium sub nocte silenti
Artibus assuetis sollicitare solet.

Canons.

If the subiect bée, then by nature, the proper adiuncts must also bée: the other that bée not proper, may bée, and may not bée.

If the subiect bée taken away, the adiunct cannot stand.

To whom you giue the subiect, to the same you giue the adiunct.

Whatsoeuer you attribute to the subiect, that you must giue the adiunct: but in due and conuenient order.

Of the subiect things bée sometimes praised and disprayсed. The house is estéemed by him that dwelleth in the house. The place giueth occasion to iudge of that which was borne in the place, as, He was borne in Bœotia, therefore hée is but a muddy-pated asse.

Explications, illustrations, amplifications, and extenuations are set from this place: So Cicero to his sonne, Thou art at Athens, therefore thou shouldest bée learned. Tis a Northerne Nagge, therefore quicke, Tis a Shrewsbury fryse, therefore the best.

From hence are almost all poeticall epithetes deducted.

As the subiect is, such is the adiunct. The place oftentimes augmenteth the crime. Locus est entis & non entis, corporum, dæmonum, &c. sic domus somni, hortus Hesperidum in loco collocantur.

2. H. 4. 19. Per touts les Iustices, que les Iustices de peace ne poyent prendre appel de nul approuer, ne de auter. Car lour commission n'extend cy auant.

9. H. 6. 5. In pleading d'arbitrement, le partie doyt monstrer le lieu ou le submission fuit fait, et les nosmes des arbitrours.

Maister Crompton, Folio. 79. 80. &c. Les Justices de peace enquirera ad chescun le lour generall sessions, de ceux que parlont irreuerentment de sacrament de corps et sanke nostre seigniour Jesu Christe. 1. E. 6. cap. 1. & 1. E. cap. 1.

Item de reteyners, liueries, mayntreiners, imbracers, bowstaues, archers, illoyall games, forestallers, regrators, vitailers et Inholders, et de chescun de eux, per, 33. H. 8. cap. 10. & 37. H. 8. cap. 7.

Item de cestuy que tue weinlinges que sont desus l'age de deux ans, al intent de vender. contr. 24. H. 8. cap. 9. & 14. El. cap. 11. Et issint de plusors auters.

Pur le subiect del lieu, Vide L. 5. E. 4. 7. 8. En annuitie vers le Prior de S. Mary Oueres in Southwarke, in le county de Surrey, le pl. count sur fait a Londres in le parish de S. Dunstane, in le garde de Faringdone, et le fait est dated, in domo capitulari eiusdem domus. Per Choke, ceo ne poet estre per comen entendement, que le Chapter del S. Mary Oueres in Southwark que est in Surrey ferra le fait in Fleetstreete in Londres &c. mes per speciall matter monstre il poet, car vbi personæ, ibi Capitulum: Mes si le date esset, in monasterio domus prædictæ, ceo per null intendement serra prise alibi, que in Southwarke ou le meason est, car le material meason n'est remouable, come le Chapter est.

Accessorium sequitur suum principale, hinc versus
Quicquid plantatur, seritur, vel inædificatur,
Omne solo cædit, radices si tamen egit.

Sublato principali, tollitur accessorium. Nam, non entis non sunt qualitates. Jeo enditera vn home pur asporter ieunes pigeons hors de mon Columbier, ou ieunes goshauks engendres en ma parke, car le propertie est in moy et ieo poy eux prendre a mon pleasure, car ils ne poyent aler dehors. Contrà del auncient haukes ou pigeons que poyent fuer. Sic ieo enditera pur prisel des pikes ou tenches hors d'un ponde ou troncke, causa qua suprà, contrà sils soyent prises en le ryuer, coq; a ore ieo ay null propertie in eux, 18. E. 4. 8.

Elenchs.

The Lawe abhorreth such thinges as are done without authoritie or commission, coram non iudice. So 10. H. 4. 2. Præmunire facias issist de ceo que le def. auer sue al court de Rome de chose dont conusance apertient al court le roy. Sée the booke called, Diuersities des courtes et lour Jurisdictions, wherein the matter subiect of the Marshalsea, Kings bench, Common place, Chauncery, Eschequer, Cinque portes, &c. is distinctly put downe. For the authoritie of courts is limited, neyther is it lawfull to intrude sophistically, or iniuriously incroache one vppon another. Vide 3. 4. P. & M. 14. Dyer. Fuit enact, que les quarter sessiõs de Anglesey serront tenues in Beaumaris: et les Justices de peace teigne eux ad Newburghe, et la preigne inditements de felony: ceux inditements fueront voyde, et coram non iudice. Vide 22. E. 4. 33. a. b. Commission est direct as certeine homes de oyer tantum, et ils oyont et determinont, cest coram non iudice: Sic s'ils oyont matters hors del compas del commission. Sic si in common bancke vn appele de mort ou robbery soyt port, &c. et le party est attaint, cest coram non iudice, car lour patent ne dona al eux cest poyar et autoritie.

The eight Chapter.

Of the Adiunct.

An adiunct is that wherunto something is subiect.

An adiunct is eyther Inherent in the subiect, or adherent to it.

The adherent adiunct doth eyther affect the subiect: or is affected by it. So vertues, vices, learning, and all such qualities are adiuncts to mans minde.

And as euery place is the subiect of the thing placed: so, time, that is to say, the continuance of euery thing, is the adiunct of those thinges which doo continue in time.

So all qualities which eyther bée proper, as laughing to a man: or common, as whitenesse to a stone, and a wall, are truely called adiuncts.

Finally euery thing which agréeth vnto an other, béeing neyther the cause, nor the effect thereof, is an adiunct of the thing wherevnto it doth agrée.

Colyn Clowt in Ianuary sayth.

All as the sheepe, such was the shepheardes looke,
For pale and wanne hee was, alas the while.
May seeme he lou'd, or els some care hee tooke, &c.

Thenot in February of himselfe,

Selfe haue I worne out thrise thrittie yeares,
Some in much ioy, many in many teares:

Where the thrise thritty yeares, bée an adiunct.

In March Thomalin argueth the spring to bée at hand, by these adiunctes.

The grasse now gins to bee refresht,
The swallow peepes out of her nest,
And clowdy *Welkin* cleareth.

In July Thomalin describeth Abell by his adiuncts compared.

As meeke hee was as meeke mought bee,
Simple, as simple sheepe:
Humble, and like in eche degree
The flocke which hee did keepe.

And in the same discourse displaying the demeanour of oure shepheardes and their pompe and gorgeous attire.

But now (thanked be God therefore)
the worlde is well amend,
Their weedes bene not so nighly wore,
Such simplesse mought them shend.
They bene yclad in Purple and Pale
So hath their God them blist.
They reigne and rulen ouer all,
And Lord it as their list
Ygyrt with belts of glitter and gold, &c.

In August Perigot describeth his boúcing Bellibone by hir attire.

I saw the bouncing *Bellibone*
hey ho *Bonnibell*
Tripping ouer the Dale alone,
Shee can trip it very well.
Well decked in a frock of gray.

Hey

Hey ho, gray is greete.
And in a kirtle of greene say
The greene is for maydens meete.
A chapelet on her head she wore
Hey ho chapelet:
Of sweete violets therein was store,
Shee sweeter then the Violet.

In November Colyn vseth this argument very oft in declaration manner, where hee bewayleth Didoes death, as

Coloured chapelets.
Knotted Rusheringes.
Gilt Rosemary.
Mantled Meadowes &c.

Thomalin in Iuly.

The hils where dwelled holy saintes
I reuerence and adore,
Not for themselues, but for the sainctes,
Which haue bee dead of yore.

By consideration of all these agreeable argumentes, thinges that differ one from an other, are called one, the same, or agreeable.

So before, Colyn in January, was sayd to haue the same looke that his sheepe had,

All as the sheepe such was the shepheardes looke,
For pale and wanne he was, alas the while &c.

Meaning one in adiunct, not in essence. And so in like maner of the rest of the agreeable argumentes wee may say.

Fol. 357.a. Et quant al ceo, ils disoient que fines oũt estre de tresgrand antiquitie al comen ley. Car ils ount este si longement come ascun court de record ad estre. Et ils fueront per le comen ley assurance pluis fort, et de plus grande force et puissance. Et issint sont terme per lestatute de modo leuandi fines. &c.

Fol. 413. b. Le deuisour serra accoumpt inops consilij, pur ceo que voluntes de pluis souent sont faites quant homes sont gisant en extremes et faudront councell. Et pur ceo le ley enterpretera les parols, et directera sa operation accordant al entent del partie.

Fol. 101. b. Et donques icy, quant il fuit arraigne pur le tuer del home sur malice prepense, le substance del matter fuit, s'il luy tue ou nemy, et le malice prepense n'est que del forme ou circumstance de tuer. Et coment que le malice prepense fait le act plus odious, et pur ceo cause l'offendour de perder diuers aduantages que autrement il aueroit, come sanctuary et clergy, et tiels semblables, uncore il n'est auter que le manner del fait, et nemy le substance del fait. Car le substance del fait est le tuer de luy: et adonques quant le substance del fait et le manner del fait sont mise en issue ensemblement, si les iurors troueront le substance, et nemy le manner, uncore iudgement serra done sur le substance. Come si home arraigne assise pur disseisin oue force, et le defendant plede al generall issue, et les iurors troueront le disseisin, mes nemy oue force, uncore le pleintife auera son iudgement: car le torcions expulsion fuit le substance, et le force, le manner. Et adonques quant le substance est troue, il auera iudgement pur ceo, et serra acquite del force, &c.

Fol. 381. Et quant al auter point, il dit que coment que le rent charge est nouel rent commenceant per graunt, uncore il est issint appropre al office que il ne serra seuere del office cy longement come le office continue: issint que si le office ne serra forfeite, le rent que est annexe al ceo ne serra forfeite. Car si un grant estouers a un autre d'estre arse en tiel meason, il est appurtenant al meason. Et issint comen graunt en tiel lieu a un pur ses auers leuant et couchant en son ferme de Dale, le commen est fait appurtenant a ceo, issint que il que ad le meason per quecunque title que il vient a ceo apres, auera les estouers: et il que apres viendra al ferme, auera le comen: et les estouers ne poient estre seuere del meason, ne le comen del ferme, si non per extientisment. Car s'il que ad le meason voile graunter les estouers a un auter reseruant a luy le meason, ou le meason a un auter, reseruant a luy les estouers: les estouers ne serront seperate del meason per ceo, pur ceo que serront expende en mesme le meason. Et issint le fee icy est graunt pur le exercise del office, et l'office fuit receiue en respect del fee, & sic officium & foedum sunt concomitantia, et l'un ensue l'auter et le fee continua

tinua oue l'office come incedent inseperable : & quæ sequuntur in eodem loco, del annuitie graunt pro consilio impendendo; de office del roy de Haroldes, graunt a Garter, cum fœdis & proficuis ab antiquo &c. 5. E. 4. Fol. vltimo. Et del graunt de x. li. à Garter ad terminum vitæ suæ ratione & causa officij. 7. E. 4. Fol. 23. et del annuitie graunt per le roy, Iohanni clerico coronæ, ad terminum vitæ suæ; en queux cases, le fee est annexe al office, et est determinable oue l'office.

Fol. 26. b. Si vn reteigne vn auter a seruer pur an pur le salary de xx.s. la si le seruant demand les xx.s. il doit monstrer que le temps est passe, cest assauoir, l'an expire, et doit ceo pleder certeine, pur ceo que son action est done en respect del an passe, et del chose fait en tempe, et le temps est parcell del cause del demaunde, et precede le demaunde.

Annotations.

ADiunct :] The same almost which the Græcians call περιστασία, and περίστασις, circumstances, if you take that word largely for whatsoeuer is added to a thing after it is once framed and made of his essentiall causes, and some of them procéede from the vniting and coniunction of the forme and matter immediately, which are commonly inseparable, as laughing to a man &c. Some are but hangbyes and remouable, or separable, and, as it were, tenants at wil, as white, blacke to the wall, &c.

Adiuncts therefore, not Accidents are they heere called: for Accidens is of it selfe, infinite and vndeterminate, and doth properly apperteine to the accidentall cause, which we before tearmed chaunce, hap, or hazard : and it conteyneth effectes, adiunctes and comparates; so that the name béeing neyther fitte, nor applyable to this place, I haue displaced it purposely.

[One and the same :] Héere is Logically put downe all that, which others peruersly teach in their diuers sortes of Idemtitie, as, Genere, Specie, Numero.

Some there bée that giue a proper and peculiar place to signes and coniecturall tokens : but friuolously. For they belong all eyther to this of adiuncts, or that other of effectes, or els they bée testimonies and witnesses.

Canons.

If the proper adiunct bée, then the subiect must commonly bée: and if the subiect bée, the proper adiunct must also bée.

To whome soeuer you ascribe the adiunct, to the same you must attribute the effect procéeding from the same adiunct.

That which is rightly applied to the inherent adiunct, must bée applied also to the receiuing subiect.

Here are gathered diuers phisiognomicall coniectures, as that of Martiall.

Crine ruber, niger ore, breuis pede, lumine lœsus,
 Rem magnam præstas, Zoile, si bonus es.

Hence are also set prayses and disprayses, deliberations and consultations. Herein are conteined all those Rhetoricall places concerning the giftes and qualities of body and soule, as also externall and those of fortune.

If the adiunct bée occupied or exercised, then the subiect must bée that exerciseth the same.

To whatsoeuer you ascribe the adiunct which is occupied, to the same you must giue the subiect: and what you apply to it, you must also attribute to this.

Sometime the adiunct together with the subiect is taken but for one onely argument, as when I say: The murthering and vsurping Tyrant, Richard the third, was deseruedly slayne: and yet neuerthelesse here the subiect is argued in some respect by the adiunctes, in that it is thereby described and declared.

Some adiunctes bée antecedent or going before, some againe present and conioyned, lastly some others consequent and following. Therefore some other Logicians haue made these thrée kinds of adiuncts, thrée seuerall kindes of arguments, as Antecedentia, adiuncta, consequentia.

Naturall Philosophers, Phisitians, Astronomers, and other professors vse much this place: as when they dispute of chaunge of weather, diuersitie of causes and occasions of diseases, signes of stormes and tempestes, as, vento rubet aurea Phœbe, when the Moone is red, shée betokeneth wind. These common adiunctes bée called τὰ κοινῶς συμβεβηκότα, τὰ ὡς ἐπὶ τὸ πολὺ, τὰ μὴ ἀεὶ ἑπόμενα.

10. H. 6. 21. Merchant est bon addition, & eadem lex de wydowe, ou single woman.

Seruant n'est addition, car est trope generall. L. 5. E. 4. 22. Vide 14. E. 4. 7. quel serra le addition d'un feme, que est ne mayde, widow, ne wife.

Vide 31. & 32. H. 8. 5. Dyer. Spynster est addition cy-bien al home, come al feme, car per Spylman in Norfolke sont diuers homes qui sont worsted spynsters.

Maister Lambard. Iustit. lib. 2. cap. 5. M. Marrow sayth, that fiue principall things bee most commonly requisite in presentments before Iustices of peace.

1 The name, surname, and addition of the party indited.

2 The yeare, day, and place, in which the offence was doone.

3. The name of the person to whome the offence was doone.

4 The name and value of the thing in which the offence was committed.

5 The manner of the facte, and the nature of the offence, as the manner of the treason, murder, felony, or trespasse.

Ad: Temp. Maister Lambard. Iust. lib. 2. cap. 19. Touching the continuance of these quarter sessions, I haue shortly but this one thing to say: that almost two hundred yeeres ago, it was ordeined by statute (12. R. 2. cap. 10.) that they should bee continued three dayes together, if neede were, vpon paine of punishment. And yet, in these dayes of ours, wherein the affayres of the sessions bee exceedingly increased (and consequently more neede to continue them now then before) many doo skantly afforde them three whole houres, besides that time which is spent in giuing of the charge.

Maister Crompton. Iust. Fol. 65. hath a number of adiuncts, effects, subiects, &c.

Inprimis couient consider le qualitie del home, lequel, il est semble a faire tiel felonious act, ou nemy.

Item quel chose doyt luy mouer d'attempter tiel enterprise.

Item lequel il fist le murder, sur ascun displeasure deuant conceue, ou sur sodein anger.

Item lequel il expect per son mort, d'auer ou receiuer ascun cõmodity, come terre, office, argent, ou ascun auter gaine.

Item lequel il est vn que ne regard le tuer de home, ou sil ad eu pardon ou ad estre acquite pur tuer de home auant cest tẽps, car tiels choses face homes d'auer luy in suspicion.

Item le pais ou home fuit nee, declare ascun foits son naturall inclination, come si l vst etre née, ou educatus enter les homes de Tyddesdale et Ryddesdale, poet estre plutost suspect.

Item dequel tradé il est, et per quel occupation il viue.

Item lequel soit gamester ou haunter de alehouses, ou vn companion inter ruffians.

Item dequel abilitie il est, et coment il auient a ceo que il ad, sil ad ascun chose.

Item quel apparel il vse, et lequel il ama daller brauement ou nemy.

Item dequel nature il est, lequel soit hastie, heady, ou prest de quarreler.

Item queux shyftes il ad de temps en temps, et quel chose luy moue de fayre tiel haynous act.

Item lequel le home fuit tue in le haut chemyn ou en boys, ou perenter deux hilles, ou lequel prochein vn hedge, ou auter secret lieu.

Item lequel fuit en le matyne, ou sere en le nuite, et lequel fuit view la circa tiel temps.

Item lequel il senfua apres l'act commit, ou auera ascun sank sur luy, ou sil tremble ou staggar, ou soit contrary en disant de son tale, et coment il gard son countenaunce.

Item lequel auer esperance de garder son fact secretment per reason del place, temps, et le maner de son secret feasans.

Item dauer tesmoignes examines de son esteant en ceo place, ou en auter place, al temps del act fait.

Item compare le force de murderer oue le weakenes, armor oue le nakednes, stoutnes oue le simplicity d'auter.

Item son confession demesne, Wilson Rhet. Fol.17.

Item si soit vagarant, & nullam exercens artem, nec laborem, ou si certein desbiens embles fuer in son possession. 7. E. 4. 10.

Item

Item siquis appellatus fuerit à probatore, & fugerit propter appellum, & mortuo probatore redierit, est suspiciosus per *Bracton*.

Item fama quæ suspicionem inducit, oriri debet apud bonos & graues, non quidem maleuolos & maledicos, sed prouidas & fide dignas personas, non semel, sed sæpius; quia clamor innuit, & defamatio manifestat, & vanæ voces populi non sunt audiendæ. Idem *Bracton*.

Item si ascun soyt imprisone pur suspition de felony, et eschapa, ou fait tout que en luy est, de eschaper, est grand suspition que il est culpable. Stamf. 180.

Item si quis noctu cubauerit in domo solus cum aliquo qui interfectus sit, vel si duo vel plures ibi fuerint, & hutesium nō leuauerint, nec plagam à latronibus vel interfectoribus in defensione facienda acceperint, nec ostendunt quis, de se, vel de alijs hominem interfecerit, his casibus mortem dedicere non possunt. *Bracton*.

Item si quis notum vel ignotum in domum suam acceperit, qui viuus ingredi visus sit, verum postea nunquam nisi mortuus: dominus domus, si tunc domi sit, vel alij de familia qui tunc interfuerunt, pœnam capitalem subibunt, nisi fortè per patriam fuerint liberati. Idem.

Item communis vox & fama est sufficient cause de suspition de felony, sans auter especiall matter alledge. per Curiam. 5. H. 7. 2. H. 7. 6.

Item si home soit robbe, ascuns voile prender le measure de les pæs de les robbers, et de les chiuals, et si cesty que est robbe ad suspition d'ascun il voile causer le measure d'estre mis al pæ de tiel person, et son chiuall, et sils accorde, il poet estre suspitious.

Item si home appelle auter traitour, et il dit rien a ceo, il est cause le luy arrester pur suspition, et pur ceo couient que il responde a ceo. Fitz. coro. 24. 37. H. 6. per les Justices, issint semble ou home appelle auter thæfe, et il dit rien a cell, &c.

Item Nota, il est vse, ou home est suspect d'auer murdre auter, d'amesner luy al mort corps et sur cel il ad estre view, que le corps ad nouelment met hors sanke, videlicet, hath bled freshly, ssicome vst este nouelment tue. Et sur ceo il ad este pris, et condemne, et quant il ale al executiō, il ad conus le fact.

Adiuncts bée more plentifull, saith Ramus, but subiectes more forcible in arguing, as, hée lookes, ergo hée loues, it followeth not so well, as thus, hée loues, ergo hée lookes. Yet some like not of this note. For, say they, if you consider the subiect and the adiunct Logically, then the one dooth equally argue the other, but if phisically, then that is heterogeneum and impertinent.

As the place, so the time may inhaunce or diminishe the value of thinges. So that, as a man may plus petere loco, so may hée also tempore. Qui tardius soluit, minus soluit, sic qui commodori loco. Qui citius petit, plus petit, sic qui loco magis remoto. Nam vt dies est pars obligationis, sic tempus.

11. H. 4. 31. b. Hill. Home priest mon fits bien vestue, luy dispoyle, et dona a luy vn drape, ieo auera le drape quia ieo auera le corps que il couer: sic adulter vest ma feme &c.

A les Iustices pertient pur doner iudgment, oyer, recorder, agarder proces &c. a les Clerkes pur escriuer ceo que les Iustices agardont, a le vicount pur returner briefs a luy directes &c. 7. H. 6. 30. Hals.

Si action de wast soit ore done generalment vers tenant in tayle apres possibilitie dissue extinct, treble dammages serront recouer vers luy sans plusors parols, car ceux sont adioynts a ceo per le former statute: et quant ceo est done in nouel case, tout que est adioynt a ceo est done ove ceo similiter.

Donatio officij del Exigenter de London &c. pertinet ad dispositionem capitalis Iusticiarij pro tempore existentis, vt incidens inseparabile ad personam dicti capitalis Iusticiarij spectans, & hoc ratione praescriptionis & vsus. 1. & 2. Elis. 25. Dyer.

1. H. 4. 6. per Gascoigne, si le roy per parols generals graunta choses a queux auters sont incidents queux ne sont seuerables, les incidents passont. Come sil graunta moy terre cum pertinentijs, a que comon est appendant, le comon passa.

Tyrwit dit, si le roy graunta moy le foundation d'un

abbey,

abbey, le corody passa: Issint sil graunta fayre, ieo auera vn court de pipouders incident a ceo.

Vide Parkins page. 24. Des incidents que passont per le graunt des principals: come fealtie est incident al homage et al rent, rent al reuersion, aduouson al manor.

Acquitall est incident al franckalmoigne, Littleton, 32. a. acquitall et garrantie sont incidents al Homage auncestrel, Little. 32. Distresse al rent seruice, 57. Distres al rent reserue sur egalitie del partition, 55. Suruyuor al Joyntenancy. 62.

Vide 12. H. 8. 7. 8. 9. Brooke Justice sayth that, le person ad le fœsimple in iure ecclesiæ, whereunto agreeth Elyot. Brudnell, semble que le person ad le fœsimple, car le patron n'ad ascun interest mes solement le presentment. But Pollard will haue it in the Patrome.

Elenchs.

This place, as others, is then abused, when false adiuncts bée applied, or others not orderly applyed.

The ninth Chapter.

Of the diuers or different.

Hitherto of argumentes agéeable, now followe the disagréeable.

A disagréeable argument is that which disagréeth from the thing which it dooth argue.

The one of these ioyned or compared with the other appeareth more plainely.

Disagréeable argumentes bée eyther diuers or opposite.

Diuers or different are disagréeable argumentes which differ onely in respect, and are onely fit for declaration: they are often in authors, and many of them be expressed by these signes, Not this, but that.

Colyn in January, Colyn lo'ude not Hobbinol, but Rosalinde.

Maister Plowden: Fol. 82. a. Car parols, que ne sont auter, que le verberation del ayer, ne sont l'estatute, mes solement

ment le image del statute, et le vie del statute rest en les ments del expositors del parols, quels sont les feasors del statute.

Annotations. Elenches.

ONely in respect:] not indeede, and naturally, in respect of the thinges themselues, which may very well oftentimes concurre in one, but onely in respect of his meaning, that so put them downe. Therefore the vse of diuers argumentes is in dinstinction, and euident explication, not in confirmation. L. 5. E 4. 7. per Bryan: les walles, timber, couerture, pieres &c. del Chapterhouse, ne serront dits proprement le Chapterhouse, mes lou le couent et Chapter sont, la proprement est le Chapterhouse. In that saying of Christ, I come not to send peace, but the sword, if wée entend this conclusion, I come to send the sword, therefore not peace, then the argumentes bée repugnant, sayth Wasserleider: but if wée take it as spoken onely for explication and distinction, then they bée vsed as diuers.

Ramus first found. diuersa: Rodolphus Agricola, disparata, which he calleth differentia.

This place is abused, when such thinges bée put downe for diuers, which are not diuers properly.

The tenth Chapter.

Of Opposites.

OPposites are disagréeable argumentes which disagrée both in respect, and in matter it selfe, and therefore cannot agrée vnto the same thing, according to the same part, respect, or time, as the same man cannot bée hote and colde in the same part of his body, at the same time. So Socrates cannot bée father and sonne to the same man: sicke and whole at the same time: Insomuch that if one of them bée affirmed, the other must bée denyed, and contrarily: but necessarily in the first; contingently in the second.

Opposites

Opposites are eyther Disparates or contraries. Disparates are sundry opposites wherof one is equally and in like manner opposed vnto many.

Hobbinoll in Aprill in his song of Elisa.

Bring here the Pincke and purple Cullambine
with Gelliflowres:
Bring Coronations, and Sops in wine
worne of paramours.
Strow me the ground with Daffadowndillyes,
And Cowslyps, and Kingcups, and loued Lillyes,
The prety Paunce,
And the Cheuisance
Shall match with the faire Flowredelice.

All which herbes bée equally differing one from another, and are therefore Disparates.

M. Plowden Fol. 170.a.b. Mes vn grosse nosme poet conteigner diuers choses corporall, come Manor, Monastery, Rectory, Castell, Honor, et tiels semblables. Car eux sont choses compound, et poyent conteyner tout ensemble, messuages, terres, prées, bois et tiels semblables.

Annotations.

Æqually:] not as though one Disparate shoulde differ equally from all the other. But equally signifieth vicissim, simul, alike, in like manner, againe, &c. Wasserleider.

Disparo signifieth to seuer, or separate. Of that word commeth Disparata, that is, thinges seuered, or put a sunder one from another.

Canons.

If one Disparate bée equally opposed to many, then certeinly, if one of them bée affirmed, all the rest must be denied. But if one among all bée denied, you cannot straightwayes infer any other what you list, but some one of the same kind of thinges. And therefore, from the first part of the Canon, commeth a necessary axiome, but from the seconde, a contingent. What then if I should thus reason?

If this man bée not a Lawyer, hée is a Diuine.

Or thus, out of Virgill.

If the Spartane mayd bée not a woman, shée is a goddesse. Bée these axiomes false or no ? I answere, they bée not altogether false, but contingent. And therefore I said before, that if one of them bée affirmed, the other must bée denyed, and contralily, that is, if one of them bée denyed, the other must bée affirmed: for, as in this argument, so in many others, the common Logicians very rashly say, it dooth not followe, if it doo not follow necessarily: Wheras notwithstanding it may follow, although it follow contingently. So then the one affirmed, the other is denyed necessarily: but the one béeing denied, another shall bée affirmed contingently, as I sayde in the text.

Maister Lambard. Iust. lib. 1. cap. 12. Capitall or deadly punishment is doone sundry wayes, as by hanging, burning, boyling, or pressing.

Not Capitall is of diuers sortes also, as cutting of the hande or eare, burning or marking the hande or face, boaring through the eare, whipping, imprisoning, stocking, setting on the pillory or cucking-stoole, which in olde time was called the tumbrell, and of olde, but not now, pulling out of the toong for false rumors, cutting off the nose for adultery, taking away the priuy partes for counterfeiting of money.

Pecuniary punishmēts bée diuers, as issues, fines, amerciaments, and forfeiture of offices, goods, and lands &c.

The Romanes vsed specially eight sorts of chastisements, Damnum, vincula, verbera, talio, ignominia, exilium, seruitus, mors.

Elenchs.

When diuers bée put downe as Disparates. So in Martiall.

> Pinxisti venerem, colis, *Artemidore, Mineruam,*
>
> Et miraris opus displicuisse tuum ?

For both these things might bée doone together by Artemidorus well ynough, and yet his worke displease no man.

The

The eleuenth Chapter.

Of Contraries.

Contraries bée such opposites, whereof eyther one is onely opposite to one, or one to two, but more to the one of them, than to the other. They bée Relatiues or repugnant. Relatiues are contraries, whereof the one is so opposed to the other, as yet there may bée in other respects a mutuall consent and reciprocall relation betwéene them, whereupon they bée called Relatiues, as father, sonne, husband, wife, &c.

In May Palinode.

So schooled the gate his wanton sonne,
That aunswered her mother, all should be done.

Maister Plowden. Fol. 121. b. Le greinder est in respect del meynder: et issint en ceo que il affirme le conusance del greinder number, il affirme auxi le conusãce del meynder &c.

Repugnant arguments bée such contraries, whereof one is so opposite to one, or at the most to two, as that there can neuer any agréement bée found betwéene them. So Warre is onely opposite to peace: but couetousnes to liberality and prodigalitie, yet more to prodigality.

Sheepheard I list none accordance make
With sheepheard that does the right way forsake:
And of the twayne, if choyse were to mee,
Had leuer my foe than my friend to bee.

Colyn in December.

Loue they him called that gaue mee checkmate,
But better mought they haue behot him hate.

Perigot in August.

Ah *Willy*, when the hart is ill assayde,
How can bagpipe, or ioynts be well apayde?

Maister Plowden Fol. 467. a. Et issint il apiert diuersitie, (hée should haue sayde rather Repugnancy) enter les deux equities, car l'un abridge, l'auter enlarge: l'un dymynisha, l'auter amplifie: l'un tolle de le letter, l'auter ad al ceo.

Fol. 274. a. Car hors de memory et hors de conusance, est

tout vn. Et ambideux ces phrases signifie ignorance del temps: et quant le partie prist conusance del temps, il n'estoit en sa bouche a dire, que il est ignorant de mesme le temps. Car ignorance et science sont contraries repugnant, et d'affirmer contraries, null serra suffer per nostre ley.

Under Repugnant arguments be conteined Priuatiues, as blindnes is opposed to sight; darkenes to light; death to life.

Piers in May.

For what concord han light and darke sam?

Villen et franck home sont priuatiues. see Plowden 397.a.

And thus much of disagreeable argumentes, by which one thing is sayd to bee different from another.

Annotations.

This word, Contrary, betokeneth no distinct and speciall determinate argument, but is a generall affection incident to diuers specials. Therefore in Iudgement we should not say, the argument is from the contrary, but from this or that kind of contrary, for all contraries argue not alike. And so in other arguments wee must not sticke in the generalitie, but descend to particulars, as, what cause, what subiect, what adiunct.

Cum res duę ità comparantur, vt ex earum altera affirmata, affirmetur altera, ex altera negata, negetur altera, tum illæ sunt consentaneæ, vt *Aegistus* est otiosus, ergò adulter: Efficiens non habet instrumenta ad ædificandum, ergò non potest ædificare: Causa & efficiens vtrobiq;: Sed cum ex vna affirmata, altera negatur, vel ex vna negata altera affirmatur, tùm sunt dissentaneæ, vt *Sophroniscus* fuit pater *Socratis*, ergò non filius: & *Socrates* fuit *Sophronisci* filius, ergò non pater: hìc causa & effectum sunt, sed considerantur, vt dissentanea: quià ex altero affirmato negatur alterum. Et non est absurdũ, quod vna eademq; res, diuerso respectu, sit & consentanea & dissentanea. Itaq; teneamus Relata. *Piscator.*

Scribonius would haue the nature of Relatiues generally put downe immediatly after the generall definition of an argument in the first Chapter. Because, as a father cannot bee

somuch

somuch as imagined without a sonne, nor a sonne without a father, so no more can a cause without a thing caused, thing caused without a cause, subiect without adiunct, adiunct without subiect &c.

Sometimes the Relatiues haue both distinct names, as father, sonne, sometimes but one name, as a brother is hee that hath a brother, a disparate is that which hath a disparate.

One Relatiue doth define and expound another. So the cause is defined by the thing caused, and this by that &c.

Relata sunt simul natura, for though Dauid were Dauid before Salomon was borne, yet Dauid was neuer Salomons father, before Salomon was Dauids sonne.

Relata ita contraria sunt, vt non sint sine medio: nam inter patrem & filium, est medius, qui neq; pater, neq; filius est.

I. Guyer fuit endite deuant le Coroner super visum corporis, del mort Emeline Guyer sa feme. Et l'enditement fuit, que le dit Emelyne fuit in pace domini regis, quousq; antedictus I. Guyer, vir præfatæ Emelyne Guyer &c. cest inditement fuit challenge. Car il poet estre intend assets bien per l'enditement, que le feme n'est occise, mes est in vie, et issint repugnant en luy mesme, coq; le dit I. Guyer est appelle vir præfate Emelyne, ou il serroyt, nuper vir, car vir est correlatiue al feme, et ne poet estre vir nisi in respectu vxoris &c. 31. 32. H. 8. 3. Dyer.

Il ne est possible, que vn person poet estre souereigne et subiect. 4. Elis. 22. Dyer.

That which agreeth with one of the Relatiues, commonly agreeth with the other, as if it bee honest to teach, it is no shame to learne.

Relatiues in our law bee, as, seignior tenant, paramount per auayle, playntife defendant, demandant tenant, garde gardeine, feffor feffee, donor donee, grauntor grauntee, lessor lessee, disseisor disseisee, conuser conusee, baron feme &c.

Repugnants.

If one repugnant argument bee denyed, the other must bee affirmed, if there bee no third thing put betweene them.

Although Contraries cannot bee applyed vnto the same thing, yet the same thing may be applied vnto contraries.

Priuatiues.

Priuatiues they call those whereof one denieth onely in that subiect whereunto the affirmatiue agreeth by nature (affirmatiue is that which doth affirme and lay down some thing to bée or imagined to bée) and héere the affirmatiue is called the habite, the negatiue the priuation thereof. A stone therefore cannot bée called blinde, for that it was neuer framed of nature to bée capable of sight, but it may bée called, not séeing.

Crompton: Fol. 29. Home tua auter quant est ebrius, il serra pendus quant est sober.

Priuatiues be, In prison alarg, compos mentis, non sane memorie: aueugle surde, mute. &c.

Priuatio presupponit habitum, vnde illa consectaria, non videtur rem amittere cuius propria non fuit. Non potest videri desisse habere, qui nunquam habuit. Quod quis, si velit, habere non potest, id repudiare non potest. Eius est non velle, qui potest velle. Expressa nocent, non expressa non nocent. Qui tacet, non vtiq; fatetur, sed tamen verum est eum non negare. Cum architecti quidam palatium ædificarent in via publica, & cum proiecto lapide proclamassent, quidam iter illac faciens, lapide vulneratus, architectos omnes in ius vocauit: ab his consultus Pyleus, animaduertit, eos probare non posse, quod proclamassent: itaq; non ius, ait, deficit, sed probatio. Cum igitur cras in iuditium veneritis, cauete, ne verbum proferatis, sed me solum loqui sinatis: die igitur iudicij constituto, cum à iudice accusationi respondere iussi essent, & *Pyleus* illos vt mutos excusaret, ibi aduersarius id pernegare cæpit, quoniam ipsos, cum vulneraretur, clamantes audisset, vt sibi caueret: quæ verba *Pyleus* statim ad acta referri iussit, & ita eos à lite liberauit. *Baldus* in sua pract. tit. de cautelis.

As for contradictories, it were vtterly impertinent to make any discourse of them in this place, as wholy belonging to axiomaticall disposition, whereunto all contradictions are naturally incident, howsoeuer Beurhusius distinguish in this case.

Elenchus.

In relatiues, Omnia castor emis, sic fiet vt omnia vendas.

Martiall.

Martiall. Indéed if Castor buy all, some body must néeds sel all: but it followeth not that therefore, Castor must sell all.

In Repugnant: Whitenes is a colour, therefore blacknes is no colour. It followeth not. For, as I sayd before, contraries generally are not such, of the which one and the same thing cannot bée affirmed, but such as cannot be affirmed of one and the same thing.

So in Relatiues. Tibullus lib. 1.

At vos exiguo pecori, furesq;, lupiq;
Parcite: de magno est præda petenda grege.

It followeth not, that because a pray is to bée taken of a great flocke, therefore nothing is to bée taken of a little one.

So in Priuatiues,

Hee that seeth is aliue, therefore
Hee that is blinde, is dead.

The 12. Chapter.

Of secondary Argumentes.

Thus much of originall and first arguments. The secondary remayneth which is made of the ioyning togither of the first, and argueth as the first doe from whence it is deriued, as the cause therefore argueth absolutely, so such secondary arguments as are made of the cause, and so in the rest, according as their seuerall kinde of arguing is.

The Argument made of the first is eyther Distribution or Definition.

Annotations.

Ramus to these two which I haue put downe, addeth other two, Coniugates, and Notation, as argumentes made of the first. As for Coniugates, I sée in them no new different force of arguing, as hée is iust, for hée dealeth iustly: héere is nothing in effect, but the cause and the effect. For as for the deriuation of this word, Iuste, from Iustice, it séemeth altother grammaticall: and whereas they both do fitly allude in the ende and falling, thus, Iustice Iust, Iustly, that commeth from a Rhetoricall figure, called Polyptoton, which concerneth the elegancie that is in the diuers fallinges and terminations of words.

So in Notation, the interpretation of the name, seemeth rather the dutie of a dictionary, then of any Logicall institution, as Argumentum ab arguendo: where againe there is no force of arguing but from the cause and the thing caused. For as for the pretty and conceipted chaunge of the word, argumentum ab arguendo, it seemeth also a Rhetoricall agnomination: yet as not fully resolued heerein, I leaue them in these Annotations.

Coniugates or offsprings, bee wordes diuersly deriued from one head, as Iustice, Iust, Iustly, hee dealeth Iustly, therefore hee is iust. The primitiue word conteineth the cause of his offsprings, as here Iustice of iust dealing.

Aristotle commendeth this place highly 7. topic.

Canons.

If you put downe or remoue one Coniugate, you must put downe, or remoue the other: That which is giuen or taken, to or from the one: is giuen or taken, to or from the other: but here Contingency is more vsuall then necessitie, therefore heede is to bee taken in distinguishing the one from the other.

In 4. H. 7. 9. b. Un briefe de partitione facienda del terre et rent fuit port. Et Keble pleade pur le rent, que le def. fuit sole seisie, sans ceo que il tient pro indiuiso oue le pl. et per Bryan, cest bon plee, car il n'auera partition del chose dont il ne ad ascun parte.

Coniugates from the cause.

Terence in Hecyra Act. 3. scoen. 4. Dedecet iam ira hæc, etsi meritò iratus es. This anger becomes you not, although you haue cause to bee angry.

From the thing caused.

Tully in his oration for his house: Primùm dico, Senatoris esse boni, in Senatum venire. First I say, it is the part of a good Senator, to come into the Senate house.

From

From the subiect.

Tully to Atticus, Quia homo es, humana tibi ferenda est ratio. Because thou art a man, thou must beare such thinges as are incident to men.

From the adiunct.

Tully in his epistles: Rege interfecto, regios omnes nutus tuemur. The king béeing killed, wée mainteine euery kingly becke and countenance.

Elenchs.

Some learned men bée lewd liuers, therefore learning is lewd: Where it should bée thus; Learned men liue lewdly, therefore they bée lewde: or thus, Learning maketh men lewd, therefore it is lewd.

Notation.

Notation or Etymologie, is the interpretation of the word. For words bée notes of thinges, and of all words eyther deriuatiue or compound, you may yéelde some reason fet from the first arguments, if the notation bée well made. It is called Originatio, quod originem verborum explicet: and Etymologia, id est, veriloquium.

Nomina sunt argumenta, non quatenus ad rem significandam referuntur, sed quatenus referuntur vel inter sé mutuò, vt coniugata: vel ad suæ originis interpretationem, quæ Notatio dicitur. Sed sic non considerantur vt nomina, id est symbola, sed vt res quędam, seu ὄντα quędam. *Piscator.*

Grammatica notatio exponit vocū adsignificationē: Logica verò causam explicat, cur hoc nomen huic rei sit impositū.

Piscator putat, à nomine ad rem significatam argumentari, nihil aliud esse quàm a testimonio argumentari: vt Christus in scriptura dicitur Deus, ergò est Deus.

Canons.

To whome the interpretation of the name agréeth, to that also the name it selfe and contrarily. Yet, sayth Corasius, ab interpretatione ad nomen ipsum deriuatum, sicuti est à genere ad speciem, desumpta argumentatio inanis est, quod etymologia latiùs pateat, quam nomen ipsum. Certè reciprocatio in his obscura & incerta est. Sed à deriuato ad deriuationem argui melius potest, vt tutor est, ergò tueri debet.

When the name is false, vnknowne. or ambiguous, then the reason is daungerous.

That which agreeth with the one, agreeth with the other.

Quips, taunts, iests, and conceipts are often fet hence.

All Platoes Cratilus is spent in the interpretation of words after this manner.

Nihil ambigi potest, ait *Cicero*, in quo, non aut res controuersiam faciat, aut verbum, in dictionibus igitur æquè atq; in rebus versatur Dialectica. *Hottoman.*

Examples of notations. From the cause.

Billinsgate, a gate in London builded by king Belus.

From the effect.

Prouident, of foreseeing future chaunces. And so in the rest.

Gospell, a good spell, or Gods spell, or saying. A Lordane signifieth an imperious idle fellow, of a lord Dane. Winchelsea, of wind, chilly, and sea: so in Latine it is called Frigmareuentus, of frigus, mare, ventus. Little Iohn, for that hee was wonderfully tall and bigge, heere the notation is from the contrary, as Lucus, quia non lucet, parcæ, quia non parcunt, Bellum, quia non bellum, & so of Ludus, Eumenides &c. Mutuum quasi meumtuum.

Victima, quæ dextra cecidit victrice, vocatur:
Hostibus à domitis, hostia nomen habet.

Arist. 2. Rhet. Draconis leges, non hominis, quod erant asperę. Dracoes lawes were a Dragons lawes, for their crueltie.

Territorium dicitur, quia magistratus eius loci, intra suos fines, terrendi, id est, coercendi ius habent.

The Court of pipowders incident to fayres, is called Curia pedis puluerisati, for fayres commonly are dusty. 13. E. 4. 8.

Choke in 17. E. 4. b. Conclude que null contract serra, si non ambideux les parties simul consentiant. Car contractus dicitur à con, quod est simul, & traho, to draw together.

Seruus a seruando, as well as of seruiendo, quia seruabantur capti in bello, vt postea venderentur. Manumissio, quasi è manu dimissio. Mancipia, quasi manu capta. *Bracton* lib. 1. Fol. 4.

Dyer

Dyer semble que vn remaynder al feme pur vie apres le mort le baron, ne poet estre termed ne prise pur vne joynture, purceoq; el doit prendre estate joyntment oue son baron accordant al etymologie del parol, joynture. 17. Elis. 50. Dyer.

Per Needham 4. E. 4. Præcipe quod reddat gist proprement vers le tenant del terre, de terris ou tenementis, car la il poet reddere: contra del comon de pasture appendant ou in grosse; la quod permittat gist que il suffer le demandant occupier son comon &c. Socage à soca. Littleton. 26. 7.

Fearmes, quasi feormian, qu'est vn Saxon paroll, significant pur fæder ou render vittayle, car les auncient reseruations fueront pur le plnis part in vittayles et nemy argent. Termes of the law. pag. 967.

Aulnage, ex quo Aulnager, est le measure et le metter per le yarde, in Latine, Vlnagium & vlnator, ab vlna. 13. & 14. Elis. 49. Dyer.

Shyrréue, of two Saxon wordes, Geresa, a ruler, and Scyran, which is to cut: as it were the ruler of the shire. For the Realme is diuided and cut, as it were, into such partes, called hérevpon shires, and allotted to seuerall shyrréues as their shires. In Latine hée is called Vicecomes, quasi vicarius comitis, in séeing iustice executed in the shire, and the kinges reuenues brought in ærarium. Which the Counte, Earle, Comes himselfe should, but could not by himselfe, as attending for the most part vpon the king in warres, as the name beareth, Comes quasi comitans principem.

Constable, quasi Kyninstaple, or Kingstaple, the stay and hold of the king, for so was the Lord great Constable of England, who had authoritie in matters of warre within & without the Realme. Out of which office this lower Constableship was first set. 13. E. 3. Stat. Winchester: where two constables in euery Hundred were appoynted to take view of armour.

Tythingman, Headborough, Chiefepledg, Borsholder, is in a manner all one with a petite Constable. Although before William Conquerour it was ordeined, that all frée borne men should cast themselues in companies by ten in ech company, and that euery of the ten should bée pledge and surety for his fellow, and amerced for his default if he escaped. Hereof these companies bée called Boroes or Borhes, a pledge, and Tything of ten. And because ten of these companies sometimes met for matters of weight, and ten times ten is an hundred, their generall assembly was called an hundred. The speaker and chiefe man was called the Tythingman, the Borsholder, quasi elder Boroe, and head-borohe, chiefe pledge. In these méetings among other things it was obserued, that euery of these pledges should yearely bée presented by the chiefe pledge at a generall assembly, yet called the view of Frankepledge, visus Franciplegij, or the Léete court. Maister Lambard.

Lathes, Rapes, and Wapentakes, be so called of the diuisions of partes of shires. Lathe is a barne, Rape a reaping. Sir Thomas Smith thinketh them to bée names of seruice, for that so many townes met in one day to reape or carry the Lords corne into his barne, and Wapentake of taking weapons, for that in those assemblies, hée that could not find suretie for his good abearing, had his weapon taken from him.

But M. Lambard in legibus Edwardi regis, writeth thus.

Totus ille conuentus dicitur Wapentac, eo quod per tactum armorũ suorum ad inuicem confederati sunt: of *Wepun* & *Tac*, tangere vel confirmare, quià omnes pręsentes cum lanceis suis tangebant hastam prefecti ipsius Wapentachij, & ità se confirmabant.

Bracton. Dicitur ideò breue, quia rem de qua agit, & intentionem petentis, paucis verbis breuiter enarrat, &c.

Maister Plowden. Fol. 357. a. Quia fines in curia nostra leuati finem litibus debent imponere & imponunt, ideò fines vocantur maximè. Sic Fol. 368. b. ex *Bracton*. Finis est extremitas vniuscuiusq; rei, hoc est, idem in quo vnaquęq; res terminatur, & ideò dicitur finalis concordia, quià imponit finem litibus.

Fol. 250. a. b. Et le nosme del estate fée tayle fuit done sur le certeintie del inheritance, come Littleton dit, car il dit, que Talliare, idem est, quod in certitudinem ponere. Et pur ceoq; en le done il est expresse de que corps les heyres que enheritont, isseront, pur cel cause il prist, que il fuit appelle tayle.

tayle. Ou plustost puit auer le nosme de cest Francois paroll, tayler, lequel est decowper, car a tayler boys, est a cowper boys, et purceoq; l'estate est docked, ou cut off (car deuant il fuit fee simple, et a ore le fee est decise de ceo, et l'estate per ceo est docked, cut off, ou fait meynder) il poet bien estre dit estate tayle, cestascauoir, estate decoupe, decise, ou deminue.

Fol. 193. a. Terres venues en mains des homes de religion, sont appelle en ley de viender en mortmayne, per le resemblance (come Weston Justice dit) al tenure d'un home en extremes, que tient en son mayne queconq; que il soit, tanq; que il soit mort. Et issint le continuance del inheritance en ceux de religion est suppose ey longement, que le meason continue. Vide Doctor & Student accordant oue ceo. pag. 172. a.

Fol. 198. b. Et le paroll, Expiration, est propernient breathing vp, ou yeelding vp the breath, come le seigniour Dyer dit, et est apply al home ou auters choses animate: et est vse pur le mort d'un home; car quant il yeelde vp his breath, adonques il morust, car sans son breath il ne poet viuer. Et comentq; il est propernient vse a choses animate, que breathont, vncore per vn similitude il est referre al choses inanimate. Come vsomus en nostre ley, Reuerter, que est properment vse in choses animate que soy remouent: mes ascun foits nous vsomus ceo in chose inanimate, come diomus, lou tenant en tayle morust, le terre reuertera al donor. Et issint expiration vse icy per similitude del choses viuant, implye fine queconq;. Car come signifiomus per expiration le mort del home, et son darreine fine, queconque voy, que il vient, issint ceo paroll, expiration, adde al estate pur ans, poet aptement signifier le fine de ceo queconq;. Et issint expiration del estate pur ans, et fine del estate pur ans, est tout vn.

Court baron, of Barones, quasi virones, magnates, among the Saxons called Thani. Court Leete, of the Saxon word Lant, which is law, so Lant-day by corruption of speech is come to be called Law-day. Barrettor, of the French Barat, deceipt: or of the Latine, Baratro, or Balatro, a vyle knaue. Apprentice of Apprendre to learne. Sessions à sedendo. Acquittance, quasi acquietantia, &c.

Indictement, of the French word, Enditer, which Stephanus

phanus, deriueth from the Gréeke ἐνδείκνυμι, defero, accuso, postulo in iudicio, and ἐνδείκνυμαι, deferor, causam dico quod circa publica secus aliquid admiserim. Hereof is ἔνδειξις, delatio, and ἐνδείκτης, delator, quadruplator. Maister Lambard in his Iustice of peace. lib. 2. cap. 5. sayth thus. The vnderstanding or knowledge which the iustices of peace doe take by the trauaile of these enquirours is by the meane of their report, put in writing, and commonly called an enditement, or presentment: betwéene the which two wordes (howsoeuer they bée confounded in common spéech) mée thinketh that there dooth easily appeare a certaine difference. For I take a presentment to bée a méere denuntiation of the iurors themselues or of some other officer without any other information: and an enditement to be the verdict of the iurours, grounded vpon the accusation of a third person. So that a presentment is but a declaration of the Iurours, or officers without any bill offered before, and an enditement is their finding of a bill of accusation to bee true. The one séemeth to come of the Gréeke ἐνδείκνυμι I accuse, the other of the French, presenter, to offer vnto a man, or set before him.

Maister Lambard: Iust. lib. 2. cap. 16. Hereof also the fine tooke first his name, of the Latine Finis, because it maketh an ende with the Prince for the imprisonment, for the offence committed, against his law, and in that respect chiefly dooth it differ from an amerceament. For when the offender hath not so déepely trespassed, that thereby hée deserueth not any bodily punishment at all (as if hée bée nonsuite in an action, or doe commit any such like default) hée is sayde to fall into the kinges mercy, because hee is then mercifully to bée dealt with. And by the great charter, cap. 14. that amerciament and summe of money which hée is to pay for ý same, ought to bée assessed and affeered by the good and lawfull men of the neighbourhood, which also Glannil, lib. 9. cap. 11. affirmeth to haue bene the lawe of the land long before that time, saying misericordia domini regis est, qua quis per iuramentum legalium hominum de vicineto eatenus amerciandus, ne aliquid de suo honorabili contenemento amittat. But when the offence or contempt falleth out to bee so great, that

it

it asketh the imprisonment of the body it selfe, and that during the kings wil and pleasure, then is the party to redeeme his liberty with some portion of money, as he can best agree with the king or his Iustices for the same, which composition is properly called his fine, or his ransome, and in Latin Redemptio, as may be plainly seene by the statute of Marlebridge. 52. H. 3. cap. 1. 2. 3. & 4. and by the statute called Ragman, and diuers other auncient statutes.

The humanitie and conscience which Christian religion dooth teach, hath ingendred a certeine feare and scruple in the hartes of our men, to haue slaues and bondmen. Yet necessity on both sides, of the one to haue helpe, and the other to haue seruice, hath kept a figure or fashion thereof. So that some would not haue bondmen, villeins in grosse, as ye would say immediately bond to the person and his heires; but ascriptitios glebæ, or agris censitos, and villeins regardant and bond to the manor or ground, as members belonging to the place, and following him who had the place; to the intent their seruice might bee furnished, and that the country beeing euill, unwholesome, and otherwise barren, should not be desolate. Others afterwards found out the wayes and meanes, that not the men, but the land should bee bound, and bring with it such bondage and seruice to him that occupyeth it, as to carry the Lords dunge unto the fieldes, to plow his ground at certeine dayes, sowe, reape, come to his court, sweare faith unto him, and in the ende to holde the land but by the copy of the Lords Court roll, and at the will of the Lord. This tenure is called also in our Law, villeine, bond, or seruice tenure. Yet, to consider more deepely, all land, euen that which is called most free land, hath a bondage annexed unto it, not as naturally the lower ground must suffer and receiue the water and filth which falleth from the higher ground, nor such as Iustinian speaketh of de seruitutibus prædiorum rusticorum & vrbanorum; but the lande dooth bring a certeine kinde of seruitude to the possessor. For no man holdeth lande simply free in England, but he or she that holdeth the crowne of England: all others holde their land in fee, that is upon a fayth or trust, and some seruice to another Lord of a mannor as his superior, and he againe of a higher Lord, till it come to the prince and him that holdeth the crowne. So that if a man die, and it bee founde that he hath lande which he holdeth, but of whom no man can tell, this is vnderstood to be holden of the crowne, and in capite, which is much like to knights seruice, and draweth vnto it three seruices, Homage, ward, and mariage: that is he shall sweare to be his man, and to be true vnto him of whome hee holdeth the land. His sonne who holdeth the land after the death of his father, shalbe married where it pleaseth the Lorde. He that holdeth the land most freely of a temporall man (for francke almes and francke mariage hath an other cause and nature) holdeth by fealtie onely, which is, hee shall sweare to bee true to the Lord. So that all free land in England is holden in fee, or fedo, which is asmuch to say, as in fide or fiducia, that is, in trust and confidence, that hee shalbe true to the Lorde, of whome he holdeth it, pay such rents, doe such seruice, and obserue such conditions, as were annexed to the first donation. Thus all, sauing the Prince, bee not veri domini, but rather Fiduciarij domini & possessores. This is a more likely interpretation then yͤ which Littleton doth put down in his booke, who sayth that fœdum, idem est quod hæreditas, which it doth betoken in no language. This happeneth many times to them who bee of great wit and learning, yet not seene in many tongues, or marke not the deduction of wordes which time doth alter. Fides in Latine, the Gothes comming into Italy, and corrupting the language, was turned first into fede and at this daye in Italy they will saye, in fide, en fede, or a la fe. And some vncunning lawyers that would make a newe barbarous Latine worde to betoken land giuen in fidem, or as the Italian sayth, in fede, or fe, made it, in feudum, or fedum. The nature of the word appeareth more euident in those which wee call to feffe, feoffee or feoffees, the one be fiduciarij possessores, or fidei cōmissarij, the other is, dare in fiduciam, or fidei commissum, or, more Latinely, fidei committere. The like error is in Wythernam, which some interprete vetitum nauium: whereas in trueth it is in playne Dutch, and in our old Saxon language

wyther

wyther nempt, alterum accipere : iterum rapere:nâm is,pignoris ablatio, wyther, signifieth altera. But to returne thither where wee did digresse: yee see that where the persons bee free, and the bodies at full libertie and maxime ingenui, yet by annexing a condition to the land,there bee meanes to bring the owners and possessors thereof into a certaine seruitude, or rather Libertinitie: that the tenantes, besides paying the rent accustomed,shall owe to the Lord a certaine fayth, duetie, trust, obedience, and, as we terme it,certaine seruice, as Libertus or cliens patrono: which, because it doth not consist in the persons, (for the respect in them doth not make them bonde) but in the land and occupation thereof,it is more properly expressed in calling the one tenant, the other Lord of the fee, then either Libertus or cliens can doe the one,or Patronus the other: for these wordes touch rather the persons, and the office and duetie betweene them, then the possessions, but in our cause, leauing the possession and land, all the obligation of seruitude and seruice is gone.

So much haue I collected out of sir Thomas Smith, concerning this word fee. lib.3. cap.8.

Maister Lambard. Iust. lib. 2. cap. 14. Arraignement seemeth to haue borrowed the name out of the worde Arraye, which is the pannell or iurie, because hee that is arraigned, must be tried by them, being first called, sworne, and tryed in order for that seruice.

Maister Lambard. Iust. lib. 1. cap. 13. This sauing then, or deliuery of a person out of prison, before hee hath satisfied the law, is vttered by three tearmes in our statutes, that is to say bailement,mainepriseor manucaption,and repleuine: and they bee indifferently vsed to expresse that suretie,which the prisoner is to finde in such a case. Neuerthelesse it seemeth that a repleuine had his original of the word, pledges, which denoteth them that vndertake for the partie, that hee shall abide to be iustified by lawe: and it is vsed in diuers other cases, as in repleuine of cattell vpon distresse, repleuine of fraunchises in a quo warranto, repleuyne of land vpon a grand cape in olde time, and repleuine of the person of a man in case of villenage.

Baylement is deriued from the French terme Bayler, and that also commeth of the Greeke βάλλειν, they both signifying to deliuer into hande. For hée that is bayled, is taken or kept out of prison, and deliuered, as it were, into the handes of his friendes, as sureties for him. Whereof also the worde Manucaptio, or Mainprise, which is all one, giueth good euidence, the one mentioning the deliuery, the other the receyuing. And in this respect, the booke of the Norman customes calleth baylement, a liue prison, for that the party thereby becommeth prisoner to his fréendes that doo vndertake for him.

Maister Lambard. Iust. lib. 1. cap. 21. As in olde time euerie killing of a man was of the effect, called Murder, because death ensued of it (and of the Hebrew word Moth, saith Postellus, commeth the Latine Mors, which the Saxons our elders, called Morth and Morthor, as wée yet found it) so was that wilfull manner of slaying with malice prepensed, long since, and most properly, called Felony, because it was doone felleo animo, in malitious heate and displeasure, and therefore per feloniam, as the statute at Marlebridge cap. 15. dooth plainely tearme it.

Maister Lambard. Iust. lib. 2. cap. 19. Riot séemeth to come of the French worde Rioter, which signifieth to brawle or scolde; for that commonly Riots indéede, doo follow of brawling in word. And it is taken to bée where there is any vnlawfull assembly (An vnlawfull assembly is the company of thrée persons or more gathered togither to doo such an vnlawfull act, although they doo it not indéede) of men gathered together, and going about to commit an vnlawful act, and they doo execute it indéede, as to beate a man, or to enter vppon a possession forcibly, or such like.

Our Rout is the same which the Germains yet call Rot, meaning a band or great company of men gathered togither, and going about to execute, or executing indéede any Riot or vnlawfull act. And, sayth Marrow, it is saide properly of the multitude that assemble themselues in such disorderly sorte for their common quarrell: as if the inhabitants of a towneship doo assemble to pull downe a hedge or pale, to haue their common, where they ought to haue none, to beate a man that

hath

hath done them some publike offence or displeasure.

M. Lambard. Iust. lib. 1. cap. 17. The wordes Affray and Assault bee indifferently used of most men, and that in our booke cases, but yet in myne opinion, there wanteth not a iust difference betweene them. For Affray, is deryued of the French, Effrayer, which signifieth, to terrifie, or bring feare, and is the more hainous trespasse: for the Law understandeth it to be a common wrong, and therefore it is enquirable and punishable in the turne of the shiriffe, and in a leete, 4. H. 6. 10. and 8. E. 4. 5. Otherwise it is of an assault, as it seemeth by those very bookes. Yet may an affray bee without word or blow giuen: as if a man shall shew himselfe furnished with armour or weapon, which is not usually worne and borne, it wil strike a feare into others that be not armed, as hee is, and therefore both the statute of Northampton. 2. E. 3 cap. 3. made against the wearing of armour and weapon, and the writ thereupon grounded, doo speake of it, by the words, Effray del pais, and, in terrorem populi.

But an Assault, as it is fetched from another fountayne, namely from the Latine Assultus, which denoteth a leaping or flying upon a man: so can it not bee performed without the offer of some hurtfull blow, or at the least of some fearfull speech. And therefore to rebuke a collector with fowle words, so that hee departed for feare without dooing his office, was taken for an assault. 27. lib. Ass. Pl. 11. And to strike at a man although hee were neither hurt, nor hit with the blowe, was adiudged an assault. 22. lib. ass. pl. 60. For this assault dooth not alwayes necessarily imply a hitting: and therefore in trespasse of assault and battery, a man may bee founde guilty of the assault, and yet excused of the battery. 40. E. 3. 4. and 45. E. 3. 24.

Estreates are called of the word Extracta, because they bee short notes or memorials, extracted or drawne out of the Records by the Clarke of the peace, and by him indented and deliuered sunderly to the shiriffe, and to the barons of the Escheqer, bearing this, or the like title: Extracta finium, amerciamentorum forisfactorum, ad generalem sessionem pacis tentam apud Maydstone &c. coram &c. For the whole forme of the making héereof, there is full direction giuen to all clerkes of estreates, by the statute. 7. H. 4. cap. 3. whereunto I referre them.

I haue purposely inserted a number of notations, for that I would make it plain, how the notion of the thing is oftentimes expressed by the notation of the word, contrary to the preiudicate opinion of some séely penmen, and illogicall lawyers, who thinke it a fruiteles poynt of superfluous curiositie, to understand the words of a mans owne profession.

Elenchs.

A Woman is a woe man, because shee worketh a man woe. Agreamentum, quasi aggregatio mentium. But all the sport is to heare the Monkish notations of wordes both Gréeke and Latine, whereof they knew neither sence nor signification, as Diabolus, of Dia, that is two (say they) and bolus, which signifieth a morsell, because the deuill maketh but two morsels of a man, one of the soule, and another of the body. Hypocrisis, of ὑπὸ, which is ouer, and χρυσὸς, gold, because hypocrites bée cloaked with a golden shew ouercast: whereas the one commeth of διαβάλλειν, to cast in accusations; the other of ὑποκρίνομαι, to dissemble.

The 13. Chapter.

Of Distribution.

IN Distribution and Definition there is a most necessary reciprocation or conuersion: in distribution, of all the parts with the whole: in definition, of the thing defined, with the definition it selfe.

A distribution is, when the whole is distributed into his partes. And as the distinguishing of the whole into his parts, is called Distribution: so the collection or gathering together of all the parts to make up the whole, is named Induction.

Distribution is made of arguments which are agréeable to the whole, but disagréeable among themselues: so that it is so much the more perfect distribution, by how much the

partes

partes doo more agrée with the whole; and disagrée among themselues.

Annotations.

Reciprocation :] In other arguments not necessary. For it is not in all causes, but onely betwéene the forme and the thing formed: not in all subiects, but betwéene the subiect and his proper adiunct, not in all contraries, but onely in Relatiues. Whereas in distribution and definition, the reciprocation is perpetuall.

Such is the excellency of distribution and definition, that almost they alone doo suffice for the absolute putting downe of any art. Therefore Socrates in Phædro Platonis sayth, that if he finde any man who can cunningly diuide, he will follow his steps, and admire him for a God.

[Induction :] Therefore as the one is an argument, and no argumentation, so also is the other. Nam Inductio arguit distributum siue totum, sine vlla dispositione tertij argumenti.

[More agree with the whole :] For in distribution of the subiect and adiunct, the partes and the whole doo not essentially agrée, as we shall sée héereafter. Therefore by this rule the best diuision is from the cause and effect. Againe, the more that the partes doo disagrée among themselues, the better is the diuision. By which it appéereth that the best diuision must be of partes that be most repugnant, which can bee but two, therefore Dichotomia is most excellent, a diuision consisting onely of two partes. For, as among agreeable arguments the cause and thing caused doo best agrée, so of all disagréeable; the repugnant be most disagréeable. But as in the most generall and subalternall, Dichotomia must bee obserued, so in the most speciall it is not to be exacted.

Elenchs.

Plato in Phædro compareth inartificial diuiders to bungling Cookes, who in stead of artificiall caruing, vse rudely to breake and dismember thinges. This is a lamentable want in our law, I meane exact diuisions, in place whereof wee haue nothing els, but eyther A B C methode without coherence, or primo notandum, 2. not. 3. not. 4. not. & so on stil till hée come to decimotertiò notandum, like dunses in schooles, and séelly bablers in pulpits: that a man were farre better make a new spéech, than remember their waste and confused Schediasmata. Lyttleton did what hée could in this behalfe, although it were but litle, as in those his distinctions, Estate taile is generall or speciall: Dower is per le comen ley, per custom, ad ostium ecclesiæ, ex assensu patris, de la pluis beale. Villen per prescription ou confession: Item in gros ou regardant. Rent est rent seruice, charge, seck. Conditions in fayt, en ley. Garrantie, lineall, collaterall, per disseisin, &c.

Well then, one generall Elench in a distribution, is the not vsing of it, when the matter requireth. Another is, when wée vse it, but inartificially, when any thing eyther wanteth in it, or is superfluous. Want, as in that which Virgil hath 5. Aeneid. where hée propoundeth in his distribution onely foure kindes of exercises, but afterwards expoundeth fiue.

Prima citæ Teucris ponam certamina classis,
Quiq; pedum cursu valet, & qui viribus audax,
Aut iaculo incedit melior, leuibusq; sagittis,
Seu crudo fidit pugnam committere cestu,
Cuncti adsint, meritæq; expectent præmia palmæ,
Ore fauete omnes, & cingite tempora ramis.

For besides these foure, followeth the fift, not named here in the distribution, and that is the race of horses.

For superfluitie, that shall serue which Tully hath in his second booke De finibus, where hée speaketh thus of Epicurus.

Quomodo autem philosophus loquitur tria esse genera cupiditatum? Naturales & necessarias, naturales & non necessarias, nec naturales nec necessarias. Primùm diuisit inleganter: duo enim genera quæ erant, fecit tria: hoc est, non diuidere, sed frangere rem. Qui si diceret, Cupiditatum duo esse genera, naturales & inanes: naturalium quoq; duo, necessarias & non necessarias, confecta res esset. Vitiosum est enim in diuidendo, partem in genere numerare.

The

The 14. Chapter.

Of Distribution of Causes.

Distribution is made eyther of argumentes fully agréable, or agréable in parte: fully as first of the cause.

The distribution made of the cause is, when the partes are the causes of the whole. And this is called partition, when the whole integrall is diuided into his members.

Hobbinoll confuteth Diggon Dauy in September, prouing by a distribution of England into her parts, no Wolues to bée in England.

> Fye on thee *Diggon*, and all thy fowle leasing,
> Well is knowne, that sith the Saxon king,
> Never was Woolfe seene, many nor some,
> Nor in all Kent, nor in Christendome.

For most parte of England béeing Christian in Ethelberts time, Kent onely continued in Paganisme, and was therefore counted no parte of English Christendome. So that partition is vsed both in a distinct propounding of partes, where any long matter is to bée handeled of Poets, Orators, Preachers, Lawyers, &c. and also syllogistically in arguing eyther the whole by the partes, or the parts by the whole.

Maister Plowden. Fol. 170. a. Terre ne poet perteigner al messuage. Car messuage consist de deux choses, del terre et structure, et terre ne poet perteigner al terre, &c.

Fol. 151. a. Reuersion del terre consist des deux choses del terre, et del residue ou remnaunt estate. Come Manor del seruices et demesne; stag.num del terre et eawe; Piscaria del eawe et terre &c.

Annotations.

E Causis singulis distributio esse potest. Ex efficiente, vt ius est naturale, ciuile, gentium; ex materia: vestes sunt laneæ, lineæ, &c. Ex forma, lanx est, quadrata, rotunda, &c. Ex fine, vestes sunt induendi causa, vel præcingendi, insternendi, &c.

For the Elenchs touching distribution of the integrall, see before in the tractate of the integrall.

The 15. Chapter.

Of distribution of Effects.

THe distributiō of the thing caused or of the effects is, whose parts are effects of the whole, and this is properly called Diuision, when as the generall or vniuersall is diuided into his specials. And as the first called Partition; so this called diuision is handeled as well in forme of Distribution, as in arguing the one by the other.

Maister Plowden. Fol. 132. b. Il n'est rente: car si serroit rent, adonq; il couyent de necessitie d'estre rent charge, rent seck, ou rent seruice, car ne sont plusors rents que ceux trois, et rent charge il n'est my, car null distres est done, nec ascun terre charge oue ceo, nec seck ou seruice, quia n'est issant hors d'ascun terre, Ergò n'est rent.

Elenchs.

Althusius thus diuideth vnlawfull pleasures: into stuprum and adulterium. Stuprum inter personas solutas, and is voluntarium or violentum. Voluntarium fit ab extraneis, aut à consanguineis, vt incestus. Ab extraneis, naturaliter, vel contrà naturam: naturaliter à mare & fæmina. Contra naturam, à mare cum mare, à fæmina cum fęmina, aut cum bestiijs. Adulterium est cum alterius coniuge vel marito. The whole constitution of this diuision is erroneous. For most of the things which are conteyned vnder stuprum, may as wel, and doo as well belong vnto adulterium. Fenners diuision therefore is farre better: where hée sayth they bée

Præter naturam, or secundum naturam: præter naturam est vel coufusio tum specierum, tum sexuum, vel incestus. Specierum, cum bestiæ verè vel spiritus specie hominibus miscentur voluptatis causa; sexuum, confusio est, cum mares maribus, fæminæ fæminis miscentur. Incestus sunt, cum propinqui carne miscentur etiam in coniugio.

Secundum

Secundum naturam est scortatio vel adulterium : Scortatio est, cum matrimonio soluti illegitimè miscentur. Adulterium, cum altera persona saltem sit desponsata. Nam si vtraq; sit desponsata, grauiùs est adulterium.

It is all one whether the generall bée diuided into his specials, or into the formes of the specials, as Animal is eyther rationale or irrationale, where the specials bée as significantly put downe as if they were expressed by their owne proper names, man and beast.

The 16. Chapter.

Of Distribution of argumentes after a certeine maner agreeable.

The second kinde of Distribution is made of arguments agréeable after a certeine manner, as of subiects and adiuncts.

The Distribution made of the subiect is, when the partes are set from the subiect.

Hobbinoll in his song of Elysa, diuideth her beauty being the adiunct, into her seuerall subiects, as, face, eye, chéeke, &c.

Tell mee, haue yee seene her angelike face
like *Phœbe* fayre ?
Her heauenly hauiour, her princely grace
can you well compare ?
The red Rose medled with the white yfeare,
In eyther cheeke depaynten liuely cheare :
Her modest eye,
Her maiestie,
Where haue you seene the like but there ?

M. Plowden Fol. 279. b. Et quant a ceo, troys y sont (come Walshe dit) que ount a intromitter oue les biens del mort, cestassauoir, l'executor, le ordinary, et les administrators &c.

The Distribution of the adiunct is, when the partes are set from the adiuncts.

Diggon in September.

For either the shepheards bene idle and still,
And led of their sheepe what way they will,

Or they bene false or full of couetise:
And casten to compasse many wrong emprise:
But the more bene fraught with fraud and spite,
Ne in God nor goodnes taken delite.

Maister Plowden Fol. 328. Mynes de plumbe sont fertile, ou sterile, &c.

Annotations.

PIscator would haue some diuisions to bée of thinges, as those that Ramus hath put downe: and some of wordes, to distinguish the diuers acceptions of ambiguous wordes, as Littleton pag. 51. in this word Assise, which he saith is equiuocum, &c. But that belongeth rather to a Dictionary-maker, then a teacher of Logike, saith one. And, indéede, as another aunswereth, words bée diuided together with the things: as Liberty and fréedome is eyther bodily or spirituall: where, as well the thing, as the word is diuyded.

All Logike is generall, and applyable as well to thinges imagined, as things that bée extant in truth: and therefore to words also, as wordes haue causes, effectes, subiectes, adiunctes, and other arguments to bée considered. Logicus, saith *Hottoman,* insitam vocum inter se rationem, habitum, respectum, affectionem: Grammaticus tantùm accidentia, & popularis sermonis in ijs iungendis consuetudinem exquirit, &c.

Sith these two last kindes of distribution bée sayde to bée made of argumentes agréeable after a certeine manner; wée are to vnderstand, that neyther the whole héere, is of the essence of the partes, nor the parts of the nature of the whole: so that this is no true distribution indéed, but rather an imagined distinction. And these bée partes, not of any whole, but rather of order, distinction, and particular rehearsall or enumeration.

Canons.

Therefore if you affirme or deny, either the adiunct which is the whole, or the subiects which bée the partes, you may contingently affirme or deny the one or the other.

And so in the other of the adiunct, the adiunctes as partes béeing affirmed, the subiect as whole may be also affirmed.

Distrib. in Sub.

Stamford

Stamford. prærog. reg. cap. 1. For which cauſe the lawes doo attribute vnto him (the king) all honour, dignitie, prerogatiue and preheminence, which prerogatiue dooth not onely extend to his owne perſon, but alſo to all other his poſſeſſions, goods, and cattels. As, that his perſon ſhall bée ſubiect to no mans ſuite, his poſſeſſions cannot bée taken from him by any violence or wrongfull diſſeiſin: his goodes and cattels are vnder no tribute, toll, or cuſtome, nor otherwiſe diſtreignable.

Elenchs.

If a falſe adiunct bée diuided into falſe ſubiects: as arguments bée eyther affirmatiue or negatiue. Or if a falſe ſubiect bée diuided into vnfit adiuncts, as ſpirits ſome be white, ſome blacke.

The 17. Chapter.

Of a Definition.

A Definition is that which declareth what a thing is: it conſiſteth on two parts, the generall and the difference. Whereof the firſt is common to the thing defined, and all his other fellow ſpecials, but the difference is proper onely to the thing defined, and diſtinguiſheth it from all other his fellow ſpecials.

A definition is perfect or vnperfect; whereof the firſt, for the excellency, is called definition by the common name: the ſecond is tearmed a deſcription, by a more ſpeciall tytle or woord.

A perfect deſcription is that, whoſe difference is ſet from the formall cauſe of the thing defined, as, A man is a ſenſible creature endued with reaſon, where, ſenſible creature is the generall, and endued with reaſon, is the difference: ſo that whatſoeuer is in a definition placed after the generall, that I call in this place the difference.

By an argument from the definition, Piers in May proueth hyrelinges, to bée no ſhepheardes, becauſe the true definition of a ſhepheard agréeth not with them.

Thilke same bene shepheards for the Deuils stead,
That playen whilest their flockes be vnfead.

Where after followeth a definition (a cuntrey definition) of an hirelyng, by application whereof vnto them, hée proueth them to bée hyrelings.

Well is it seene their sheepe be not their owne,
That letten them run at randome alone:
But they bene hyred, for little pay,
Of others that caren as little as they,
What fallen the flocke, so they han the fleece,
And get all the gaine paying but a peece.

Maister Plowden Fol. 54. b. Car couyn, solonq; le vray definition de ceo, est vn secreate assent, determine en les cœurs de deux ou plusors homes, al preiudice d'auter. Come si tenant pur vie voyle secretement conspirer oue vn auter, que l'auter recouera en preiudice de cestuy en reuersion. Car per ceo son reuersion serra toll. Et ceo conspiracy est et poet estre terme, et dit couyne; car touts les parts del couyne sont la perimplies. Car la est vnitie de lour deux cœurs; et est secretement fayt, et est en preiudice del tierce person, et issint perfect couyne sans mayheme ou blemish.

Fol. 261. a. Et quant al qualitie del offence, quel le offendor icy ad fayt, il dit, que est in degrée del murder, et nemy de manslaughter. Car manslaughter est le occider del home feloniousement sans malice prepense. Mes murder est occider del home sur malice prepence. Et icy le occider de luymesme, fuit prepence et resolue en sa ment deuant le act fayt. Et auxi il agrée in auter point oue l'auncient definition del murder, que fuit tiel, Murdrum est occulta hominis occisio, nullo præsente, nullo sciente. Issint icy sir Iames Hales secreatement surround luymesme, ne auterment il serroit stay ou interrupt de ceo fayre.

Fol. 359. a. Le seigniour Dyer define clayme en tiel maner; Clayme est challenge per ascun home del proprietie ou ownership del chose que il ne ad en possession, mes que est deteigne de luy per tort.

Annotations.

Definition is not set among the last, as though it were one of the worst, but because it is made of those other going before, and therefore cannot bee conceiued without them. Heere wee teach what a definition is, and how to make it, therefore it commeth after the other argumentes of which it is made: but in the tractate of Methode, wee shew how and where to place a definition already made; and therefore according to her excellency, we allow her the first place.

Diuisio est quasi sectio rei in partes: Definitio contra, quasi collectio & comprehensio partium ad rem explicandam.

Theloall hath taken some more paines in defining and diuiding a writ, than eyther the author of the Register, of old Natura breuium, or Fitzherbert. Theloals definition is alreadie put downe elsewhere.

Tenant in feesimple est celuy que ad terres ou tenements a tener a luy, et a ses heyres a touts iours. Littleton pag. 1. Disseisin est vn tortious ousting del francktenant per entree nyent congeable. 62. a. Plowden.

Nous voulons que prisone soyt tenue place per nous bounde dedeins certeyne bounds assignes pur le garde del corps del home. Brytton. 17. Appele est pleynte de home fait sur auter, ouesq; purpose de luy atteyndre de felony par mots a ceo ordeynes. Brytton, when hee had thus defined marrymony, Fol. 246. Matrimony est assembly de home et de feme, a lour deux assents par ioynture de saynt eglise, pur demorer ensemble auxi come vn chayre a touts lour vies, sans espoyre de partir: afterwardes, Fol. 252. hee prooueth that if a man haue two wiues, the second is not feme de iure by this definition, thus; et deux ne poyt il my auer a vne foits, sicome apiert per le definition de matrimony, ou est dit, que matrimony est assembly de home et de feme, et nemy de home et femes, ou feme et homes, mes singulerment feme et home. It is shame that Brytton were not newly printed, and pittie that hee and Bracton bee no more reade: for though the Law bee much altered since their time, yet there is no essentiall part of the Law, which hee and Bracton doo not define, diuide, and handle accordingly. So that by discretion a man shall by one chapter of Brytton more plainely perceyue the nature of Garde, villen, &c. then by turning and tossing of forty vncoherent cases in yeare-bookes, which doo not expound the nature of, Gard, villen, &c. but are spent in the determination of some obscure poynt touching Gard, villen, &c. and doo presuppose a generall notice of them, before wee come to the examination of particular difficulties discussed in yeere-bookes. And indeed it seemeth a preposterous thing to iangle of moote conceiptes in Essoyne, Protection, &c. not knowing what an Essoyne is, what a Protection meaneth. But as in Vniuersities, so in Innes of Court, the greedy desire of a superficiall shew in vnnecessary tryfles maketh vs want the true substance: they for hast to get a prebend by a degree, make light worke and run ouer two or three Epitomes; and wee by a moote booke and a Brookes abridgement climbe to the barre, & bar our selues vtterly from the substance of the cōmon Law. But omnis definitio in iure ciuili periculosa est, and so in the common Law. Thats true, but M. Theloall, as also Freigius, who is of the same minde, mistooke the word; for I thinke Vlpian, by this word, Definitio, meaned not the Logical definition which expoundeth the nature of a thing, but breuem & circumscriptam quandam iuris sententiam, quam iurisconsulti regulam, Dialectici *Thesin*, seu positionem; Medici *Aphorismum* nominant. And yet, bee it as it may bee, I doubt not but who so attempteth to make Logicall definitions in the Law, shall finde it somewhat daungerous, because it is very difficult.

Cambiparticipes sunt, qui per se vel per alios placita mouent, vel mouere faciunt, & ea suis sumptibus prosequuntur, ad cambipartem, vel pro parte lucri habenda. Stat. an. 33. E 1.

Toftum est ou meason ad este, et ore est nul mesuage, mes le site del meason apiert. Curtilagium est vn soyle ou garden apperteignant a vne mease, quasi curta pecia terræ. Fayrfax. 21. E. 4. 52.

Glanuil. lib. 9. Fol. 7. Dicitur autem purprestura, vel porprestura propriè quando aliquid supra dominum regem iniustè occupatur, vt in dominicis regis, vel in vijs publicis obstructis, vel in aquis publicis transuersis a recto cursu, vel

quando

quando aliquis in ciuitate super regiam plateam aliquid ędificando occupauerit,&c.

24.H.7.12. Reade. Misprision properment est lou vn chose est agrée destre bray, come nosme del ville ou del person, et puis en mesme cel plée, cel chose est autrement nosme, Come ou ieo sue nosme en formedome R. Reade, a que ieo face defence, et en mon barre ieo moy entitle per le nosme del T. R. ceo serra amend, car serra entend que le clerke fuit ignorant que ceo escript issint. Mes si en briefe vers moy per le nosme de R. ieo dy, vous aues cy le dit T. ceo nest misprision amendable.

In stead of geuing a true definition or explication of the nature & essence of any thing in our lawe, these single-solde Lawyers and golden Asses aunswere, ὡς εν τυπω : put downe a particuler case, as if I shoulde aske what is a man: A man, say they, is such a thing as Willy the milman: Robin the pannierman, &c. Where a generall definition being put downe, woulde giue a speciall light to the matter in hand.

Accurata definitione vtendum est in artibus, & cum doctis hominibus: in vulgus autem, & imperitorum sensus, descriptiones aptiores sunt.

Heriettum est quædam præstatio, vbi tenens liber vel seruus in morte sua dominum suum respicit de meliori auerio suo, vel de secundo meliori: quæ quidem præstatio magis de gratia quam de iure fit. Fleta: lib. 4. cap. 3. Elis. 58. Dyer.

Collegium est societas plurium corporum inter se distantium: & dicitur collegium propriè, cum simul habitant, quoniam simul colliguntur, & collegium constituitur in ecclesia vel per priuilegium concessum a superiori post fundatam ecclesiam, vel si a principio fuit ordinatum, quod ecclesia esset collegiata, vel si longo tempore vixerint collegialiter & sunt in quasi possessione collegij. Item ecclesia potest fieri collegiata cum consensu episcopi & patroni. 9. & 10. Elis.13. Dyer.

If some of these examples by mee collected seeme rather good descriptions, then perfite definitions: thou that so thinkest, must thinke this also, that I could finde no better.

Therefore Si quid nouisti rectius istis,
Candidus imperti: si non, his vtere mecum.

A definition is called of the Grecians, ὅρος, ὁρισμὸς, ὁρισμὸς λόγος. Which is a translated worde from boundes and limittes of grounde. For as they hedge in and include the ground: so doth a definition limite and circumscribe, or, as it were binde in the nature of that which is defined.

And that also is the naturall signification of this worde which the Latinistes vse, finire, or definire: from whence come finitio, and definitio: Which we now vse as an English word. Finis is an end, finire, and definire, signifie to limite and end, or circumscribe one from an other, that so it may be knowne from other. The chiefe vse then of a definition is, to shew and make playne: yet an argument prouing may bée set both from the definition to the thing defined, and from this to that, negatiuely, and affirmatiuely, and so it is in descriptions.

[The difference :] This difference is sometimes set from the very internall forme and essentiall cause of the thing defined: which is best, but hard to bée found: and therfore, instead thereof, sometimes the ende is vsed, sometimes the proper adiunct, sometimes many adiunctes togither, sometimes the subiect.

One Relatiue doth define an other.

Canons.

If the definition bée, then the thing defined must bée, and contrarily: but if not that, then neyther this, and contrarily.

To whatsoeuer, the definition eyther may or may not bée applied, to the same also the thing defined eyther may, or may not bée attributed, and contrarily.

Whatsoeuer agréeth, or not agréeth with the definition, the same thing eyther will agrée or not agrée with the thing defined and contrarily.

In genere asciscendo satis erit proximum ponere, neq; altius a capite repetere. Nam qui proximum genus posuit, is etiam superiora omnia posuisse intelligitur. Quandoquidem (ait *Aristoteles* in topicis) in inferioribus ea quæ suprà sunt intelliguntur. *Hottoman.*

Maister Lambert: Iust. lib. 1. ca. 1. Iustices of the peace

bée

be Iustices of record appoynted by the Quéene to bée iustices within certaine limites: for the conseruation of the peace, and for the execution of sundrie thinges comprehended in their commission, and in diuers lawes committed vnto them.

The 18. Chapter.

Of a Discription.

AN imperfect definition or description, is that whose difference is set elswhere then from the formall cause, and it is sometimes briefe, sometimes more largely amplified.

Thenot in Februarye describeth the oake, thus,

There grew an aged tree on the greene,
A goodly oake sometime had it beene,
With armes full strong and largely displayde,
But of their leaues they were disarayde:
The body byg, and mightily pyght,
Throughly rooted and of wondrous hyght:
Whilom had bene the king of the field,
And muchel mast to the husband did yeeld,
And with his nuts larded many swyne,
But now the gray mosse marred his ryne.
His bared boughs were beate with stormes,
His top was balde and wasted with wormes,
His honour decayde, his braunches sere, &c.

In May Piers describeth the kid.

She set her yongling before her knee
That was both fresh and louely to see,
And full of fauour as Kid mought bee.
His vellet head began to shoot out,
And his wreathed hornes began to sprout.
The blossoms of lust to bud did begyn,
And spring foorth rankly vnder his chyn. &c.

Where afterwards followeth the description of the counterfayt pedler, the fox, by adiuncts, effects, &c.

It was not long after she was gone,

But the falſe fox came to the doore anone,
Not as a Foxe, for then he had bee kend,
But as a poore pedler he did wend,
Bearing a truſſe of tryfles at his backe,
As bels, and babes, and glaſſes in his packe.
A biggen he had got about his brayne,
For in his headpeece he felt a ſore payne.
His hinder heele was wrapt in a clowte,
For with great colde he had got the gowte.
There at the doore he caſt me downe his packe,
And layd him downe, and groand, alacke, alacke.
Ah deare Lord, and ſweet ſaint Charitee,
That ſome good body would once pity me. &c.

Maiſter Plowden Fol. 273. a. Terminus, ſi ſit referre al temps, eſt le fine del ceo, come Weſton dit: et poet eſtre referre al lieu, come le ſeignior Dyer dit, come terminus loci; et adonques il eſt priſe come precinct ou lymite del vn lieu, come bounde eſt inter terres de diuers homes, et iſſint ad meſme le ſentence, come certeintie ad, ſoit il referre al tẽps, ou lieu: et terminus loci poot eſtre dit certeintie en lieu: terminus temporis eſt certeintie en temps.

Fol. 88. a. Et moy ſemble que pretenſed droyt ou title neſt forſque en vne caſe, et ceo eſt l'ou vn eſt en poſſeſſion de terres, ou tenements, et auter que eſt hors del poſſeſſion, claym ceo ou ſue pur ceo; ceo eſt pretenſed droyt ou tytle.

Fol. 368. b. Deſcription de peace per Catlyn, et Fol. 195. a. Deſcription del fearme per Browne et Dyer &c. Ibidem, Le Comen ley, n'eſt que comen vſe.

Annotations.

As breuity is commended in a perfect definition, ſo copious amplification is fitteſt for a deſcription: yet ſo as ſwelling ſuperfluitie bée alwayes auoyded.

Deſcriptio is called of the Græcians περίφρασις, τύπος, σκιαγραφὴ, ὑπογραφή. Some call it in Latine, Alluſio: it hath of diuers men, vppon ſundry occaſions diuers names. Sometimes ὑποτύπωσις, as it were a certeine delineation: if any perſõ be deſcribed, they call it Proſopographia, if a place, Topographia.

Topographia, if a nation, Chorographia, if the earth Geographia, if the water, hydrographia, if the wind, Anemographia, if a trée, Dendographia, if the time, Chronographia, &c.

Aristoteles ait, neq; vnam duarũ rerum, neq; vnius rei duas definitiones esse posse. οὔτε γὰρ ἕνα δυοῖν, οὔτε δύο τοῦ αὐτοῦ ὅρους δυνατὸν εἶναι. Nam cum vnius rei vna natura sit, quæ definitione explicatur, rectissimè à *Galeno* scriptum est, ἐνεσι πάμπολλους ὁρισμοὺς ποιεῖν ἑνὸς πράγματος ἐν ταῖς φωναῖς μόνον, οὐκ ἐν τοῖς νοήμασι διαφέροντας. Licet plures vnius rei definitiones conficere vocibus tantum differentes, non rationibus.

Quod *Zeno* de Dialectica & Rhetorica dixit, illam pugno, hanc palmæ similem esse, idem de definitione dici & definito potest, idq; multò magis accomodatè. Re namq; sunt eadem, sed alterum euolutum, alterum inuolutum.

M. Lambard. Iust. lib. 1. cap. 16. Budæus in his Gréeke Commentaries is of the opinion, that the French worde Arrest, which with them signifieth a decrée or iudgement of a court, tooke beginning of the Gréeke ἀρεσόν, that is Placitum, and, as wée might say, the pleasure or will of a Court. And albeit that it were not out of our way, to thinke that it is called Arrest, because it stayeth, or resteth the party, yet I beléeue rather that wée receiued the name from the Norman lawes, because wée vse it in the same sence with them: for commonly with vs, an Arrest is taken for the execution of the commaundement of some Court, or of some officer in Iustice. But howsoeuer the name began, An arrest is a certayne restraint of a mans person, depriuing it of his owne will and liberty, and binding it to become obedient to the will of the lawe; and it may bée called the beginning of imprisonment. The precepts and writs of the high courtes of lawe, doe vse to expresse it by two sundry wordes, as, Capias, and Attachias, which signifie to take or catch holde of a man. But this our precept noteth it by the wordes duci facias, cause him to bée conueyed &c. for that the officer hath after a sort, taken him before, in that hée commeth to him, and requireth him to goe to some iustice of the peace.

Ibidem. Suretie of the peace is an acknowledging of a bond to the prince, taken by a competent iudge of recorde for the kéeping of the peace, and it is called suretie of the word securitas, because the partie that was in feare, is thereby the more quiet and secure.

Idem. Lib. 1. cap. 13. The Latine men vse, Recordor, when they will signifie, to kéepe in minde, or to remember, in which sence the poet sayd:

Si ritè audita recordor.

And after the same sence also doth our lawe vse it: For Recordes bée nothing els but memorials or monumentes of thinges done before Judges that haue credite in that behalf.

One may affirme a thing, and another may deny it, but if a Record once say the word, no man shall be receaued to auerre or speake against it. For otherwise there would neuer bée any ende of controuersies.

Stamford. lib. 2. cap. 38. Sanctuary est vn lieu priuilege per le prince, ou soueraigne gouernour, pur le safegard de vie de home qui est offẽdour, et est foũdue sur la ley de mercy, et sur le grand reuerence, honor et deuotion, que le prince ad al lieu, deins quel il granta tyel priuiledge, &c. An issue is sayd to bée status causæ, it is called Issue, of an issue in some vessell, whence onely the water is voyded &c.

Elenchs of all definitions.

First, if it want where it should bée: Then if it bée, but bée false: or bée obscure, as that of the snayle, where the definition is more obscure than the thing defined, and that in Pacuuius, Testudo est quadrupes tardigrada, agrestis, humilis, aspera, capite breui, ceruice anguina, aspectu truci, euiscerata inanima, cum animali sono.

Arist. in 6. Top. compareth an obscure definitiõ to the pictures of old bungling payntersm, τῶν ἀρχάιον γραφέων; which had the names of the things paynted, put ouer the pictures, or else they would neuer haue béene taken to bée the pictures of such things.

Homo est animal bipes, implume, quod erectum ingreditur, q. Plato. And the next day after comes mée Diogenes with a cocke pluckt cleane without feathers, and throwing him into Plato his schoole, sayd, Ecce hominem Platonicum, lo héere is Platoes tall man, a twoo-footed creature, without feathers, going vpright.

Agayne

Agayne, if it eyther want, or haue too much.

In an vnperfect definition, the conuersion and reciprocation of it with the thing so defined is not precisely to be exacted : but in the other, it is necessarily required, the wants whereof is an infallible token of a sophisticall definition.

The 18. Chapter.

Of the argument borrowed.

Sith wée haue sufficiently discoursed of the nature of inherent arguments, it now remayneth to speake of the borrowed elsewhere, which is properly called a testimony or witnesse, and is only fit for proofe or confirmation. First, a testimony is either a famous sentence, as prouerbs, &c. or a law. A law is eyther naturall, or written.

Secondly a testimonie is either simply propounded, as an edict, &c. or written before.

Thirdly, a testimony is either with oath, or without oath. So much of the common affections of a testimonie: the specials follow.

A testimonie is either of God, or of man. Of God eyther immediately, or by prophetes, Aungels, &c. of this kinde bée diuinations, &c.

That of man, argueth not of it selfe, but by the vertue of some inherent argument : and in exquisite searching out of the truth of any thing, is but of small force, but in ciuill affayres it much preuayleth, when the testimony of any man is beléeued, by reason of his vertue, wisedome, &c. which indéed bée inherent arguments.

In May, the Fox would proue himselfe kynne to the Kid, because his grandsyre tolde him so.

And if that my Grandsyre tolde me be true,
Siker I am very sib to you.

Morrell in July.

Besides (as holy fathers sayne)
there is a hilly place,

Where *Titan* riseth from the mayne,
to ren his dayly race.

And Thomalyn in July vseth a prouerbe to confute Morrell, the commender of hils.

Ah, God shield man, that I should clymbe,
and learne to looke aloft,
This reede is rife, that oftentime
great clymbers fall vnsofte. And agayne,
To kerke the nar, from God more far,
hath beene an olde sayd saw,
And he that striues to touch a star,
oft stumbles at a straw.

Mans testimony is eyther of one man, or of many. That of one, is eyther obligation or confession. To obligation bée referred pledges or sureties. So in August the two shéepeheards, Perigot and Willy, for want of better arguments to proue their skill in singing, lay downe wagers, the one a cuppe, the other a spotted lambe. This is commonly called the fooles argument.

Willy. Then loe, *Perigot*, the pledge which I plight,
A mazer ywrought of the maple warre,
Wherein is enchased many a faire sight
Of Beares and Tygers, that maken fierce warre,
And ouer them spread a goodly wyld vyne,
Entrayled with a wanton yuy twyne.
Thereby is a lambe in the wolues iawes,
But see how fast renneth the shepheards swayne,
To saue the innocent from the beasts pawes,
And here with his sheepehooke hath him slayne.
Tell mee, such a cup hast thou euer seene?
Well mought it beseeme any haruest queene.

Perigot. Thereto will I pawne yonder spotted lam,
Of all my flocke there nis syke another,
For I brought him vp without the dam,
But *Colyn Clowt* raft me of his brother;
That he purchaste of mee in the playne field.
Sore against my will was I forst to yeelde.

I remember Diggon in September sweareth by his soule,

soule, to giue credite to his assertion; which I should haue put before.

They say they com to heauen the nigher way,
But by my soule I dare vndersay,
They neuer set foot in that same troade,
But balke the right way and strayen abroade.

Maister Plowden Fol. 5. a. b. Et quant al distinction de Brytton parenter inheritance et purchase, sir ieo n'ay grande regarde a ceo, car son lyeur conteigne mults errours.

Mes le lyeur de Lyttleton, que est solonque le primer edition, en que les nouels additions sont omise, que est le verey et pluis sure regiſter del fundaments et principles de nostre ley, define, quod fœdum simplex idem est quod hæreditas legitima vel pura. Et issint il prist chescun fee simple deste inheritance. Et il dit que ceo parolle, inheritance, n'est solement entende lou home ad terre per discent, mes auxi chescun fee simple, ou tayle, que home ad per son purchase, est inheritance tamen vis verbi hoc non vult.

Fol. 161. b. Et le cauillation oue les parols contrary al simple entent, come Tullius dit en son lyuer de officijs, est calumnia quædam & nimis callida, sed malitiosa iuris interpretatio, ex quo illud, summum ius, summa iniuria. Come il mist exemple de vn que auoyt prise truce pur 130 iours oue son enemy, et en le nuyct il destruist et depopulate ses possessions pur ceo, come il dit, le truce fuit pur iours, et nyent pur les nuyctes. Lequel Tullius accompt mere iniury et iniustice.

Fol. 321. b. Et ialemeins fuit dit per Gerrard que en le lyuer appelle expositiones vocabulorum, que fuit mise en print 40 ans passe, il est declare que mynes de ore et argent en quecunq; terres, que ils sont, afferont al roys del ceo realme. Issint Wray dit, que Hesket apprentice que fuit bien apprise en le ley, en son lecture extant sur lestatute de charta foreste, affirmast, que si fueront mynes de ore et argent en terre del subiects deins le forest, que ceux afferont al roy. Issint il dit, que il auoyt vieu les leyes de S. Edward le Confessor, en queux fuit conteigne, quod Thesauri de terra pertinent domino regi. Et issint dit Barham del leys William conqueror, queux'il auoyt veu, queux auoyent semblables parols.

The offering of triall and proofe, belongeth to this place, as when a man seeing his words not beleeued, biddeth them trie and then trust, as in Terence of the boy, fac periculum in literis, fac in musicis, fac in palestra : quæ liberum scire æquum est, solertem dabo : trie the boy in learning, try him in singing, trie him in wrestling : I will vndertake you shall finde him sufficient in whatsoeuer belongeth to a free borne boy.

Annotations.

ADrianus rectè rescripsit, se testibus, non testimonijs crediturum, itaq; testium dignitas consideranda est : neq; enim quia affirmatum sit, aut negatum, ideo erit, aut non erit, *Arist.* de interpret : but because he that spake it, was so honest and wise a man, as that hee woulde not affirme an vntruth. Arist. 20. Rhet.

God is to be beleeued without exception, because God spake it: but men are so much either more or lesse credited, by how much their behauiour & learning is more or lesse esteemed. Therefore the Pythagorians were very foolish in thinking their maister Pythagoras so wise, as that it were a sufficient argument, the thing were so, because Pythagoras said it was so, αυτος εφα ipse dixit : ipse autem erat *Pythagoras*. Those men, saith Plato in Protagoras that vse the authoritie of others instead of argumentes of their owne, are like to seely soules of the country, when they keepe their wakes: quum enim propter inscitiam nequeant inuicem propria voce suisq; sermonibus ipsi colloqui, mercede exhibita tibicines introducunt, vt aliena voce, id est tibiarum flatu, conuiuium transigant. Vbi autem boni, præclariq; & eruditi viri conueniunt, neq; tibicines, neq; saltatrices, neq; cantatrices vllas videas, sed voce propria, remotis ijs nugis iocisq, conuiuium celebrare & alternis interrogationibus responsionibusq; modestè disserere, etiamsi vinum abunde bibant. And in Gorgias hee saith truely, that in these borrowed testimonies there is no reason or perswasion, but rather violence and compulsion. Therefore, in Charmide, he biddeth vs consider,

sider, not who speaketh, but how true that is which is spoken. So sayde Aristotle of his owne mayster Plato, Amicus *Socrates*, amicus *Plato*, magis amica veritas. I loue Socrates and Plato well, but I like the truth better. So in 5. E. 4. 112. est dit, que precedents et course ne rule le ley, mes le ley rulera eux. Et pur ceo la fuit dit, que un utlagary fuit reuers, quia il fuit ad Com. Lancaster ibidem tent. et ne dit apud Lancaster, ou tiel lieu certeyne, a que le ibidem poet estre refer, nient obstant que furont 100 precedent de cel retorne. Donq; à fortiori, d'un precedent, quia vna hirundo non facit ver. 1. & 2. M. 14. Dyer.

Canons.

Heere, they are usually woont to say, Vnicuiq; in sua arte perito, credendum est. Euery man is to bee beleeued in that art which hee professeth, and wherein hee hath skill and experience.

The Rhetoricians dispute with, and against extort testimonies, as present occasion is euer offered unto them.

In our law, twelue bee chosen and sworne; their verdict is quasi verèdictum. The suspected men may bee ousted by challenge. Heereupon wee haue challenge peremptory, challenge per cause, &c.

Maister Lambard Iust. But especially there ought to appeare such Iurors, as be returned by the shiriffe, and warned by his bayliffe, whether it bee for enquiry or tryall: and in this behalfe, both the commission, the common forme of the precept, and the Law it selfe (11. H. 4. cap. 9.) willeth that they should bee probi & legales homines. For if any of them be discredited in Law, as by attainder in conspiracy, attaint, Decies tantùm, subornation of periury, or such like, they bee not probi, and their presentment is voyde by it, unlesse there bee 12. besides them, that are not so blemished. Agayne, if they bee outlawed, abiured, condemned in a Præmunire, or attaynted of treason, felony, or such like, then bee they not legales, and their presentment is meerely voyde also, as it may bee gathered upon the case. 11. H. 4. 41.

And women, infants under fourteene yeeres of age, aliens, and such as bee within orders of the ministery of the clergy, cannot bée impannelled amongst others. Generally also, these Jurors ought either to bée inhabiting within the shire, or els to haue landes there: for, the commission willeth, that they should be such per quos rei veritas melius sciri poterit: which must néedes bée understoode of such, as haue cause to know the countrey: and the precept is usually according to the same forme. But especially in the countie Palatine of Lancaster, each Jurour ought to haue to the yearely value of fiue poundes by order of the statute. 33. H. 6. ca. 2. Now by 27. Elis. euery Juror must haue iiij. pound by the yeare.

But these men bée not truely Jurors, till they bée sworne, as their name pretendeth; and otherwise their presentment is utterly voyde.

Each Jury of Enquiry ought to conteine twelue in number at the least, & if there bée 18 or moe, it shal not bée amisse. Yea the common order with us is, to haue them of an odde number, as 17. 19. or 21. to the ende (as it séemeth) that if they shoulde dissent in opinion somewhat equallie, yet there should bée allwayes one, to wey downe the side, and cast the ballance: but if 12. of them doe agrée, the gaynelaying of the residue cannot hinder the presentment. Les Jurors tryeront le fayt, et nemy le ley, quia sont ignorants: mes les Judges le ley, itaq; trauers est prise sur le matter in fayt et non sur le matter en ley. Vide Plowden. Fol. 231.

Fortescue, Lord Chauncellor, in Henry the sixt his time, preferreth this order of triall before that used in the Ciuill Law. His comparison is to this effect.

Si coram Iudice contendentes, ad litis perueniant contestationem super materia facti (quam legis Angliæ periti exitum placiti appellant) exitus huiusmodi veritas per leges ciuiles, per testium depositionem probari debet, in qua duo testes idonei sufficiunt. Sed per leges Angliæ veritas illa non nisi duodecim hominum de vicineto vbi factum huiusmodi supponitur sacramento, Iudici constare poterit: and afterward.

Per leges ciuiles pars quæ in litis contestatione affirmatiuam dicit, testes producere debet, quos ipsemet ad libitum suum nominabit. Negatiua autem probari non potest, videlicet directè; licet posit per obliquum. Ex illis quippè creditur

creditur esse potentiæ, minoris quoq; industriæ, qui de omnibus, quos noscit hominibus, duos reperire nequit ita conscientia & veritate vacuos, vt timore, amore, vel commodo, omni velint contraire veritati. Hos potest tunc ipse in testimonium producere in causa sua; & si contra eos pars altera dicere velit, vel contra eorum dicta, non semper continget eos, eorum quoq; mores aut facta apud contradicere volentem agnosci, vt ex eorum fœditate & vitijs testes illi possint reprobari. Et dum eorum dicta affirmatiuam contineant, non facilè poterunt illa per circumstantias aut obliqua alia improbari. Quis tunc poterit suorum aut suijpsius sub lege tali viuere securus, dum cuilibet sibi inimicari volenti lex tale præstat subsidium? Et qui iniqui duo tam incauti sunt, quod facti de quo ipsi examinabuntur in iudicio, non, antequam in testes producantur, occulté fingant imaginem & figuram; componant quoq; eidem omnes circumstantias, quales sibi affuissent, si illud in veritate constitisset? Prudentiores namq;, vt dicit Dominus, sunt filij huius mundi, quam filij lucis. Sic *Iesabel* sceleratissima, testes duos filios *Belial*, contra *Nabot* in iudicio produxit, quo ipse vitam perdidit; & *Achab* rex, eius vineam possidebat. Sic duorum senum etiam Iudicum testimonio, mortua fuisset pro adulterio vxor castissima *Susanna*, si non eam miraculosè liberasset Dominus inexcogitabili prudentia, quam à natura non habuit puer iunior nondum ætate prouectus. Et si ipsos depositione sua varia conuicerat puer ille esse falsarios, quis nisi solùm Dominus nouisse poterat eos in dictis suis taliter variaturos? dum non de arboris natura sub qua imputatum facinus fiebat, lex aliqua eos arctabat reminisci, quia testes sceleris cuiusq; considerare non putantur omnia vmbracula & cætera vicina illi facto, quæ ad aggrauationem vel detectionem criminis illius minimè operantur. Sed dum de arborum speciebus, Iudices illi nequam vltrò deponentes variabant, eorum dicta ipsos veritatis fuisse præuaricatores demonstrabant, quo & talionis pœnam merito incurrerunt. **And so forth in the example of one** Iohn Fringe, **that at his death protested hée was not guilty of the fault, whereof two men accused him.** Et alibi. Non igitur contenta est lex Franciæ, in criminalibus vbi mors imminet, reum testibus conuincere, re falsidicorum testimonio sanguis innocens cōdemnetur. Sed mauult lex illa reos tales torturis cruciari, quoúsq; ipsi eorum reatum confiteantur, quam testium depositione, qui sæpè passionibus iniquis, & quandóq; subornatione malorum ad periuria stimulantur. Quali cautione & astutia, criminosi etiam & de criminibus suspecti tot torturarum in regno illo generibus affliguntur, quod fastidit calamus ea literis designare. Quidam verò in equuleis extenduntur, quo eorum rumpuntur nerui, & venæ in sanguinis fluenta prorumpunt. Quorundam verò diuersorum ponderum pendulis dissoluuntur compagines & iuncturæ: & quorundam gaggantur ora, vsq; dum per illa tot aquarum infundantur fluenta, vt ipsorum venter montis tumescat more, quo tunc venter ille fossorio vel simili percussus instrumento, per os aquam illam euomat ad instar balęnæ quæ cum halecibus & alijs pisciculis mare absorbuit, aquam despumat, ad altitudinem arboris pini. Piget, proh pudor, iam penna exquisitorum ad hæc cruciatuum enarrare immania. Nam eorum variatus numerus vix notari poterit magna in membrana. Leges etiam ipsæ ciuiles deficiente testium copia, in criminalibus, veritatem consimilibus extorquent tormentis, qualiter & faciunt etiam quamplurima regna. Sed quis tam duri animi est, qui semel ab atroci tanto torculari laxatus, non potius innocens ille omnia fateretur scelerum genera, quam acerbitatem sic experti iterum subire tormenti; & non semel mori mallet, dum mors sit vltimum terribilium, quàm totiens occidi, & totidem gehennales furias morte amariores sustinere? **Then followeth an example of one that by torture confessed thinges vntrue &c.** Taliter, proh dolor, & quamplures alij miseri faciunt, non veritatis causa, sed solùm vrgentibus torturis artati. Quid tunc certitudinis resultat ex confessionibus taliter compressorum?

Cæterùm, si innocens aliquis non immemor salutis æternæ in huiusmodi *Babylonis* fornace, cum tribus pueris benedicat Dominum, nec mentiri velit in perniciem animi sui, quo iudex eum pronunciat innocentem, nonne eodem iudicio iudex ille, seipsum reum iudicat omnis sęuitiæ & pœnarum quibus innocentem afflixit? ô quàm crudelis est lex talis, quæ dum innocentem damnare nequit, iudicem ipsum condemnat?

Et

Et alibi. Preterea si ex contractibus illatisue iniurijs, vel hæreditatis titulo, ius accreuerit homini, agendi in iudicio, si testes non fuerint, vel si qui fuerint, moriantur, succumbet ipse agens in causa sua, nisi ius suum probare valeat ineuitabilibus coniecturis, quod facere crebrò non contingit. Quare de dominijs & alijs possessionibus iure ciuili regulatis similiter & in omnibus actionibus cadentibus sub eodem iure, actiones agentium pro defectu testium quampluries suffocantur, ita quod earum vix pars media optatum finem sortiatur, &c.

The order of our common law followeth.

Regnum Angliæ per comitatus, vt regnum Franciæ per Balliuatus distinguitur, ita vt non sit locus in Anglia, qui non sit infra corpus alicuius comitatus. Comitatus quoq; diuiduntur in Hundreda, quæ alicubi Wapentakia nuncupantur. Hundreda verò diuiduntur per villas, sub quarum appellatione continentur & burgi atq; ciuitates. Villarum etenim metæ non muris, ædificijs aut stratis terminantur sed agrorum ambitibus, territorijs magnis, hamletis quibusdam, & multis alijs, sicut aquarum, boscorum, & vastorum terminis, quæ iam non expedit nominibus designare, quia vix in Anglia est locus aliquis qui non infrà villarum ambitus contineatur, licèt priuilegiati loci quidam infrà villas, de eisdem villis pars esse non censentur. Preterea in quolibet comitatu est officiarius quidam vnus regis vicecomes appellatus, qui inter cætera sui officij ministeria, omnia mandata & iudicia curiarum regis in comitatu suo exequenda exequitur. Cuius officium annale est, quo ei post annum in eodem ministrare non licet, nec duobus tunc sequentibus annis ad idem officium reassumetur. Officiarius iste sic eligitur. Quolibet anno in crastino animarum, conueniunt in Scaccario regis omnes consiliarij eius, tam domini spirituales & temporales, quàm alii omnes iusticiarii, omnes barones de Scaccario, clericus rotulorũ, & quidam alii officiarii, vbi hi omnes cõmuni assensu nominant de quolibet comitatu tres milites vel armigeros, quos inter ceteros eiusdem comitatus, ipsi opinantur melioris esse dispositionis & famæ, & ad officium vicecomitis comitatus illius melius dispositos: ex quibus rex vnum tantum eliget, quem per literas suas patentes constituet vicecomitem comitatus de quo eligitur,

T.

gitur, pro anno tunc sequente. Sed ipse antequàm literas illas recipiat, iurabit super sancta Dei euangelia, inter articulos alios quod benè, fideliter & indifferenter exercebit & faciet officium suum toto anno illo, neq; aliquid accipiet colore aut causa officij sui ab aliquo alio quàm à rege. His iam sic prẹsuppositis, ad eorum quæ quærimus, indaginem procedamus.

Quotiescunq; contendentes in curijs regis Angliæ ad exitum placiti super materia facti deuenerint, concitò, Iustitiarij per breue regis scribunt vicecomiti comitatus in quo factum illud fieri supponitur, quod ipse venire faciat coram eisdem Iustitiarijs ad certum diem per eos limitatum, duodecim probos & legales homines, de vicineto, vbi illud factum supponitur, qui neutrum partium sic placitantium vlla affinitate attingunt, ad recognoscendum super eorum sacramenta, si factum illud factum fuerit, sicut vna earundem partium dicit, vel non, sicut altera pars negat. Quo adueniente die, vicecomes returnabit breue prẹdictum coram eisdem Iustitiarijs vna cum panello nominum eorum quos ipse ad hoc summoniuit, quos, si venerint, vtraq; pars recusare poterit, dicendo quod vicecomes panellum illud fauorabiliter fecit pro parte altera, viz. de personis nimis indifferentibus. Quæ exceptio, si comperta fuerit vera per sacramentum duorũ hominum de eodem panello ad hoc per Iustitiarios electorum, mox panellum illud quassabitur, & Iustitiarij tunc scribẽt coronatoribus eiusdem comitatus, quod ipsi nouum faciant panellum. Quod cùm fecerint, si & illud consimiliter repertum fuerit viciatũ, etiam & illud quassabitur: & tunc iustitiarij eligent duos de clericis curiæ illius, vel alios de eodem comitatu qui in præsentia curiæ per eorum sacramenta facient indifferens panellum, quod deinde per nullam partiũ illarum calumniabitur. Sed cùm venerint sic impanellati in curiam, quęlibet partium excipere potest contra personam cuiuscunq; eorũ, sicut & potest in omni casu & omni tempore, quo aliquis qualitercunq; impanellatus comparuerit in curia super veritate exitus huiusmodi iuraturus: dicendò, quod impanellatus ille est consanguineus vel affinis parti alteri, vel amicitia quacunq; tali sibi coniunctus, quod indifferens ipse non est ostendere inter eos veritatẽ: qualium exceptionum tot sunt genera & species, quod non

licet

licet eas breui explicare sermone : quarum si aliqua reperta fuerit vera, non tunc iurabitur ille contra quem exceptio illa proponitur, sed cancellabitur nomen eius in panello. Sic quoque fiet de omnibus nominibus impanellatorum, quousq; duodecim eorũ iurentur ita indifferentes, quod versus eos neutra partium habeat aliquam materiam calumniæ. Horum autem duodecim ad minus quatuor erunt de hundredo vbi villa in qua factũ de quo contenditur, fieri supponitur, sita est. Et quilibet iuratorũ huiusmodi habebit terras vel reditus pro termino vitæ suæ ad minus, ad valorem annuũ 40. s. (now 4. li. by stat. 27. Eli.) Et hic ordo obseruatur in omnibus actionibus & causis criminalibus, realibus & personalibus, pręterquam vbi damna vel debitum in personalibus non excedunt 40. marcas monetæ anglicanę. quia tunc non requiritur, quod iuratores in actionibus huiusmodi tantùm expendere poßint. Habebunt tamen terram vel reditũ ad valorem competentem iuxta discretionẽ iustitiariorum, alioquin ipsi minime iurabũtur, ne per inediam & paupertatem iuratores huiusmodi de facili valeant corrumpi & subornari.

Et si per tales exceptiones, tot iuratorum nomina in panello cancellentur, quod non remaneat numerus sufficiens ad faciendam inde iuratam, tunc mandabitur vicecomiti, per breue regis, quod ipse apponat plures iuratores : quod & sæpiùs fieri potest, ita quod inquisitio veritatis super exitu placiti, non remanebit ob defectum iuratorum &c.

Iuratis demùm in forma prędicta duodecim probis & legalibus hominibus habentibus vltra mobilia sua, possessiones, vt pręd icitur sufficientes, vnde eorũ statum ipsi continere poterint, & nulli partium suspectis nec inuisis, sed ijsdem vicinis, legetur in Anglico coram eis per curiam totum recordum & processus placiti quod pendet inter partes : ac dilucidè exponetur eis exitus placiti de cuius veritate iurati illi curiam certificabunt. Quibus peractis, vtráque partium per se vel consiliarios suos in præsentia curiæ referet & manifestabit eisdem iuratis, omnes & singulas materias & euidentias quibus eos docere se posse credit veritatem exitus taliter placitati. Et tunc addúcere potest vtráq; pars corã eisdem iustitiarijs & iuratis omnes & singulos testes quos pro parte sua ipsa producere velit, qui super sancta Dei euangelia per iusticiaros onerati, testificabuntur omnia quæ cognoscunt probantia veritatem facti de quo partes contendunt. Et si necessitas exegerit, diuidentur testes huiusmodi, donec ipsi deposuerint quicquid velint, ita quod dictum vnius non docebit, aut concitabit eorum alium ad consimiliter testificandum. Quibus consummatis, postquàm iuratores illi deindè ad eorum libitum super veritate exitus huiusmodi, deliberatione quantam ipsi optabunt, colloquium habuerint, in custodia ministrorum curiæ in loco eis ad hoc assignato, ne interim eos aliqui subornare valeant, reuenient illi in curiam, & certificabunt iustitiarios super veritate exitus sic iuncti, in præsentia partium, si interesse velint, & maximè, petentis. Quorum iuratorum dictum per leges Angliæ, Veredictum nuncupatur; & tunc secundũ huiusmodi veredicti qualitatem, iustitiarij reddent & formabunt iudicium suum. Tamen, si pars altera, contra quam veredictum huiusmodi prolatum est, conqueratur se per illud iniustè esse grauatum, prosequi tunc potest pars illa versus iuratores illos, & versus partem quæ obtinuit, breue de attincta. Virtute cuius, si compertum fuerit per sacramentum viginti quatuor hominum in forma prænotata retornatorum, qui multò maiora habebunt patrimonia quàm iuratores primi, quod ijdem iuratores primi falsum fecerunt sacramentum, corpora eorundem primorum iuratorum prisonæ regis committentur, bona eorum confiscabuntur, ac omnes possessiones eorundem in manus regis capientur; domus quoq; eorum & ædificia prosternentur, bosci succidentur, & prata arabuntur, ipsi etiam iuratores primi extunc infames erunt, nec alicubi recipientur in testimonium veritatis, & pars quæ succubuit in priori placito, restituetur ad omnia quæ ipse perdidit occasione eius. Quis tunc, etsi immemor salutis animæ suæ fuerit, non formidine tantæ pœnæ, & verecundia tantæ infamiæ, veritatem non diceret sic iuratus? Et si vnus forsan tantus sui honoris prodigus esse non pepercerit, aliqui tamen iuratorum tantorum famam suam non negligent, neq; bona & possessiones suas taliter distrahi patiētur propria culpa sua. Nonne iã hic ordo reuelandi veritatem potior & efficacior est, quàm est processus qualem pariunt ciuiles leges? Non hìc pereunt causæ aut ius alicuius

per

per mortem, aut ob defectum testium, non hîc producuntur testes ignoti, conductitij, pauperes, vagi, inconstantes, aut quorum conditiones vel malitiæ ignorantur. Vicini sunt testes isti de proprijs viuere potentes, famæ integræ, & opinionis illesæ, non per partem in curiam ducti, sed per officiarium nobilem & indifferentem electi, & coram iudice venire compulsi. Isti omnia sc unt quæ testes deponere norunt, & isti testium productorum agnoscunt constantias inconstantiasq; & famam. Quid vltra? Verè nihil est quod veritatem dubij de quo contendi poterit, detegere valebit, quod iuratoribus talibus latere quomodolibet potest aut ignorari, dummodo possibile sit, illud venire posse in cognitionem humanam.

And then after, de causis criminalibus. Si reus quispiam de felonia aut proditione in Anglia rettatus, crimen suum coram iudicibus dedicat, mox vicecomes comitatus vbi facinus illud commissum est, venire faciet coram eisdem iudicibus viginti quatuor probos & legales homines de vicineto villæ vbi illud factum est, qui rettato illi nulla affinitate attingunt, & quorum quilibet centum solidatus habeat terræ & reditus, ad certificandum iudices illos super criminis illius veritate. Quibus comparentibus, rettatus ille eos calumniare potest eadem forma qua in actionibus realibus fieri debere superius describitur. Et insuper reus ipse, in fauorem vitæ suæ calumniare potuit olim trigintaquinq; homines quos ipse maximè formidat, qui ad eius calumniam cancellabuntur in panello, aut signis talibus notabuntur, quod (vt verbis legis vtar) illi super eum non transibunt, licet ipse nullam causam assignare sciat exceptionis seu calumniȩ suȩ. Quis tunc mori possit iniquè in Anglia pro crimine, cùm tot iuuamina habere ille poterit ob fauorem vitȩ suȩ? Et non nisi vicini eius, probi & fideles homines, versus quos ipse nullam habet materiam exceptionis eum condemnare poterunt? Mallem reuera viginti facinorosos mortem pietate euadere, quàm iustum vnum iniustè condemnari.

Nec tamen reum quempiam sub hac forma, reatus sui pœnam euadere posse suspicandum est, dum eius vita & mores timori deinceps erunt eis qui eum sic purgarunt à crimine.

In hoc equidem processu nihil est crudele, nihil inhuma-

num, nec lædi poterit innocens in corpore aut membris suis, quarè nec formidabit ille calumniam inimicorum eius, quia non torquebitur iste ad arbitrium ipsorum. Igitur sub hac lege viuere, quietum & securum est &c.
Somuch I thought good to borrowe of Fortescue, concerning witnesses and testimonies, tortures, rackinges, and suche other greeuous & extort confessions vsed, as he saith in France and elswhere. The rudenesse of the time wherein he wrate, must excuse the manner of his writing, which is not ouer elegant.

Reade the statutes made, 17. E. 2. and there see the othe of a villeine doing fealtie vnto his Lord: from whence Littleton, hath set the prescript formes of oathes to be vsed of freemen in doing homage, and fealtie to their Lords, partition, 91. 85. 86. 87. 88. 89.

Of the writing, ensealing, and deliuering of deedes and euidences, Parkins hath a special tractate cap. 20. Where the misdating, rasing, interlyning, adding new letters vpon the old, hāging in the smoke, breaking of ẏ seale, vtter quashing of the print, heating of the waxe and fastning therof to the Labell from whence it was once seuered, with other such imperfections, make the deede suspcious.

Of the auncient manner of sealing with crosses and such markes, of Edward the thirds fashion in biting the waxe with his tooth, reade the exposition of our Lawtearmes.

Elenchs.

A false testimonie is descried by the wickednesse, and malicious nature of him that gaue witnesse. The worlde is full of false forswo rne knaues, desperate careawaies, and rascallike swashbucklers, that borrow citizens gownes to sell hired oathes, to the vtter subuersion of Iustice, and vndoing of wel-meaning neighbours. So that no one thing is more common then that damnable speech, Iuraui lingua, mentem iniuratam gero, and Iura, periura, secretum prodere noli.

The

The 20. Chapter.

Of compared argumentes.

Hitherto then of the first diuision of argumentes. Now secondly, an argument is eyther simple, or compared. Simple is that which is simply considered without any respect of comparison. Compared is that which is compared with another. Compared argumentes are sometimes briefly expressed by plaine and euident signes, and sometimes largely distinguished by two partes, whereof the first is called the proposition, which propoundeth and putteth downe the first part of the comparison in the first place: the second is the Reddition, which addeth the second part, and applyeth it vnto the first.

Comparison is eyther in qualitie, or quantitie. Qualitie is that whereby thinges compared are called eyther like, or vnlike.

Like are those which haue the selfe same qualitie: this likenesse is called Proportion, and the thinges like proportionable. The signes be these, like as, euen as, so, and a deniall of the vnlike.

Diggon in September.

They looken big, as Buls that bene bate,
And bearen the cragge so stiffe and so state,
As Cock on his dunghill crowing cranck.

Agayne

Well away the while I was so fond,
To leaue the good that I had in hond,
In hope of better that was vncouth,
So lost the dog the flesh in his mouth:

And below.

Thus chatten the people in their steds,
Ylike as a monster of many heads:

The gate of her kiddy in May:

For euen so thy father his head vphelde,
And so his hawtie hornes did he welde.

Piers in May.

Sike mens folly I cannot compare.

Better then to the apes foolish care,
That is so enamoured of her yong one,
And yet, God wot, such cause hath shee none:
That with her hard hold and straite embracing,
Shee stoppeth the breath of her yongling.

Sometimes there bée no notes at all, as, Thenot in Februarye.

For youth is a buble blowne vp with breath,
Whose wit is weakenesse, whose wage is death,
Whose way is wildernesse, whose Inne penance,
And stoope-gallant age the hoste of greeuance.

The parts of a similitude are sometimes more largely put downe, and that by thrée partes and dégrées of comparison, or els by foure. The first is called a continued similitude. the seconde a distinct and seuered similitude: For the first, Cuddy in Februarye hath this:

The keene could blowes through my beaten hide,
All as I were through the body gryde:
My ragged rontes all shiuer and shake,
As doone high towers in an earthquake.

Where one part must be twise repeated to couple and continue the similitude, thus, As towers shake in an earthquake, so my ronts shake, where this word, shake, is twise mentioned.

Colyn in January vseth a distinct similitude with foure tearmes.

You naked trees, whose shady leaues are lost,
Wherein the byrds were woont to build their bowre
And now are cloathed with mosse and hoarie frost,
Instead of blosmes wherewith your buds did flowre:
I see your teares that from your bowes do rayne,
Whose drops in dreary Isicles remayne.
Also my lustfull leafe is drie and seare,
My timely buds with wailing all are wasted.
The blossome which my branch of youth did beare,
With breathed sighes is blowne away and blasted.
And from myne eyes the drizling teares discend
As on your boughes the Isicles depend.

Fayned

Fayned similitudes haue like force with others : and here in these similitudes thus largely put downe, Esopicall fables haue very good grace. So Menenius Agrippa vsing the tale of the rebellion betwéene the belly and other partes of the body : and comparing that with the rebellion betwéene the common people and senators of Rome, perswaded those that were fled to the holie hill, quicklie to returne home to Rome, and become conformable citizens.

Maister Plowden. Fol. 31. b. Semblable reason semblable ley.

Fol. 369. b. Et Catlyne resemble le fine per ceo act, al Ianus, quel, il dit, fuit Noe:mes les Romaines sur occasion luy nosme Ianus, et vse de picter luy oue deux faces, vn aspectant arere, s. backward, en respect que il auoit view le former monde que fuit peri per le inundation, et auter, aspectant auant, s. forward, in respect que il comence nouel monde commenceant de le inundation et procedant dillonques en euant. Et pur ceo ils luy appelle Ianus Bifrons et auxi portant clyffe en sa mayne, signifiant per ceo clyffe son poyar per son generatiō de renouater le nouel monde. Issint ceo act fait vn inundation, per quel tout former droit deuant le fine serra merge per non claime, car non claime est le flud et le fine produce nouel generation, quel est le nouel droyt. Car le fine fait nouel droit, et est le commencement de nouel monde, quel procede del temps del fine en auant.

Fol. 272. Et il dit que il y ad diuersitie enter lease conditional, et condition, d'auer lease. Car lease conditional est bone tanques le condition est enfreint, et la le lease va deuant, et le condition vyent apres. Mes en condition d'auer lease, le condition va deuant, et le lease vient apres, et le lease ne serra vnques aiudge destre lease, tanque le condition soit primes performe. Come si ieo graunt a vous que si vous faces tiel chose, vous aueres lease en tiel mon terre, la, il dit, le condition precede le lease, come le nedle precede le file, et sicome le nedle tray le file puis luy, issint fait le condition le lease la.

Fol. 465. a. De cest iudgement, et le cause poyes veyer, (lecteur) que les parolles del ley, ne sont le ley, mes le internall sence. Et nostre ley, come touts autres leyes, ad deux parts, cestassauoir, carnem & animam. Le letter de le ley est le chaire de le ley, et le sence et reason del ley, est le alme de le ley, quià ratio legis est anima legis. Et le ley poet estre resemble a vn noix, que ad vn test, et vn cerneau deins. Le letter represent le test, et le sence le cerneau; et sicome ne serres le meliour pur le noix si arrestes sur le test, nyent pluis serres pur le ley, si arrestes sur le letter. Et sicome le fruyt et profite est en le cerneau, et nient en le test, issint le fruyte et profite de ley est en le sence pluis tost que en le letter, et souent foits quant vous saches le letter, vous ne saches le sence. Car ascun foits le sence ne serra cy large come le letter est, et ascun foits le sence serra pluis large que le letter: et equitie, que en Lattin est appelle, æquitas, amplifie, ou demenuist le letter, come sa direction veult.

Fol. 486. a. Car soyt le atteinder per statute, ou per commen ley, le forfeyture al roy ensue, come le umbre ensue le corps, come Dyer le terme.

Fol. 529. b. Et il dit, sicome femme que ad recouer dower, ne poet entrer, mes doit auer seisin deliuer a luy per le viscount. Et sicome vn copyholder, a que vn copyhold tenement est discende, doit estre admitte per le seigniour auant que il auera seisin in iudgement del ley. Issint cesty que est admitt, ou institute al prebend, parsonage, ou vicarage, ne poet auer seisin, ne est plein incumbent, tanque le archdeacon ad luy induct, ou, si soit prebendary, deuant que le Deane et le chapter del Cathedrall eglise lou sa prebend est, ont luy enstalle.

Annotations.

Fayned similitudes bée very populare and plausible, and haue in them this one good thing, that where as it is somtimes hard to finde out true similitudes, it is an easie matter, to fayne some odde parable. But like examples of things done in déede bée best. Aristo. 2. Rhet. hath that of the bridled horsse, and hungry flies.

Bracton: descendit ius quasi ponderosum quid, cadens deorsum recta linea, vel transuersali, & nunquam reascendit ea via qua descendit post mortem antecessorum: à latere tamen

ascendit

ascendit alicui propter defectum hæredū inferius prouenientium. Maister Lambard Iust. lib. 2. cap. 1. As a man that hath receiued hurt in his body by a stroake whereof hée bléedeth freshly, will be content for the present to admit the help of any leeche or surgeon comming next to hand, for the stanching of the bloud and binding vp of the wounde, and yet would more gladly haue vsed the conference of diuers expert surgeons for dooing the same if the danger of the hurt woulde haue graunted the time, that will be lost in calling them together: so also, the common counsaile of this realme, finding that the body thereof may bée deeeply wounded in some one member, and perceiuing that some euils must bée resisted at the very first (least otherwiso they grow past helpe and ware incurable) hath many times thought it good to commit to one or to a few Iustices of the peace (for that they bée ready and at hand) the stopping of the bloud, as it were, and first dressing of the wound by repressing of force and other outrages that doo sodainly arise: and hath yet neuerthelesse, when as the time and matter will permit, politikely established an assemblie and conference of all the Iustices, at certayne times in a full court and open session.

When it appeareth that the thinges which we compare togither, be like, because that thing wherein they be compared, may be applied to them both; then wée looke whether it be applied to them in equal proportion and quantitie, or vnequall: if in equall, then they bée pares, equall: if in vnequall, then impares, of the which the one is the more, the other is the lesse, which is the comparison of quantitie: therfore I haue put qualitie before quantitie. For it were absurd to aske wheather Higs of Balkot, or Shepheard of Tugford, were the falser knaue, vnlesse it were first graunted that they were both false knaues.

Affectio similium inter se, (vt cæterorum argumentorum) est ἀνάπαλιν καὶ ἐναλλάξ: Inuerse & alterne. Inuerse quando inuertitur ordo propositionis & redditionis tantum, aut etiam terminorum. Itaq; si quædam similia fuerint, inuersè similia erunt, vt aurum ad ignem, sic fides ad periculum, ergo vt fides ad periculum, sic aurum ad ignem, Item ergò, vt periculum, ad fidem, ſic ignis ad aurum. Alternè, quando ſimilitudinis antecedens antecedenti, & conſequens conſequenti comparatur: ſi quædam ſimilia fuerint, alternè ſimilia erunt, vt aurum ad ignem, ſic fides ad periculum, ergò, vt aurum ad fidem, ſic ignis ad periculum.

I haue made a ſecond generall diuiſion of argumentes, into ſimple, and compared, as perceauing the nature of comparison to bée incident to euery argument that is not ſimple.

Canons.

One like argueth an other: as this is in reſpect of that, ſo the other in reſpect of the other: As this is in that, ſo an other in another.

Of likes there is like reaſon. Lykes agrre to like.

Vbi eadem ratio, ibi idem ius. 19. H. 6. 18. b. Newton & Littleton, que ſont en ſemblable reaſon, ſont en ſemblable ley. pag. 301.

Vide 9. H. 6. 24. b. Bab. Home poet deuiſer que ſa terre ſerra vendue per les executors, et iſſint home auera francktenement de ceſtuy que ne auera riens, come home auera fire dun flynte, et vncore null fire eſt in le flynte. Sic in 19. H. 6. 24. Mark: Executors poyent doner choſe que ils n'auoyent, come vn whetſtone, que done ſharpenes a vn cuttell, et vncore null eſt en luy.

Si cui ſimpliciter via per fundum cuiuſpiam concedatur vel relinquatur, quà primum viam direxerit, ea demum ire, agere debet, nec amplius mutandæ eius poteſtatem habet, argumento riui, quem primò qualibet ducere licet, poſteaquam ductus eſt, transferre non licet.

Elenchs.

As a new coate is better than an old: ſo new friendſhip, and new wine; theſe bée not like.

The 21. Chapter.

Of the vnlike.

The vnlike is that whoſe qualitie is vnlike. The notes are theſe, vnlike, differing, otherwiſe, and the deniall of the like.

Thomalin in July.

But

But nothing such thilke shepheard was,
whome Ida hill did beare:
That left his flocke to fetch a lasse,
whose loue hee bought too deare.

The notes bée oftentimes omitted, and the dissimilitude more fully enlarged.

Colyn in June.

O happy *Hobbinoll*, I blesse thy state,
That Paradise hast found which *Adam* lost,
Here wander may thy flocke early or late:
Withouten dread of woolues to beene ytost,
Thy louely layes here mayst thou freely boste:
But I vnhappy man whome cruell fate
And angry Gods pursue from coaste to coaste,
Can no where finde to shrowde my lucklesse pate.

Maister Plowden Fol. 76. b. Et quant a ceo que est dit, que en le briefe de droyt, quandò capitalis dominus remisit curiam, que l'assent del seigniour est primes conus, et issint en le Recordare, le clause est, si causa sit vera, aliter non: sir, ceo est bon reason, et nyent semblable a nostre case. Car la, est parcell del inheritance del seigniour d'auer le plée tenus en son court, et d'auer les profites et casualties veignant per ceo, lequel n'est reason a toller de luy sans cause. Mes en nostre case le viscount n'est forsques minister al roy per luy appoynt, et n'ad ascun profite, mes solement allowance pur son labor, s. les fées vsuall pur le execution del briefes: et si auter serue les briefes, le viscount ne perde riens, car il ne prist ascun labor. Et issint si le roy change son officer, n'est ascun tort fayt al officer, et issint il ne poet estre semble a les auters cases. So much of Qualitie.

Annotations.

Dissimilitudinis explicatæ redditio, hîc appellatur ἀνταπόδοσις, dissimilis redditio. *Ramus*.

The difference betwéene argumentes vnlike and arguments diuers, is, that in diuers, the simple and absolute disagréeing of two thinges is considered: but in vnlyke arguments, the vnlike comparison of foure termes, that is of two things, and the two qualities of the ſame. In diuers wée affirme the one, and deny the other after a certeine manner; in vnlykes wée deny neither, but onely diſtinguiſh the one from the other by the difference in quality. So that all diſagréeable arguments may bée handled as vnlyke, if the diuers qualitie bée reſpected.

Canons.

Of vnlikes there is vnlike reaſon.

Vnlikes agrée with vnlike, &c.

Examples bée euery where extant of likes and vnlikes in our lawe.

Elenchs.

Golde is tryed in the fire, but not ſo, is truſt and fidelitie in aduerſitie. This is falſe: for theſe thinges bée like, not vnlike.

The 22. Chapter.

Of the Aequall.

QUantitie is that whereby things compared are ſayd to bée of this or that quantitie.

Quantitie is either equall or vnequall. Equal are thoſe whoſe quantitie is equall. And therefore it is an argument from the equall, when one equall is argued or declared by an other.

The equall hath certeine proper ſignes, whereby it is often expreſſed in authors, and may, if they want, alwaies be added, for the playner declaration thereof, as, Equall, Alike, The ſame that, Aſwell as; Somuch howmuch; Somany howmany; No leſſe, no greater; and ſuch like. Yet equals are ſometimes expreſſed without any note at all.

Thomalin in July vſeth notes.

Al ſoone may ſhepheards clymbe to skye,
that leade in lowly dales,
As gotheard proud that ſitting hye
vpon the mountaine ſayles.

Willy in Auguſt.

Neuer

Neuer dempt more right of beauty I weene
The shepheard of *Ida*, that iudged beauties queene.

Maister Plowden Fol. 15. a. Car come proprement come il appent al office del brasier en l'auter case a weyer et metter en view le dit belle, ou al office del taylor, a shaper le panne; cy propermeut il appent al office del collector a weyer chose pur que le subsidie serroyt pay.

Fol. 7. a. Issint si home est tenus in un obligation sur condition de enfeoffer I. St. et il fayt lease pur ans, et release a luy en fee, il ad performe le condition, coment que il n'ad performe les parolles. Et uncore les parolles d'un condition d'obligation doyent estre performe cy straytment come les parols dascun statute: mes entant que l'entent et effect est performe et ceo que counteruaylera les parols, il suffist.

Annotations. Canons.

This Logical quantity is most generally to bee understood. And therefore all those wordes bee utterly reiected, which are not ample ynough to expresse the generall nature of this Logicall quantity: As ὕπαρξις, facilis, difficilis, credibilis, incredibilis. Aequè, magis, & minus probabilis; &c. As though no argument were of the more or greater, but that which were rather in, which had more probabilitie, which were more easie: And so in the lesse and equall. If a man will restrayne the generall nature of this quantity in this sort, hee shall finde himselfe intangled with repugnant examples in such sort that for his heart hee shall not bee able to ryd himselfe out. If any thinke I doo but ieast, let him reade the third part of Beurhusius, and make a tryall of his owne skill.

Canons.

Of things that be equall, there is equall reason and iudgment.

Of equals, if one eyther bee, or not bee; the other must in like manner bee, or not bee.

Equall things agree with equall.

Such thinges as are equall to any other thing, are also equall among themselues. This holdeth not in unequals, as 3. and 3. are unequall to 2, and yet equall among themselues.

If

If you doo either adde or detract equall things from things that bee equall, the whole, or remnant will bee equall.

You shall, as is sayde, sometimes meet with equals without any notes at all, as in Terence.

Quando ego non curo tuum, ne cura meum. Sith I meddle not with thine, meddle not thou with mine.

Agayne, the equall is returned against the equall nowe and then, without any forme.

If any one thing bee, or seeme to bee in some two thinges equally: then if it bee not in the one, it shall not bee in the other, but if it bee in the one it shall bee in the other. For the last part, take this example.

If a tutor must bee faithfull, then also a procurator.
But a tutor must;
Therefore the procurator must also.

Or thus more briefly in a contracted syllogisme called an Enthymeme.

A Tutor must bee faythfull and true,
Therefore a procurator must bee so also.

Other Logicians commonly, to confirme and proue the consequence in the Enthymeme, bring in the Canon before alleaged out of Aristotle, if any one thing &c. But I had rather say, that this connexed syllogisme is good and artificiall, so that no man ought to doubt of the consequence, which is already determined by the lawfulnes of the syllogisme, which is the onely rule of all consequence and coherence.

Now for the partes of this consequence, I meane the proposition and the assumption; I say, the proposition is true, and that I proue by the definition of the equall. Because there is one and the same, or equall quantity, that is to say, an equall reason in a tutor, and in a procurator. And as for the assumption, it is allowed by the ciuill law.

Yet wee are not altogether to reiect these rules and Canons, but to vse them in writing and speaking, as certaine corollaries, or fruites of this art: and not to put them downe in the art, for that most of them bee too particular, or doubtful and contingent, and also vnnecessary and superfluous.

The second Canon is this. If two things bee equally in a third;

third; then if the one bée, the other shall bée: if not this, neyther that. As, he vseth to lye, therefore to steale. It is not proper and peculiar to man for to sée, therefore neyther to heare.

The third and last. If two bée equally and indifferently in twoo, then if this bée not in that, the thirde shall not bée in the fourth: but if that bée, then this also, as in that out of Terence whereof wée spake before, Demea saide to his brother Mitio:

Quando ego, non curo tuum, ne cura meum. Sith I care not for thy sonne, Aeschinus, meddle not thou with my sonne Ctesiphon.

To this place also belonge those consectaries, which procéede from contraries, but are handled by a certaine comparison of equals, as that in Martiall.

Tum seruum scis te genitum blandeq; fateris
Cum dicis dominum, *Sosibiane*, patrem. Sosibian calleth his father maister, therefore hée confesseth himselfe to bée a seruant.

Arist. 2. Rhet. Iphicrates, when hée saw his yongest son, because hée was bigge and tall, preferred to office; said thus. If you take great boyes for men; you will surely make litle men boyes.

4. E. 4. 33. b. Ardern. En precipe vers vn que n'ad riens in le dd. iour del briefe, mes puis il enter in le terre ou purchase ceo, ore per son fait demesne il ad fait le briefe bon. Donq; come le fait le tenant fait mal briefe bon, per mesme le reason, le fait le demandant fra vn bon briefe male, come en le case al barre, si le demandant enter en parcell del demaunde pendant le plée ou briefe.

Choke in 8. E. 4. 21. b. confuta Markam: Fol. 11. 4. Que sic argua, les parties que submittont &c. ne dischargeront les arbitrors sans notice, Ergò les arbitrors ne chargeront les parties sans notice. A que Choke dit, que ceux ne sont contraries, s. discharger les parties sans notice: et charger les parties sans notice: mes charger les arbitrors sans notice, et discharger eux sans notice sont contraries, car come le charge, ne serra sans notice, issint le discharge ne serra sans notice.

This kinde of arguing is not allwayes effectuall, as a man is mortall, therefore a beast is immortall : it holdeth best when the argumentes be repugnant.

Elenchs.

Martiall in his first booke.

Quod *Alpha* dixi, Codre,penulatorum,
Te nuper aliqua cum iocarer in charta,
Si forte bilem mouit hic tibi versus,
Dicas licebit *Beta* me togatorum.

These bée not equall. For although Alpha and Beta séeme neighboures in the Gréeke Alphabet, yet they are nothing equall in signification. For Alpha signifieth the chiefe or principall : whereas Beta eyther signifieth that which is second, or els hath no signification at all.

The 23. Chapter.

Of the Greater.

Hitherto of Equalles. Unequals are those which haue not the same quantitie.

Unequall is either more or lesse.

The more is that whose quantitie is the greater: The signes bée such as these. Not onely, but also: Rather this, then that: more then : if this, much more that: and also the Grammaticall comparison.

Diggon in September.

For lyker beene they to plucke away more,
Then ought of the gotten good to restore.

And after

Yet better leaue of with a little losse,
Then by much wrestling to leaue the grosse.

Maister Plowden: Fol. 85. a. Le roy poet wayuer vn issue, et demurrer en ley, et contra : et auters prerogatiues il y ad, mes vncore, per misrecitall,ou misuser, ou misconceiuer del action, il serra lye, et sur tiels matters les briefes abateront, come en les cases de comen persons. Et si le ley soit tiel lou le roy est sole partie, à multo fortiori sera tiel, lou auter person est partie oue le roy.

Fol.

Fol. 160. Et si le habendum donera estate en chose nyent donc deuant, et a person nient nosme deuant, et altra l'estate donc deuant, adonques il mieux puit declarer le sence del parolles en les premisses en nostre case, et nosmant ou les premisses comprehende le chose en le habendum, come il fait en nostre case. Here is oftentimes a Logicall gradation, sometimes ioyned with a Rhetoricall climax.

Annotations.

When this note is in the consequent, much more, then it is an argumēt from the lesse, that is, from the lesse probable. But when it is said, Much lesse, it is an argument frō the greater, that is, from the more probable. This is Piscators iudgement. So that all argumentes from the greater should bée negatiue; and, affirmatiue from the lesse. But, as I haue already shewed, so I now affirme againe; that wée may reason as well affirmatiuely as negatiuely frō equals, greater, lesse, and all other arguments whatsoeuer, except diuers. For Ramus doth not tye this Logicall quantity, to such particuler consideration of probability, as Piscator doth imagine and teach out of Aristotle (for if hée so did, contrary examples would confute him) but leaueth it frée and generall, applyable to any thing whatsoeuer wée can imagine to bée equall, more, or lesse in any respect or consideration whatsoeuer, and as fit for confirmation as confutation.

This Logicall quantity therefore may bée attributed to any thing incident and conuenient to our purpose, as, to dignitie, praise, reproche, abilitie and power, greatnes, multitude, conueniency, commoditie, opportunitie, facilitie, difficultie, care, neglect, excellencie, vilenes, and in a worde, to whatsoeuer may bée saide to bée equall, more, or lesse.

They that doo otherwise determine of this matter, are, as I sayd, woonderfully troubled with repugnant examples, contrary Canons, and variety of opinions.

They that will haue all arguments of the more to bée negatiue and onely fit for confutation; all of the lesse, affirmatiue and seruing for assertion, doo put downe these Canons out of the 4. chapter of the 2. booke of Aristotles Topikes.

When two thinges are affirmed of one, if that which is more like to bée in it, bée not in it, neyther shall that which is lesse lyke, as,

Satrapes, si siet amator, nunquam sufferre eius sumptus queat: nedum tu posis.

If a Lord were her louer, hée could neuer mayntaine her; much lesse thou.

When one thing is spoken of two, if it bée not in that, wherein it is more like to bée, neyther shall it bée in that, wherein it is lesse like to bée: as, If the iust shall scarse bée saued, where will the wicked appeare?

When two thinges are affirmed of two thinges, if that which is more like to bée in the one, bée not in it, neyther shall the other bée in the other: as, You breake not the saboth day in loosing your oxe, and bringing him to the water; therefore much lesse I in loosing the daughter of Abraham from the bands of Satan.

Others, as Cicero, Quintilian, and sometimes Ramus, would haue the greater onely to serue for confirmation, and the lesse, for confutation: taking that to be the greater which is the more excellent, more difficult and more incredible: that to bée the lesse which is more abiect, easie, and sooner beléeued: and therefore they lay downe these Canons.

That which hath force in the greater, must haue also force in the lesse, as,

Wée haue suffered worse things then these;

Therefore these that bée lesse may bée borne of vs.

Ramus in his last edition leaueth this place frée, loose, and at liberty, fit for affirmations and negations. An affirmatiue argument from the greater, is this out of Virgil, which I put downe last.

If the Troianes haue suffered greater thinges, they may also suffer lesse.

But the Troianes haue suffered greater daungers then these.

Therefore they may also beare these lesse.

The proposition is true, as gathering the lesse of the more. For if the greater bée, the lesse will also bée: and in this

this place, that is called the greater, which is more vncredible and intollerable, as to suffer greater mischiefes.

The sillogisme it selfe is connexed, and artificiall, therefore the consequence is good. A Negatiue example is, that in Terence.

If a Lord cannot mayntayne her, much lesse thou. But a Lord cannot, therefore neither thou.

Fayned argumentes from the greater haue good grace as in this last example.

From this place bée deriued pretty gradations conioyned sometimes with a Rhetoricall climax, and sometimes alone without it. With it as,

Neq; verò se populo solùm, sed etiam senatui tradidit: neq; senatui modò, sed etiam publicis præsidijs & armis: neq; his tantùm, verumetiam, &c. *Tully* pro *Milone*.

Without any climax, is that in Terence betwéene Thraso and Gnatho.

Th. Magnas verò agere gratias Thais mihi? *Gn.* Ingentes. *Th.* A'in tu? læta est. *Gn.* Non tam ipso quidem dono, quàm abs te datum esse: id vero seriò triumphat.

Where, (although there séeme to bée nothing but a simple exposition) is conteyned a syllogisticall probation, thus.

> Thais giueth you excéeding great thankes, and shée triumpheth for ioy, that the gift came from such a giuer.
> Therefore, no doubt, shée thanketh you, and is glad that you bestowed this on hir.

Sometimes the greater is vsed without any notes or signes at all, as in that of *Virgill*.

Talibus insidijs periuriq; arte *Sinonis*,
Credita res, captiq; dolis, lachrimisq; coactis:
Quos neq; *Tydides*, nec *Larißæus Achilles*,
Non anni domuêre decem: non mille carinæ.

Counterfayt teares circumuented them, whome neyther the cruell Diomedes, nor fierce Achilles, nor ten yeares warre, nor a thousand ships could ouercome.

Canons.

If a greater quantitie bée (I take quantitie generally, as I sayd before) then the lesse may also bée: but if the greater bée not, neyther shall the lesse bée.

If the greater and more valiant cannot performe a thing, neyther can the lesse and weaker. But if the greater can doo it, it followeth not straightway that the lesse shall also doe it.

If any chaunce unlooked for, happen to the greater, it may more easily light upon the lesse and inferiour.

Si grammatica comparatio addatur ei quod comparatur & in quæstione versatur, reddit idipsum maius, vt id cui comparatur, sit minus, argumentumq; sit a minori: si vero addatur ei, quod ad arguendum adhibetur, argumentum est à maiori, itaq; tam in maiorum quam in minorum collocatione locum habet. Nam comparatiuus & superlatiuus superant positiuum, & id cui adduntur, maius esse significant, vt etiam verba quæ similem vim habent; vt malo, præstat &c. *Waßerleider.*

Falsum est, sayth *Snellius,* quod vulgò dicitur, propositionem hìc continere maius, redditionem minus: imò respiciendum est perpetuò ad id quod arguit, si enim illud est maius, argumentum est à maiori, sin minus, a minori, quocunq; in loco ponatur.

In maiori inest minus. Non debet, cui plus licet, quod minus est, non licere. Vnde illa consectaria: Cuius est donandi, eidem & vendendi, & cõcedendi ius est, plus enim est donare: (quod profusionem quandam patrimonij continet) quam vendere (quod administrationis & vtilitatis est propter pretium) aut concedere, quod amicitiæ est, vt in commodato aut precario. Et illud, cum quis poterit alienare, poterit & consentire alienationi.

3. E. 4. 24. Danby lesst: de 8. H. 6. ca. 9. Done treble dammages vers cestuy que enter oue force, ou teigne oue force. Et si lessa: done treble dammages pur l'un tort tantum, à fortiori pur ambideux. Issint le briefe bon que ioyne vtrumq;.

Hée that may doe the more may doe the lesse: Doct. Stud. pag. 114.

The 24. Chapter.

Of the lesse.

THe lesse is that whose quantitie is lesse. The signes of it are these. Not this onely, but not that. The denying of the equall, or equality: a grammaticall comparison.

In August, Perigot and Willy.

A chapelet on her head she bore,
hey ho chapelet:
Of sweet Violets therein was store,
she sweeter then the Violet.

Thenot in November.

She, while she was (that, was, a wofull word to sayne)
For beauties prayse, and pleasaunce had no peare.

Maister Plowden Fol. 57. a. Et quant a ceo que fuit auri dit per luy, que si le party serroyt force a monstre coment il auoit tytle, que donques poet estre, que il auoyt duble tytle (come en le case mise) et le monstrans de ceo fairoyt le plée double: sir, quant a ceo, les plaintifes ont preuent ceo assets bien: car pour doubt que le plée serroit double, ils ount monstre riens: et ore il est pier que double plée: car double plée ad matter de substance, mes icy n'est ascun matter de substance.

There is also a gradation sometimes from the lesse.

Annotations.

AS before in the greater, so héere in the lesse, the common Logicians differ. Some wil haue that to bée lesse which is lesse probable: briefly, when the antecedent in the Enthymeme is lesse probable than the consequent. These men will haue all arguments from the lesse, to bée affirmatiue; and they frame axiomes héereof accordingly, correspondent to those of the greater.

If any thing bée in that, wherein it is lesse like to bée, it shall also bée in that, wherein it is more like to bée, as, If brute beastes loue their young ones, how tender a care should we haue of our children?

If that bée in a thing which is lesse like to bée in it, then that must bée in it, which is more like to bée in it, as, God careth for the fowles of the ayre, therefore much more for you.

If two thinges séeme to bée in two, the one in the other: and that bée in, which is lesse like to bee in, then the other shall bée in the other.

If wée, béeing enemies to God bée reconciled vnto him by Christ his death, then
Wée, béeing now reconciled vnto God, shall be saued by Christ his life.

Others, (whome Ramus followed in two editions of his Logike) take that for the lesse, which is lesse difficult, which may sooner bée in the thing: Where they might perceiue, if they marked, that indéede, such things as are more easily in, bée commonly the greater in strength, power, and dignitie. But they, not regarding this, haue framed such an axiome or Canon.

If a thing bée not in that, wherein it is most like to bée, then it shall not bée in that, wherein it is lesse like to bée: so that, according to their mind this place should serue onely for negatiue arguments, they vse this example.

A Lord cannot kéepe her, therefore neyther thou.

Where the argument is rather from the greater.

Ramus therefore at the length left this place also generall and appliable aswell to affirmation as negation. An affirmatiue is this out of Ouid.

If thou care for the body, much more wilt thou care for the soule:
But thou doest that: therefore this.

A Negatiue.

If God doe not reiect the sparrowes, much lesse you:
But he contemneth not them: therefore not you.

As the argument of the equall is vsed oftentimes in opposing one equall against another, so these of vnequalles, bée sometimes in a very long continued spéeche matched together, as in Ouid, where hée by a continued comparison of his owne miseries with those of Vlisses, inferreth that which he

intended

intended, that hée was more to bée lamented then Vlisses: And these may bée fayned also, as ante leues ergò &c. in Virgil. Héere is also sometimés a gradation, as in this, facinus est vincire ciuem Romanum: scelus verberare: propè parricidium necare: quid dicam in crucem tollere? *Ramus.*

Glanuil chiefe Iustice in H.2. dayes, lib.7. ca.10. Notandum quòd si quis in capite de domino rege tenere debet, tunc eius custodia ad dominum regem plene pertinet, siue alios dominos habere debeat ipse heres, siue non, quià dominus rex nullum habere potest parem, multò minus superiorem.

Elenchs.

As when you take that for lesse which is not lesse. As if a boy can paynt, then a man can paynt, for although a boy bée lesse then a man, yet a boy may sometimes sooner paynt then a man.

So then by these generall heades thus distinguished, wée haue the meanes and way of inuention put down. Although Menon make a great shewe of proofe that there is no art or order in inuention: for it were in vaine, quoth hée, to séeke for that which wée haue found alreadie, & it is impossible by search to find ý which we know not when wée sée it: Socrates goeth about to dissolue this Dilemma, by I cannot tell what mistery of Pythagoricall philosophie, and saith that our Discere is nothing els but Recordari; and that our soules were adorned with perfection of all knowledge from eternitie, but enclosed in this fleshly dungeon of the body, waxed dull, yet by the application of one thing to an other, remembred that againe which they had forgotten before.

Aristotle aunswereth it after an other maner, and saith, that hée who séeketh, knoweth generally what hée séeketh, though not in particularitie: so by this generall note and marke hée may obserue the speciall, whereof hée was ignorant before. And this is true in part, for when wée haue conceiued the generall precepts of any art, then doe wée search the particularities by the generall direction of those rules. But if Menon should goe further, and bring in that first inuention of man, when there was no obseruation either of generall or speciall, how would this aunswere suffice? Therefore, for a finall resolution, I say, that mans soule hath in it a naturall power and abilitie, whereby it is apt to conceiue any thing, if it bee directed, turned, applied, and bent thereunto: so saith Aristotle. 2. de demonst. that our soule brought not with it into the body the knowledge of thinges, as Socrates imagined, but onely a facultie and power of vnderstanding; as our eyes haue not the distinct kindes of colours ingrauen in them by nature, but onely an abilitie of seeing colours. So then, as a man looking on colours, seeth: in like maner by applying his spirit and vnderstanding to thinges vnknowne, he may by the diligent perusing of these generall heades, finde, what hee seeketh now, and knew not heeretofore. But to him onely, as Tully sayth, will these generall predicamentes or Categories of argumentes become profitable indeede, which hath beene a trauailed and a well experienced man in matters of importance, which age and continuance of time affoordeth, or hath read much and heard more, which studie and diligence yeeldeth. Subacto enim ingenio opus est &c.

If we shall for exercise sake vse to draw any one word through these generall places of inuention, it will breede a great plentie and varietie of new argumentes, while wee marke what be the causes, effects, parts, whole, generall, speciall, subiectes, adiunctes thereof, and so foorth in all the rest: and this either in making and enditing our selues, or els in resoluing, and as it were dismembring that which others haue done.

For the first, let that example of Nobilitas, serue, put downe by Sturmius: For the later, we will take, Amicitia, out of Tullies dialogue, called Lælius. The examples be placed according to the vsuall distribution of arguments framed by Ramus, not according to this lately put downe by my selfe. The matter is not great: it may soone bee altered, and should haue bene now, if time had suffered.

Causæ efficientes Nobilitatis. καθόλου τα.

Maiorum pręclara facta, & generis diuturna comprobatio, stirpisq; antiquitas atque amplitudo: hæ procreantes, conseruantes istæ.

Virtus

Virtus & continentia in posteris, quæ maiorum laudibus respondeat.

ἄιτια συνεργοῦντα.

Liberalitas, fortitudo, clementia, cęteræq; virtutes cum corporis pulchritudine copulatæ.

Destruentes.

Morum turpitudo, ignoratio, inhumanitas, vultus Centauricus, & habitudo *Polyphemi* Cyclopica.

Materia.

Ipsa generis antiquitas, & propria virtutis præstantia, frequenti actionum celebritate confirmata.

Forma.

Ista ipsa nominis amplitudo, longinquitate temporis confirmata, & hominum comprobatione stabilita.

Finis.

Vt quæ à maioribus præclarè iacta sint nobilitatis fundamenta, à posteris perficiantur, vt & sibi honori, & amicis voluptati & reip. emolumento esse possint.

Effecta.

In Tyrocinio & exercitationibus militaribus aut cæteros æquales superasse viribus & virtute, aut melioribus & magnis, industria fuisse parem : Sub literarum magistris magnam & diuturnam operam nauasse, & progressus magnos in doctrina fecisse : summa semper temperantia & sobrietate præditum fuisse : optimis & clarissimis imperatoribus stipendia fecisse: In nullo nisi iusto bello militasse : in hostem lenem & misericordem, non sæuum & crudelem extitisse : in acie & oppugnandis ciuitatibus semper inter primos visum fuisse : Duxisse exercitum : Appellatum imperatorem à militibus : Parua manu magnas copias sæpè fudisse : Sese pro patria deuouisse, aut voluisse deuouere, si permisissent milites : Ex pręda, vel nullam pecuniam accepisse, vel cęteris parem : Res à se gestas historia complexum esse : Domi & in pace prudentem senatorem, charum suis, iucundum omnibus sese prębuisse : Principem senatus fuisse : Bis triumphasse : Tertiò consulem fuisse : semper fuisse verum & constantem, nunquam vanum & leuem.

The first Booke.

Subiecta.

Animus reuera nobilis & magnanimus, & virtutum præsidijs vndiq; circumseptus.

Adiuncta.

Clarum esse, & illustrem: omnium gentium literis ac linguis celebrari: deduci: assurgi: &c.

Diuersa.

Non omnem à maioribus habuit nobilitatis opinionem, sed & suis virtutibus exornatam.

Disparata.

Non in simulata ementitæ nobilitatis vmbra delitescit, non pecuniarum copijs euectus est, sed & suis & suorum factis illustratus.

Relata.

Nobilitas est rei nobilitatæ nobilitas.

Aduersa.

Nobilitas & obscuritas: nouitas & antiquitas: humilitas & amplitudo.

Priuantia.

Nobilis & ignobilis. Clarus, obscurus.

Paria.

Claritas & splendor: Antiquitas & vetustas.

Maiora. Minora.

Pulchrius est fieri, quàm creari nobilem.

Ortus preclarus est exoptandus, multò magis itaq; animus generosus, & mens excelsa.

Similia.

Ciuitas in qua nobiles non sunt, similis est ijs hortis, in quibus flos nullus est insignior.

Dissimilia.

Non vt herbæ vitiosæ abijciuntur, ita si quis nobilis vitiosus aliqua in parte sit, spoliari debet auito nomine.

Coniugata.

Nobilitas, nobilis, nobilitare, nobilitari, nobile factum, homo nobilitatus, & virtus nobilitata; nobili loco natus, & natus nobili genere, & nobilissima familia, aut stirpe antiquissima ortus, & generosa stirpe procreatus.

Notatio.

Notatio.

Nobilitas indè nominata eſt, quod eorum qui nobiles ſunt, nota virtus eſſe debeat.

Diſtributio ex cauſis.

Nobilitas in ciuitatem, familiam, gentem diſtributa eſt.

Ex effectis.

Nobilitas alia vera, orta ex clara familia, & virtutibus maiorum reſpondens, alia noua quidem, non adiuta maiorum gloria, bona tamen & induſtria, & cupida honeſtatis. Tertia, calida & malitioſa, quæ non virtute, ſed ſimulatione, & falſa ſpecie virtutis ſibi nomen conatur comparare. Quarta verò quæ vitijs atq; flagitijs dedita eſt, dedecus familiæ ſuæ, profundens omnes opes, amittens domeſticam laudem, profligatæ audatiæ atq; malitiæ. *Ex ſubiectis.*

Nobilitas, vel *Græcorum* eſt, vel *Romanorum*, vel *Perſarum*, vel *Medorum*, vel gentium aliarum.

Ex adiunctis.

Hominum alij nobiles, alij ignobiles.

Definitio.

Nobilitas eſt generis antiquitas, ortum habens vel à diuino aliquo principio, vel maiorum virtute pręclara, humanę ſocietatis conſenſu comprobata.

Deſcriptio.

Nobilitas eſt nominis amplitudo, virtutis comes, virtute conformata, quæ breuitatem vitæ poſteritatis memoria conſolatur, quæ facit vt abſentes adſimus, viuamus mortui : cuius deniq; gradibus homines in cœlum videantur aſcendere.

Teſtimonia.

Malo, pater tibi ſit *Therſites*, dummodò tu ſis
Aeacidæ ſimilis, *Vulcaniaq;* arma capeſſas;
Quàm te *Therſitæ* ſimilem producat *Achilles*.
Inquit *Iuuenalis*.

Nobilitas ſola eſt, atq; vnica, virtus. Vt rectè Poëta.

Non domus dominum, ſed dominus domum nobilitare debet, ſi fidem *Ciceroni* adhibeamus.

Thus haue we drawne this argument, Nobilitas, throughout moſt of the places of Logicall Inuention: which ſhall ſuffiſe at this time for an example of Geneſis in this firſt part of Logike. Now let vs in order of Analysis. apply such arguments to this word, Amicitia, as wee can readily find in the forenamed Dialogue.

Causa efficiens. Natura, Virtus.

Quapropter à natura mihi videtur potius quàm ab imbecillitate orta amicitia, & applicatione magis animi cum quodam sensu amandi, quàm cogitatione quantum illa res vtilitatis esset habitura &c.

Quod si tanta vis probitatis est, vt eam vel in eis quos nunquam vidimus, vel, quod maius est, in hoste etiam diligamus, quid mirum si animi hominum moueantur, cum eorum, quibuscum vsu coniuncti esse posʃint, virtutem & bonitatem perspicere videantur?

Causa adiuuans.

Quanquam, confirmatur amor, & beneficio accepto, & studio perspecto, & consuetudine adiuncta, quibus rebus ad illũ primum motum animi & amoris adhibitis, admirabilis quædam exardescit beneuolentiæ magnitudo, quam siqui putant ab imbecillitate proficisci, vt sit per quam quisq; assequatur quod desideret, humilem sanè relinquunt, & minimè generosum, vt ita dicam, ortum amicitiæ, quam ex inopia atque indigentia nasci volunt &c.

Adiungitur etiam & rerum conuenientia, & morum similitudo, & voluntatum summa consensio.

Destruens.

Contentiones, luxurię conditiones, vel commodi, honoris ambitus, pecuniæ cupiditates, iniquę postulationes, morum disʃimilitudo: dispares enim mores dispaia studia sequuntur: quorum disʃimilitudo dissoluit amicitias, &c.

Materia.

Id in quo est omnis vis amicitię, voluntatum, studiorum, sententiarum summa consensio.

Forma.

Ipsa animorum coniunctio.

Finis.

Vt vsu eius quem diligere cęperunt, fruantur & moribus; sintq; pares in amore, & ęquales, propensioresq; ad benè merendum quàm ad reposcendum. Et infra.

Aliso

Alios autem dicere aiunt etiam multò inhumanius, quem locum breuiter perstrinxi paulò antè, præsidij adiumentiq; causa, non beneuolentiæ neque charitatis, amicitias esse expetendas.

Effecta.

Cui potest esse vita vitalis, vt ait *Ennius*, qui non in amici mutua beneuolentia conquiescat? Quid dulcius, quàm habere quocum omnia audeas sic loqui vt tecum? Quis esset tantus fructus in prosperis rebus, nisi haberes qui illis æquè ac tu ipse gauderet? Aduersas verò res ferre difficile esset sine eo qui illas grauius etiam quàm tu, ferret. Deniq;, cęterę res quæ expetuntur, opportunæ sunt singulę rebus ferè singulis: diuitiæ, vt vtare; opes, vt colare; honores, vt laudere; voluptates, vt gaudeas. Valetudo, vt dolore careas, & muneribus fungaris corporis: Amicitia plurimas res continet, quoquò te verteris prestó est, nullo loco excluditur, nunquam intempestiua, nunquam molesta est. Infra.

Nam et secundas res splendidiores facit amicitia, & aduersas patiens cõmunicansq; leniores. Cumq; plurimas & maximas commoditates amicitia contineat, tum illa nimirùm pręstat omnibus, quod bona spe prelucet in posterum, nec debilitari animos aut cadere patitur: verum enim amicum qui intuetur, tanquàm exemplar quoddam intuetur sui. Quocirca & absentes adsunt, & egentes abundant, & imbecilli valent, &, quod difficilius dictu est, mortui viuunt: tantus eos honos, memoria, desiderium prosequitur amicorum, &c.

Subiectum.

Sed hoc primum sentio, nisi inter bonos amicitiam esse non posse. Et

Quanta autem vis amicitiæ sit, ex hoc intelligi maximè potest, quod ex infinita societate generis humani quam conciliauit ipsa natura, ita contracta res est, & adducta in angustũ, vt omnis charitas aut inter duos, aut inter paucos iungeretur.

Et,

Itaq; verę amicitię difficilimè repeiiuntur in ijs, qui in honoribus req, publica versantur.

Adiuncta.

In amicitia autem, nihil est fictum, nihil simulatum: &

quicqud

quicquid in ea est, idem verum & voluntarium est. Et,

Vt igitur & monere & moneri, proprium est veræ amicitiæ, & alterum liberè facere, non aspere; alterum patienter accipere, non repugnanter, sic habendum est, nullam in amicitijs pestem esse maiorem, quàm adulationem, blanditias, assentationem.

Diuersa.

Suis autem incommodis grauiter angi; non amicum, sed seipsum amantis est.

Disparata.

Quocircà, mœrere hoc eius euentu, vereor ne inuidi magis quàm amici sit.

Relata & Coniugata.

Sed vt tum ad senem senex de senectute, sic in hoc libro, ad amicum amicissimus de amicitia scripsi.

Aduersa.

Quæ enim domus tam stabilis, quę tam firma ciuitas est quę non odijs atq; dissidijs funditùs possit euerti?

Priuantia.

Beneuolentia, amor, affectio, & απαθεια.

Paria.

Itaq; non aqua, non igni, non aëre, vt aiunt, pluribus locis vtimur quàm amicitia. Et,

Verum enim amicum qui intuetur, tanquam exemplar quoddam intuetur sui. Et,

In amicitia, ęquè nefas sit, turpè aliquid & facere rogatum, & imperare.

Maiora. Minora.

Apertè enim odisse magis ingenuum est, quàm fronte occultare sententiam. Et,

Quid enim potest esse tam flexibile, tam deuium quàm animus eius, qui ad alterius non modò sensum ac voluntatem, sed etiam vultum atq; nutum conuertitur?

Quod si hæc apparent in bestijs, volucribus, agrestibus, natantibus, cicuribus, feris, primùm se vt ipsę diligant (id enim pariter cum omni animante nascitur) deindè vt requirant atq; appetant ad quas se applicent eiusdem generis animantes, idq; faciunt cum desiderio, & cum quadam similitudine amoris humani,

humani, quantò id magis in homine fit natura, qui & seipse diligit, & alterum requirit, cuius animum ita cum suo commisceat, vt efficiat poenè vnum ex duobus?

Similia.

Est igitur prudentis, sustinere, vt cursum, sic impetum beneuolentiæ: quò vtamur quasi aquis tentatis, sic amicitijs, aliqua ex parte periclitatis moribus amicorum?

Et illud.

Veterimæ quęque, vt ea vina quę vetustatem ferunt, esse debent suauissimæ: verumq; illud est quod vulgò dicitur, multos modios salis simul edendos esse, vt amicitiæ munus expletum sit. Nouitates autem, si spem afferunt, vt tanquàm in herbis non fallacibus fructus appareat, non sunt illę quidem repudiandę, vetustas tamen suo loco conseruanda est.

Dissimilia.

Nec enim illa prima vera est, vt quemadmodum in se quisque, sic in amicum sit animatus.

Coniugata.

Plurimùm in amicitia amicorum benè suadentium valeat autoritas.

Notatio.

Vtrumq; enim, & amor & amicitia, dictum est ab amando.

Diuisio.

Sed nescio quo pacto, ab amicitijs perfectorum hominum, id est sapientum, ad leues amicitias deflexit oratio.

Definitio.

Est autem amicitia nihil aliud nisi omnium diuinarum humanarumq; rerum, cum beneuolentia & charitate summa consensio.

Descriptio breuis.

Amare autem nihil aliud est nisi eum ipsum diligere, quem ames, nulla vtilitate quęsita.

Descriptio explicata.

Equidem ex omnibus rebus quas mihi aut fortuna aut natura tribuit, nihil habeo quod cum amicitia *Scipionis* possit comparari. In hac mihi de Republica fuit consensus, in hac rerum priuatarum consilium, in eadem requies plena oblectationis fuit. Nunquam illum, ne minima quidem re offendi, quod quidem sensciim, nihil audiui ex eo ipso quod nollem: vna domus erat, idem victus, isq; communis: neq; solùm militia, sed etiam peregrinationes, rusticationesq; communes. Nam quid ego de studijs dicam cognoscendi semper aliquid atque discendi? In quibus remoti ab oculis populi, omne otium tempusq; contriuimus?

Testimonium.

Agrigentinum doctum quendam virum, carminibus Grecis vaticinatum ferunt, quæ in rerum natura totoq; mundo constarent, quæque mouerentur, ea contrahere amicitiam, dissipare discordiam. Et,

Rectè *Ennius*, Amicus certus in re incerta cernitur.

Et illud.

Verum igitur illud est, quod à *Tarentino Archita*, vt opinor, dici solitum, nostros senes commemorare audiui, ab alijs senibus auditum; si quis coelum ascendisset, naturamq; mundi & pulchritudinem syderum perspexisset, insuauem illam admirationem ei fore, quæ iucundissima fuisset, nisi aliquem cui narraret, habuisset. Postremò

Sed nescio quo modo verum est, quod in *Andria* familiaris meus *Terentius* dicit, Obsequium amicos, veritas odium parit.

Thus much for these two wordes, Nobilitas and Amicitia. The like would I haue all Logicall Lawyers to attempt in our common Lawe. At the first it will seeme harde and troublesome: but vndoubtedly the speedy profite accompanyed with a sweete delight, will soone ouertake, and quite ouercome the paynes before susteined: and so much the rather, for that it is impossible, any profession whatsoeuer, to bee more Logicall then is the Law. For proofe; if you take but that little tractate of Villenage in Maister Littleton, you shall finde, if not all, yet not many lesse then all these arguments, vsed in the same discourse, within the compasse of eight little leaues, whereof some bee bestowed on some other matters.

THE

THE SECOND BOOKE.

Of Dispositiоn.

THE FIRST CHAPTER.

HEtherto of Exposition of Arguments called Inuention, the first parte of Logike: Now foloweth the second, which is Disposition.

Disposition is the second part of Logike concerning the disposing of Arguments, thereby to iudge well of them: and therefore this second part is called both Judgement and Disposition.

Annotations.

TAξις among the Grecians, is Disposition with the Latinistes. So then the second part of Logike is called Disposition of the forme of the same second part, for that, as in Grammer Syntaxis béeing the second part, ordereth & disposeth simple wordes handled in the first; so τάξις, Disposition in Logike doth artificially place, settle, and dispose single argumentes one with an other, and that first axiomatically, in seuered axiomes: then, procéeding forwardes to a Syllogisme and methode, as occasion shall serue. For examples sake, this sentence, a villeine regardant is a villeine, is true English, because the nominatiue case and the verbe be placed Grammatically, according to the prescription of Syntaxis: so the same sentence is a true Logicall axiome, because the generall is affirmed on the speciall, in a simple axiome, according to Art in Disposition. Now, this second part of Logike is also called κρίσις, Iudicium, Judgement, of the vse, commoditie, and ende thereof. For that, by a certeine direction, rule, and prescription of Disposition, ariseth iudgement of the trueth or vntrueth of any axiome; the consequence or inconsequence of any Syllogisme: and the perspicuitie or confused obscuritie of any methode or procéeding.

The ſecond Booke.

The ſecond Chapter.

Of Axiomes affirmatiue and negatiue.

DIſpoſition is either of one ſentence, called Axiomaticall: or of more then one, called Dianoeticall. An Axiome or propoſition is a diſpoſition of one argument with an other, whereby wée iudge a thing to bée, or not to bée.

An Axiome hath two partes, the bande, and the partes bound: the band is that, which bindeth the other partes togither. The partes bound, be either the former or the later. The former is that which goeth before, and is called the antecedent: the later, that which followeth, called the conſequent, As

Ah God that Loue ſhould breede both ioy and paine.

Where, Loue, being the cauſe and firſt part, is coupled, by the band, ſhoulde bréede; with his effectes, both ioye and payne, the latter part.

An Axiome is either affirmatiue or negatiue, affirmatiue when the bande of the Axiome is affirmed. Negatiue, when it is denied, and although in Engliſh, the negation come after the bande, yet in reaſon it goeth before, and denyeth the bande aſwell as in other languages.

From this affirmation and negation ariſe all contradictions, when the ſelfe ſame Axiome is both affirmed and denied, As,

Dido my deare, alas, is dead,
Dido n'is dead, but into heauen hent. Dido is dead, Dido is not dead.

Maiſter Plowden. Fol. 10. b. Les ſtatutes doyent eſtre conſtrues ſolonq; les reaſons del comon ley: the negation whereof will make this contradiction, les ſtatutes ne doyent eſtre conſtrue ſolonq; les reaſons del comon ley.

Annotations.

SIcut νοητικὸν, à verbo νοεῖν, ſic διανοητικὸν, à διανοεῖσθαι dicitur. Illud verbum à nomine νοῦς, mens; hoc à διάνοια, mentis agitatio.

agitatio. νοῦς apud *Ariſtotelicos* eſt cognitio principiorum indemonſtrabilium. διάνοια verò, mentis ſeu rationis quidam quaſi diſcurſus, qui aliter λογισμός, ratiocinatio dicitur, cùm ratio ex quocunq; propoſito aliud deducit, mouens ſe ab vno ad aliud inueſtigandum, vt præpoſitio declaret motus tractum, ac tranſmiſsionem ipſius νῦ.

[An Axiome:] The Gréeke worde, ἀξίωμα, ſignifieth dignitie, authoritie. The Logicians, as it ſhould ſéeme, tooke it for any thing ſpoken, pronounced, tolde, as it were, with authority. It héere ſignifieth any ſentence or propoſition whatſoeuer, wherein one argument, reaſon, conceipt, thing, is ſo conioyned with, or ſeuered from another, as that thereby wée iudge the one eyther to bée or not to bée, the cauſe, effect; whole, part; generall, ſpeciall; ſubiect, adiunct; diuers, diſparate, relatiue, repugnant, diſtribution, definition, teſtimony, like, vnlike, equall, more or leſſe to the other.

[Affirmatiue:] It is proper then to axiomes, not to ſimple arguments, to affirme or deny: as it is to a ſyllogiſme, to confute or confirme. Affirmatio & negatio enunciati, nihil aliud eſt quàm partium compoſitio & diuiſio.

[The bande:] The bande in a ſimple axiome is alwaies a verbe: but this verbe is ſometimes put betwéene the two arguments, ſometimes of it ſelfe it ſupplyeth the place of the ſecond argument, as will appeare if you reſolue ſuch implicate propoſitions thus, Plato diſputeth learnedly, Plato is a learned diſputer.

[Contradiction:] In our Trauerſe, which tooke name of the French Trauerſe (that is de tranſuerſo, on the other ſide) there is alwaies a manifeſt example of an exact and Logicall contradiction betwéene two axiomes, the one affirming, the other denying the ſelfe ſame thing that was affirmed: Sée Maiſter Lambard Iuſt. lib. 2. cap. 13.

Home n'auera expreſſe auerment encounter le returne del vicount, quia il eſt officer al court, itaq; le court doyt doner credence a luy. Mes ſi le vicount returne attache, le party dira encounter ceo, nyent attache per 15 iours: iſſint ſ'il returne, que le ten. eſt ſummons, le tenant poet dire, nyent ſummons ſolonq; le ley del terre, car ceo ne trauerſe expreſment

ment le returne del vicount, mes estoit oue ceo assets bien sans ascun contradiction.

Vide 1.H.6.8.Rolf. Enseint et nyent enseint, bon issue.

The third Chapter.

Of a true and false Axiome.

SEcondarily, an axiome is either true or false. True, when the thing is euen so as it is sayde to bée: false when contrarily: and héere according to the affection of the arguments, we must graunt the true, and deny the false, absolutely.

Both these bée eyther Necessary, or Contingent. Necessarie, when an axiome is eyther true or false without exception: (yet to a generall axiome, exceptions may bée added to make it generally true.)

What euer wanteth changeable rest,
Must needes decay when it is at best. This is necessarily true, and his contrary, necessarily false, so this:

There is no greater estate, then fée-simple. Contingent is, when it is true in such sort, as it may bée false, or so false, as yet it may bée true. As,

Great climbers fall vnsoft. This is doubtfull and contingent.

So Maister Plowden: Fol. 50. Femes facile sont illudes et entice al couyne: For although some great climers haue great falles, and many women bée seduced, yet oftentimes it falleth out, that many of the first escape from falling: and more of the second preuent illusions. Here we must neither absolutely affirme nor deny, but distinguish. The iudgement which wée can haue of this Contingent or doubtfull Axiome, is called Opinion, which in thinges already past or present, may bée certeine vnto man; but in thinges to come, it is altogether vncertaine, although to God there is no such difference of thinges in respect of time, to whome all thinges be present.

All preceptes of Artes are or ought to bée necessarily and

alwayes

allwayes true without exception, and so rules of truth: but besides this, they must also bée rules of iustice, as it were, and also of wisedome or discretion, or compendious breuitie.

A rule of iustice is an axiome which giueth vnto euery thing his owne, in coupling those thinges together which agrée naturally, wherein vsually are disposed together, the formall cause and the thing formed; the generall and his speciall; the subiect and his proper adiunct.

A rule of wisedome, discretion, or breuity, is an axiome wherein the arguments disposed may bée mutually affirmed one of another. So that, as the later is verified of the former, so the former may bée of the later. The iudgement of these thrée kindes of axioms is most certeine and infallible knowledge.

Annotations.

THe first rule which Ramus calleth a rule of truth is tearmed of the Græcians κατὰ παντός, of the Latinists, de omni, because it is absolutely and in most generall manner pronounced of all, without any exception. And it must bée affirmatiue. For a negation doth but depriue and take away; and not imprint in mans minde the knowledge of any thing certeinly. So that no negation, although it bée generally true, is fit to make any precept of art, exactly put downe: whose duety is, to teach truth; not vnteach vntruths, or to tell what is not true. Therefore sayth Aristotle, an affirmation is more honourable then a negation.

As a true axiome is eyther contingent, or necessary: so the false axiome in like wise is eyther variable, or els necessarily false, that is impossible. For, the necessary false hath a proper and distinct name, to wit, impossible: but the necessary true hath no seuerall name: but is called necessary, by that generall word.

The second rule of artes is the rule of iustice: so called of Ramus, for that according to the nature of iustice, in this axiome euery argument hath that adioyned vnto it which is by naturall right, his owne, as the forme his thing formed, the subiect his owne proper adiunct, the generall his speciall: examples whereof I thought it nothing necessary to heape vp in the text, for that in the chapters of the forme and formed, subiect and adiunct, generall and speciall, they are already discoursed vpon: and there wanteth nothing but the putting of them together in an axiome, which may sone bee perfor- med by the direction of rules of axiomaticall iudgment. This rule is called in Greeke καθ' αὑτὸ, in Latine, per se: for that both the argumentes in this kinde of axiome, bee essentially and by themselues, their owne nature, force, power, vertue, and inclination linked together. Of these Latine wordes, per se, Paulus Venetus, and other schoolemen, haue framed this dunsical word of art, Perseitas, and therof made many kinds, and long discourses.

The thirde and last rule, is named of Ramus, the rule of wisedome or discretion; of the effect which it worketh in vs, which is wisedome, sayth Rodingus. For, then onely are wee wise, then onely haue wee the perfect knowledge of any thing, when wee know it by the first causes, that is, by such which are immediate, equall, neyther higher, nor lower, nei- ther too generall, nor too speciall, but iumpe, fit, meete, that is, first, and therefore reciprocall: and this is performed by this rule. This rule is therefore the rule of wisedome; teaching generall things in their due place, once, and generally: Spe- ciall thinges in their conuenient time and order, specially, with their seuerall specials. Whereas, if a man teach a spe- ciall thing generally, in generall, and in a generall place: or a generall thing in speciall, specially, and in a speciall place, hee shall bewray his folly and want of discretion in troubling the auditors with his grosse errour, and tedious Tautologie: Error, in applying a speciall and peculiar thing to a general and vninersall matter: Tautologie and vayne inculcation of the same thing, in repeating that many times confusedly, which both might and shonld haue beene taught but once, and distinctly. For if I teach a generall thing specially, that is, in a speciall and inferiour place, I must of necessitie repeat that so many times, as there bee speciall things to which it is applyable, because I left it out in the beginning: whereas if I had put it downe generally, in his higher place, aboue his specials, this once putting downe had sufficed for all: because it is placed as a generall; and euery generall includeth the whole societie of his specials, and to euery of them is equally appliable, by the order of art and nature.

The Grecians call this rule, καθ' ὅλου πρῶτον: the Latinistes, vniuersaliter primum. καθ' ὅλου πρῶτον, is then, as I said before; when in an axiome, both the argumentes ioyned together bee iumpe, fit, meete, first, equal and therefore reciprocall: equall I call them, which are as generall or special, the one as the other: so that the one conteineth no more then the other, neither is the one higher then the other, such an one is this, A man is apt to laugh: A man is reasonable: A villeyne is either, in grosse, or els regardant: Logike consisteth in Inuention, and Disposition: Logike is an Arte of reasoning, for here either the definition and the thing defined, or the subiect and his proper adiunct; or the forme and the thing formed, or the generall and his specialles, or els whole and partes bee ioyned togither. Such as these, bee according to this rule, καθ' ὅλου πρῶτον. And it is so called because the second part of the axiome (in this, A man is apt to laugh) is verified of no other thing before man in generall, but first of man, then secondarily of singuler men, as Plato, Socrates, &c. and whatsoeuer is thus spokē first of the whole antecedent, must needes be reciprocall with the same antecedent. Herevpon, I say, was it called καθ' ὅλου πρῶτον, vniuersaliter primum.

Prima regula, sayth one, falsos; secunda peregrinos; tertia nimis elatos aut abiectos ciues è ciuitate philosophica excludit. The first excludeth all false and lame preceptes, which if it were obserued in our lawe, then all repugnant dreames of Serieantes and Counsailers that serue the time and speake for money shoulde not runne so currant for good law: nay euery iudgement geuen either without reason, or with partialitie, should not stand for Iustice: euery Semble, should not passe for a sentence, nor euery Dictum fuit, for a Dictators constitution.

It is not necessary that euery axiome κατὰ παντός, should be general, saith Scribonius, for, in astronomy, there be many particulers, but it is therefore called De omni, for that it is necessarily true, with affirmation, without exception. Yet a general rule with his particular exception is κατὰ παντος, nam exceptio non solùm restringit regulam, sed etiam confirmat.

The second rule reiecteth all impertinent matters which are not coherent, nor sutable to the proposed argument, but discrepant and disagréeable, as precepts of Rhetorike among axiomes of Logike, as in a discourse of Garrantie, to talke of Rickhils remaynders: in a chapter of releases, to lay downe the pleading in a writ of right: in the explication of conditionall estates, to declare the nature of a déede indented, and a déede polle: among the preceptes of tenants in common, to cast in péeces of releases; as the custome is among litle grand mootemen, who cast case vpon case, as Carters doo billets vpon billets, and for euery collaterall trifle, run ouer all the 633. titles of Brookes abridgement.

The third rule, as it is in practise hard, so in obseruation it is most commendable, and if it bée violated, it argueth a most grosse ouersight in the vnskilfull artificer. As if a professor of Logike should say, that a cause is euer inherent, or, as it were, ingrauen in, and together with the thing caused; this were absurdly spoken, for in teaching a speciall thing generally, hée applyeth that generally to all causes, which is appropriate naturally to one cause, and onely one cause, I meane the forme, which is alwayes inherent in the things formed, and imprinted in the same, whereas other causes bée not so. Agayne, if the same Logicall Doctor should say, that the materiall cause were the fountayne of all knowledge, or should affirme the same of all the other kindes of causes specially and in seueralty, hée might iustly bée reprehended for a double fault, the one, for making a generall adiunct bée restrayned and tyed to one peculiar subiect: the other, for vainlie repeating that in diuers specials, which was in generalitie to haue béene layd downe but once for all. There is in effect no part of our Law that euer was ordered according to this rule: yet it appeareth that the founders of our Law had a liking thereof, in that they detested the contrary vice. Car nous eyomus vne erudition, que si home ad briefe framed in le Register pur son speciall case, præter le generall briefe, et

il

il use le generall briefe pur son speciall case, ceo briefe abatera. Et vide 7. H. 7. In trespasse per le baron et feme, et count del trespas fayt al feme dum sola fuit, ceo abatera le briefe. 7. E. 6. 80. Dyer.

Aristoteles affectiones has tres ad propositiones syllogismi Demonstratiui restrinxit, sed *Ramus* eas ad omnia artium precepta rectius accomodauit. In Logike, saith Scribonius, wee are not to giue peculiar preceptes fit onely to put downe arts (as Ramus in this place seemeth to doo, where hee maketh the foresaid rules of Truth, Justice, and Discretion, proper and peculiar directions for the conformation of arts) but generall for Ens, and non Ens. So that hee would haue no mention made of the constitution and framing of artes purposely and ex professo, for that were impertinent, but onely obiter, and by the way, in manner of a Corollary or Consectary, that it might bee the more tollerable and Homogeneum, that is, the more sutable and coherent. And so I make it heere no distribution at all, but onely a Corollary.

Impossibile quadruplex, sayth one, Naturæ, vt cœlum digito attingere: Iuris, quod bonis moribus & rationi repugnat: Contradictionis: Facti; hinc imposibilium nulla est obligatio, the like whereof is in Parkins and diuers yeare bookes.

The fourth Chapter.

Of a simple Axiome.

Thus much of the common proprieties of axiomes, the specials follow.

An axiome is either simple or compound: Simple is that whose partes bee coupled together with a verbe.

In July. They beene yclad in Purple.

Maister Plowden. Fol. 497. a. Le prior de. S. Iohns auoit l'estate del templers.

In Nouember, *Dido* n'is dead.

M. Plowden. Fol. 5. a. Ex nudo pacto non oritur actio, And this is the first disposition of argumentes inuented.

In the first affirmatiue example, the former part is the subiect: the later the adiunct: In the first negatiue, Dido, the former part, is opposite vnto deade, which is the later parte: and deade is opposite vnto Dido, which is the former parte.

And as wee see in these examples the disposition of agreeable argumentes, as of the subiect with his adiunct in the first: and of disagreeable argumentes, as of the opposite with the opposite in the last: so wee may dispose after the same maner all argumentes agreeable and disagreeable: alwayes affirming the agreeable, and denying the disagreeable: except distributions and full comparisõs, such as haue three or foure tearmes or partes, and therefore cannot bee disposed in a simple axiome, but in a compound.

The simple axiome is eyther generall or speciall: Generall is when the later parte is generally referred and attributed to the former. And in general axioms, one of them contradictory to the other, is not alwayes true or alwaies false; for if they bee both variable, they may bee both false, as,

All that is lent to loue will be lost.
Nought that is lent to loue will be lost.
Chescun tuer d'un home est prohibite per le ley.
Nul tuer d'un home est prohibite per le le ley.

As also if they bee not varyable, as heere:

Euery creature is reasonable.
No creature is reasonable.
Chescun Custome est ground sur reason.
Nul Cũstome est ground sur reason.

The speciall axiome is, when the consequent or later part, is specially attributed vnto the antecedent or former parte: not generally: whereof one beeing contradictory to another, is alwayes true, or alwayes false.

The speciall is eyther particular or proper: Particular, when the later part generall is attributed vnto some of the former, but without any certaine limitation, and to this the generall is contradictory.

In May Piers, of sheepheards.

Some gan to gape for greedy gouernance.

The generall contradictory whereof, is,

None

None gan to gape for greedy gouernance.
Aſcunes mynes ſont royall
Null mynes ſont royall

The proper Axiome is when the latter part is attributed unto the former, being a proper, ſinguler, or one thing.

Diggon in September.
Indeede thy Ball is a bold bigge curre,
Whoſe negatiue and contradictory, is
In deede thy Ball is not a bold bigge curre.
Iohn vane *Salsbury* tue l'home felonioufment,
Iohn vane *Salsbury* ne tue l'home felonioufement.

Annotations.

The iudgement of this ſimple axiome is moſte naturall, but in part common to brute beaſtes aſwell as to man, as in all ſinguler matters compriſed in the axiomes called proper. For as Ariſtotle teacheth in the ſecond of his demonſtrations, euery ſenſible creature hath a naturall power and facultie of iudging, which is called ſence; & this ſence 2. Topic: is of him ſayde to bee a certayne kinde of iudgement: and without doubt, the ſence is a moſte upright iudge of ſuche thinges as are properly under his iuriſdiction, as the ſight of colours, the hearing of ſoundes, the ſmelling of ſmelles, 4. Metap.

This iudgement of the ſences is more exact and exquiſite in ſome ſortes of beaſtes, then it is in man. For although man doe ſurpaſſe other creatures in tutching, yet the Egle ſeeth more clearely than hee, the Vultur ſmelleth better, and the Mowld heareth ſooner, as *Plynie* reporteth in the ſecond of his naturall hiſtorie. So that the iudgement of a ſimple axiome is not altogether proper and peculiar to man onely, but that of the generall axiome is mans alone. For although it ſeeme that beaſtes haue ſome little ſparkes of reaſon, as Ariſtotle in the ſecond of his Phyſikes ſpeaketh of the Spider and the Ante, whereunto Galen alſo ſeemeth to yeelde, yet in truth this iudgement is nothing els in them, but only the fantaſy or imagination of ſenſible notions, neither can any beaſt conceiue any generall. And though Epicurus did ſo much abaſe mans dignitie, as to attribute the ſoueraigne iudgement,

iudgement and determination of all thinges vnto sence, not vnto reason and vnderstanding, yet wée know what an infinite & vnspeakable capacitie mans soule is indowed withal, how farre the general is more honorable then the singuler, & how wonderfully mans minde worketh of it selfe alone without any helpe of sence, whatsoeuer bée obiected by that seusuall, or rather sencelesse and brutish Philosopher Epicurus.

[And in the generall, one of them contradictory to the other, is not alwayes true or alwayes false:] this is false, sayth Scribonius, therefore we must say thus,

All that is lent to loue will be lost:

Not all that is lent to loue will be lost.

For, saith he, the generall nature of a contradiction is, to diuide betwéene truth and falshoode. But there is a generall kinde of contradiction in propositions or axiomes, when two generall axiomes are so opposed the one against the other, as what the one dooth affirme, the other denieth of and in the selfe same thing, and these can neuer bée both true, but they may be both false. This general contradiction is of Aristotle called a contrarietie in axiomes by a distinct name and title, not a contradiction.

An other kinde of contradiction there is which is special, and is called by the generall name, a Contradiction, not a Contrarietie, when ye one is a generall affirmatiue axiome, the other a particuler negatiue, or contrarilie: which indéede as Scribonius saith, can neuer bée either both true or both false; Thus then wée sée the cause of this reprehension, what it is and how much worth. The diuers acceptation of this word, Contradiction, caused an error, and this error a néedles reprehension.

Et quia quidam recognitorum modò comparentium non fecerunt visum, & quidam non venerunt, ideo iurata remanet vsq; ad proximam assisam. Ceo fuit error per troys Iustices, car l'un part del recorde est contrariant al auter: car per le primer parcel, s. quia quidã recognitorum modò comparentiũ; l'apparance de touts est affirme: et in le second part, s. & buidam non venerunt, le non apparãce del parcel des Iurors

est

eſt affirme, ſic contrariant, ſ. omnes Iuratores venerunt (car coment q le generall note, Omnes, ne ſoit la miſe, uncore eſt include et implye ſolonq; ceſt opinion :) & quidam Iuratores non venerunt. 22. E. 4. 16. 17.

33. H. 6. 26. b. Priſot. Le brieſe eſt repugnant en luymeſme, ſ. quod cum ipſe habeat quoddam Cheminum ratione tenuræ ſuæ ad eccleſiam de D. le def. leuauit quendam murum. per quem murum Cheminum habere non poteſt. Issint il reherce coment il ad un chemyne in le premis del briefe, et in le percloſe, il reherce, quod habere non poteſt, niſi ita exponas, habeat de iure, habere non poſsit de facto.

A generall :] Axioma generale eſſe poteſt, etſi nullum ſymbolum generale adijciatur, cuiuſmodi ſunt omnis, nullus, &c. Itaq; ſententia axiomatis conſideranda eſt, ſic, Malus vſus abolendus eſt, generale eſt axioma. In euery general axiome both the former and later part muſt bee a thing generall and common to many : and alſo the later part muſt bée generally attributed to the former part, that is to ſay, to all the nature of the former parte, and to all thinges conteyned under the ſame former part.

A ſimple axiome, ſayth Piſcator, is generall or ſpeciall : generall is univerſall or particular : univerſall eyther definite, as euery man is reaſonable, or indefinite, as man is reaſonable : But Ramus expelleth that uncerteine and indefinite axiome ; for euery conceipt of the mind is determinatly eyther generall or ſpeciall, and ſpeciall, eyther particular or ſingular, as in that axiome uttered by Hanck. 11. H. 4. 47. Damnum poet eſtre abſq; iniuria, the ſence is determinate, that aliquod damnum eſt abſq; iniuria, as in that caſe of the thrée ſchoolemaiſters, where the thirds diligence withdrewe all the ſchollers from the other two.

As for thoſe which they call Subcontrarias ; or under contraries, they make no true contradiction. For they may bée both true : nay they rather make an argument of partition. For, theſe axiomes :

Some men be lawyers,
Some men be not lawyers.

Be nothing els but a diſtribution of men, as if a man

ſhould diuide men into two partes, whereof the one ſhould bee lawyers, the other ſhoulde bée no lawyers: and theſe axiomes may bée both true.

The other that are called Subalternæ, bée both affirmatiue, or both negatiue, the one béeing generall, the other his ſpeciall: ſo that they make an argument, of the generall to his ſpeciall: As,

Euery knightes ſeruice draweth with it gard, mariage, and reliefe.

Some knightes ſeruice draweth with it, gard, mariage, and reliefe.

Equipollence is Grammaticall, Brian in 11. H. 7. 23. intangleth a plaine caſe with this obſcure ſophiſtry of Aequipollentia. Conuerſion of propoſitions turneth good axiomes many times out of their wit: whatſoeuer is good in it, is fet either from reciprocation in argumentes, or from ſyllogiſmes: De modalibus, they ſay, Non guſtabit aſinus: Let fine headed cloyſterers loue them, ſine riuali: they bée nothing but additions of ſeuerall affections of argumentes in an axiome. Suppoſitions are built rather vpon idle ſuppoſals of ſchoolemen, then grounded vpon any ſure foundation of naturall experience. For theſe and all like theſe, no more, but this, As good they were neuer named, as euer beléeued.

The fift Chapter.

Of the congregatiue Axiome.

Hitherto of the ſimple axiome. Now followeth the compound. The compound axiome is that whoſe parts bée coupled together with a coniunction, and the partes of the contradiction are alwayes one of them true and the other falſe. Here the turning of the parts is very vſuall.

The compound axiome, according to the nature of hys coniunction, is either congregatiue, or ſegregatiue. Congregatiue is that which gathereth or coupleth togither the agréeable and diſagreeable arguments, affirming the one, and denying the other.

The congregatiue is eyther copulatiue, or conneriue: copulatiue is that, whoſe coniunction is copulatiue, as that of Thomalyn in July.

But ſhepheard mought be meeke and milde,
well eyed, as *Argus* was:
With fleſhly folly vndefilde,
and ſtout, as ſteede of braſſe.

Maiſter Plowden, Fol. 75. b. Aſſiſes ſont le plus ſpeedy ſuites que le ley done. Et le ley plus grandement ceux fauour, et fauour auxi les choſes que ſont ſpeede et expedition en ceo, et abhorre touts delayes que ſont en retardation del aſſiſes.

The negation and contradiction is,
But ſhepheard mought not, &c. And
Aſſiſes ne ſont, &c.

The true iudgement of this copulatiue axiome dependeth on the truth of euery part: for if all the partes bee true, it is then a true axiome: falſe, if any bee falſe.

Heerevnto muſt bee referred full compariſons and ſimilitudes, wherein the coniunction is the very relation it ſelfe, as, Colyn in January.

And from mine eyes the drizling teares deſcend,
As on your boughs the yſicles depend.

Heere the iudgement is compound, as if hee had ſayd, the yſicles depend on your boughs, and the teares fall from myne eyes.

The contradiction of theſe, are the denials to euery part.

Annotations.

COmpound:] the worde, hypotheticall, which is heere commonly vſed, is neither proper nor fit for this purpoſe. For, in abſolute copulatiue and diſcretiue axiomes, there is no ὑπόθεσις, no condition at all.

Whereas I haue already oftentimes in this ſecond booke vſed theſe wordes, a Verbe, and a Coniunction: it is to be vnderſtoode, that I meane not the naked wordes; (for that were

Grammaticall, and belonging onely to speech: not Logicall, and perteyning to reason:) but the verbe and coniunction of the minde, wit, and reason: which indeede is commonly, although not alwaies, expressed by some such Grammaticall Verbe and Coniunction.

The negation in a copulatiue axiome is not the denying of the parts conioyned; but the denying of the conioyning of the partes. As thus,

Shepheardes must not be both meeke and milde, and well eyd, and vndefil'd, and stout, altogether.

Q. An copulatum axioma sit sine notis copulatiuis, vt *Titius, Meuius, Decius* heredes sunto.

In 22. E. 4. 32. In dett sur le custome de Londres de forreine attachement, le def. pleade en barre, vn copulatiue, s. le record del recouery, et auxi le custome de Londres, le pl. trauerse l'un part, s. le custome, et est troue faux per certificat, ergò tout est faux, car le nature d'un copulatyue, est que si part de luy soit faux, tout serra faux. Bryan.

Legulei aliquando accipiunt, Et, pro, aut, & contra. Vt, home bargaine ou vende sa terre a vn auter, et couenant de faire vn bone et sufficient estate in feesimple al bargainée et ses heyres in le terme de s. Michael, procheine; et deuant le terme de s. Michael, le bargaignée mourust, hic le bargaignor poet et doyt fayre estate in terme de s. Michael al heyre le bargaignée: et vncore les parolles fueront, que il fairoit estate al bargaignée et ses heyres: hic, et, est prise, pro, aut. Sed barbarismus imperitoru ne doit estre preiudiciall al art.

In omni composito axiomate, præter discretum, duplex est modus contradicendi. Primo, cum contradicitur vinculo compositionis, & tùm contradictio diuidit verum & falsum, vt *Esopus* & ingeniosus fuit & formosus, *Esopus* non & ingeniosus fuit & formosus. Secundo, cùm contradicitur compositi partibus, vt *Esopus* fuit & ingeniosus & formosus, *Esopus* nec ingeniosus fuit, nec formosus, & tum non diuidit verum & falsum ait *Piscator*.

The sixt Chapter.

Of a connexiue Axiome.

A Connexiue Axiome, is that, whose coniunction is connexiue, as, Hobbinoll in Iune.

Then, if by me thou list aduised be,
Forsake the foyle that so doth thee bewitch.

Maister Plowden Fol. 11. b. Car en 2. R. 2. in trespasse, il est tenus come vn maxime, que si ascun home ad interest a ascun chose per le graunt ou assent d'un auter: et le partie que ad tiel interest, ne poet auer le principal chose sans faire auter chose, que il poet faire le dit auter chose, et ceo iustifier, co que il est le meynes a vener a son profit.

Whose contradiction is, though thou be aduised by mee, yet thou needest not forsake the soyle &c. And, comentq; il ne poet auer le principale chose sans faire auter chose, vncore il nauera ceo &c. For, the affirmation signifieth, if the former part bee true, then the later must needes follow; wherefore the negatiue and contradictory must bee thus: if, or though the antecedent bee graunted, yet the consequent doth not necessarily folow.

Wherefore when wee iudge the connexiue axiome to bee absolutely true, wee iudge it also to bee necessary. Albeit the necessitie ariseth onely of, or dependeth vpon the necessary coupling together of the parts: which may bee when as, notwithstanding, both the parts seuerally disposed are false, as in the first example: for neyther did hee leaue the soyle, nor folow Hobbinols counsayle; which counsayle if hee had folowed, then must hee necessarily haue left that countrey: for this was his counsayle.

The iudgement of this axiome is certeine knowledge, when the connexion of the parts is necessary, but if the parts be variable, and the connexion onely probable, then our iudgment thereof is onely an opinion.

In May the gate to her kiddy:

Thy father had he liued this day
To see the braunch of his body display,

How would he haue ioyed at this sweet sight?

Hitherto must bee referred that relation which is expressed by an aduerbe of time.

In December.

> Whylom in youth when flowrd my ioyfull spring,
> Like swallow swift I wandred heere and there.

As often as thy brother offends, so often forgiue him.

Maister Plowden: Fol. 541. Quant diuers choses sont dit a vn mesme instant, et l'un ne poet prendre effect sans auter; le comen ley aiudgera ceo de preceder et ensuer, en feasant lentent des parties de prender effect.

Annotations. Elenchs.

The other axiomes are not so easily abused as this. For here the negation is of no force at all, vnlesse it be directly referred to the band which is a coniunction. Therefore although a man might thinke this to bee a Negation.

> If *Dido* liue, she is not dead:

Yet indeede, it is an affirmation, whose negation should bee thus.

Not if shee liue, therefore she is not dead, or, it doth not folow, that if Dido liue, therefore shee is not dead.

Beurhusius giueth this Canon, which seemeth strange to many. There may bee an affirmation, though both the partes be denyed, as, if hee bee not industrious, hee will not bee learned.

This is Berhusius his example: the like whereof is this.

If hee bee not in London, hee is not in Cheapeside. Ista negatio æquipollet affirmationi, s. hee that is out of London, is out of Cheapeside.

And vnlesse this bee graunted to bee an affirmatiue axiome, there will be a very good syllogisme made of onely Negatiues, contrarily to the common receaued verse: for, I can very well reason thus.

> If it bee not in London it is not in Cheapeside:
> But it is not in London, therefore
> It is not in Cheapeside.

A connexiue axiome is that also in Maister Plowden: Fol.

Fol. 10.b. Et il y ad vn principall ou foundation en le comen ley pur construction des parolles, ou clauses, ou sentences, s. que en chescun graunt, ou done, si les parolles soyent ambiguous et doubfull, que ils serra prise plus fort encounter les grauntors ou donors, et plus beneficiall a ceux as queux le graunt ou done fuit fayt.

[Connexion onely probable:] Contingens est connexio, quando partes pro sua probabilitate tantùm ponuntur, id est, neq; absolutè consentiunt, neq; planè dissentiunt. Itaq; etiam axiomatis veritas ex argumentis siue rebus dispositis, non ex sola connexione dependet: si enim necessitas ex sola connexione esset, omnis connexio esset necessaria, quod nemo dixerit. *Wasserleider.*

[Aduerbe of time:] Fit. cor. P. 385. P. 15. Quant le defendant pleda al appele de rien culpable, priss a defender per son corps, il doyt getter son gaunce in le court, &c. The same force is in an aduerbe of place in our law, as in that of 1. H. 5. 3. per Hull. Lou vn home demande certeine chateux, et per son briefe est proue, que le property est deuestue de son possession per le prise, la il couyent a luy de metter le price. Here these words, lou and la, bee in sence no more but, if, and then, or when and then.

Connexum duobus modis negatur: simpliciter quando negatio preponitur coniunctioni; apertius, quandò inconsequentia etiam exponitur; vt si dies est, lucet: non, si dies est, lucet. Et, si dies est, non ideò lucet, vel non sequitur lucere. Itaq; non satis accuratè *Boetius* dicit, ad consequentem propositionem respiciendum esse, vt affirmatiua vel negatiua, propositio connexa iudicetur: vt, si est A, est B; affirmatiua est, ait *Boetius*: si est A, non est B; negatiua: at, inquam, tam est affirmatiua secunda propositio hæc, quam illa prima. Deceptus est autor huius dogmatis dissensionis specie, quia illa enunciata dissentirent, nec simul esse vera possent, ideò contradicentia putauit. At contradictio est affirmatio & negatio eiusdem de eodem, illic, si est A, est B; affirmatio est consequentis affirmati de antecedente affirmato: hîc, si est A, non est B, affirmatio item, sed consequentis negati de affirmato antecedente: at affirmatio affirmationi non contradicit, licet opponatur alio genere.

Connexiue

Connexiue axioms bée called Conditionall: of these there bée infinite in our lawe, as may appeare by the large titles and discourses of conditions in Littleton, Parkins, Fitzherbert and Brooke. Conditio, saith one, triplex est: concipitur enim aut in præteritum, præsens, aut futurum. In futurum conceptæ sunt possibiles vel impossibiles. Possibiles sunt vel simpliciter voluntariæ fortuitæq; (vulgò potestatiuæ & casuales dicuntur) vel mixtæ.

The seuenth Chapter.

Of the disiunctiue Axiome.

The segregatiue axiome is that whose coniunction is segregatiue, and therefore is fittest to dispose disagréeable arguments, which must bée seuered.

The segregatiue is eyther Disiunctiue or Discretiue. Disiunctiue is that whose coniunction is disiunctiue, whereunto is referred the distributiue. These are fittest to dispose repugnant arguments, and diuisions of two partes.

In September.

> *Diggon Dauy* I bid her good day,
> Or *Diggon* her is, or I missay.

Touts mynes sont royall ou base mynes.

Héere the contradiction dooth not make the partes necessarily true or false: for if the disiunction or separation bée true absolutely and also necessarily without any thirde thing put betwéene, then the whole axiome is true and necessary, notwithstanding the speciall partes by themselues considered may bée contingent, as héere:

> Or *Diggon* her is, or I missay.

The disiunction is necessary; & yet *Diggon* her is, is a contingent axiome; also, I missay, is a contingent axiome. But the necessitie of the disiunction dependeth on the necessary exposition or disiunction of the parts, not on the necessary truth of the partes. If therefore the disiunction bée but contingent, or

vpon

vpon a supposition, then it is not absolutely a true axiome, as when Læander sayd, he would either bee drowned or haue his desire. Otherwise the iudgement of this axiome, when the opposition is necessary, is a certeine knowledge.

Annotations.

Piscator ait axioma disiunctiuũ præponendum esse discreto, vt copulatiuum prius est connexo. Nam in copulatiuo & disiunctiuo, pars altera notio simplex est, altera verò notionum complexio; at connexi & discreti vtraq; pars tum antecedens tum consequens non simplex notio est, sed notionum complexio enunciatiua.

Idem *Piscator* putat axioma disiunctiuum differre à distributiuo. Nam disiunctio est qua partium disiunctarum vna aliqua pro vera asseritur, ita vt cæteræ res sint falsæ, scilicet, cum partes de specie aliqua eius generis, ad quod partes propriè pertinent, enunciantur, vt *Socrates* est rationalis, aut irrationalis, sanus aut æger. At distributio est, qua partes enumeratæ omnes pro veris asseruntur, vnaquæq; cum toto quod distribuitur, particulariter disposita, scilicet cum partes de ipso genere aut integro, ad quod propriè pertinent, enunciantur, vt animal aut rationale est aut irrationale, aut sanum aut ægrum, ac si dicerem, animalium aliud est rationale, aliud irrationale, aliud sanum, aliud ægrum.

[Læander:] the verses bee these;

Aut mihi continget fœlix audacia saluo,
Aut mors solliciti finis amoris erit.

Lease fait pur ans, payant annuelment xx. s. ou vn toge. This, as also the whole title of Election dependeth on this disiunctiue axiome. The difference is now when it is but for once, or when continuall; if continuall, eliget grauntor &c. Vide 9. E. 4. & 17. E. 4.

Congregare, segregare, copulare, connectere, discernere, disiungere, bee Latine wordes, yet by vse made English. I neede not make any interpretation of them.

The necessitie of the disiunctiue axiome, as is said before, dependeth of the necessary opposition of the partes, not of the necessary truth of the same. Which thing being not considered, caused not onely Epicurus, who was but a dunsicall Logician, to bée deceiued, but those also who thought themselues great experienced men in this profession, as Chrysippus and Diodorus: for they imagined that if the disiunction were necessary, then the one or the other part of the axiome should be also necessary, and into the same error doeth Tully himselfe fall in his booke de fato.

Elenchs.

Sith the disiunction is not necessary, but when the partes haue no third thing betwéene, this axiome is false when wée thus say, *Paris* must needes eyther walke or daunce, for hée may aswell holde his peace and stand still. So this, Euery francktenement is eyther feesimple or feetayle, for there bée other freeholds, as pur terme de vie, and pur auter vie.

The eight Chapter.

Of the Discretiue Axiome.

The discretiue or discerning axiome is that whose coniunction is discretiue. Wherefore of disagréeable argumentes it is fittest to dispose those that are diuers and differ onely in respect.

In December.

> But ah vnwise and witlesse *Colin Clowt*,
> That kidst the hidden kinde of many a weede,
> Yet kyds not one to cure thy sore heart roote,
> Whose ranckling wound as yet doth rifely bleede.

Maister Plowden: Fol. 82. a. Car parols, que ne sont que le verberation del ayer, ne sont lestatute, mes solement l'image del statute.

This axiome is iudged to bée true, when the partes bée not onely true but diuers also the one from the other: false and ridiculous, when otherwise.

Annotations.

Dissentanea argumenta etiam congregatiuo axiomate enunciari possunt, vt mel & dulce est & flauum, hîc diuersa enunciantur congregatiuo copulato. Quin & simplici etiam axiomate [illegible]ate diuersa enunciari possunt, vt flauedo mellis non est dulcedo eius.

Vt occupatiua axiomata non admittunt contradictionem, ita nec discretiua; sed illa apta sunt ad respondendum & contradicendum consequentibus falsis enthymematum illlorum hominum quibuscum loquimur: hæc ad contradicendum enunciatis copulatis ex parte falsis, vt *Aesopus* & ingeniosus fuit & formosus, hoc falsum est ex parte posteriore: Si ergò hanc falsitatem velim ostendere contradicendo, non satis erit negare copulationem, sic, *Aesopus* non & ingeniosus & formosus fuit. Hinc enim nondum liquet, vtram partem falsam putem: instituenda est ergò discretio sic, *Aesopus* non fuit ille quidem formosus, sed tamen fuit ingeniosus, & hic solus est discretorum vsus.

Enunciata per, quanquam, et, tamen, videntur προληπτικα, non διακριτικα, vt,

Hic *Priamus*, quanquam in media iam morte tenetur,
Non tamen abstinuit &c. Vbi *Virgilius*, nihil discernit, sed lectoris cogitationi occurrit, & contradicit, nam lector videns *Pyrrhum* armatum, facilè obijceret, *Priamum* non audere loqui. Occurrit itaq; *Virgilius* & dicit, quanquam &c. Non tamen &c. Hic est solus horum vsus. *Piscator.*

Elenchs.

It is a ridiculous discretiue axiome wherein such things are seuered, which naturally go so together, as that they can not somuch as be seuered in respect, much lesse in deede.

The ninth Chapter.

Of a Syllogisme and his partes.

Thus much touching the disposition and iudgement axiomaticall, or of one axiome. Now followeth the disposition of more then one which is called Dianoeticall.

The disposition Dianoeticall is, when one axiome by reason is inferred of another, or drawne out of an other, and then it is called eyther syllogisme or methode.

A Syllogisme is a disposition of thrée axiomes, whereby or wherein a doubtfull question disposed with an argument inuented, and the antecedent or former part béeing put and graunted, is necessarily concluded and determined: for, where an axiome is doubtfull, it maketh a question: therefore for proofe of the truth, wée must inuent a third argument, and dispose it with the partes of the question seuerally, one with the one, and one with the other.

There bée two parts of a syllogisme: the antecedent, and conclusion: The antecedent proueth the conclusion, and hath two partes, to wit, the proposition and the assumption.

The proposition is the first part, wherein the whole question, or at the least, the latter part of the question is disposed with the argument inuented.

The Assumption is the second part, which is taken out of the proposition.

The conclusion is the last part, proued by the antecedent, and concluding the question which was in doubt.

If any part of a syllogisme bée wanting, it is called then an imperfect syllogisme, or enthymeme. If any thing bée added more and aboue these thrée axiomes appertaining thereunto, that addition is called a prosyllogisme:.

The partes also of the syllogisme are oftentimes disorderedly and confusedly disposed or placed: notwithstanding, if any doubt shall arise hereof, the axiome which is wanting must bée supplied, the superfluous prosyllogismes or additions must be cut off, and euery part orderly reduced to his owne place.

Annotations.

A Man may héere aske, why I doe not aswell put down the nature of a false syllogisme as I haue done the definition of a false axiome. I aunswere: that, truth and falshoode being incident to the nature of an axiome, both were to be put downe, for that in them both, appeareth the fruite of axiomaticall iudgement: but it is one thing to diuide an axiome into that which pronounceth trueth, and that which conteyneth falshoode: and another thing, to tell what is a false,

and

and an inartificiall axiome, made against these rules and prescriptions of Arte: the one I did, for it was to bée done: the other, as I did it not in the tractate of axiomes, so will I not doo it in this discourse of syllogismes: the ambiguous signification therefore, of this word, false, was the onely occasion of this doubt.

As in Grammer, and Rhetoricke, the naturall ordering of nownes and verbes with other partes of speach is commonly altered and chaunged into a more elegant and artificial coniunction, so in Logike the proposition is not alwaies in the first place: but is diuersly disposed, to auoyde satietie, and suspicion of Arte.

Wée perceaue héere, by the definition of a syllogisme, that the necessitie and vertue of consequence dependeth vpon the orderly disposition of the question with the argument inuented: so that, not the argument properly, but the syllogisticall disposition dooth eyther prooue or disprooue the question.

Hée is greatly deceaued who thinketh there is no part of iudgement but onely in syllogismes. For, besides methode; the first, and almost the chiefe kinde of iudgement is in axiomes, yea and the very foundation of all other iudgement. For hereby wée iudge of all the principles of all artes, of all playne and manifest axiomes. Yea all such questions to the which we cannot aunswere yea or nay (as these be: what is it? what partes hath it? where is it? what qualities hath it? when will it come?) are aunswered by this kinde of iudgement. For, if you make answere to that which is demaunded; the hearer is satisfied.

But if these axiomes bée not playne inough of themselues, they must bée sent to syllogisme, there to bée discussed, and so to methode, there to bée ordered. So that, whatsoeuer is eyther by syllogisme, or methode iudged, it is all iudged by the helpe of this first and axiomaticall iudgement. For if the premisses in a syllogisme bée not sometimes certayne and so iudged by axiomaticall iudgement, and graunted; there will bée no ende of making syllogismes: when still wée call the groundes thereof into controuersie, for want of axiomaticall iudgement.

[A Syllogisme :] σύλλογισμος is, as it were, συλλογὴ καὶ ἐπαρίθμησις, an Arithmeticall deduction of summes in accompts, and so heere metaphorically of axiomes and arguments.

The necessitie of the consequence in a syllogisme dependeth on that olde ground, that such thinges as agree in any third thing, must also agree among themselues. As then, in thinges that bee to bee measured with line or by weight, wee iudge of them as they agree both eyther in line or weight: so it is also when an axiome doth affirme or deny any thing of an other, whereof wee doubt. For, if the line or measure, I meane the third argumēt, agree with both yͤ parts of the question, it sheweth yͤ then the affirmation is true: but if it agree but with one of them, it declareth the negation to be true.

ὅταν τὸ μέσον, sayth Aristotle, ἐξ ἀνάγκης, καὶ τὸ συμπέρασμα ἐξ ἀνάγκης. Non enim ex omnibus propositionibus veris syllogismus duntaxàt efficitur, sed ex duabus necessariò consequentibus, & inter se non minus cohærentibus, quàm annuli inter se cohærent. Oportet enim conclusionem ex superiorum propositionum consecutione exprimi.

There is but one kinde of argumentation, and, that is a syllogisme. For, an Enthymeme is nothing but a contracted syllogisme. If the subiect be one and the same in both the propositions, then the Maior wanteth: but if the predicate, then the Minor. Aristotle calleth it συλλογισμὸς ἀτελής. It hath his name παρὰ τὸ ἐνθυμεῖσθαι, that is in Latine cogitare, & commentari, to thinke, to excogitate, to tosse a mans minde, and meditate. For the minde neuer rests when an imperfect syllogisme is put downe, before it hath supplyed that which wanteth, the better to iudge of the whole perfect syllogisme: whereupon the satyricall poet sayth,

aut curtum sermone rotato,
Torqueat Enthymema. *Iuuenal satyr. 6.*

Maister Plowden Fol. 361. a. Stowell le ayel fuit estrange al fine, et de pleine age al temps del fine leue, ergò il fuit lye. Adde the proposition hereunto, it will bee a playne and perfect syllogisme. So agayne in the same place;

Stowell le demandant fuit estrange al fine, et deins age al temps del fine leue: Ergò il est exempt. Adde the proposition

tion, and this also will bée a full syllogisme.

[The proposition:] in a compound syllogisme, which they call hypotheticall, the proposition, that is, the Maior, as they tearme it, conteines the whole question: but in a simple one, which they tearme a Categoricall syllogisme, it conteyneth onely the later parte of the question, which is called of them prędicatum, or attributum, the predicate or attribute, because it is spoken, affirmed, attributed or applyed to the former.

[The assumption is taken out:] as from a thing put downe and graunted, and now applied more nearely to the purpose, of the Latine, Assumo.

The schoolemen haue commonly foure kindes of Argumentations, Syllogisme, Enthymeme, Induction, Example, to the which some adde Sorites and Dilemma: others also there bée, but these are the most famous: and all these, as I sayd before, come all to one. For an Enthymeme is but a contracted and short syllogisme: An example, but an argument from the like or equall, a facto simili seu pari, and no argumentation of it selfe without the helpe of a syllogisme: An Induction, which is called the Socraticall Argumentation, is but an argument concluded by a syllogisme, from the enumeration of the partes: A Sorites, but an Enthymematicall progression by certainy degrees. Tully calleth it Penelopes telam, because it is wouen as it were, by ascending and affirming, but vnwouen againe by descending and denying: the Stoykes vsed this very much: it is called Sorites of σώρος. aceruus, a heape, because, as of many graynes is made a heape of corne, so of many degrées an argument called Sorites, by this enthymematicall progression. Whereupon the Poet sayth:

Inuentus, *Chrysippe,* tui finitor aceruí.

It is commonly called, à primo ad vltimum, but not so aptly, for as well may it bée called, ab vltimo ad primum. As in that which Themistocles was wont to vse:

The Athenians rule all the other Græcians: I rule the Athenians; my wife, mée; my boy, my wife:
Therefore my sonne ruleth all Greece. Or thus,

My

My sonne ruleth my wife; my wife commaundeth mée:
I the Athenians; the Athenians all Græce:
Therefore my sonne ruleth all Græce.

Maister Plowden Fol.229.b. hath a Sorites of diuers degrées. Le playntife derive son lease de Cocke, quel derive son title del Counte del Pembroke, quel derive son title del roy Edward, quel derive son title per discent del roy Henry le huict, quel derive son title per discent del roy Henry le sept, quel deryve son title per le fine, et per le mort del Marques sans issue. Uintq; si le plaintife ne proue sufficientment, que le Marques est mort sans issue, et que le roy auoyt estate en la terre puis sa mort, il ne proue sufficientment sa title ne interest.

Bracton. lib. 5. Fol. 335. Item, cum nulla summonitio nec defalta, nulla sequi deberet Captio: & cum Captio nulla, nulla sequi deberet possessionis amissio: Ergò à primo, vbi nulla summonitio, nulla sequitur possessionis amissio, quia vbi primum & principale, quod est summonitio, non subsistit, nec ea quæ sequuntur, locum habere debent.

Lastly, a Dilemma, is nothing els, but an argument from the contraries or opposites, or any disagréeable argument. It is called Dilemma, of δις, and λαμβανειν, to take on both the sides: because the argumentes are so set, as that there is no way left to escape, as in that of Protagoras the maister, and Euathlus the scholler: where Euathlus gaue some money in hande to his Rhetoricall Doctor Protagoras, and couenanted to pay the rest when Euathlus should win the first cause that euer hée pleaded for. Protagoras suing Euathlus for his money, saide, if Euathlus ouercome mée, then by bargaine & composition hée must pay mée the money; if hée lose, then by the course of Law. Nay qd Euathlus, if I lose, then by couenant you get nothing: if I winne, then will the iudgement discharge mée.

The like is that which Bias vsed, and was refored by Phauorine: If you marry any woman, shée must either bée faire and so shall you haue her κοινην, common: or els fowle; and then you shall finde her ποινην, [redacted]: therefore mary none at all. Nay, saide Phauorine, there bée women of middle beautie,

beautie, neyther so fine, as to make euery man to loue, nor so foule, as to make euery man hate them. Therfore a man must marry.

So in Arist. 2. Rhet. A certaine precise priest would not suffer his sonne to haue any dealing or conference with the people. For sayth he, if thou speake truth, thou shalt displease men, if untrueth, God: Nay rather feare not to meddle with the multitude, for if thou tell the truth, thou shalt please God, if untruth, men.

Plowden: Fol. 362. Browne a most Logicall Lawyer concludeth his witty disputation with this Dilemma, si Stowell fuit lie per le purvieu del statute, il est apres except: si ne'st lye per le puruieu, ne besoigne destre except, ergo il est, alarge.

I sayd before, that Exemplum, an example, was but an argument a facto simili, seu pari, and that the onely force of argumentation therin proceedeth from disposition syllogisticall: so it is in 4. H. 6. 13. briefe de mayntenance fuit port per deux, ou le tort fuit fayt al troys, la Newton proue que le briefe abatera, quia ne fuit port per touts troys, sic, si le tort fuit en comon, donque eux couyent de prendre lour action en comon. et que le tort fuit en comon, ieo prouera, car si eux fuessont nonsuit per cause del mayntenance, cest in comon: si soysoyent barres per cause del mayntenance, cest in comon, et les expenses del suite sont en comon. ergo, &c.

Neither in these, nor in that called βιαιον Violentum, and such like, is there any new disposition or art of consequence, but onely that of syllogisme.

[A prosyllogisme:] Vide 4. H. 6. 30. In repl bastardie fuit alledge in le maister le auowant, le question fuit, an il auera ayd de son maister, deuant que il reioyne al bastardy, et per Martyn, il ne auera.

Le syllogisme est issint.

- ou nul entry del ayd, la nul ayd.
- Icy nul entry del ayd, car
  - Si ascun entry del ayd icy, il serra del ceo que est devant ple, s. petit auxilium d'un tiel, sine quo ipse non potest respondere: del apres ple, s. petit auxiliũ ad manutenendum exitum, le consequens est proue,
    - ne sont plusors que deux maners de entries del ayde, d'uant ple, ou apres, l'un in reall action, lauter in personell.
    - Ergo si soyt omninò, oportet quòd sit vel hoc, vel illud.
  - mes icy.
    - il nauera lentry devant ple, s. sine quo nõ potest respondere, car il mesme ad responde, s. ad fayt Conusance.
    - Nec l'entry apres, ad manutenendũ exitum, car icy nul issue est ioyne inter eux.
  - Ergo nul entry omnino.
- Ergo nul ayd icy.

In 3. H 6. 21. b. Rolf vsa vne prosyllogisme, vide le lieu.

Canons, Elenchs.

In euery simple syllogisme that is not proper, there must be some affirmatiue and generall argument.

Interdum quoq; simplex syllogismus ex enunciatis compositis constare potest, si modo compositio ipsa argumenti simplex sit. Vt apparebit aliâs. *Freigius. Snellius. Ramus.*

Heere then generally it is a false syllogisme, when all the axiomes bee either negatiue or proper. Ex omnibus enim specialibus, aut negatis, nullus communis syllogismus in vlla figura simplici, concluditur. *Ramus.* 2. lib. animaduers.

Proximum genus syllogismi & Methodi ignoratur, itaq; ponitur dispositio.

Vt

Vt in connexo & disiuncto axiomate veritas pendet ex connexione & disiunctione, non veritate partium, sic syllogismus ex necessitate consequutionis, licet omnes partes sint impossibiles, vt, omnis arbor est lapis, omnis leo est arbor, ergo omnis leo est lapis.

In euery syllogisticall conflict and controuersie, there is a defendant & an opponent. The first is to vrge, proue, conclude; the other to repell, auoyd, and driue backe. The disputation being once begon, it is an vnorderly confusion for the same man sometimes to aunswere, sometimes to reply, and neuer constantly to playe out his owne parte: much like the two clownes in Virgill, which, when they could not aunswere what was propounded, begin a freshe with a new doubt on the necke of the olde: Dic, quibus in terris, quoth the one, and Dic, quibus in terris, quoth the other, Arreede me a riddle, sayth Damætas: and Arreede me a riddle replyeth Menalcas, thincking it a faire conquest, to haue taken and giuen blowe for blowe, as Bakers and Butchers vse to doe, who neuer care for any curious wardes, but lay on loade like good fellowes, one for one, till both begin to stagger, with their valiant bloud about their brused pates. I haue therefore in a word or two, layd downe some generall instructions and directions for orderly disputations.

Logicall exercise is that which expresseth that in particular practise which is generally put downe in art. For as art followeth nature, so exercise foloweth art. Herein let vs consider

- 1. The adiuncts & affections of it, for it is perfor-med.
  - either by writing
  - or speaking.
  - & eyther of these is eyther
    - continued, as in long discourses & tractats.
    - or interrupted as, in
      - Dialogues.
      - Disputations. Vide BB.
- 2. The specials of it. Vide AA.

BB. Disputation is an argumentable discussing of a doubtfull proposition. where note.

- 1. The disputers
  - The proponent, who defendeth the proposition or position: whereunto also the moderator and determiner of the disputation is referred, who commonly mainteyneth the position.
  - The opponent, whoe defendeth the contrary.
- 2. The duties of the disputers, eyther,
  - commõ to both them, as in
    - preparation and furniture,
      - of instruments for the disputatiion, as bee
        - Logike.
        - Rhetorike
      - things requisite for the same, it must be noted therfore.
        - 1. What may confirme or confute the position.
        - 2. What sect of philosophy the aduersary followeth.
        - 3. They must haue in memory the generall heades of artes, which are commonly vsed in disputations.
    - Cõflict and assault: they must neither
      - Wrangle about trifling wordes,
      - Nor make long and impertinent excursion and vagaries.
      - Nor seeke starting holes.
      - Nor bring in any such thing as may rather make against them, then with them.
      - Nor seeke to supplant or circumuent one another iniuriously.
      - Nor overweene themselues, or be obstinate and singuler in conceipt.
      - Nor fal to threatning and railing with vndecent tearmes.
  - Proper to eyther of them. CC.

CC. The proper dueties of the

- **Opponent be**
  1. To haue his weapons in a readines, that is, to haue his obiections framed artificially with syllogisticall disposition.
  2. Not to cast his argumentes confusedly on a heape, but to vse them distinctly, one after another.
  3. To haue Prosyllogismes in a readynes, for the confirmation of such parts of his syllogismes, as may by likelyhood, be denied.
  4. To bring in nothing which hath not some probabilitie or shew of truth in it.
  5. Sometimes to deale directly & openly: sometimes couertly, and by bringing his aduersary to an absurditie or impossibilitie.
  6. Neuer to choppe in impertinent matters, which make nothing at all to the matter in controuersie.
- **Defendent be**
  1. In choise of his position, that it be not
     - Repugnant to sence.
     - Contrary to equity & honesty.
     - Too hard and difficult.
  2. Both in
     - Repetitions of the obiections made, & that either by the selfesame words, or with the selfe same sence, in the like order as they were propounded: with a kind of curteous preface: that both himselfe may haue some meane-space of conceauing a solution, and the auditors better vnderstand what was obiected.
     - And also in aunswering of the same.

DD.

DD. The obiectiōs be aunswered,

- either
  - By skorning, and reiecting, if absurd fooleries be obiected, or such as no man vnderstandeth.
  - By graunting and confessing, when such thinges bee brought in, as make nothing against the position.
  - By affirming or denying, when any interrogation is made : or els by asking what he meaneth by his interrogation, if it be ambiguous and sophisticall.
- Or by direct solution, & that
  - either perfect, when the very cause is shewed, why the conclusion is not sufficient, and it is
    - 1. by denying either of
      - The premisses and prosyllogisms when they be false,
      - Or the consecution & consequence, when the fault is in the forme of conclusion : for the conclusion it selfe must neuer be denied.
    - 2. eyther
      - by distinguishing when eyther
        - The questions and interrogatiōs be captious and doubtfull.
        - Or the premisses bee true not absolutly, but in part. And here friuolous distinctions must be auoyded.
      - Or conditionall graunting, as I graunt, if you so vnderstand it. Sometimes the defendent doubteth of the truth of some one of the premisses, and doth therfore leaue it, of purpose to aunswere to the other that is more plaine, Thus, Let the Maior passe for a whyle, I now aunswere to the minor.
  - Imperfect by bringing in some instance, that is by taking a particular exception to a generall proposition.

A A. so much of ẏ affections of this logicall exercise ẏ specials now follow, which bee

- Analysis, in undoing & examining that which is already made, & is
  - eyther belongyng to Inuention: as
    - to search and inuent the question it selfe.
    - to picke out the arguments and proofes.
    - to refer them euery one to their seuerall heads, & there to inquire of their sufficiency as whether ẏ be used for a Cause which is no cause, &c.
  - or to Disposition & that either
    - Axiomaticall, where all the axiomes must be also brought to their heads, and their truth or falsnes diligently examined.
    - or Dianoeticall which is eyther
      - Syllogisticall, for the examination and triall of consequution, what followeth, or not followeth.
      - Methodicall, for proofe of order and Methodicall handling of the matter discoursed upon.
- Genesis, in making or framig of any thing by our owne industrie, & that eyther by
  - way of imitation and that either
    - of the whole worke
    - or of some part
    - eyther of these is
      - in wordes, called Translation.
      - in things called properly imitatiō. wee must Imitate
        - neyther all autors, but the best of all:
        - nor al things but the best, & that freely, not seruilely, as bindyng our iudgemēt to other mens fancie.
  - Or by proper Inuention, where we must
    - First peruse euery place of Logicall inuention for the inuenting of proofes and arguments.
    - then dispose them artificially both by iudgmēt
      - Axiomaticall:
      - and Dianoeticall & that both
        - Syllogisticall.
        - & Methodicall.

The tenth Chapter.

Of a simple syllogisme.

A Syllogisme is eyther simple or compound. The simple is that, wherein the later part of the question is disposed in the proposition, the former part in the assumption, and is affirmatiue when all the partes be affirmed: Negatiue, when the conclusion with the proposition, or the assumption is denied. Generall when the proposition and assumption be generall; Speciall, when one of them onely is generall: Proper, when both of them are proper or singuler.

The eleuenth Chapter.

Of the contracted syllogisme.

THere bée two kindes of simple syllogismes. The first when of the former argument in the proposition either affirmed or denied, but in the assumption affirmed, the conclusion is speciall.

Affirmatiue generall.

Da- Constancy is a vertue.
rap- Constancy is confidency,
ti. Therefore some confidency is a vertue.

Neg. generall.

Fe- Rashnesse is no vertue,
lap- Rashnesse is confidency:
ton. Some confidency is no vertue.

Affir. speciall.

Di- Some wise man is rich,
sa- Euery wise man is prayse worthy,
mis. Some prayseworthy man is rich.

Da- A wise man is prayseworthie,
ti- Some wiseman is poore,
si. Some poore man is prayseworthie.

Neg. speciall.

Bo- Some foole is not fortunate,
car- Euery foole is contemned,
do. Some contemptible man is not fortunate.

Fe- Fooles bée not happy.
ri- Some fooles bée fortunate,
son. Some fortunate men bée not happy.

Affir. proper.
Socrates is a philosopher,
Socrates is a man,
Some man is a philosopher.

Neg. proper.
Thersites is no philosopher,
Thersites is a man,
Some man is no philosopher.

But the clearenes of reason and iudgement requireth no such disposition, but is content with a more contracted kinde of argumentation. This contraction is, when the argument inuented to a particular question, is put for an example, in such sort, that it go before eyther part, and bée affirmed in the assumption, thus:

Some confidence is vertue, as Constancie:
Some confidence is not vertue, as Rashnes.

For hére the argument inuented commeth before both the partes of the question, as though it were expressed thus:

That constancie is a vertue, and confidencie a vertue,
Therefore some confidencie is a vertue. And,
Rashnes to bée no vertue, yet a kind of confidency,
Therefore some confidency to bée no vertue.

And after this manner, Use, the mayster of syllogisticall iudgement, doth alwaies contract it, and neuer otherwise expresse it. So in that example.

Ascun Husbandman tua sa file, come Saunders; which, if you expresse it, will bée thus:

Saunders poysoned his daughter,
Saunders was an husbandman,
Therefore some husbandman poysoned his daughter.

Annotations.

This chapter conteyneth the third figure of Ariſtotle.

In all thoſe artificiall wordes, Darapti, Felapton, &c. and others of the ſame kinde, there bée certeine ſignificant letters to be obſerued, as, A, ſignifieth a generall affirmatiue axiome: E, a generall negatiue: I, a ſpeciall affirmatiue: O, a ſpeciall negatiue: beſides ſome conſonantes which bée notes of Reduction, which I little eſtéeme of.

The olde verſes bée thus,

Aſſerit, A: negat, E: ſunt vniuerſaliter ambæ:
Aſſerit, I: negat, O: ſunt particulariter ambæ.

Valla reiecteth this contracted ſyllogiſme, ſo doth Scribonius, ſith, as they thinke, there is no example héereof to bée found: and by Scribonius, there is no new ſyllogiſtical diſpoſition héere, but onely an argument from the ſpeciall. But Lazarus Schonerus, adducit hęc exempla, Primum eſt in *Miloniana*. Negant intueri lucem fas eſſe ei, qui à ſe hominem occiſum fateatur. In qua tandem vrbe hoc homines ſtultiſsimi diſputant? Nempè in ea quæ primùm iudicium de capite vidit, *M. Horatii* fortiſsimi viri, qui nondum libera ciuitate, tamen populi Romani comitijs liberatus eſt, cùm ſua manu ſororem eſſe interfectam fateretur, ſyllogiſmus hic eſt,

M. Horatius populi comitijs abſolutus eſt,
M. Horatius confeſſus eſt ſe ſua manu cędem feciſſe,
Ergò aliquis à ſe hominem occiſum faſſus, eſt abſolutus.

Item in eadem. Quod ſi duodecim tabulæ nocturnum furem quoquo modo, diurnum autem, ſi ſe telo defenderit, interfici impunè voluêrunt, quis eſt, qui quoquo modo quis interfectus ſit, puniendum putet, cum videat aliquando gladium ad occidendum hominem ab ipſis porrigi legibus?

Syllogiſmus hic eſt,

Furem nocturnum interficere licet,
Furem nocturnum interficere, eſt hominem occidere,
Ergò hominem occidere aliquando licet.

Huius generis eſt illud,

Riuos deducere eſt licitum diebus feſtis,
Riuos deducere eſt opus ruſticum,
Quędam igitur opera ruſtica ſunt licita feſtis diebus.

Virgilius

Virgilius ſic iudicat, 1. *Georgic.* ſed pro argumento exemplum ſextuplex, ſubijcit particulari quęſtioni.

Quippè etiam feſtis quædam exercere diebus
Fas & iura ſinunt: riuos deducere, nulla
Relligio vetuit, ſegeti prætendere ſæpem,
Inſidias auibus moliri, incendere vepres,
Balantumq; gregem fluuio merſare ſalubri.
Sępè oleo tardi coſtas agitator aſelli,
Vilibus aut onerat pomis, lapidemq; reuertens
Incuſum, aut atræ maſſam picis vrbe reportat.

Exempla ſpecialia ſuo generi particulariter ſic interdum in artium pręceptis accommodantur, quale eſt illud de ſimilitudine, lib. 1. dialecticæ *Rameæ*, cap. 20. aliquando nota nulla eſt, *Virg. Aeg.* 2. O formoſe puer &c. Syllogiſmus hic eſt.

In hoc exemplo nota eſt nulla,
Eſt autem ſimilitudinis:
Ergò aliquando ſimilitudinis nota eſt nulla.

Sic in *Rami* Arithmetica, lib. 1. cap. 1. Numerus poteſt eſſe minimus, vt vnitas, ſyllogiſmus hic eſt.

Vnitas eſt res minima,
Vnitas eſt numerus:
Aliquis igitur numerus eſt minimus &c.

Elenchs.

Among all theſe ſyllogiſmes, there is not any one good, where the aſſumption is negatiue.

The twelfth Chapter.

The explicate Syllogiſme.

In a Syllogiſme ſimple of the ſeconde kinde the propoſition muſt bée alwayes generall or proper: the concluſion negatiue, if either the propoſition or aſſumption bée negatiue.

There bée two kindes of them: The firſt wherein the argument inuented doth follow both in the propoſition & aſſumption, and muſt bée denyed in one of them.

The firſt generall; Piers in May.

Cæ- He that plaieth while his flocke is unfed, can giue no accompt to great God Pan,

Sa- A good shepheard can geue accompt to great God Pan.

Re: Therefore a good shepheard playeth not while his flocke is unfed.

Maister Plowden Fol. 213. b.

Ce- Nul secret verdit del iurors fait le plaintif nonsue,

Sa- Chescun verdit de droit bien rendue, fait le plaintife nonsue.

Re. Ergò Nul verdit bien rendue, est secrete.

The second generall in May.

Ca- The hyreling letteth his sheepe runne at randon:

Mes- The good shepheard letteth not his sheepe runne at randon, Therefore

Tres. The good shepheard is not a hyreling.

Maister Plowden: Fol. 5.

Ca- Chescun bone agréement couvent estre perfect,

Mes. Nul incerteine agréement est perfect:

Tres. Ergo nul incerteine agréement est bone agréement.

The first speciall in Iuly.

Fes- A good shepheard is not idle:

Ti- Paris is idle, therefore,

no. Paris is not a good shepheard:

Maister Plowden: Fol. 28. b.

Fes- Nul bone remaynder poet cōmencer sur conditiō:

Ti. Cest remaynder fait per le prior de bath a William Beiushin est limite de commencer sur condition, s. si ipse habitaret, & residens esset &c. *Ergo*

No- Cest remaynder n'est bone remaynder.

The second Speciall.

Ba- Hée that sitteth safely sitteth below:

Ro- Algryn did not sit below, Therefore

Co. Algryn sate not safely.

Mayster Plowden: Fol. 34. a.

Ba- Chescune bone condition est compulsiue,

Ro- Cest limitation en William Beiushin, n'est compulsiue.

Co.

Co. Ergo ceſt limitation neſt bone condition.

The firſt proper.

Morrels brayne was not bruſed by an Egle,
Algrins brayne was bruſed by an Egle,
Therefore Algrin is not morell.

Mayſter Plowden, Fol. 101. a.

Iohn vane Salisbury ne fue Olyuer ap Dauid auec malice prepence:
Richard Salisbury fue Olyuer ap Dauid auec malice prepence. Ergo,
Richard vane Salisbury n'eſt Iohn &c. vel,
N'eſt d'eſtre acquite, come, Iohn &c.

The ſecond proper.

Paris was prowd
Moſes was not prowd, Therefore
Moſes was not Paris.

Mayſter Plowden: Fol: eodem.

Richard Salisbury fuit murderer,
Iohn vane Salisbury ne fuit murderer Ergo,
Iohn n'eſt ſemblable al Richard &c.

Annotations.

NEgatiue if:] Here vpon the ſchoolemen giue out this rule. Concluſio ſequitur deteriorem partem. For a Negation is worſe then an affirmation, as wée haue heard already. But that which they put downe generally as incident to all ſyllogiſmes is heere artificially ſet downe in his proper place.

Others haue left out theſe two laſt kindes of ſyllogiſmes; but iniuriouſly: for they are as artificiall as the reſt, and oftentimes vſed to diſcerne ſingulers that ſéeme to be the ſame. Singularia, ſay they, non conſiderantur in arte &c. abſurdè. Nam tota Aſtrologia eſt de ſingularibus de ſole &c. tamen pręcepta ſunt catholica. Sic in foro, curia, roſtris, &c. omnia ſingularia. Sic accuſare ſolemus hunc, defendere illum, &c. Omnia ſingularia.

As before, the contracted ſyllogiſme was according to the diſpoſition of the third figure put downe by Ariſtotle, where the Medium is the former part in eyther of the premisses: so this first kinde of the explicate syllogisme is the same that Aristotle comprehendeth in his second figure, where the Medium, or third argument is the later part in eyther premisse. Lastly, the second kind of explicate syllogismes, which followeth in the next chapter, is conteined in the first Aristotelicall figure, wherein the third argument is the former part in the proposition, and the later part in the assumption: according to the verse:

Sub, præ, prima: bis pre, secunda: tertia, bis sub.

Annotations. Elenchs.

No good syllogisme can bée made in this kind, if eyther all the axiomes bée affirmatiue, or the proposition bée speciall, as,

That which vseth reason is best,
The world is best,
Therefore the world vseth reason.

For so (sayth Cotta in the third booke of Cicero concerning the nature of Gods) a man may conclude, that because nothing is better then the whole world, therefore the world can play on the Lute.

Yet I say not this, as though no truth could bée concluded by the like disposition: for, true things are sometimes concluded by sophisticall and deceiptfull disposition, as that of Persius in his fift satyre.

An quisquam est alius liber, nisi ducere vitam
Cui licet, vt voluit? licet, vt volo, viuere: Non sum
Liberior *Bruto*?

Hée is frée that liues as hée list,
I liue as I list, therefore I am frée.

But it is therefore noted as sophisticall, for that, of true thinges, by the selfe same disposition, an vntrueth may bée concluded. As,

A man is a liuing creature,
A horse is a liuing creature. Therefore,
A horse is a man. Agayne,
Hée that affirmeth a man to bée a liuing creature, sayth truely.

Hée

Hée that sayth, thou art an asse, affirmeth a man to bée a
living creature, Therefore
Hée that sayth, thou art an asse, sayth truely.

Thus much for the first fallatian, when all the axiomes bée affirmatiue. The second followeth, when the proposition is speciall, as in that which was obiected against Diogenes.

Thou hast that which thou didst neuer loose,
But hornes thou didst neuer loose,
Therefore thou hast hornes.

For if you resolue it thus,

Hée hath hornes that neuer lost hornes,
Diogenes neuer lost hornes,
Therefore Diogenes hath hornes.

Then eyther the proposition will be false, if it bée generall, or the syllogisme will proue sophistical, if it be speciall.

The proper ductie therefore of a syllogisme is, to lay downe a certaine, true, and infallible rule of reasoning in such sort, that the premisses once graunted, the conclusion must in any case follow, and therefore this maner of reasoning, as all such like, is left out, as not artificiall, constant, and immutable; but, doubtfull, uncertaine, and deceiptfull. For, although sometimes thereby a trueth may bée concluded, yet séeing that it also for the most part causeth error, it is not admitted as a law syllogisticall.

The 13. Chapter.

Of the second kinde.

IN this second kinde, the argument goeth before in the proposition, and followeth affirmatiuely in the assumption.

The generall affirmatiue.

Bar- That which bringeth to good, is good.
Ba- Death bringeth to good, Therefore
Ra. Death is good.

Colyn in November.

Vnwise and wretched men to weete what's good or ill,

We-

Wee deeme of death as doome of ill deſert:
But knew wee fooles what it brings vs vntill,
Dye would wee daily once it to expert.
Faire fields and pleaſant layes there beene,
The fields ay freſh, the graſſe ay greene.
ô happy hearſe:
Make haſt ye ſhepheards thither to reuert,
ô ioyfull verſe.

Maiſter Plowden Fol. 315. a.

Bar- Les choſes pluis excellents del terre perteignont al roy,
Ba- Ore eſt le choſe plus excellent del terre:
Ra. Ergò ore perteigne al roy.

The generall negatiue.

Ce- Men muſt not bée bound to more miſery then men can beare,
La- Shepheards bée men,
Rent Therefore ſhepheards muſt not bée bound to more miſery then &c.

Hobbinoll in September.

Ah *Diggon*, thylke ſame rule were too ſtrayte,
All the colde ſeaſon to watch and wayte,
Wee bene of fleſh, men as others be,
Why ſhould wee be bound to ſuch miſery.
What euer thing lacketh changeable reſt,
Mought needes decay when it is at beſt.

Maiſter Plowden Fol. 332. b.

Ce- Ceo que vient al roy en reſpect que il eſt poſſeſſor del corone, ne paſſera per graunt del terre,
La- Ore vient al roy come poſſeſſor del corone:
Rent Ergo, ore ne paſſera per grant del ſoile.

The ſpeciall affirmatiue.

Da- Hée that hath loued, ought to pitie louers,
Ri- Pan hath loued,
j. Therefore Pan ought to pitie louers.

Colyn in January.

And *Pan* thou ſhepheards god, that once didſt loue,
Pitie the paines that thou thy ſelfe didſt proue.

Da-

Maister Plowden Fol. 64. a.

Da- Cestuy que prist obligations come vicount pour lesser home a mainprise, fayt ceo colore officij,

Ri- Lewis Dyue prist obligatiō de Iohn Maningham &c.

j. Ergo Lewis Dyue fayt ceo colore officij.

The speciall negatiue.

Fe- The pipe which pleaseth where it should not, shall not bée kept,

Ri- Colyns pipe pleaseth where it should not,

O. Therefore Colyns pipe shall not bée kept.

Wherefore, my pipe, although rude *Pan* thou please,
Yet for thou pleasest not where most I would,
And thou vnlucky muse that wontst to ease
My musing minde, yet canst not when thou should.
Both pipe and muse, shall sore the while aby,
So broke his oaten pipe, and downe did lye.

Maister Plowden Fol. 64. b.

Fe- Nul obligation fait pur ayder le vicount pur vn tort, n'est loyall,

Ri- Cest obligation de Maningham al Dyue est fait pur ayder le vicount pur vn tort,

O. Ergo cest obligation n'est loyall.

The proper affirmatiue in Iuly.

The great God Pan saued his flock with bloody sweat,
Christ is the great God Pan,
Therefore Christ saued his flocke with bloody sweate.
O blessed sheepe, ô shepheard great.
that bought his flocke so deare,
And them did saue with bloody sweat
from wolues that would them teare.

Maister Plowden, Fol. 401. a.

Richard Cole tue Elizabeth Penbrooke,
Cestuy que done le coupe le 12. iour del February, est Richard Cole,
Ergo cestuy que done le coupe, tue Elizabeth Penbroke.

The proper negatiue, in Aprill.

Elysa cannot bée blemisht with any mortall blot,
Shée that sits vpon the grassy gréene, is Elysa.

Therfore she that sits vpon the grassy gréene cannot bée blemisht with any mortall blot.

Maister Plowden Fol. 475. a.

Alexander Archer ne fuit culpable del mort del Elyanor Saunders,

Cestuy que counsel Iohn Saunders de tuer sa feme, fuit Alexander Archer,

Ergò cestuy que counsel &c. ne fuit culpable del mort del Elyanor Saunders.

Annotations.

BArbara, is fittest for a general confirmation; Celarent, for a generall confutation; Darij, serueth to proue in parte, Ferio, to disproue in parte, according to those two olde schoole verses which I rehearsed before.

As for that kinde of demonstration of syllogismes which is done by Reduction, it is more troublesome than néedfull. For, syllogismes, if they bée once artificially made, néede no further demonstration, as béeing of themselues sufficiently confirmed by their seuerall definitions, diuisions, examples, and explications.

Elenchs.

The syllogisme is héere nought, if eyther the proposition bée speciall, or the assumption negatiue, as,

Aliquod animal est equus:
Omnis homo est animal:
Homo igitur est equus. And,

Omnis homo est animal:
Nullus equus est homo
Nullus igitur equus est animal.

The 14. Chapter.

Of the first kinde of a connexiue Syllogisme.

THus much for the simple syllogisme. The compound syllogisme is that wherein the whole question maketh the one part of the proposition affirmed and compounded; And the argument inuented

ted, maketh the other part of the proposition, or is conteyned in it.

To deny or remoue any part in a compound syllogisme is to set downe the speciall contradiction thereof.

The compound syllogisme is eyther connexiue, or disiunctiue.

The connexiue is that whose proposition is connexiue, and is made after two sortes.

First when the former part of the proposition maketh the assumption, the later part the conclusion. As in this,

And if that my grandsire mee sayd bee true,
Sycker I am very sib to you.
If my grandsire tolde mee truth, I am sib to you,
But my grandsire tolde mee truth,
Therefore I am sib to you.

Maister Plowden Fol. 76. a.

Si le briefe est fait en le nosme du roy, et seale oue son seale, adonques est le fait le roy.
Mes icy, ceo briefe, est fayt en le nosme &c.
Ergò est le fait del roy.

Here oftentimes the former parte of the proposition maketh not the assumption, but that which is greater, and of more force to conclude then it is, as,

If there were none but other beasts thine enemies, yet oughtest thou to take heede,
But now the Fox also, the maister of collusion, is thine enemy,
Therefore much more oughtest thou to take heede.

Piers vseth this in May, in the gates speech to her little one.

Kiddy, quoth she, thou kenst the great care
I haue of thy wealth and thy welfare,
Which many wilde beastes liggen in wayte
For to intrap in thy tender state:
But most, the Fox, maister of collusion,
For he has vowed thy last confusion.
For thy, my kiddy, be ruled by mee,
And neuer giue trust to his trechery.

And if he chaunce come, when I am abroade,
Sperr the yate faſt, for feare of fraude:
Ne for all his worſt, nor for his beſt,
Open the dore at his requeſt.

Maiſter Plowden: Fol. 11. a.

Si nul forſques vn comen perſon eſt grauntée, ou donée, uncore les parolles ambiguous ſerra priſe pluis beneficialment a luy.

Mes icy, le roy meſme eſt grauntée ou donée,

Ergo, a multo fortiore, les parolles doubtfull ſerra pluis beneficiall a le roy.

The ſame kinde of ſyllogiſme or reaſoning is framed by a coniunction of time, with the ſame force, which this connexiue hath, As

When night drawes on, it's time to goe homeward,
But now night drawes on, Therefore
it's now time to get homeward.

Willy in March.

But ſee, the Welkin thicks apace,
And ſtouping *Phebus* ſteepes his face,
It's time to haſte vs homeward.

Mayſter Plowden: Fol. 263. a.

Quant ſir Iames Hales metts luymeſme en le eawe, donques il forfetoit ſes biens.

Mes il mette luymeſme en le eawe, quant il fuit en vie,

Ergò, quant il eſtoit en vie, adonques il forfetoit ſes biens.

Annotations.

THe ſpeciall contradiction:] when that which was affirmed in generall, is denyed in ſpeciall: or contrarily, affirmed, when it was denyed: and when the ſame thing in ſpeciall, is both affirmed before and denyed after.

[Connexiue or diſiunctiue:] So then of an axiome copulatiue or diſcretiue, wée vnderſtand, that no ſeuerall and peculier diſpoſition ariſeth.

Vide 10. E. 4. Lyttleton contra Danby: ſi le propertie des biyns le mort ſoit en aſcun, tunc ſerra in le teſtator, vel

vel in les executors : mes eſt en aſcun , ergò in l'un ou l'auter : ceſt connexiue : Then agayne :

Le propertie eſt in le teſtator, ou in les executors,
Mes nemy in le teſtator,
Ergò in les executors : ceſt vn diſiunctiue.

In compoſito ſyllogiſmo, aſſumptio, præter argumentum, nihil aſſumit quæſtionis; quod tamen fit ſemper in ſimplici ſyllogiſmo.

If not the whole queſtion, but onely the latter part of it bée conteyned together with the argument inuented, in the propoſition, then the ſyllogiſme is ſimple, although the propoſition bée compound. For as I ſayd elſwhere, whenſoeuer the diſpoſition is ſimple, there the ſyllogiſme is ſimple, though the partes bée compound. So that in Catullus is a ſimple ſyllogiſme. 1. Gen.

Si quicquam cupidoq; optantiq; obtigit vnquam &
inſperanti, hoc eſt gratum animo propriè.
Quarè hoc eſt gratum nobis, quoq; charius auro,
quod te reſtituis, *Lesbia*, mî cupido,
Reſtituis cupido, atq; inſperanti ipſa refers te
nobis : ô lucem candidiore nota.
Quis me vno viuit fœlicior ? aut magis hac quid
optandum vita dicere quis poterit ?

Ramus format ſic :

Quod optandum redierit, gratum eſt,
Lesbia Catullo optata redijt :
Optata igitur eſt.

So in 2. Gen.

Si quicquam ſit homo, tum erit animal,
Lapis non eſt animal,
Lapis ergo non eſt homo.

Nay, which is more, the ſyllogiſme may bée ſimple, though all the partes bée conditionall and compound, thus :

Si ſit honeſtum, erit laudabile,
Si ſit iuſtum, erit honeſtum,
Ergò ſi ſit iuſtum, erit laudabile. As Ramus more at large putteth downe in his French Logike.

Elenchs.

There bée two other conuersiue syllogismes different from these already rehearsed : but because they are not certayne, constant, and alwayes infallible : therefore they be not put downe in the text, as precepts of Art : yet are they diligently to bée obserued, for they are often in autors : especially the first, which is very vsuall : but the second is not so common.

The first kinde is that which taketh away the former part, that it may also take away the later. Terence in Adelphis.

Dem : Cæterum.

Placet tibi factum Mitio? Mi : Non, si queam mutare : nunc cum non queo, æquo animo fero.

Cicero for *Muræna*.

Etenim si largitionem factam esse confiterer, idque rectè esse factum defenderem, facerem improbè, etiamsi alius legem tulisset. Cùm verò nihil commissum esse contra legem defendam, quid est quod meam defensionem latio legis impediat?

Ouid in his second booke of sorrowfull songs.

Si, quoties peccant homines, sua fulmina mittat
Iupiter, exiguo tempore inermis erit :
Nunc vbi detonuit, strepituq; exterruit orbem,
Purum discussis aëra reddit aquis.
Iure igitur, genitorq; deûm, rectorq; vocatur :
Iure, capax mundus nil *Ioue* maius habet.

Cæsar in *Salust*. Si digna pœna pro factis eorum reperitur, nouum consilium approbo : sin magnitudo sceleris omnium ingenia exuperat, his vtendum censeo, quæ legibus comparata sunt.

Colyn in June hath the like.

But if in mee some little drops would flow
Of that the spring was in his learned head,
I soone would learne these woods to wayle my woe,
And teach the trees their trickling teares to shed.
Then should my plaints, causd of discurtesie,
As messengers of this my plainfull plite,
Flye to my loue where euer that she bee,

And

And pierce her hart with poynt of worthy wite,
As she deserues that wrought so deadly spite.
And thou *Menalcas* that by trechery
Didst vnderfong my lasse to wexe so light,
Shouldst well be knowne for such thy villany.

But since I am not as I wish I were,
Ye gentle shepheards which your flocks doo feede,
Whether on hils, or dales, or otherwhere,
Beare witnesse all of this so wicked deede,
And tell the lasse whose flower is waxe a weede,
And fautles fayth is turnd to faythles pheare,
That she the truest shepheards hart made bleede
That liues on earth, and loued her most deare.

For, although all the examples of this kinde bée not false and deceiptfull, but good and sufficient, as in these now rehearsed; yet, false may bée concluded by the selfe same disposition, as

Si arbor equus est, viueret:
Sed arbor equus non est:
Non igitur arbor viuit.

In which example, the proposition and assumption are both true, yet the conclusion is false: but it is the office of a syllogisme, as hath béene sayde, to lay downe, a necessary, perpetuall, and immutable rule, by the which, vppon the premisses once graunted, the consequence must bée necessary.

The second, which is not so vsuall, is that which taketh the latter parte, that it may also haue the former concluded, as in that of Ouide in the fourth booke of his transformations.

Quem si cura deûm tam certa vindicat ira,
Ipse precor serpens in longam porrigar aluum:
Dixit; et, vt serpens, in longam tenditur aluum.

The argumentation is thus:

Si dij statuêrunt vindicare *Cadmum*, fiat serpens:
Sed fit serpens:
Ergo dij statuêrunt vindicare *Cadmum*.

Take

Take an other example, and you ſhall ſée, that by the ſame rule you may conclude that which is ſtarke falſe, As

Si arbor equus eſſet, viueret:
Sed viuit arbor:
Ergo, arbor equus eſt.

For héere the forerunning axiomes being both true, the concluſion for all that, is manifeſtly falſe. This is called of Ariſtotle an Elench of the conſequent: yet in trueth it is no Elench of argument, but of argumentation: when wée are perſwaded fooliſhly that the conſequution is reciprocall, and that the putting downe of the one bringeth in of neceſſitie the other, and contrarily, As,

Si cygnus eſt, albus eſt color. This followeth.
Sed albus eſt color,
Cygnus igitur eſt. } It followeth not.

So, that of Meliſſus.

Si quid factum eſt, habet principium,
Ergo ſi principium habet, etiam factum eſt

The conſequution, ſayth Ariſtotle, is not reciprocall.

Ramus in the 20. of his Logicall animaduerſions, the firſt Chapter ſayth thus.

Theophraſtus autem & *Eudemus* docuerunt in connexo, Antecedentis negati, & conſequentis affirmati tolli poſſe antecedens, vt tollatur conſequens: & conſequens retineri, vt retineatur antecedens. In quo genere, etſi rarus error eſt, eſt tamen aliquando: Vt,

Si nullum animal eſt irrationale, omnis homo eſt rationalis.
Sed aliquod animal eſt irrationale:
Ergo aliquis homo non eſt rationalis.
Item,
Sed omnis homo eſt rationalis,
Ergo nullum animal eſt irrationale.

Cum maius aliquid concluditur, videntur eſſe tres termini, ſed reuera, res illa maior continet rem ante propoſitam in ſe, & quiddam amplius: Itaq; tres tantum termini ſunt.

The 15. Chapter.

Of the second kinde of a connexiue syllogisme.

The second connexiue is, wherin the later part of the proposition is remoued in the assumption, that the former also may bee remoued in the conclusion, As

If thou hadst bene ruled by mee, thou shouldest haue left that vnlucky soyle.
But thou didst not leaue that vnluckie soyle:
Therefore thou wast not ruled by mee.

Mayster Plowden: 281: a.

Si apres le mort le testator, fambien l'ordinary, come l'executor aueroit le propertie del biens le testator, adonques serront deux properties d'une chose.
Mes deux properties ne sont d'une chose,
Ergò apres le mort le testator &c.

The 16. Chapter.

Of a disiunctiue syllogisme.

The disiunctiue is that whose proposition is disiunctiue: and is framed after two sortes also.

The first doth remoue one part of the proposition in the assumption, and inferreth the other in the conclusion.

Or Diggon her is, or I missay,
But I doo not missay,
Therefore her is Diggon.

Maister Plowden Fol. 295. b.

Ou Iohn Carrell ayel al enfant de part son pere, ou Elisabeth Cuddington ayels al enfant de part sa mere, doit estre gardeine in socage al dit enfant en manor de Suytterton:
Mes nemy Elisabeth Cuddington:
Ergo Iohn Carrell.

The second is that which maketh the assumption of one

parte of the proposition béeing affirmed, and remoueth the other in the conclusion, as,

> Or Diggon her is, or I missay,
> But her is Diggon,
> Therefore I doo not missay.

Maister Plowden, Ibidem.

> Ou Iohn &c. ou Elisabeth &c.
> Mes Elisabeth doit estre gardeine &c.
> Ergò nemy Iohn &c.

The same syllogisme is also made of a copulatiue proposition béeing denyed, because it hath the same force with a proposition disiunctiue béeing affirmed, as,

> Shepheards cannot liue in pleasure and paine at once:
> But they must liue in pleasure:
> Therefore not in paine.

Maister Plowden Fol. 281. a.

> Le executor, et le ordinary ne poyent auer le profite del byens le testator ensemble, apres le mort le testator:
> Mes le executor le auera:
> Ergo nemy le ordinary.

Annotations. Elenchs.

For the first, if the assumption conteine not a speciall, but a generall contradiction, the syllogisme will bée sophisticall.

For the second, if the proposition haue not all his partes affirmatiue, the syllogisme is sophisticall.

The proposition in a syllogisme is commonly set from some grounds of liberall arts, as Logike, Rhetorike, Ethike, Physike, &c.

It is not a syllogisme, vnlesse it conclude and iudge necessarily: yea, notwithstanding, the premisses of themselues bée false.

Syllogisme is onely proper and peculiar to man; whereof, no beast doth in any respect participate.

Strict syllogismes bée neuer lightly vsed among authors, but eyther contracted or amplified, or els inuerted, as I sayde before. The quicknes of mans wit is such, that it conceaueth the

the whole sometimes without any proposition, another while without any assumption, and now and then it preuenteth and foretaketh the conclusion.

Ramus in his French Logike reduceth all the Oration which Tully made in defence of Milo to these thrée lines, making one simple syllogisme.

Le guetteur et espieur meschant est iustement occis :

Car l'autoritè du peuple, et des iudgements du Senate, de *Marie*, de la ley naturelle et humaine le tesmoignent : et n'y a aucune ley contraire ny du Senate, ny de *Pompée*. Tel est le prosyllogisme de la proposition.

Or Clode est guetteur et espieur meschant :

Car il a espiè *Milon*, esmeu d'vtilité, de haine, de mauuaises meurs, d'esperance d'impunitè: Ce qui a este entendue per ses parolles et fayts. Et qu'il ayt estè meschant, les faicts contre hommes et les dieus, le demonstrent. Tel est le prosyllogisme de l'assumption, dont est conclu.

Purtant Clode est iustement occis.

This is the briefe summe of all that long oration.

The 17. Chapter.

Of Methode.

Thus much for a Syllogisme. Now followeth methode.

Methode is a disposition of diuers coherent axiomes, whereby the most generall is euer first placed : and of diuers syllogismes whereby the best and principall is first put downe, in such sort that thereby all of them may bée the more easily perceaued and better remembred. I call that the principall syllogisme which prooueth and concludeth the principall question; and that the principall question which was first propounded to bée concluded.

So then, as an axiome determineth truth and vntruth, and syllogisme consequence or inconsequence, in like maner is methode the onely iudge of order or confusion.

This methode is then obserued, when as that which is

best knowne, is placed in the first roome, and those which bée lesse knowne of themselues, doo follow in order, as euery one is better knowne then an other.

Therefore this methode descendeth alwayes from the generall to the specials, euen to the most singular thing, which cannot bée diuided into any more parts.

The most generall definition is first to bée placed, and distribution next, which, if it bée manyfold; partition into the integrall parts must bée set downe first, and the generall proprieties of the thing so parted; then diuision of the specials must follow. And these partes and specials are in the same order to bée handled, as they were diuided.

If the discourse bée long, it must bée knit together, with transitions, telling briefly what is doone, and what is to bée doone, for confirmation of memory, and recreation of the reader.

This methode onely, and none other is to bée obserued, so often as wée teach any art or science, or take vpon vs to intreate perfectly of any generall matter.

Historiographers, Poets, Orators, and such other speakers or writers, are not bound so strictly to obserue the perfection of the first methode: but may, according to their matter, meaning, purpose, time, place, persons, wisely obserue the best for their intent, altering, hiding, adding, detracting, when and how they list. Poets séeke to please the multitude, a beast of many heades. Therefore Homer, maketh not an historicall narration of the Troian warre, from the beginning to the ending thereof, but so mingleth truth with tales, and tempereth them both with a probable shew, and delightsome continuation, that neyther the middle doo séeme discrepant from the beginning, nor the ending from the middle.

And Virgil beginneth the Narration of Æneas his voiage from Sicile: making him declare the rest at supper in Carthage with Quéene Dido. Comicall poets also, albeit they very exactly diuide their Comedies into Acts and Scenes, yet for the pleasure of the people, bring in euery thing in such order, as though it were by chaunce, hap, or hazard, come so to passe.

Orators.

Orators, as referring all to perswasion and victory, omit orderly distributions; obscure thinges purposely; amplifie; digresse; flatter; insinuate; alter; chaunge; and turne all upside downe, placing the best arguments first and last: leauing the worst, in the middle of their speech altogether, the one to helpe the other; that with forcible thinges in the beginning, the auditors may bée wonne; and with as good in the ending, haue their minde and memory wholy occupyed.

This is called the concealed or hidden methode: the methode of wit and discretion, for that it is rather séene in the prouident conceipt of him that writeth or speaketh, then perceaued by any generall rule of art, or precept whatsoeuer. So it is a good policie, if thy cause bée honest and good, to use such Exordiums and beginnings, as may make the matter best knowne and understood plainly and simply: but, if not so good, as thou couldst wish, then to passe away slily with a smoothing insinuation.

In like manner, if thou bée to speake before thy enemies, and such as thou fearest, discretion must bée used, in putting this generall note which I haue now deliuered, in particular practise. Socrates in this sort cogged with the olde Græcian Sophisters, making them say and unsay, and therefore say this, that hée was a wrangler, an inchaunter, a dissembler, a deceiuer. In one word, it is not amisse, to imitate the cunning Surgeon, who hideth his knife, because his patient should not be discouraged. So let us in this poynt shew our selues skilfull in art, that wée may use art, without any suspition of art.

Yet, notwithstanding all this licence upon such necessary occasion, graunted to these people pleasing men, they must, asmuch as they may, follow and expresse generally, the methode which I first put downe: and that somuch the rather, because it is easie to bée practised in some part; and unto reason most agréeable.

Annotations.

SOme thinke, the rule καθ' ὅλου πρῶτον, to belong to methode; but it is not so. For, axiomaticall iudgement considereth the axioms alone, and seuerall by themselues; but Methode, the coherence of many distinct axiomes together. The rule καθ' ὅλου πρῶτον doth simply and onely shew, what axiome is generall, and to bée taught generally; what speciall, and specially to bée put downe, because such onely be reciprocall: but it telleth not which of these axiomes must in order haue first or second place, which onely is Methodicall.

μεθοδος, of μετα which signifieth, with; and οδος, which is a way. For this is the right and compendious way, in writing or speaking to bée obserued. The word therefore is metaphorically applied to any orderly procéeding.

Methode then, as wée take it héere, is an ordering of dyuers axiomes already inuented: not a direction how to finde out axiomes. The inuenting of Artes came by obseruation of particulers; but the teaching and conformation of them now inuented, beginneth at the vniuersall. For, it both geueth more light then the speciall, and may be knowne without the speciall: but not the speciall without it: as a tree, in respect of a pearetree.

Of a little sparke commeth a great flame. Yet the sparke is not therefore more cleare then the flame: so although the knowledge of generals commeth by obseruation of particulers; yet these particulers giue not more light then the generals.

Examples are alwayes lastly to bée put downe, for that they are most speciall; and cannot bée diuided into any other specials: as béeing nothing els but the singuler obseruation of this and that proper and peculier thing.

Methode is like to Homers golden chayne, whereby thinges are sweetly vnited and knit so together, that if one Lynk fall of, the whole chayne is broken and dissolued. And Plato calleth it Vinculum artis &c.

As farre as man excelleth a brute beast, by the iudgement syllogisticall; so farre doth one man surpasse an other by disposition methodicall. As then the practise is harde, the praise most excellent, so the Elench in Methode, causing obscuritie, and tautologie, is most foule and detestable.

Homer is noted for his peruersion of Methode, insomuch

that

that Tully writing to Atticus, where hee purposed to aunswere the last question first, said hee would talke of the last question first, ὕστερον πρότερον ὁμηρικῶς.

As in the other parts of iudgement, so in this especially, vse, practise, and continuall exercise worketh all in all, hee that hath a generall sight in Logike, hath but the shadowe. He that is acquainted with the particuler practise, is the onely true and perfit logician.

I will neuer call him a Musitian that neuer sang: a Carpenter that neuer builded house: a Souldier that neuer fought, notwithstanding the generall speculation of the first in Musicke, of the second in building, of the third in fighting: no more will I thinke him worthie of the title & name of a Logician, that neuer put his generall contemplation of logicall precepts in particuler practise. For, as it is not yenough to know what vertue is, vnlesse you liue vertuously, and expresse your learning by your liuing, so it is but a fruitlesse ostentation to bragge of a generall conceipt, without continuance in speciall and particuler exercise.

What precepts soeuer the common Rhetoricians put downe for ordering of Exordiums and framing and disposing of the whole course of their speeche fitly and according to cause, auditors, time, place, and such like circumstances; all those I say, are altogether Logicall, not in any respect perteining to Rhetoricke, but as a Rhetor may bee directed by Logicall precepts of iudgement and disposition.

[Coherent axiomes:] For otherwise a man may say heere, as Horace did of a Poeme patched lyke a beggers cloake, wherein no one peece is like another.

Humano capiti ceruicem pictor equinam
Iungere si velit, & varias inducere plumas,
Vndiq; collatis membris, vt turpiter atrum
Desinat in piscem mulier formosa superne;
Spectatum admißi risum teneatis amici?
Credite, Pisones, isti tabulæ fore librum
Persimilem, cuius, velut egri somnia, vanæ
Fingantur species, vt nec pes, nec caput vni
Reddatur formæ, And after,

Sed

Sed non vt placidis coeant immitia, non vt
Serpentes auibus geminentur, tigribus agnæ.

[Most generall:] Le chose generall serra toustours mise en demande ou pleynt deuant le chose speciall, et l'entier deuant ses partes, Come terre est genre a prée, pasture, bois, &c. et serra mise in pleint ou demaunde deuant eux.

Issint bois est vn genre de terre ou tours maners de arbres crescent, et pur ceo serra mise en demaunde deuant alnetum & salicetum, que ne sont que especes de bois. Theloall. lib. 8. cap. 20. Fol. 129.

Notiora sunt, saith *Wasserleider*, non quæ facilius percipiuntur, sed quæ percepta & intellecta plurimum notitiæ & cognitionis afferunt, vt vniuersalia, quæ pluribus insunt & conueniunt. Sic obscuriora, non quæ difficilius percipiuntur, sed quæ percepta & intellecta singula parum lucis & scientiæ prębent, vt singularia, & specialissima, quæ etiam sensibus percipiuntur. Hereupon is the distinction of notiora naturæ, and notiora nobis. But this is confuted of others.

[Syllogismus:] Nam est quędam methodus in syllogismis. Methodus inueniendæ artis dicta est in genere & specie. Hîc agitur de methodo disponendi.

[Definition first:] for it giueth light to all that followeth.

[Partition first:] for it is made of causes, whereas diuision is of effects.

[Transitions:] Transitio inter figuras Rhetoricas à *Cicerone* numeratur, cum sit planè logica. Transitio reficit auditorem, certo singularum partiũ fine, non aliter quàm facientibus iter multùm detrahunt fatigationis notata inscriptis lapidibus spatia: Nam & exhausti laboris nosse mensuram, voluptati est: & hortatio ad reliqua fortius exequenda, scire quantum supersit: nihil enim longum videri necesse est, in quo, quid vltimum sit, certum est. Transitio imperfecta est conuenientior, quando longa partis disputatio non fuerit, vt memoriæ renouatione minime sit opus.

Crypsis methodi est in Elleipsi vel redundantia. Elleipsis est, non omnium amissio, sed quarundam in methodo. Redundantia est Heterogenia vel Tautologia. In perfecta methodo docendus est auditor, in crypsei fallendus & mouendus. Sic enim

enim mutato auditoris stomacho, salubria fiunt venenata, & contra.

As an Enthymeme is a defect of a ful syllogisme, so Elleipsis is in methode; as a prosyllogisme is superfluous there, so digressions heere: as the inuersion of the premisses is in the one, so the intangled circumduction is in the other. Wherof, besides Homers Iliades, and Virgils Æneis, the Ethiopicall history is a sweet example.

Argumentum semper disponitur, nunquam disponit: Methodus semper disponit, nunquā disponitur, vt summū genus & infima species: sed enunciatū & syllogismus sunt vt subalterna. Nam enunciatum disponit argumenta, disponitur in syllogismo, syllogismus disponit enūciata, disponitur à methodo.

Vbi materia nulla est, ibi forma nulla esse potest, vt si pars Rhetorices imperfecta in pronunciatione docenda sit, methodus perfecta non est desideranda.

Socrates compareth the oration which Lysias made of loue, to the foure verses which were written on Mydas tombe, wherein the matter did so wisely hang together, that the first might bee last, and last first without any daunger.

χαλκῆ παρθένος εἰμὶ &c.
Aenea virgo sum, Midæ sepulchro imponor,
Quamdiu & aqua fluet, & longæ arbores virescent.
Ipsius hîc manens lamentabili in tumulo,
Nuntio prętereuntibus, *Midas* quod hîc sepultus est.

And like to Lysias speech, or Mydas epitaph, be all our balductum and vncoherent pamphlets, all our yeare-bookes and abridgements.

Imagine, sayth Ramus, that all definitions, diuisions, and rules of any art, as of Logike, were already inuented and allowed for true, and euery rule were written in a seuerall schrole, euery schrole beeing put into an earthen pitcher, as they vse in lottaries, and there shuffled together: what part of Logike now must order these confused rules and scattered schroles. Not Inuention, for they bee found out already: not axiomaticall Iudgement, for they bee iudged and allowed as true, euery Axiome seuerally: nor Syllogisticall; for nowe euery question is aunswered, all controuersies concerning these rules, bée discussed: onely methode remaineth, by the direction wherof, I will séeke in this pot for the definition of Logike, and will set it in the first place: then for the diuision thereof into Inuention and Disposition, placing it in the second roome. This doone, I will take the definition of Inuention and put it in the third degrée; and consequently the definition and diuision of arguments, vntill all the first part of Logike bée thus put downe, by defining, diuiding, exemplifying, and binding together the seuerall tractates by conuenient transitions. Then will I in like manner procéede to Disposition.

Methode and order is the chiefest helpe of memory: therfore sith all methode is altogether Logicall: instructions for memory, if they belong to any art, must néedes bée Logicall. Therefore, Sit puer, sayth *Ramus*, qui querimoniam *Penelopes* apud *Ouidium* epistola prima de *Vlyßis* absentia post euersam *Troiam* memoriæ commendare velit.

Sed mihi quid prodest vestris disiecta lacertis
Ilios, & murus, quod fuit antè, solum,
Si maneo qualis *Troia* durante manebam,
Virq; mihi dempto fine carendus abest?
Diruta sunt alijs, vni mihi *Pergama* restant,
Incola captiuo quæ boue victor arat.
Iam seges est vbi *Troia* fuit, resecandaq; falce,
Luxuriat *Phrygio* sanguine pinguis humus.
Semisepulta virûm curuis feriuntur aratris
Ossa, ruinosas occulit herba domos.
Victor abes, nec scire mihi quæ causa morandi,
Aut in quo lateas ferreus orbe, licet.
Quisquis ad hęc vertit peregrinam littora puppim,
Ille mihi de te multa rogatus abit.
Quamq; tibi reddat, si te modò viderit vsquam,
Traditur huic digitis charta notata meis.
Nos *Pylon*, antiqui *Neleia Nestoris* arua
Misimus, incerta est fama remissa *Pylo*.
Misimus & *Sparten*, *Sparte* quoq; nescia veri,
Quas habitas terras, aut vbi lentus abes.
Vtilius starent etiam nunc mœnia *Phœbi*:

Irascor

Iraſcor votis heu leuis ipſa meis.
Scirem vbi pugnares, & tantùm bella timerem:
Et mea cum multis iuncta querela foret.
Quid timeam ignoro, timeo tamen omnia demens,
Et patet in curas area lata meas.
Quęcunque ęquor habet, quęcunque pericula tellus,
Tam longę cauſas ſuſpicor eſſe morę.

Hunc totum locum cum viderit puer primo connexo ſyllogiſmo comprehenſum, partes ſingulas notabit, earumq; pręcipuas exornationes. Propoſitionem igitur aſpiciet initio in quatuor primis verſibus poſitam.

Sed mihi quid prodeſt veſtris diſiecta lacertis
Ilios, et, murus quod fuit ante, ſolum:
Si maneo qualis *Troia* durante manebam,
Virq; mihi, dempto fine, carendus abeſt?

Deinde ſequitur aſſumptionis ſententia: At tu abes: & amplificatio ex adiunctis ruinis euerſę *Troiæ*: vbi ſex ſunt verſus.

Diruta ſunt alijs, vni mihi Pergama reſtant,
Incola captiuo quę boue victor arat.
Iam ſeges eſt vbi *Troia* fuit, reſecandaq; falce
Luxuriat *Phrygio* ſanguine pinguis humus.
Semiſepulta virûm curuis feriuntur aratris
Oſſa, ruinoſas occulit herba domos.

Dehinc repetitur aſſumptio, & augetur à maiori: non modò abes, ſed ita abes, vt ſcire nequeam vbi lateas. Quod exaggeratur factis *Penelopes*, interrogo, ſcribo, mitto in omnes orbis partes, nec quicquam de te audio. Decem ſunt hîc verſus.

Victor abes, nec ſcire mihi quę cauſa morandi,
Aut in quo lateas ferreus orbe, licet.
Quiſquis ad hęc vertit peregrinam littora puppim,
Ille mihi de te multa rogatus abit.
Quamq; tibi reddat, ſi te modò viderit vſquàm,
Traditur huic digitis charta notata meis.
Nos *Pylon*, antiqui *Neleia Neſtoris* arua
Miſimus, incerta eſt fama remiſſa *Pylo*.
Miſimus & *Sparten*, *Sparte* quoq; neſcia veri
Quas habitas terras, aut vbi lentus abes.

Concluſionis ſententia tandem viceſimo primo ſecundoq; verſibus per contrarium ſignificatur.

> Vtilius ſtarent etiam nunc mœnia *Troiæ*,
> Iraſcor votis heu leuis ipſa meis.

Sed & ipſi concluſioni amplificatio accedit ex adiunctis : ſex ſunt verſus :

> Scirem vbi pugnares, & tantùm bella timerem,
> Et mea cum multis iuncta querela foret.
> Quid timeam ignoro, timeo tamen omnia demens,
> Et patet in curas area lata meas.
> Quęcunq; æquor habet, quæcunq; pericula tellus,
> Tam longæ cauſas ſuſpicor eſſe moræ.

Quamobrem cum hac interpretationis diligentia puer totam ſententiam diſtinxerit, vel à diligenti pręceptore diſtinctam acceperit,& ex octo & viginti verſibus, quatuor propoſitioni, ſexdecim aſſumptioni,& octo concluſioni tribuerit,hac ſyllogiſmi deſcriptione non ſolùm partes,ſed partium quoque ſententiam ſibi repræſentabit. Nam cum ſcierit hic primo loco propoſitionem, ſecundo aſſumptionem, tertio concluſionem eſſe, ſciet itidem ex cognitis ſyllogiſmi legibus quæ vis cuiuſque partis eſſe debeat : quinetiam hac ratione facilimè φαντασίας animo concipiet, per quas, imagines rerum abſentium ita ſubijciet animo, vt cernere oculis ac preſentes habere videatur. Vt in hoc exemplo concurrent antiquæ vrbis ruinæ, agricolæ, oſſa, nautę, mulier ſollicitè interrogans, tabellarij, bella, naufragia, cędes. In longioris autem orationis & diſputationis ambitu, pręſertim ſi methodus ſeruata ſit, memorię pręſidium pręcipuum erit. Exemplum noſtra dialectica cōmodiſsimum erit, vt dialectica ſuijpſius inprimis memoriam confirmet,quę alijs opem confirmandę memorię pollicetur. Figuretur igitur hîc primis rerum notis, artis dialecticę ſumma & vniuerſa partitio,quę quod dicimus, oculis etiam ſpectandum proponat.

Logike

[**]

Itaq; propoſitis hoc modo diſtributiſq; rebus, vt verborum quoq; contextus facilius ediſcatur (qui ab arte auxilij nihil admodum capit, niſi forte quod res ordine diſtributæ ſua vocabula ſecum rapient,

Verbaq; prouiſam rem non inuita ſequentur) accedat, ſi placet, meditatio, vt per partes paulatim memoria ducatur: quinetiam modica voce in meditando animus excitetur, vt duplici motu dicendi & audiendi memoria iuuetur: tum ſiqua ratio memoriam poſsit adiuuare, illa diſpoſitionis admonitio iuuabit: licebitq; philoſophis & oratoribus, qui locis & imaginibus artem quandam memorię confinxerunt, per nos quidem valere: nihil enim pollicentur, quod non vberius multò faciliuſq; teneamus. Aiunt enim ordinem prodeſſe memorię, ſed externis & commentitijs eam ſignis & ſimulachris inſtruunt, nos ordinis rebus inſiti doctrinam certiſsimam & veros locos pro rerum gradibus & generibus diſtinctos, rerumq; veriſsimas imagines adhibemus: illi verborū memoriam infinitate formarum conturbant, dum propter ſingula verba ad ſingulas ſpecies eſt reſpiciendū: Nos hanc partem rerum compoſitione & collocatione, quantum natura ſert, adiuuamus. Quapropter quicquid eſt, quod ad confirmandam memoriam doctrina poſsit efficere, id totum dialecticę diſpoſitionis doctrina prę ſtabit.

Hitherto Ramus concerning the helpe of memory by Logicall diſpoſition: to the which counſayle of him, if we adde ſome comfortable ſimples, & haue a careful heed ỳ we diſtemper not our ſelues either with vnorderly dyet, or vnhoneſt exerciſe, I am perſwaded it will be more auaileable, then all the volumes of the art of memory.

Examples of the perfect methode, appeare in the artificial putting downe of Arts (as in this type of Ramus his Logike already drawn) & alſo in ſome other philoſophicall diſcourſes.

For our Kalender, although ſhepheardes bee not woont to binde themſelues to any ouerſtrict methode in ſpeaking, yet that ſong of Colyn Clowt rehearſed by Hobbynoll in May, may make vs beleeue, that euen ſhepheardes, by the light of nature, did, aſmuch as in them lay, expreſſe this methode in their ſpeeches. For there he, after a poetical inuocation, and generall proposition of that which ho hath in hand, I meane the prayses of Elysa, commeth nearer ẏ matter, and first putteth downe the causes, then adiunctes, and other arguments, incident to Elysa.

Instead af a definition we may vse this generall propounding of the matter: then deuide it into some fewe heades: and orderly discourse of euery head, vsing the places of inuention, the helpe of iudgement &c.

Sir William Stamford in his crowne plees doth first define and propound, thus:

Plées del corone sont les ples queux conteignōt l'offences faits encounter la corone et dignitie le roy, perque pur le mieulx entendement de eux, est requisite a veier queux sont les dits offences: et puis de la maniere coment ils serront pledus, et darreinement de la manier coment ils serront tries et iuges. And so goeth on forward, defining, diuiding, and making playne by examples all the speciall sortes of offences against the crowne.

Bracton foloweth the order of the ciuill law altogether, insomuch that he that hath seene the one, may easily iudge of the other.

Perkins in euery of his seuerall tractates doth, as Stamford, propounde, diuide, and adde examples.

Lyttleton in like maner, by definitions, diuisions, and induction of speciall cases insteede of so many examples, made vp his booke.

Maister Theloall tooke occasion (as in his preface to the Lord Chancellor he confesseth) by Stamfords good motion, to make a more methodicall discourse of writtes, then was extant heeretofore. I will vse his owne wordes to shew hys owne order.

Pour ceo que mon entent est de entraiter de briefe, et des choses concernantes briefe, il moy semble conuenyent de commencer per la definition de briefe, et de monster quelle chose il est.

And afterwards, J'ay enterprinse de framer vn definition, ou plustost discription de briefe solonq; le forme et doctrine d'eux, que le art de ceo professont, per les genres, differences, pro-

proprieties, en tiel manner, &c. The definition I haue put downe in the first booke.

Then hauing defined it, he saith, me boyes a diuider mon briefe.

After the diuision hee vseth a transition, wherein he briefly telleth, what hee hath doone, and orderly declareth what remayneth to bee doone moreouer.

Which kinde of Transitions, wanting in Lyttleton, make the coherence of his discourses somewhat obscure, as in that tractate of estates sur condition, where hee first diuideth conditionall estates, thus:

Estates que homes ont en terres ou tenements sur condition sont de deux maners, s. ou ils ont estate sur condition en fait, ou sur condition en ley. And after the laying downe of so many seuerall cases of the first part, as could be conteyned within the compasse of sixteene leaues: hee immediatly, if not abruptly, proceedeth to the explication of the second, without any transition at all: Neither telling what was done, nor what was to be done. So also in the discourse of releases, he first deuideth releases thus. Releases sont in diuers maners, s. releases de tout le droyt que home ad en terres ou tenements; et releases d'actions personels et reals et auters choses. And then hauing bestowed ten leaues wholly vpon the first member of his distribution, hee sets vpon ẏ second part sodenly without any warning giuen at all.

Digressions be sometimes tolerable vpon necessary occasion: but impertinent, or rather repugnant imaginations continually cast in, marre all. A man taketh vppon him to reade vpon the statute of fines, and hee thrummeth in 50. scattered & vndigested cases of estate tayle in possessiō, and as many of the same in reuersion, with a cluster of other sophisticall and vncoherent poynts, much like a foolish paynter, who because he had some litle skill in paynting a peare tree, but no cunning at all in expressing any thing els, would be sure to make a peare tree grow on euery mans wal. So this fellow hauing met with some odde learnings of estate tayle, will needes haue vtterance for it. An other maketh euery case haue one idle poynt of a fine, for fashion sake, whereas hée foysteth in 6. 8. 10. 12. or more extrauagant conceipts, as well agréeing with the nature of a fine, as a Harpe doth with a Harrow; yet, who but hée? Non equidem inuideo: miror magis, at the frenzie of the reader, and folly of the hearer. For if the readers intent be to explayne the statute, then quorsum hæc tam putida tendunt? but if hée meane to make ostentation of all his imaginations, me thinks he should not make a well meaning statute the cloake of two hundred ambiguities. I graunt the matter may bée well worth the hearing, but Nunc non erat his locus: Therefore as Horace sayth,

Amphora cæpit,
Institui, currente rota, cur vrceus exit?

To conclude I could heartily wish the whole body of our law to be rather logically ordered, then by Alphabeticall breuiaries torne and dismembred. If any man say, it cannot be, he should adde, by himself: if hée thinke it should not bée, then I doe not somuch enuy his great wisedome, as pitie his rusticall education, who had rather eate Acornes with hogs, then bread with men; and preferreth the loathsome tossing of an A. B. C. abridgement, before the lightsome perusing of a Methodicall coherence of the whole common law.

Yet I am not hée, that will once open my mouth, generally to condemne the contracting and abridging of dispersed & tedious cases: But as, Lyttleton, Parkins, Stamford, Theloall, Bracton and Britton haue excelled the abridgers in light and order, so the paynefull abridgements of Statham and those reuerend Iudges Fitzherbert, and Brooke, are more conuenient for many purposes, then those vast heapes of scattered discourses, throwne into euery corner of our yeare bookes: Which, notwithstanding, are diligently to be reteyned: but the matter may bée, for the benefite of studentes, more orderly contriued.

It is not my purpose, at this time to dispute, whether the law of England, being one onely proper, and singuler law, appropriate to our nation, consisting of so many particularities, being subiect to such continuall change and alteration, can bée made an art: But that the confusion of writers may bée remoued, the maner reformed, the matter better ordered,

I doe

I doo surely beléeue, because I know assuredly.

Thus haue I at last, made an end of a confused meditatiō, patched vp, I feare mée, rather in great hast, then with good spéed. Wherein I thinke the art of Logike to bée as I haue put downe: but the precepts of the same must bée continually practised, as I haue elsewhere sayde, or els the generall contemplation thereof will proue a fruitles conceipt & naked speculation. Let vs folow therefore the counsell of Apelles; Nulla dies sine linea. Let no day passe without some practise, either in making, framing, and inuenting of our selues, or in resoluing & dissoluing of things doone by others, for the triall of their skil, and confirmation of our owne. Neither would I haue this practise continued onely in reading or writing, but in euery ciuill assembly or méeting: wherein yet I will not bée so seuere a censor, as to exact euery spéech to the formall rules of axiomes, syllogismes, &c. It shall bée sufficient for vs to folow a more easie and elegant kinde of disputation, ioyning Rhetorike with Logike, and referring that precise straitnesse vnto Philosophicall exercises.

Neyther let any man thinke, that because in common méetings and assemblies the wordes and tearmes of Logike bée not named, therefore the force and operation of Logike is not there vsed and apparant. For, as in Grammer wée name neyther Noune, Pronoune, Verbe, nor any other parte of spéech: and as in Rhethorike, wée make mention neyther of Metonymia, Synecdoche, Exclamatio, nor any other Rhetoricall figure or trope: yet vse in our spéech the helpe of the one in speaking grammatically, and the direction of the other in talking eloquently: so, although in common conference wée neuer name syllogismes, axiomes, propositions, assumptions, & other words of art, yet doo wée secretly practise them in our disputations, the vertue whereof is, to make our discourses séeme true to the simple, and probable to the wise.

I haue, for examples sake, put downe a Logicall Analysis of the second Aegloge in Virgill, of the Earle of

Northumberlands case in Maister Plowdens reportes, and of sir William Stamfords crowne plées. For the Aeglogue although the verses of Virgill be better knowne in Latine, then I can make them vnderstoode in English, (especially obseruing the same order of verse) yet I haue attempted the interpreting of the same by a poeticall Paraphrasis, for the contentation of such as vnderstand no Latine: & withall inserted the Latyne verses, for their pleasure, that disdayne the English.

Alexis 2. Aegloga Virgilij.

FOrmosum pastor *Corydon* ardebat *Alexin*
Delitias domini, nec quid speraret, habebat.
Tantùm inter densas, vmbrosa cacumina, fagos
Assiduè veniebat. Ibi hæc incondita solus
Montibus, & syluis studio iactabat inani.
O crudelis *Alexi*, nihil mea carmina curas;
Nil nostri miserere; mori me deniq; coges.
Nunc etiam pecudes vmbras & frigora captant:
Nunc virides etiam occultant spineta lacertas:
Thestylis & rapido fessis messoribus æstu
Allia, serpyllumq; herbas contundit òlentes.
At mecum raucis, tua dum vestigia lustro,
Sole sub ardenti resonant arbusta cicadis.
Nonne fuit satius tristes *Amaryllidis* iras,
Atq; superba pati fastidia, nonne *Menalcam*,
Quamuis ille niger, quamuis tu candidus esses?
O formose puer, nimium ne crede colori:
Alba ligustra cadunt, vaccinia nigra leguntur.
Despectus tibi sum, nec quis sim, quæris *Alexi*,
Quàm diues pecoris niuei, quàm lactis abundans.
Mille meæ Siculis errant in montibus agnæ.
Lac mihi non æstate nouum, non frigore defit.
Canto, quę solitus, si quando armenta vocabat,
Amphion Dircæus in *Actæo Aracyntho*.
Nec sum adeò informis, nuper me in littore vidi,

Cum

Cum placidum ventis ſtaret mare,non ego *Daphnim*
Iudice te metuam, ſi nunquam fallit imago.
O tantùm libeat mecum tibi ſordida rura,
Atq; humiles habitare caſas,& figere ceruos,
Hædorumq; gregem viridi compellere hibyſco.
Mecum vnà in ſyluis imitabere *Pana* canendo.
Pan primus calamos cera coniungere plures
Inſtituit : *Pan* curat oues,ouiumq; magiſtros.
Nec te pæniteat calamo triuiſſe labellum,
Hæc eadem vt ſciret,quid non faciebat *Amyntas* ?
Eſt mihi diſparibus ſeptem compacta cicutis
Fiſtula,*Damætas* dono mihi quam dedit olim,
Et dixit moriens, te nunc habet iſta ſecundum :
Dixit *Damætas*,inuidit ſtultus *Amyntas*.
Prętereà duo, nec tuta mihi valle reperti
Capreoli,ſparſis etiam nunc pellibus albo,
Bina die ſiccant ouis vbera,quos tibi ſeruo.
Iampridem à me illos abducere *Theſtylis* orat :
Et faciet, quoniam ſordent tibi munera noſtra.
Huc ades,ô formoſe puer,tibi lilia plenis
Ecce ferunt nymphæ calathis : tibi candida *Nais*
Pallentes violas,& ſumma papauera carpens,
Narciſſum,& florem iungit benè olentis *Anethi*.
Tum *Caſia*,atq; alijs intexens ſuauibus herbis,
Mollia luteola pingit vaccinia caltha.
Ipſe ego cana legam tenera lanugine mala,
Caſtaneaſq; nuces,mea quas *Amaryllis* amabat :
Addam cerea pruna ; & honos erit huic quoq; pomo :
Et vos, ô Lauri, carpam,& te, proxima myrte ;
Sic poſitæ quoniam ſuaues miſcetis odores.
Ruſticus es,*Corydon*,nec munera curat *Alexis* :
Nec ſi muneribus certes,concedat *Iolas*.
Eheu quid volui miſero mihi ? Floribus auſtrum
Perditus & liquidis immiſi fontibus apros.
Quem fugis ah demens ? habitarunt dij quoq; ſiluas,
Dardaniuſq; Paris. *Pallas* quas condidit arces,
Ipſa colat ; nobis placeant ante omnia ſiluæ.

The ſecond Booke.

Toruа leæna lupum ſequitur; lupus ipſe capellam;
Florentem Cithyſum ſequitur laſciua capella,
Te *Corydon*, ô *Alexi*: Trahit ſua quemq; voluptas.
Aſpice, aratra iugo referunt ſuſpenſa iuuenci,
Et ſol creſcentes decedens duplicat vmbras:
Me tamen vrit amor, quis enim modus adſit amori?
Ah *Corydon*, *Corydon*, quæ te dementia cępit?
Semiputata tibi frondoſa vitis in vlmo eſt.
Quin tu aliquid ſaltem potius, quorum indiget vſus,
Viminibus, molliq; paras detexere iunco?
Inuenies alium, ſi te hic faſtidit *Alexis*.

The ſame in Engliſh Hexameters,
verſe for verſe.

SEelly ſhepheard *Corydon* lou'd hartily faire lad *Alexis*,
His maiſters dearling, but ſaw no matter of hoping.
Only amid the foreſt thick ſet with broad-ſhadoe beachtrees
daily reſort did he make: thus alone to the woods, to the moũtains
With broken ſpeeches, fond thoughts moſt vainly reuealing.
O hardharted *Alexis*: I ſee my verſe to be ſcorned,
My ſelfe not pitied, my death by thee laſtly procured.
Now do the beaſts cũn ſeeke for cooling ſhàde to refreſh thẽ,
Grene lyzards now too in buſhes thorny be lurking,
And for faint reapers by the ſuns rage, *Theſtylis* haſtning,
Strong-ſmelling wilde thime, and garlyke beates in a mortar.
But whilſt I trace thee, with ſun beames all to beſcorched,
Groûes by the hoarſchirping graſhoppers yeeld a reſoũding.
Waſt not far better t'haue borne with ſurly *Menalcas*,
And ſore diſpleaſed, diſdainfull, prowd *Amaryllis*,
Although thou white were, although but ſwarty *Menalcas*?
O thou faire white boy, truſt not too much to thy whitnes:
Faire white flowers fall downe, black fruits are only reſerued.
Thou câr'ſt not for mee, my ſtate thou knowſt not, *Alexis*:
What flocks of white ſheepe I do keepe, of milke what abũdance.
On *Sicil* high mountains my lambs feed more then a thouſãd:
New mylke in ſummer, new mylke in winter I want not.

My

My ſong's like *Thebane Amphions* ſong, when he called
His wandring bullocks, on Greekiſh mount *Aracynthus.*
Neyther am I ſo fowle: I ſaw my ſelfe by the ſeaſhore,
When ſeas al calme were: I doubt not, but by thy cenſure,
Daphnis I ſhall ſurpaſſe, vnles my face do deceaue mee.
O, let this be thy will, to frequent my ruſtical harbors,
And ſimple cotages, and ſticke in forkes to vphold them,
And driue on forward our flocke of kids to the mallowes:
Wee wil amid the foreſt contend *Pans* ſong to reſemble:
Pan was firſt that quils with waxe ty'de ioyntly together.
Pan is good to the ſheepe, and *Pan* is good to the ſheepſman.
Neither think it a ſhame to thy ſelf t'haue plaid on a cornpipe:
For, that he might do the ſame with skil, what did not *Amyntas*?
Damætas long ſince did giue me a pipe for a token,
Compact of ſeűn reedes, all placed in order, vnæquall:
And thus ſayd, when he dy'de: One vſed it onely beefore thee.
Thus ſayd *Damætas,* this greeued fooliſh *Amyntas.*
Alſo two prety kids doe I keepe, late found in a valley
Dangerus: & their skins with mylke white ſpots be bedecked,
Of dams milke not a drop they leaue; & for thee I keepe them,
Theſtylis of long time hath theſe kids of me deſired;
And they ſhalbe her own, for that thou skornſt what I giue thee.
Come neare, ô faire boy, ſee the nymphs bring here to the lillies
With full ſtuft baskets: faire *Nais* now to thy comfort
White violets gathering, and poppies daintily topping, (Dill.
Daffadil ads to the ſame, & leaues late pluckt fro the ſweete
Then mingling Caſia with diuers ſauory ſweet flowrs,
With yelowiſh Marygold, ſhe the tender Crowtoe bedecketh,
Ile plucke hoare quinces, with ſoft downe all to beſmeared,
And Cheſſnuts which were loűd of my ſweet *Amaryllis.*
Add wil I wheateplumbs too: for this fruit will be regarded,
And you laurell leaues wil I plucke, and thee, prety myrtle
Next to the laurell leaues: for ſo plâſt yeeld ye the ſweet ſent.
Th'art but a foole *Corydon,* for firſt gifts mooue not *Alexis,*
Then, though thou giue much, yet much more giue wil *Iolas.*
But what alas did I mean, poore foole? I do let go the ſouthwind
Into the flowrs, & boares ſend forward into the cleare ſprings.

Whom flyêſt thou mad man? Many gods haue alſo reſorted,
And *Paris* of olde *Troy*, to the woods. Let towers by *Minerua*
Built, by *Minerua* be kept; and woods of vs onely regarded.
Grim Lioneſſe runneth to the wolfe, & wolfe to the yong gote,
And wanton yong gote to the flowring tetrifol haſtneth,
And *Corydon* to *Alexis*: a ſelfe ioy draweth on each man.
But ſee the plow coms home hangd faſt by the yoke, to the bul-
And ſhadoe by *Phœbus* declining double appeareth: (locks,
Yet do I burne with loue: for what meane can be to louing?
Ah *Corydon*, *Corydon*, what mad rage hath thee bewitched?
Thy vin's ſcarſe halfe cut, peſtred with leaues of her elme tree:
Leaue this churliſh boy, and bend thy ſelfe to thy buſnes,
With twigs and bulruſh ſome needefull thing be a making:
Thou ſhalt find others though th'art diſdaind of *Alexis*.

There bee, saith Freigius 2. partes of the Aeglogue.

- First the propounding of the argument, which is of the incontinency of a louer lamenting his loue in solitary places,
- Secondly the complaint and lamentation of Corydon the louer, speaking
  - First to his loue, and that by
    - Accusing his crueltie, which is argued
      - First by comparison of the vnlikes, the proposition consisteth of three vnlikes, the beastes, Lysardes, and reapers seeke shade: the reddition is, but yet I burne with loue.
      - 2. By the lesse Amaryllis and Menalcas are too cruell, but thou more cruel then they.
      - 3. By the cause of his pride, whiche was his beautie, and ẏ is extenuated by a simily. As white primprint fales, but blacke Violets bee gathered, so beautie decayes, and blacknes remaines.
    - Enticing him to come to his house to sing, to driue the kids to the Mallowes, &c. and that by praysing of himselfe by his adiunctes. AAA
  - DDD

A A A Corydons adiuncts be these: he is

- Rich, and his riches be proued by specials
  - his lambs
  - his mylke.
- Skilfull in singing, and that is proued.
  - By a comparison of the equall, in that hee is equall to Amphion: and heere an obiection is preuented by a comparison also of the equall: neither thinke it a shame to play on a pype, for Amyntas thought well of it. Then the prayse of his singing is continued by his pype, and his pype by the autor that gaue it, which was Damætas, and another that enuyed it, to wit Amyntas.
- Faire & comly: it is proued by
  - The adiunct of his image in the water
  - Comparison of the equall, as was Daphnis.
- Franke and free, which is proued by his sundry giftes.
  - 1. His kydds, commended by their adiunctes, in that they were white spotted, well sucking, and desired of Thestylis.
  - 2. His basket of sweete flowers gathered by the Nymphes, they be hearbs and also flowers, as,
    - Lillyes.
    - Violets.
    - Poppy.
    - Dylle.
    - Daffadil.
    - Cassa.
    - Marigold
    - Crowtoe
  - 3. His diuerse kindes of
    - Fruits as
      - Quinces.
      - Chesnuts.
      - wheatplums.
    - Boughs as bee
      - The Lawrell.
      - The Myrtle.

DDD. Secondly to himselfe, by resisting himselfe, as it were, and here is conteyned both a

- doble correction or calling backe of himselfe.
  - the first is both of the
    - adiunct, pride, and contempt of hys gifts and here is
      - First a double exclamation: and here
        - in the first hee noteth Alexis his pride by two similies, ÿ south winde, and the boare.
        - in ÿ secōd he entreateth againe, by the equals, as Paris, and ÿ gods &c.
      - Secondly a permission by the unlike. Let Pallace keep her Pallaces, and wee the woodes which is our delight. The reddition is made playne by comparison of lykes: where also the generall is concluded by the specialles in a Clymax of three degrees, Grimme Lyonesse to the Wolfe &c.
    - More, or greater, for Iolas gaue more largely then hee.
  - the second is of the adiunctes both of
    - The tyme, where there is a Periphrasis of night, and an argument of the diuers, albeit the heate of the sunne is mitigated by the comming of the night, yet I burne still with loue: the reason followeth of the adiunct of loue: for loue hath no meane.
    - his businesse neglected, where is a double negligence: of
      - his vine halfe cut
      - his elme full of boughes
      - for both be naught.
- Remedy of loue by cōtraries which be:
  - businesse in making some needefull thinge of twigs and bulrush.
  - and hope of some other louer, if Alexis should still thus disdaine him.

For the Earle of Northumberlands case, I haue rather shewed what is donne by maister Plowden, then what might haue béene donne by a better Logician. Le matter fuit argue en Leschecquer M.9.& 10. Elis. deuāt touts les Justices d'angleterre et Barons deschecquer, per Onslow Sollicitor, Gerard Atturney, Wray & Barrham seriants le roigne, del part le roigne: et per Shirborne et Bell. apprētices et Meade seriants del part le Coūte. Le case fuit tiel; l'attorney le roigne informe le court, que ou le roigne doyt auer touts mynes de ore et d'auter mettail conteignant ore per prerogatiue, el 10. Martij. An. 8. regni sui esteant seisie en son demesne, come de fée en droit la corone, del wast dit Newland, in com. Northumberland, en queux certene veynes de quyure sont, conteignants ore; assigne T. & D, de fower &c. queux fowont 600000 poys &c. et le Counte eux disturbe: le Counte, protest: que le roigne ne doit auer per prerogatiue &c. pro ple dit, que quant al 500000 parcel del 600000, le terre in que &c. fuit done al counte per patent le roy et roigne P. & M. dat. a Richmond, le 15 del August 4. & 5. An. reg. &c. ex gratia speciali, certa scientia, & mero motu suis &c. et que il disturbe &c. et auerra, que cest veyne fuit ouert primes puis le dit 15 iour del August. an. 4. & 5. reg. &c. s. I. April. an. 7. Elis. et trauerse le seisine le roigne le dit 15. iour del March. Et pur les auter 100000, residue del 600000, il plede patent le dit roigne del honor del Cokermouth, oue wrecks, mines, &c et que le myne in que &c. fuit ouert iour del date del patent et deuant &c. issint il disturbe prout bien a luy list. sur que l'atturney le royne, demurre en ley. Les points sont generall, ou speciall. les general points sont deux: le primer, si touts mynes d'ore et argent in terres del subiects, oue poyar de fower le terre et asporter le ore &c. apperteigne al roy per prerogatiue, car nest in le treatise de prærogatiua regis, et le fower tutch le francktenement et l'inheritance d'auter. Le second, si mynes de Copper conteignant ore ou argent, perteigne al roy vt supra. Le proper et speciall poynt que immediatement concerne le case del Counte, est, si les mynes de quyure cōteignāt ore ou argent, perteigne al roy per prerogatiue, Vtrum le graunt P. & M. del terre en le primer case, et de touts et singuler mynes en l'auter case per patent de gratia &c. fait les mynes de passer del eux al dit Counte, on nemy.

Or doncques primerment est a dire de les arguments de les

dits

dits seriants et apprentices, puis de le iudgment et opinion des Justices.

Les arguments del primer point, pur le roigne, sont in confirmando, ou confutando: les confirmant arguments sont inherent ou borowed, come testimonies et autorities: les inherents sont quater, et Onslow fait troys de eux, et Gerard le quart.

- Le primer. est deryue del adiunct excellency del roy et de ceux mettayles, &c. sic,
  - Les choses plus excellents del terre perteigne al person pluis excellent que est le roy: probatur a pari,
    - Les choses plus excellent del mer et eawe perteigne al roy per comon ley. A A.
    - Ergo et ceux del terre, come ore et argent,
  - Mes ore et argent sont le pluis excellent choses del terre:
  - Ergo ore et argent perteigne al roy, &c. et les mynes eux conteignants &c.

A A.

Cest premier part del enthymeme est confirme per nouel syllogisme, conteignant vn argument del special, issint constitute.

Le comen ley approprie al roy sturgions et baleynes que sont deins le mere en engleterre: s. les braches del mere: et ceo est proue per deux testimonyes.

Le primer est de treatise de prærogatiua regis, cap. 11. (que n'est nouel ley, mes declaration del comon ley) s. Rex habebit balenas & sturgiones captos in mari, vel alibi infra regnum.

Le second est del Britton que escry long temps deuant le treatise de prærogatiua regis et il monstre en son chapter de trouours que le roy auera les pisches per prerogatiue per le comen ley en son temps.

Mes del choses de la mer, les pisches, et de pisches, les sturgions et baleines sont plus excellentes.

Ergo le comen ley appropie al roy les choses plus excellentes de la mere et eaw.

Le second argument est del causes principalls et coadiuuants: s. le roy, et le treasure: queux ambideux deuont concurrer al mayntenaunce del realme:

Il est reason que il que ad le regiment et tutel del people come principall cause, queux il ne peuit defender sans adiuant et instrumentall causes, auoit ces aydes et causes adiuuants.

Mes l'office le roy que le ley a luy apoint est de defender ses subiectes: et le treasure, que est terme les senows del guerre, est le adiuuant cause pour defender eux vers tout hostilitie.

Ergo il est conuenient que le roy auerope le treasure et mynes de ore et argent, en queux consist cest treasure.

Le tierce conteigne un final cause et use del money que est, d'estre coigne, printe, et value. Car donques solement il est currant pur le cõmoditie del subiects en lour mutual commercion ou traffique

A que il apperteigne de metter certeine print et price sur le ore et argent issint que il poet estre disperse enter les subiects, per entercourse de merchandise, vender achater &c. A cestui il apperteigne daver l'ore et argent.

Mes ces choses tant solement apperteignont al roy mesme, et a nul auter. Car il fuit graund treason per le comen ley devant l'estatute de Anno. 25. E. 3. ca. 2. come il apiert per 23 E. 3. lib. ass. ou feme fuist arse pur fauxer ou counterfeiter money

Ergo al roy apperteigne les mynes et owres del ore et argent.

Gerard fait le quart argument, conteignãt les pernicieux effects del cest donation de ore et argent al subiects.

Ceo que ouste le convenientcy et bone proportion del members del bien publique en feasant le subiect et servant greinder que le roy et governor: doyt estre remove hors del bien publique, come chose pernicieux et causant rebellion, contempt, et honor en le subiect, mes deposition, peril, et danger en le roy.

Mes le graunting del mynes de ore et argent al subiects fait &c.

Ergo ceo doit estre remove hors del bien publique.

Ore est adire del testimonies queux sont de deux genres: les primers sont matters de record, et charters le roy: les auters sont escripts, dicts, et edicts del certeine homes: primermēt pur les primers, mittomus cest foundement derive del effects et uses et custumes del predecessors, et certeine adiuncts incidents a les dits choses.

- Ceo que est use de temps del un roy puys auter, oue l'assent del iudges et auters sages del ley, et dont les charters et recordes sont enrolles en leschequer, come choses de effect, et come foundations al accoumpts, ne poet estre dit tortious. Car ley n'est sinon per usage, et usage proue que il est ley.
- Mes que mynes de ore et argent, en auters soyles sont al royne per prerogatiue, est consonant al use &c. Vide, A A A.
- Ergo il n'est tortious.

A A A.

Le minor est confirme per diuers precedentes, et matters de record hors de leschequer q; est le court del reuenues le roy en tēps de diuers royes: les records sont

- primerment recitees et sōt en troys maners,
  - ascuns sont charters fait de graunt de mynes de ore et argent en auter soyle: Vide, OO.
  - Ascuns prouont accoumpts de reuenue del tyel mynes en auter soyle, d'estre rendue al roy. R R.
  - Ascuns prouont que le roy ad impled pernours del profite des owres &c. in terre de auters. N N N.
- Puys, lour auctoritie est confirme. B B.

OO. Les

OO.
Les recordes del 1. genre sont huyct:

1 En temps le roy. E. 3. 32. Anno.
2. Fuit charter le roy: R. 2. 8. en le explication du quel, est conteigne cest syll:

Si le owre de ore et argent est al roy, le ley done a luy meanes de vener a ceo, que est per fower.

Mes le owre de ore et argent est al roy.

Ergo le ley done a luy meanes de vener a ceo, que est per fower.

3. Per le roy: H. 4. 2
4. Per le roy. H. 6. 5.
5. Per le roy. H. 6. 11.
6. Per le roy. E. 4. 15.
7. Per le roy. E. 4. 18.
8. Per le roy. H. 7. 1.

RR.
Ceus de second espece sont deux:

L'un accoumpt fuit fait et rendue en l'escheequer sur le lease del mynes de ore et argent et quiure fait per le roy Ed. le tierce a Iohan Balauncer, et VValter Goldbeater: per quel apiert que le roy fuit responde del 20. markes pur le primer an, et riens pur le second an, pur ceo que les lessees moreront, et le roy auoyt graunte les mynes as auters.

Lauter accoumpt fuit fait per Henry euesque de VVinchester Cardinal d'engleterre, un del executors Iohn Duke de Bedford, fermour de les mynes de ore et argent en les counties de Deuon. et Corn. de le 15. part del pure argent reserue sur le graunte, f de le 15. iour de December an: 22. H. 6. iesques al 16. iour de August an. 23. mesme le roy: et sur ceo accoumpt il rende trent size lyuers pois de pure argent, et deux ounces surdant de mesme le 15. part.

NN. N'est forsques, un example de pernours del owre, impledees per le roy. 36. H. 6. f. ceo de Roger Chambernoume, que pur son discharge fuit chase de suer al roy pur pardon, sachant per son counsel, que il ne puyst defender le matter per le comen ley.

BB. Lauto.

BB Lautoritie del recordes auandits est confirme en deux maners 1. per vn generall axiome. que est tiel, les Recordes de chescune court sont le pluis effectuall proufes del ley en choses treates en ceo court: et ceo que est vse en vn court, est ley en touts courtes, et per tout le realme: sic hic, nul proofe del reuenue le roy est pluis fort que les recordes del court en que le reuenue est rend s. Leschequer. le axiome auantdit est proue per le particuler enumeration de les special matters subiects del courts le roy, Car

Quant al matters del corone, s. en appeales de felony, et enditementes de murder et treason, et tyels semblables, si question surde, quel est ley en tyels choses et quel non, les Recordes del bank le roy, sont le pluis effectuall proofe de ceo: et ceo que est vse la doit estre prise come proofe del ley per tout le realme. Car ceo court treate de tiels choses et a iurisdiction de eux, et les recordes la, sont tesmoignes del ley en ceux points.

Et les Recordes et precedentes del comen banke, in le propertie del biens ou chatels reals ou personals, ou droits ou tytles en terres et tenementes.

Ergo eodem modo les Recordes del eschequer, pur choses concernants le reuenue le roye, et que apperteignont al roye et que port ou attreit reuenue al roy. et ceo est confirme per le recitall del special cases dont iugement fuit done accordant al Recordes del exchequer. M. M.

M.M. Les

MM.
Les speciall cases sont ceux

Primerment le case de Littleton cap. socag. que action de accoumpt ne gist vers executors pur ascun, si non pur le roy tantsolement, est prove per le Records del eschequer, lou accoumpts pur duities le roy sont discusse & responde, et que accoumpera, et que nemy.

2. In le case touche per Littleton cap. de grand seriantie, hors del. 11. H 4. Cockein chiefe baron demaund des iustices del comen bank, si vn tient del roy a trouer a luy vn home al guerre deins les 4. meres, si fuit grand seriantie ou nemy, ou fuit responde, que fuit: et adonques il demaund si le roy auera reliefe solonque le value del terre ou nemy, ad quod non fuit responsum, car ils ne besoigne de responder luy a ceo, pur ceo que si fuit grand seriantie, il poet scyer per le vsage en le eschequer, quel summe il payera &c.

3. Et dillonques vient le notice del ley a Littleton, que si le villeine le roy purchase biens, et alien eux deuant seiser, que vncore le roy poet eux seiser apres, car tyelment fuit le vsage del eschequer, en quel court tiels biens fueront responduc al roy, et la il apprise, quòd nullum tempus occurrit regi.

4. Issint en le case sir William Sentlow, que a mary le feme de sir William Candish, mise per Gerard per que il apiert. que si ascun est accoumptant al roy, ou si ascun money ou biens ou chatels personals del roy, veigne al mains dascũ subiect per matter de record, ou matter en fait, que le terre de tiel subiect est charge pur ceo, et subiect al seisure le roy, en quecunque mains que il veigne apres, soit il per discent, ou purchase, ou anterment.

5. Et sur semblable reason le case est rule in 50. lib. Ass. lou vn R. auoit receaue certeine biens de sir Hugh Spencer que fuit atteint, per que les deniers attient al roy. R. que auoit les ioyntenent oue sa feme, morust: et per agreement de touts les iustices, le terme en les mains le femme suruiuor fuit charge al execution le roy pur les deniers. Car le roy puit auer execution de ceo en le vie le baron, que fuit garrant per moults recordes en le eschequer.

Mm. Iesques

Iesques icy nous auons propose le confirmation del Recordes, per vne generall axiome prouee per diuers specials: ore est a dire del secōd proofe, que est vn argument a fortiore.

Les reports de nostre ley sont fait pur le pluis grand part de les parols et dits de les iudges, et ceo en que ils assentont est prise de estre le ley.

Ergò a fortiori lour iudgements et lour affaires entres de Recorde en courtes, doyent estre prise de cy grand, ou pluis grande effect, que lour parols, ou dits.

Ore est a dire de second kinde de testimonyes s. de les escripts, dicts, et edicts de certeine homes, Et sont quater. le quart de queux est illustre per vn argument a diuersis.

1. Fuit dit per Gerard que en le lyuer appelle expositiones vocabulorum que fuit mise en print 40. ans passe, il est declare que mynes de ore et argent en quecunque terres que ils sont, afferont al roys de realme.

2. Issint Wray dit, que Hesket apprentice que fuit perbien apprise en le ley, en son lecture extant sur le statute de charta forrestæ, affirmast, que si fueront mynes de ore et argent en terre del subiects deins le forrest, que ceux afferont al roy.

3. Issint il dit que il auoyt view les leys de saynt Edvvard le confessor, en queux fuit conteigne, quòd thesauri de terra pertinent domino regi.

4. Issint dit Barrham del leys William Conquerour queux il auoyt view, queux auoyent semblables parolles, queux leys fueront recites a luy per les sages del realme a ceo iures, que ils deuant mesme le roy W. Conquerour verament reciteront les leys del terre, nihil prætermittentes.

Queux parolles Thesauri de terra, les dits seriaunts pristeront pur owres de ore et argent, et nient pur treasor troue. Car disoyent que ils sont appelles, Thesauri in terra, et nemy de terra, et issent diuersa.

Assets

Touts les prerogatiues le roy sont conteines en le treatise de prærogatiua regis.

Mes que le roy aueroyt les owres &c n'est conteigne en le treatise de prærogatiua regis.

Ergò n'est ascune prerogatiue le roy.

assets est dit de les arguméts que fueront in confirmando, or est besoigne de dire de les arguments in confutando. Car il poet estre dupliciter obiect 1. tyelment per vn argument a toto.

Primerment, le treatise de prærogatiua regis n'est ascun cause per quel le roy aueroyt ceux prerogatiues. Car le'effect ne poet preceder le cause. Mes les prerogatiues la recitees en maner touts fueront al roy deuant le dit treatise escrye. Ergò ceo treatise n'est cause del prerogatiues le roy, le minor, ou assumption est proue ab adiunćto temporis, car le pluis grand part de eux est recite per Britton en son lyeur en le chapter de trouers et de droits le roy quel lyeur fuyt fayt deuant le treatise de prærogatiua regis.

A cest obiection il est dupliciter respondue: Car le proposition, s. le maior est false pur deux causes.

2. N'est ascun argument a toto ad partes, car le treatise auantdit n'est totum, en respect del particuler prerogatiues le roy. Car ceo treatise ne conteigne touts les prerogatiues le roy, mes part de eux: et issiut le argument nient conclude. Et il est proue que ceo treatise ne conteigne touts les prerogatiues le roy, per vn induction de moults special prerogatiues, nient comprehends en ceo treatise, tielment, NN.

NN.

1. Le roy auera action ou suite d'accoumpt vers les executours del testator le roy, per prerogatiue donc a luy per le ley.

2. Il auera les biens son villeine vende deuant seisur.

3. Il seysera le terre que fuit a cesty que doit render accoumpt a luy, ou que auoyt receu ascune biens ou chateux del roy, en quecunque mains que mesme le terre veigne apres.

4. Il poet wayuer issue, et demurrer en ley, ou econtra, poet wayuer demurrer, et pleader al issue.

5. Il auera treasure troue.

6. Il auera escheate de eux atteint de treason.

7. Deuant l'estatute de 1. Ed. 3. il aueroyt en fee le terre tenus de luy, et alien sans licence.

8. Il auera, pur satisfaction de sa det, ceo que est deliuer en court en execution al dettour le roy. Ed. 3. 43.

9. Si le patron ne present deins 6. moys, et le euesque et apres luy de metropolitane suffer le laps, ou si euesque patrone, et le metropolitane suffer le laps, le roy auera le presentment, per son prerogatiue: 27. E. 3.

Et uncore ceux prerogatiues ne sont recite en le treatise de prærogatiua regis.

Ergò le treatise de prærogatiua regis ne conteigne touts les prerogatiues le roy.

Le second obiection est tyel ab adiuncta iniuria.

- Ceo que touche le francktenement et inheritance del subiect, ne doyt estre fayt per le roy.
- Mes de fower terre, et prender dillonques le owre, quel est part del soile, touche le francktenement le subiect.
- Ergo le roy ne doit ceo faire. LL.

LL.
Le maior, le proposition du cesty syllogisme est false : que poet estre proue per deux arguments.

Le primer est a pari, a le pareil.

Car sicome prescription et vsage poet doner tytle ou interest al subiect en le franktenement ou inheritance le roy, come in commen, ou voy, ou estouers clayme per prescription en le terre del roy, ou en wayues, estrayes, wrecks, ou tiels semblables pertinent de droyt al roy, et uncore clayme per prescription per les subiectes : Issint et per mesme le reason, prescription et vsage poet doner al roy tytle ou interest en auter franktenement: car il ne serra de pyer codition que le subiect, que auera ceo per prescription vers les subiects et vers le roy.

Le second est derive del vn enumeration de speciall prerogatiues que le roy ad en franktenements dauters. FF.

FF.

1. Deuant le'estatute de magna charta, le roy per son prerogatiue puit entrer en auter boys et prendre arbres pur reparation de ces castels.

2. Deuant l'estatute de charta forestæ. cap. 2. le roy puit afforester le boys del auter home per que il fuit restraygne de succider son boys demesne sans licence.

3. Il apiert P. 7. H. 3. que le roy, et auter per son commaundement poet enfreinder un stewe, que est auter francktenement, et prendre le pische pur son prouision per force de son prerogatiue.

4. Villeine, que est le francktenement et l'inheritaunce d'un auter, vient en le presence le roy: le seigniour del villeine, ne puit luy prendre en le presence le roy, 27. lib. Ass. Car le presence le roy est protection pur luy pur le temps.

5. Si le roy ad rent charge en fee hors del ascun terre il poet distreyner pur ceo per son prerogatiue, en tout auter terre de cesty que le doyt payer: 13. E. 4.

Mes en touts ceux cases, le francktenement et inheritance del auter est touche.

Ergò le roy poet per prescription auer prerogatiues touchant le francktenement dauter.

Touts ceux arguments fueront faits del part le roygne. Ex parte comitis, Shirbourne sole, alledge le opinion de Newton: 19. H. 6. per implication deste al contrary: ou il dit, que si home done terre en fee que ne vault 40. d. et percase le terre per casuel aduenture en cell, come per myne de ore ou argent troue, vault per an 100. li. Si l'impledee vouche le feoffor al garranty, il poet monstrer coment le terre ne vault forsques 40. d. al temps de feoffement, et a cel il est prist dentrer en le garranty, ceo serra bon plee, et ne garrentera pluys que fuit al temps del feoffment. Mes sil enter generalment en le garrantie, il rendra in value tant come il est ore: ex que dit (il dit) que fuit imply per l'intent del Newton, que le myne de ore et argent serra recouer oue le terre, et ne serra al roy.

Quant

Quant al second general point fuit inferre pur le roygne, que si issint soit que le roygne auera per prerogatiue touts les mynes de ore et argent en les terres de subiects, que de ceo il voet ensuer en maner come consequent, que il doyt auer ceux owres et mynes de quiure ore en question, s. cybien le cinquecent mille pois contenus en le primer ple en barre, come l'auter cent mille pois contenus en le second barre: plusors sont reasons.

Le primer est quasi a parte precipua que trayt a luy le tout

Si le ore et argent appertaine al roy, donques les quiure apperteigneroit: car le ore ou argēt et le quiure sont ensemble, et en le soile indiuisible, et leur commixture fait eux come vne chose entier: & omne magis dignum trahit ad se minus dignum, come ore et argent le quiure: cest confirme per treys speciallcs que sont semblables. (4.)

Mes le ore et argent apperteigne al roy, et est confesse que mesme sixcentmille pois de quiure conteigne en soy ore ou argent.

Ergò le quyure a luy apperteigneroit.

Le secōd est ab adiuncta absurditate,

Si quiure apperteigne al' subiects que ne poet estre seuere mes per foundre, issint le roy serroit seruant al subiect pur fower et foundre son quyure.

Mes ceo est tout irreasonable et absurde.

Ergò il ne apperteigneroit al subiects, mes al roy.

(4)

A A.
Selõ l'exposition auant dit, ils

primerment interpretont

Ceux parolls, aliquid auri vel argenti habeatur, issint que ceo aliquid soit tant que vault le charge del Fower et fercher &c. car autermēt cest aliquid, n'est aliquid, mes cest aliquid nihil est, et meyns que nihil, Car ex nihil home auera nihil, mes icy de cest aliquid il auera perde, si pur acquirer le ore de value de 4. d. il serra al charge de 5. d.
Et le maxime, quòd omne magis dignum &c. Car ceo est intendible ou le chose pluis digne est de ascun value, ou de pluis value que le base chose est. Car de minimis non curat lex, come en action de wast del 2 d le plaintife nauera iudgement: et cest lour interpretation de ceux parols de etre intelligibles lou fuit grand abondance de ore en les mynes est confirme per le reseruation del roy H. 4. S. Nonam libram de argento puro inde proueniente, issint que le roy intende grande quantitie de argent de estre en les mynes, entant que il n'ad reserue ascun part dauter mettall.

puis reprehendont l'information per argument a descriptione. Car,

Information pur le roy est le declaration le roy, quel doit conteiner certeintie, issint que le partie auera perfect scyence a quel chose respõdera, et le court de quel chose il adiudgera.

Mes icy per l'information et le respons est disclose et confesse que le counte ad prise sizecentmille pois de owre de quiure conteignant en soy ore ou argent troue et fowe en son terre demesne, s. cinquecentmille pois en myne apert puis que le counte fuit seigniour del soile, et centmille pois en myne en son soile apert deuant que il fuit seigniour del soile: et ne apiert si le ore et argent en tyel owre fuit de greinder value que le quyure, ou al meyns d'ascun value ouster le charge de acquisition, et ouster le base mettell, pur sac... le loyaltie del fayt del counte.

Ergò n'est bon Information.

Iesques

Iesques icy del general points ore est a dire del speciall, que est proue del part le counte per vn enthymeme conteynant leffect et graunt le roy et royne: a partibus ad totum.

Le roy et royne P. et M. ont en l'une case graunt al counte le terre en que le owre fuit, et en lauter case le myne per le nome de touts et singuler mynes. Car le vaine dont les 500000. pois &c. ne fuit myne al temps del date al counte, eo que fuit close, pur ceo passera per graunt del soile, come part de soile. Mes en le second plec le vaine passera per nome de mynes, car le vaine fuit patent &c.

Cest antecedent del enthymeme est pleinement illustre per vn amplification del obiections que poent estre fait del auter parte encounter le counte: et cest preoccupation est derive del diuers adiuncts incidents al patents le roy et royne QQQ.

Ergo tout ceo que est conteigne en l'information perteigne al counte.

Le quatt est deduct hors de les dits recordes et est a genere, Issint,

Touts mynes en quex est ascun argent ou ore, apperteigne al roy,

Mes les mynes de quyure conteignont argent, Car nul myne d'estayne est voyde d'argent:

Ergò touts les mynes de quyure apperteigne al roy.

Et ceo est confirme per charter le roy Edw. le primer graunt al subiects del counte de Cornewale, cõfirme per le charter le roy R. 2. que fuit mitigate per lestat: de 50. E. 3. per queux apiert que lour autoritie en Cornewale et Deuon. de fower et de auer estayne fuit deriue del roy: et certaine quantitie del estayne est payable al corone pur tyel libertie tesque a ceo iour: come en ascun lieus en le countie de Darby le roy ad certayne quantitie del plumbe sur consideration que argent est en ceo, et que il abstepnera de vser le extremitie de son prerogatiue. Mes en Darbyshire et ailours ou sterile mynes de plumbe ont este apiert tout temps, et le roy nauoyt ascun profite, les subiects la poient prescriber pur ceo vers le roy, et le fower et prisel del plumb sans payment, est prescription pur le pays, et come Hesket auantdit tient, le prescription en tiel case est bone. Car il y auoit diuersite del mynes de plumbe, car ascunes fueront fertile, cestassauoir, conteignants en eux ore ou argent: et ascuns sterile, cestassauoir, sans ore, ou argent.

Iesques

Iesques icy del part le royne: ore est a dire del respons fait per part le counte, et ceo en deux maners. Car

Primerment ils, supposant le autoritie de Recordes estre tresgrande, donont a eux vn reasonable expositiō. Car il ny ad ascune myne de estayne, de quiure, ou de plumbe, ne de ferre, mes que ascun ore ou argent poet etre treate ou finate hors de ceo (et issint le roy aueroit touts mynes de base mettale deins le realme, que est absurde) denques icy le roy auera ceux prerogatiues, ou le ore et argent que est en le base mettale, excede le value del base mettale, ou al meins suffist al porter touts les expences destre defray entour le acquisition de ceo, et selon cest exposition ils primerment interpretont les parols del records et le maxime de magis digno, puis print exception contre l'information. A A.

1. ils denyont tam bien.

Le autoritie de Recordes, come choses faits al importunate request de eux que fueront al royes pur gaigner, et tollerate per les subiectes, eo que ils aueront part del gayne, issint ils vituperant l'effect pur le cause &c.

Come ceo que est collect del charter le royes al ceux de Cornewale: Car appert per les parols del charter que lour libertie ne prist original comencement, mes tantsolement confirmation et direction per ceux charters et coment que le roy ad ascun profite, ceo nest en respect de ascun interest en le chose, mes pur porter le charge des officers, s. tryers, controllers &c. scome il ad del merchants, car il appoint serchers &c. queux auont stipends de les merchants &c. tamen nont ascun property in lour merchandise &c.

En ceuse del charters del inheritance estcantes en un cyste ou boxe enseale, si le possessor ent morust, les charters afferont al heyre, et le boxe, si fuit ouert, al executours: Mes entaunt que est enseale, et issint les charters, et le boxe sont fait une chose entier, et les charters sont pluis precious que le boxe le heyre que ad propertie al charters, auera le boxe auxi, et nyent les executors, sur le reason auantdit.

Issint si une chariot que est traye oue sixe chiuals eschue sur un, et luy tue: les chiualles serront forfayt al roy come Deodand eybien come le charyot que tue l'home, pur ceo que ils fueront attache al chariot, et issint fueront come un chose ensemble, que occasionont son mort.

(4.)

Issint si obligation est fait a deux, ou deux sont possesse d'un chyuall, et l'un est attaint, le roy auera le obligatiō, et tout le duitie, ou le chyuall, pour ceo que il est chose entier.

Donques per semblable reason et ley, pur ceo que le ore ou argent et le quiure sont ensemble, et en le soile indiuisible, et lour commixture fait eux entier, le roy auera tout ensemble. Quia magis dignum &c.

3. A generaltyelment,
- Touts mynes et owres portāts ore ou argent et base mettayle ensemble que sont en soyle dauters perteignont al royne: et ceo est proue per specials.
- Mes le information conteine que cest myne côteigne en luy ore et argent auec le quiure: et n'est dedit per respons, mes pleinement confesse.
- Ergò cest mine ē le terre le counte perteigne al royne:
  - 1. Records dont le
    - Primer est an. 7. E. 3.
    - 2. 17. R. 3.
    - 3. 7. H. 4.
    - 4. 17. H. 6.
    - 5. 30. H. 6.
    - 6. 31. H. 6.
    - 7. 33. H. 6.
    - 8. 34. H. 6.
    - 9. 2. E. 4.
    - 10. 8. E. 4.
  - 2. accoumpts rende al roy dont,
    - Le primer fuit fait per William Wymoundham del profits del mynes en les counties de Deuon. et Corn. del 12. iour de August. An. 22 E. 1. iesques le 23. de September, 25. eiusdem regis.
    - Le second per William de Aulton clerke pur les profits del mynes en les counties de Deuon. et Corn. del quart del March, 26. E. 1. iesques le 18. de Aprill, 27. eiusdem regis.
    - Le tierce, per Mathew Crawthorne, de les mynes in Deuon. et Corn 15. E. 3.
    - Le quart per Iohn Maneron que succede Crawthorne, fait del 19. E. 3. iesques al 23. Eiusdem regis.
    - Le sinque per vn Robart Glouer.

An. Le

QQQ.
Les adiuncts incidents al fait et patents sont,

- primerment recites briefement, et opposes encoũter les obiections del auter part car les parols,
  - De gratia sua speciali, pretend grand fauour le roy, et son bountifulnes vers le patentee.
  - Ex certa scientia pretend pleine intelligence de roy et royne en le matter, et exclude tout ignorance.
  - Ex mero motu, testifie, que il nauoit ascun suyt ne suggestion de patentee, mes que le primer motion, et tout le sequel al perfection del patent procede del roy mesme, et pur ceo, le effect del patent serra le pluis amplement extende al benefice le patentee.
- secondement pluis amplifies,
  - Tam bien per vn distinct proposition de les obiections et seueral applying de respons. BB,
  - Come de nouel confirmation de ceo per induction de specialls. SS.

B B. Dōques le,

- Primer
  - obiection est tyel, car,
    - Ascun de part le roy et royne poet dire, que quant ils granteront le terre, que ils ne conusteront que tyel vayne de owre fuit en ceo, ou quant ils graunteont omnes & singulas mineras, que ils ne conusteront que ore ou argent fuit en les mynes.
  - respons est,
    - 1. Propose tielment.
      - Sir, ils mesme ont tesmoigne le contrary, south le grand seale dengleterre, que est tesmoigne de verite, et nient impugnable en exedit. Car, ont dit, ex certa sciētia, que est tant a dire, que ils ont conusance de chescune chose materiall.
    - 2. Confirme per vn argument, a maiori.
      - In 43. E. 3. Thorp dit, si vn manor a que vn auowson est appendant soit en le mayne le roy per escheate, ou purchase, si le roy a ceo iour done le manor a vn home auxi entierment come vn tiel tenoyt devant que il vient en nostre mains per voy descheate, ou que vn tiel tenoit que nous enfeoffa, le auowson passera, sans dire, cum fœdis & aduocationibus: et le cause est pur ceoque le ley entēd en tiel case, que le roy est apprise de sa droit, quòd curia concessit Ia, et si serra dit issint en ceo case, lou n'est prise mes per implication que le roy est apprise de son droyt: a fortiore serra prise issint, l'ou le roy issint dit per expresse parolles.
- Second, O.
- Tierce, R.

O.
Le second

- obiection, — Si ascune voet dire que les parolls serront straitement prise vers le patentee, et beneficialment vers le roy et le royne.
- respons, — Sir, ceo patent fuit fait per le roy et royne de gratia sua speciali : per queux parols ils signifiont lour fauour et grace al patentee, et per ceo donont intelligence que les parolles serront fauorablement interprete et largemente extende a son benefite et commoditie, et estraitment vers le royne.

R.
Le tierce,

- obiection, — Si home voet dire que le patentee ad done information al roy et royne, et ad fait suit de auer grant, et pur ceo chescun parol serra prise estraitement vers luy.
- respons: — Sir, le roy et le royne ont tesmoigne le contrary, car ils ont dit, que le graunt est fait ex mero motu suo, per quel ils voilent, que ceo fait de loure mere motion prendra effect amplement.

S.S.
Le nouel confirmation est per induction de sis special cases, eu ceux parols, ex gratia speciali, certa scientia, et mero motu, sont semblablement expoundes.

1. Per Hussey. 9.H. 7. 2. que prist difference inter patent ex certa scientia, et per informamur.
2. 1. H. 7. 13. en charter de pardon.
3. 3. H. 7. 6. en case de prior de Norwich.
4. 22. E. 4. 44. en case abbe de Waltam.
5. 36. et 37. H. 6. 24. en le case de Quatermaynes.
6. 41. E. 3. lib. Assis. 19. Licence de doner en mortmaine. A cest derniere case est adioigne vn auter reason, que si le counte nauera les mynes, donques riens passera per ceux parolles, omnes & singulas mineras &c. et en le generall conclusion est dit que le patent fuit fait deuant lestatute de 4. et 5. de le raygne de les dits roy et royne, fayt touchant lour letters patentes, & sic, est mult ayd per cest statute, que patents serront beneficialment expound pur le patentee, nient obstant le defect del very nosmer de les natures, genres et sorts de les hereditaments conteynes in tiels letters patents.

Le

Le counsel le roy encounter ceo, et consider deux points

Le primer est, si per le graunt de soile en que le owre fuit, fait ex gratia speciali, certa scientia & mero motu, le owre de quyure conteignant ore, ou argent (le vayn de quel ne fuit apert, mes secret) passera al patentee, ou nemy, et semble a eux, que nemy, Car.

1. Issint arguont,

Ceo que vient al roy en respect que il est possessor del corone, ne passera per graunt de terre Vide, L. L. L.

Mes le owre de ore et argent apperteigne al roy come il est possessor del corone, et nemy del terre: et en ceo respect il ad le owre en son soile, et en soile d'auter.

Ergò ne passera &c. Car sil alien le soyle, il n'ad per ceo alien ceo point de prerogatiue sa corone en sa soile.

2. Issint, et est respons al dit argument sur ceux parolles ex gratia speciali &c.

Car le patent que est issint fait, serra prise fauorablement al patentee: mes ceo est quant al chose expresse en le patent, que les parolles monstre de estre entende de passer, mes ceo ne voet faire auter chose de passer que n'est expresse per parolls de patent destre entende. Car si le roy graunt et entende vn chose, tiels parolls ne poyent faire deux choses de passer, come est en le case de Prior de Wenlocke: Non, ui natura bre: Fol. 232.

Le second est, si per le graunt fait de touts mynes, oue les parols susdits, si ceo myne de quiure conteignant ore ou argent passera al patentee ou nemy, et semble a eux que nemy.

P. P. P.

L. L. L.

Cest maior, seu propositio est proue per enumeration de,

- Particuler choses del prerogatiue que ne passont per done le soile, come
  - Wayue,
  - Estray,
  - Wreck,
  - Et tyels semblables choses que sont collaterall a le terre.
- Speciall cases ceo confirmants dont le
  - Primer est de manor deins vn forest le roy escheate al roy et done per le roy al auter &c.
  - Second est le lyuery grant al heyre de tenant le roy en capite, en quel le clause de salua al feme sa Dower per le roy assignanda, n'est conteigne.
  - Tierce est en 31. E. 3. de vn aduowson, descend a troys copercenerss et Fitz: Quare impedit 1.

P.P.P.

P P.P.
Quant al secōd point, et le graunt specifie en le second plee, s. de omnibus & singulis mineris, il est tielmēt argue encounter le counte,

1. Issint.

Termes en patentes de roys que comprehendont choses annexe al corone ou prerogatiue royall, ou de grand importance et chose de pluis base degree, serront prise et construe de faire les choses base solement de passer al patentees, et ceo est confirme per special cases. R.R.R.

mes en ceo patent est issint. Car sont deux maners de myns

Mynes royall que consist de ore ou argent ou de base mettalles conteignant en soy ore ou argēt.

Base mynes que consist solement de base mettalle et substance s. quyure, estayne, plumbe ferre ou carbones, et neyant en eux ore ou argent.

Ergò en ceo patent les termes serront construe de faire le base mynes passer, et nemy le royall.

2. 4. 4. 4.

3. 4. 4. 4.

R.R.R. Speciall cases.

1. En. 22. E. 3. lib. ass. 45. En grant al mayster de S. Lenard de bonis felonum, vbi excipitur treitor.

2. En returne de touts maner de briefes graunt albn, ou somons sont except, car touche le roy.

3. En graunt de fynes, issues &c. de ses tenants; il nauera fynes del home que est tenant de luy et del auter.

4. En 3. E 3. Fitz assise 445. de pount eschue et destre repaire ou generall charter le roy ne excuse le abbe que fuit charge per speciall cause.

5. En 9. H. 6. 56. En graunt le roy de terres en fee oue garrantie, le patentee ne recouera en value sans expresse parols. Car garrantie ad deux effects, l'une a rebutter, et ceo il fra la: lauter a recouer en value, et ceo ne fra en le case le roy sans precise parols.

6. En 2. H. 7. 6. En le case del counte de Northumberland, lou le graunt le roy des amerciamentes en tyel countie, ne trayt les amerciamentes del vicount, coroner, ou auter grand officer pur son misdemeanour, car ceux sont royall amerciaments.

7. En 43. E. 3. 15. lib. ass. En graunt le roy del duchy de Cornewale a son eigne fits, ou per generall graunt, vn speciall gard ne passa.

8. 5. E. 2. Fitz Quare impedit. 165. ou le roy pur aduowson en le countie Palantine de Durrham suist Quare impedit en le comon banck, lou pleder al iurisdiction del court graunt per le roy, ne excuse le pleadar.

9. 3. E. 3. Fitz. Graunt: 102. Ou le roy auoyt grant a vn abbe que il puit amortiser terres al value de 100. s. et vncore ne puit purchase auowson tenus del roy en chiefe. Cest case differ del case en 4. lib. ass. cite del auter part: car la, le charter le roy nosme le mease &c issint que ne poet estre entende, que il fuit ignorant del tenure, mes icy in 34. E. 3. Le patent est generall que il amortisera terre de value le 100. s. &c. Come dit Wray apprentice: mes auters ceo denyent, car le aduouson fuit hic nosme auxi.

10. 19 Fitz: Graunt: 58. Lou licence le roy de appropre l'aduowson ne puit faire aduowson tenus del roy destre appropre.

11. 1. H. 7 23. et 26. En case del sanctuary, ou le charter le roy generall ne fuist sufficient de faire sanctuary pur treason.

12. 18. H: 8: Brooke Estates: 84: et Patents, 104. En le case de Bowrehall en Essex, l'ou fuit tenus, que nul estate de inheritance passera, nyent obstant les parolls de gratia speciali, &c. per queux le roy auoyt grant ceo a vn home et ses heyres males. Donques les parols en charters le roy enureront al comen entent, et ne deuesteront del roy, choses de haut degree, ne choses annexe al corone in point de prerogatiue.

Car quant a ceo que Shirborne dit, que si le counte naucera les mynes royall, il auera ryens per le parolle, Mynes, car le base mynes passeront per le graunt del terre. Sir, que adonques ? ils sont parols de surplisage pur mines en mesme le terre, come sont les parols de graunter gards, maryages, et escheates, que sont plusors foits mise en patentes : ou autermnent poient prendre effect pur mynes que Henry le counte auoyt en terres dauters.

'4 4 4. Secondment ils respõd a ceo q; est dit del auter part.

Et quant a lestatute de 4. et 5. P. et M. Barrham dit, que voyer est q; l'act fait les letters patents bon nyent obstant le defect, del very nosmer de le natures, genres, et sortes de les hereditamentes : mes ceo serra solõq; le tenor de mesme les letters patentes. Et voyer est que l'act dit que les letters patentes serront expounde pluis beneficialment pur les patentees, mes solonques les parols et purport de les letters patents, et sur ceo ils issint conclude.

Si en le parol, terre, en lun case le owre royall nest graunt: ne en le parol, mynes, en lauter case : donques, la act nextende mes al base owre : et pur ceux serra beneficialment expounde en auantage del patentee : car ceo est, solonque le tenor et purport del patents.

Mes en le parol, terre, en lune case &c.

Ergò le act nextend mes al nature del base owre &c. car dextender al owre royall, serra contrary al purport del patent.

7.7.7.
3. Deux several opinions de ceux de ceo part sont recite, car ascuns arguont

- Issint
  - Ceo que est incident al corone inseparablement, ne poet estre graunt ou severe del corone, per expresse paroll.
  - Mes ceo myne, est cant myne royall, est incident al corone inseparablement, come escheate pur treason:
  - Ergò per expresse parolles ceo myne ne puit estre graunt ou sever del corone, multo minus sans expresse parolls.
- Ascuns encounter ceo, à maiori.
  - Si le ley soit tiel que le roy poet graunter point de sa prerogative a auter, à fortiore il le poet en nostre case, ou le chose n'est que revenue ou profite del corone, que poet estre ley bien lease ou demise a auter, sans rent, come pur rent.
  - mes le ley est tyel: que est proue per deux speciall cases
    - Le primer est en 20. E. 3. Fitz. Corone. 12. 5. lou le roy auoyt graunt as cytisens de Loundres que nul gagera battaile vers eux en appeale et uncore ceo est un chose annexe pluys procheine al prerogative le roy, et al person le roy.
    - Le second est issint: si home prist les biens le roy torciousment le roy poet prendre ou seiser ses biens tanque il ad fait restitution, come le comen use del eschequer est, uncore le roy graunt ceo al ville de Lynne. 8. R. 2. Fitz. Graunt placito ultimo.
  - Ergò multo magis il poet en nostre case &c.

Hactenus

Hactenus des arguments in vtramque partem: ore del opinio des Justices que est concernant,

- Le matter en ley, in les poins.
  - Generall, et
    - Pur le primer ils agreont.
      - Que touts mines d'ore et argēt, en quecunq; soyle, perteigne al roy per prerogatiue, oue libertie de fower, caryer &c.
      - Que mynes de quyure, estayne, plūbe, ou ferre sans ore ou argēt, perteigne al proprietor del soyle, car en base mettayle, null prerogatiue.
      - Et per Baron Freuil, q; sil y ad quiure in vne veyne sans ore, et in fower outer il apiert ore, et petite d'auter mettayle, ceo serra dit myne de quyure de ore, et nyent de quyure solement.
    - Pur le second, fuit agree per Harper, Southcot, et Weston, que si le value de ore ou argēt ne excede le value del base mettayle, tout affiert al proprietor del terre: mes si excede, tout est al roy, et serra dit Myne Royall.
  - Speciall,
    - Fuit agree per touts, que touts mynes Royall, soyent de pure ore ou argent, ou soyent de base mettayle conteynant ore ou argent, poyent per apt parolls estre graunt, car ne sont inseparablement incident al corone.
    - Fuit agree per touts forsque les troys auantdits, et per eux auxi, si ceux mynes in question sont royall mynes, que les owres in le primer ple specifie per grant del soile, ne le myne in le second per graunt del mynes, ne passeront al counte per le patent, mes besoigne d'auer speciall parolls, car soile et myne icy serront prise al comon intent pur base mynes &c.
    - Lact del 4 et 5. P. et M. ne ayd: car l'intēt del charter est del mynes base, et nextend al mynes royal, mes per Dyer si null myne soit forsque royall, donq; passeroit, car auter les parols serroint voyd, mes icy sont auters mynes, s. base perq; &c. et per mesme le Dyer comēt q; le myne in le primer ple ne fuit apiert al temps del date del patēt, vncore serra dit myne, car de Mineris aliquæ sūt occultæ, & aliquæ apertæ, Catlyn dit, que, les parols ad humilem petitionem eiusdem comitis, diminuont le force des parols, ex gratia speciali &c.
- Le pleading et information.
  - L'information fuit challēg per Mead, quia ne fuit mōstre en quel vil ou Hamel Newlands gist: mes fuit respōd, q; ne besoigne, quia n'est en effect forsq; pur trespas, et nul serra recouer forsq; dāmages: contra in action real, car l'a sur recouery, le vicount ne puit luy metter en seisin sans notice del ville &c.
  - Le pleading del part le counte fuit vicious: car doit auer mōstre q; le mine conteigne forsq; petite ore, ne tant come serra les charges: mes ceo il ne ad fait, iaq; per le general confession q; il ad ore, serra prise pluis beneficialmēt pur le roigne encoūter le pleadant, q; il ad effects del ore. Imò touts forsq; les troys auantdits agree que tout serra al roigne, coment q; le base mettayle soit de greinder value, coq; est confesse que ascune ore et argent fuit en ceo.

Plees

A Logicall Analysis of

Pleas del corone, sont q̃ contiegne offences faits encounter le corone et dignitie le roy atque hic Stanford agit.

1. Del nature des dits offẽces, ubi fait ascauoir q̃ les accessories deuant, s. les procurers, ou apres s. les receiuors ou fauorers, pari pœna plectentur. Stanf. 40:41:42.43: Home poet estre accessory al accessory, sil felonice receaua un accessory, 43. b. et la, 44: Licet un statute que fait ascune chose felony, ne parle des procurers et receiuers, uncore serront deins l'estatute. Offẽces encounter le corone sont.

- Felony, que est offence del corone, immediatè vers un comon person, et cõcerna les
  - Biens, A. A.
  - Le person, B:B:
- Treason, que est offence del Corone immediatè encounter l'estate le roy & roy-alme, est q;
  - Grand
    - Come compasser ou imaginer le mort le roy, sa roigne, lour eigne fits, violare le reigne, ou leigne file le roy nyent mary, ou le feme l'eigne fits le roy; Leuer guerre, adhererans enemies le roy: counterfeiter le grãd ou priuy seale, ou sa money: porter faux money in le realme-coũterfait au money dengleterre, tuer Chauncellor, Treasuror, Justice dascun banck, en eyre, ou assises, doyer et terminer, seants in lour place, et ce per Lest. de 25. E. 3. cap: 2: de proditionibus: Item counterfaitter de priuy seignet 1. M. cap: 6: vide lest: de Elis: ca: 11 et 18. Elis. ca. 1. de clippers, washers, filers, roũders, et lour abettours, quelconque soit le coyne, dummodo soit currant icy.
  - Petite
    - Vide mesme lest: de 25. E. 3: ca: 21: que n'est que explication del comõ ley. Come, Quant un seruant tua son maister, feme sa Baron, home seculer son prelate: feme sa mystres per 12. Ass. p. 30. 10. H. 6. 47. comẽt que soit hors de seruice dũmodo fit de malice conceaue in seruice. Fitz: 210. Imo les abbettors hic puniuntur eodẽ modo. Fitz: 216. Itẽ mitter excommengement south bul le pape, 30: Ass. 19. Item utlage debrusa le prison et amesne prisoners, 1: H: 6: 5: Vide Stamford, pag: 10. a. b.

2. Des penalties de mesmes offences. Q Q.

Huc refer misprision, s. le concealing de felony ou treason come, Justice de peace enrolla un bille denditement nyent troue per le pais: Estranger utter faux money, 3. H. 7. 10. Home trahe son espee de Ferir Justice seant en son place 22: E. 3: 13: Ferir ou bater un Juror, in presence des Justices Fitz: Iudg. 174, un ferist auter en le sale de West. Fitz. Cor. 280. Vide lest. 33. H. 8. ca. 12. Pur drawing blood in le meason le roy. Item per Britton, Ribaud ferist un honorable home, Justice arresta un que fayt fray deuant luy, et un auter luy rescussa. 22. E. 3. 13.

A. A.

A. A. Felony in biens est

In bonis abductis

Del person dascun home hinc surdont,

Robbery scilicet,

Sil prist de mon person licet soit south xii. d., Del lieu, ou ieo suis present. Sil manace de moy occider, ou fit moy iurer: Item sil gist en agayst, olim, contra hodie.
Hic de scinsors de burses: de queux Britton, 24, b.

Hic de Hue et Crye: Vide lest. de West. cap, 9. an, 3, E, 1. Lest, de Winchest, 13. E, 1: Lest, de. 28, E. 3, ca, 11. Et 27, Elis. ca: 17,

Pyracy Vide lest. 28, H, 6, ca. 13, Rastall, Tryall, 8.

Vel aliter, & est Larceny si supra xii. d. aliter n'est felony, mes petit Larceny per Stanford, q. atq; hic,

1. Agit in genere de Larceny, vbi,

Primum explicat naturam rei, & definit Larceny, et mette diuers cases et exemples: Larceny est fraudulenta rei alienæ pluris quam 12. d. valentis tractatio, animo furandi: inuito illo cuius res illa fuerit. Vide pag. 24. 25.

Deinde latius illustrat furtum per les adiuncts Vide, C. C.

2. De certis speciebus furti p statuta.

Recordes emblees, 8. H. 6. ca 12. Prisel del feme inuitz, 3. H. 7. cap. 2. Hunting in painted visors pur stealer Venison, et denier ceo 1. H. 7. ca. 7 Seruant prist les biens son maister, except prentises, et ceux que sont deins le age de 18. ans, 21. H. 8. cap. 7. Selling horses into Scotland, que est vn stealing d'eux hors D'england: 23 H. 8. cap 16. & 1. Elis. cap. 8. Souldier steale away sans licence, 2. E. 6. 2. Multiplication, 5. H. 4. ca. 4. Prisel de castels le roy, towers, ships, armor, ou practise de prendre: 14. Elis. cap. 1. Seruant stela les biens son mayster apres sa mort, et ne voet aperer apres proclamations, per lest. de 33. H 6. ca 1. Escipper lane forsq; a Calice, 18. h. 6. 15

Destructis et ceo per

Arsons des measons felonice, ou des Barnes adioinant al measons. Bourglours, que felonice in temps de peace debrusont measons, eglises, mures, towres, ports noctantes, licet riens import. Huc refer Drawlatches, Wastors, Robeardes men, que seront arrestes pur suspicion, per lest. 5, E. 3. 14.

C C. Illustrat Larceny per ses adiuncts. f.

De queux choses Larceny ne serra, Come de

Beastes sauages, columbes hors del douecoate, poysons in le ryuer, car nulluis in bonis. Cor. 185. 18.H.8.2. contre del debruser del douecoate, et prender les yong pigeons, 18: E:4:8. 10.E.4.15. embleer domesticall dame, felony. q. sil ne conust destre domestical, mes sil prist mort, cest felony.

Item serra de personel choses, et neiny de reall; itaq; si home succida arbre et prist, nest felony, contra si fuit succide deuant, Cor. 119. Box oue charters null felony, 10 E. 4.15. treasure troue, wrecke, del mere, wayf, stray prise, null felony: Cor. 187. 265. car incertum, quis dominus: contrà de bonis capellæ, Endit. 15.

Poet estre de ses proper biens, come beploy [sic] stela biens baylees, & tamen le propertie fuit en luy semper, 7.H:6: 45.13.E.4.10.

Larceny le possessiō estcant in le owner. q. pag 26.

Quis non potest cōmitter Larceny, s. quis ne serra dit larson comentque il prist &c.

Feme per coertion ou commandement son Baron, q. vt nec ioyntment oue son baron: car serra l'act le baron: mes feme poet, inscio viro. Item feme ne serra accessory pur receiuer son Baron.

Infant de tender age, come deins 12. ans per Bracton: mes contra hodiè.

Huc pertinet le tractate de Theftboote, quant home reprist ses biens emblees: mes propermient est, quant home prist ses biens dun laron pur luy fauorer: nest felony mes punishable per ranson & imprisonment. Ass. 346: tamen, Cor. 353. fuit felony. Biens confisques, que sont dones al roy, quia ne sont claymes per ascun auter, mes disauowed del laron. Vide Stanf. 186. diuersity inter biens confisques, et biens forfets. Wayf, quant le laron sur hue & crye & pursuite, pur easer luymesme del portage, wayua les biens ou part d'eux perque les officers le roy, ou auter in droit le roy seisist les biens, la le roy eux retiendra come waife, si non que le owner fait fresh suite, car donq; il reauera ses biens, issint, si le laron ne wayua, mes home in droit le roy prist eux de luy pur suspicion, le owner reauera sur fresh suyte. Null wayfe des biens prises per trespas: null wayfe de biēs d'un qui ad saufeconduite in bonis & corpore. 13.E.4.10. Freshsuyte, quant le party pursue le laron cy hastymēt que il luy apprehend oue le manor, et sur ceo port son appeale et luy conuince per verdit, mes hodiè suffist sil fait son deuoyr, comētque ne soit prise deins vn an apres, ou soit prise al suite d'un auter, et suffist conuiction sans atteynder. Mes per lest. 21.H. 8: ca. 11 il auera ses biens sur lenditement del felon, imò sil procure euidence destre done, sans ascun fresh suite, et semble, que si le seruant soit robbe, le mayster poet doner euydence et reauer &c.

B. B. Felony in le person, et ceo vel.

- in parte
  - Sublata come in
    - Couper des langues
    - Ouster des oyeles,
      - Vtrumq; felony per 5, H, 4, cap, 5,
        - Hic del Mayme, vbi le pl: poet eslyer de fayre chescun principal, ou solemēt cestuy que luy ferust, et les auters accessories. Mayme per Britton, est ou ascune member est toll dont home est pluis feble a cōbater, come oyel, mayne, pee, teste debruse, anterior dents: mes dents molliers, oraillés, neese, n'est mayme, eins blemishe, hic lex talionis, est lex Dei: mes nostre ley agard tout in dammages.
  - Corrupta per carnalem copulā: hæc copula est
    - Contrà naturā, & hæc vel,
      - Confusio.
        - Specierum, home ou feme oue brute beastes,
        - Sexuum, home oue home, feme oue feme,
          - ceo est Buggery, et est felony per lest: 25, H. 8, 6, & 5, Elis: cap: 17.
      - Incest, inter gradus prohibitos.
    - Secundùm naturam.
      - Scortatio inter personas solutas,
      - Adulteriū, cum altera persona est desponsata, vel vtraq;.
        - Si violence soit vse, dicitur Rape: fuit felony al comon ley: puis, trespas per lest: West: 1: cap: 13, tempore E. 1: postremò idem rex p West: 2: ca. 34, fist ceo felony, comētq; le feme assent apres: vide lest: de 6, R, 2, cap: 6, feuerall punishment vers le feme que consenta apres.
- In toto, D: D:

D.D. In toto, s. in occisione, cùm quis iniustè priuatur vita, hîc vide Stanf: del coroner et son poyer de veyer le corps, a pag: 48. ad. 53. et del vicount, que si decolla vn home ou doit luy pender, cest felony: Hîc agit.

- 1. De certen statutes come,
  - Per lest. de 3. H. 7. ca. 13. si ascun del hostell le roy conspire le mort le roy, seigniour de priuy counsayle, Steward, Treasorer, Controller del hostell, cest felony.
  - Wilfull poysoning est fayt felony, s. est fayt wilfull murder, per lest: de 2. E. 6. ca. 2.
  - Si Gaylor per dures fayt home apprauer, cest felony per lest, de 14. E. 3. ca. 9.
    Vide lest. de 1. et 2. P. et M. ca. contrà ægyptios: & 5. Elis. cap. 16. que fait conuration felony.
    Britten dit, que sorcerers et miscreants serront arses.
- 2. Del comen ley vbi,
  - 1. Breuiter describit ex Bracton, Homicidium est hominis occisio ab homine facta: sed ista descriptio nimis est specialis, & excludit Deodanda.
  - 2. Explicat latius per species, s.
    - Homicidium, manslaughter, sance malice prepence: hîc si ascun chose q; n'est home, tua home, le chose mesme, & tout q; est moue oue ceo. serra forfet come vn Deodand.
      - hîc volūtas olim fuit felony sans act, contrà hodiè.
      - Olim le stryking d'un feme pregnant, fuit felony, si il causoit abortum, mes hodiè doit estre in rerum natura, et deuy deins l'an & tour puis le coupe.
    - murder, auec malice prepence: hîc de felo de se.

Q.Q. Dictum est del offences: dicendum de penalties, et de maner vse in punishing, vbi considerantur.

- Le nature del suyt et ceo tùm
  - In le commencement del suyte, vbi docetur
    - Que serra iudg in le suyte, s. Iustices del banck, d'assise: et steward del hostel del chose deins le hostéll.
    - Que serra le meane de suer, s. per,
      - Appeale: G.G.
      - Inditemēt. P.P.
  - In le prosecuting del ceo, atq; hîc:
    - Del order in pleading. N.N.
    - Maner del tryall. T.T.
- Finall iudgement et determination del suyt. X.X.

A Logicall Analysis of

- G.G. Appeale atq; hic.
  - 1. Le general nature de appeles exponitur.
    - 1. Per vn briefe definition ex Brytton.
      - Appeale est pleynte del home fayt sur auter, ouesq; purpose de luy attaynder de felony, per motes a ceo ordeynes.
    - 2. per vn large explication conteynant
      - Certeyne generall adiuncts del apeles
        - Come, vers queux Appeale gist, s. vers touts, que poyent fayre felony.
        - Deins quel temps serra port, s. deins l'an et iour, in appeale de mort.q. de robbery et Rape.
        - Deins quel county. s. ou le felony fuit fayt. Vide lest. de 2. et 3. E. 6. ca. 24.
        - Deuāt queux. s. Coroner. vicount, Iustice de banck, et gaole deliuery, Iustice de peace.
        - Ou vn auera diuers appeles pur vn felony. Olim licuit auer vn vers le principall, et auter vers l'accessory. contra iam. Tamen in speciali casu licet, come si vn in vn county procure auter de robber moy en auter county.q.
        - Ou vn respondra al diuers appeales, s. home committ seuerall robberies as seuerall homes, il respondra al appele de chescune q. in mort ou rape.
        - Si l'appellant surcessa son appele per nonsuyte, releas, retraxit, mariage apres declaration, ou sil deuy, le roy pursuera, et le party ne irra alarg, mes serra arraigne al suit le roy sur mesme le declaratiō.
      - Le proces en appeale. M.M.
  - 2. Les particuler properties del singuler appeales:
    - Mort. S.S.
    - Robbery 4.4.
    - Rape. 88.

M.M. Le

- M.M. Le proces in appele ou inditemēt vt Capias, Exigent, Certiorari &c. 67: hîc le princi-pall serra primes artaint, et puis le accessary, 45. hîc
  - 1. Le maner del intreating les prisoners quant ils sont in prison, est declare
    - Vide lestatute de 14. E. 3. ca. 9. contra le crueltie de gaolers.
    - Vide lest. West. 1. ca. 13. que notorious et rebellious felons serront en pryson fort et dure.
    - hîc de Escapes. V. V. V.
  - 2. Le order,
    - del amesner eux al barre,
      - Per Britton, ils serront dischances, disceints, sans coif, en leur pure coat, hors de ferres, ne pœna faciat timidos: tamen p Bracton, propter euasionis periculum interdum compedes gestare possunt. Bract. lib. 2. Britt. fo. 14.
    - de lesser a mainprise
      - Per le comē ley ils ne serront mainprise—
        - Qui fueront prises pur mort dun home,
        - Per commandement le roy ou ses Justices.
        - ou pur le forest.
      - Per lest. West. 11. cap. 15. ne sont mainp.—
        - Utlages deuant, forjurors, prouors, prises oue le manor, debrusers del prison, notorious larons, appellees des prouors viuāt les prouors nisi soyēt de bone fame, arsōs, faussers del money, ou del seale le roy, excommēge per prier leuesque ou pur apert malueste, ou pur treason.
          - Itaq; ceux que sont indite de Larceny per inquest d'office ou pur leger suspiciō, ou pur petite Larceny, nisi sint culpable d'auter fayt, sōt mainpernables. Sic appellees del prouors puis le mort del prouor.

V.V.W.

A Logicall Analysis of

V.V.V. Escape per lest. 1 E. 2. de frã gentibus prisonam, rumper le prison n'est felony, si nõ q; il fuit imprison pur felony. Null escape devant arrest, hic,

- 1. Explicat le nature des escapes, tùm
  - Per quandam definitionem del prison, s.
    - Imprisonment n'est auter que un restraynt del libertie, itaque si home soit south arrest, come in cippes, ou in le possession de ascune home, cest un prison, et lescaping del ceo, est un debruser del prison.
    - Quin et rescus est rumper del prison, come si home prist le felon hors de ma possession.
  - per species
    - Voluntary.
      - Quant home arrest un, et puis lessa luy aler hors del boũdes del prison ou il veut, voluntariò.
    - Negligent.
      - Quãt un est arrest, et escape encoũter le volũt le arrestor, et n'est freshment pursue et repris devant que le pursuor ad perde le vieu del cestuy, que escape, Vide Stanf. 33.
- Ponit quædam generalia adiuncta.
  - Double escape, come
    - Home arreste, escape al eglise, et puis auxi fua del eglise: ceo est un doble escape.
  - Escape sans arrest, come
    - Home est murder in un ville, per le iour, ou in cytie mured, per le nuicte: le murdrer escape sans estre prise, cest un escape. Vide lest: de Winchester.
  - Que serra charge ouc lescape, s. le vicount, garden, ville, Hundred, &c. 34.
  - Coment escape serra trye et adiudge, car prisoners sont
    - per matter de recorde
      - Quant un present in court est committ al prison per le court: la si le garden n'ad luy semper prist, il est escape sans auter enquyry nisi ad reasonable excuse.
    - per matter en fayt
      - Quant un est arrest per le vicount, constable, ou auter, et escape, la il ne respondra al escape devant que l'escape soit present devant Justices.
  - Le penaltie
    - De voluntary, felony. De negligent, fyne. Si soit pur felony, Un hundred pound. Devant arrest, amerciament.

Particuler

Particuler appeales some sont,

- Appeale de mort. S.S.
  - Feme auera appele de mort son Baron, mes de null auter, le feme doit estre sa feme de facto & etiam de iure. Item doyt estre sole. Ou le feme poet auer appele, null auter auera ceo. Mes si le mort n'ad feme, son procheine heyre male per le comon ley auera ceo. vide 60.
- 4.4. De Robbery,
  - Seruant auera ceo.
  - Baylee.
  - Feme.
  - Infant.
  - Executors.
  - Merchauntes in comon.
- 8.8. Rape.
  - Feme sole rauy auera appele: feme couert oue son Baron: mes si el assent apres, tunc le Baron sole auera ceo, per lestat. de 6.R.2.ca.6. mes doyt estre Baron de iure & facto. Pur defaut del Baron, le pere ou auter procheine del sang auera le appeale.

A Logicall Analysis of

- F.F. Inditements. Si inditor discouer le counsell le roy, cest felony. Cor. 272. 207. hic describit.
  - 1. Le nature et forme del
    - bon Inditement
      - per lestatute
        - Vide lest. de 4. H. 4. cap. 2. 37. H. 8. cap. 8. que, les parols, vi & armis non ponentur in inditements de necessitate.
      - per comon ley, doyt estre,
        - certeine, in
          - le matter.
          - l'an.
          - le tour.
          - le lieu.
        - expresse, et nemy, per implication come
          - abduxit equum mal, sans cepit & abduxit.
          - Furatus, mal, sans felonice.
          - Carnaliter cognouit, mal sans rapuit, & tamen les auters parolls implyont tant, mes ceo formalitie serra use.
    - vicious et incerteine,
      - hic, et si ne vaut pur felony, tamen les Justices poyent fayre eux serue come inditementes de trespasse, a mitter le party al fine, et poyent agarder venire f. vers linditor d'amender lincerteintie.
  - Vide, 16. 16.

16. 16. 2. Cer

16.16.
2. Certeine adiunctes per statutes et autrement, come.

- Del statutes dinditementes in Leetes deins county Palatine, 33. H. 6. cap. 2.
  - 31. E. 3. cap. 14.
  - West. 2. cap. 13.
  - 1. E. 3. cap. 17.
  - 1. R. 2. cap. 4.
  - 1. E. 4. cap. 3.
  - Vide lest. Elis.
- Deuant Iust. de peace.
  - 1. H. 4. cap. vlt.
  - 3. H. 8. cap. 12. contra.
  - 3. H. 7. cap. 1.
- In vn county del chose fait in auter county
  - 33. H: 8: cap. 23.
  - 1: & 2: P: & M: 10:
  - 35: H: 8: cap: 2:
  - 33: H: 8: cap: 20:
  - 2. & 3: E: 6: 24:
- Le forme del inditement d'accessary, f. Que il exprescera le maner del felony, 81.
- Ou verdit in auter action ou returne del vicount serue pur Inditemēt, car.
  - verdit in auter action seruera, car il y ad vn verdit de 12. homes &c.
  - contra de returne de vicount licet soit matter de record. Vide lest: de 25: E: 3: ca: 4: de ceo.
- differēce inter appele et inditement.
  - In appele de mort, mortui nomen ponetur: contra del inditement, car le mort poet estre mangled, et issint incognitus.
  - Inditee pledra misnosmer del surnosme, et poet approuer, contra d'appellee.
  - Si appellee pria clergy, il ne vnque fra sa purgation, contra d'inditee.
  - In appeale le def. poet auer triall per battayle contra in inditement.

A Logicall Analysis of

N. N. Order in pleading, et

- 1. Le counte, que expressera le fact vel
  - come fuit fayt,
  - come le ley appoynt.
- 2. Le responce d'appellee, quel responce, vel,
  - Excuse, idq;
    - vel orderly et solonq; le ley, et ceo vel,
      - defence s.
        - Que il defenda touts maners de apeles, agaites, assauts, purpences, et quecunq; est encounter le peace le roy, sa corone et dignitie.
      - plees, que
        - vaout
          - al briefe, car le briefe abatera pur faux latyne, ou defaute del forme &c.
          - in barr, sontq; vel
            - proper
              - al appeale 333:
              - Inditemēt 444.
            - comon al ambideux, come,
              - Autersoits acquite. OO;
              - Sanctuary, RR.
              - Clergie, 555.
        - trenchont al fayt, come Rien culpable. 444.
    - perversly, hic del peine fort et dure. 10:10:10:
  - Confess. 7777777.

333 Barres

- 333. barres in appele, et hic,
  - 1. special et particuler barres, come
    - in appele de mort,
      - per le feme, a dire: que el est marye arere, que ne fuit unque accouple in loyal matrimony.
      - per le heyre:
        - Le mort ad feme in vie.
        - Il n'est heyre, eins ad eigne frere.
        - Il est bastard.
        - Ne fuit mort deins l'an et iour.
        - Le party n'est mort, eins in vie a tiel lieu &c. ou d'amesner lui in le court: ceux deux sont comon al feme.
    - In appele de robbery, a dire, que le pl: est son villein.
    - In appeale de rape per baron et feme: a dire, ne unq; accouple, ou a pleder villenage in le pl.
  - 2. generall, come a dire,
    - Le pl: est attaint de felony ou treason: est moigne: prestre, mayme per auter, insanus, surdus, mutus, lazar, ou foole naturall.
    - Le pl: auterfoits fuit nonsue in appele de mesme le felony apres declaration, ou fist un Retraxit, ou que le def: fuit attaint et acquite al suite le pl:
    - Le pl: ad releas al defendant.
    - Licet le pl: pleade issint in barre, tamen in fauorem vitæ il poet pleader ouster al felony, et son plee ne serra dooble, sinon in le case del releas, car per ceo il confesse le felony per implication: et quant le def: in appeale de robbery, pl. ade villenage in le pl: car s'il concluderoit ouster al felony, le pl: serroyt enfraunchise.

444: Barres all Inditement, come pardon le roy, vide Stanf. a pag: 99. ad 105. diuers statutes des Charters de pardon, et coment ils serront pleades.
OO. Auterfoits acquite de mesme le felony, vide Stanf. 105. &c. n'est ple iam in appele de mort per lest: 3. H. 7. cap. 1 Sic auterfoits conuict ou atteint semble bon plee, nisi il debrusoit le prison del ordinary et escape, car la il serra auterfoits arraigne sur l'inditement.

R.R. Sanctuary doit estre pleade al commencement sur l'arraignement, icy

- 1. Definit sanctuary.
  - Sanctuary est vn lieu priuiledge per le prince pur le safegard del vie del offendor.
  - Fuit founde sur le le ley de mercy, et sur le deuotions des princes al certeine lieues.
- 2. Agit del sanctuary men
  - Queux auerōt le priuiledge del sanctuary, queux non, vide plusors statutes reherses per luy, 208. &c.
  - Quomodo ils serront vse et demesnes. Vide statutes cites 115. &c. huc pertinet Abiuration, que est
    - 1. Define, Abiuration est vn serement, q; home priss quant il ad committ ascun felony et fua al eglise ou cimitory pur tuition de sa vie, eslyant pluistost perpetuall banishment hors del realme, que a estoyer al ley, et destre try del felony.
    - 2. Latius explicata, et reherse diuers statutes, 117. &c. del vsage des abiurors in Itinere &c.

555. Clergy

- 555. Clergye
  - 1. Del Clergy
    - Ordinarement per description.
      - Clergy est un auntient libertie del saynt eglise qua quiconque poet lyser, sil soyt arraine de felony devant seculer iudge, poet suer destre dismisse al ordinary, de faire sa purgation del dit offence. Liser come clerke, est lyser tout le verse. Licet speller.
    - Largely per adiuncts
      - Quant Clergy serra pleade,
        - Non sur son arraignement, vt quondam, eins il serra mise al responder al felony, et sil soyt troue culpable a son mise demesne, donq; il demandera sa Clergy; si non que le prisoner voyle Wayuer le benefite del ceo, et prier son. lyeur sang oyer le verdit.
      - Que serra iudge d'allower ou disalower ceo, s. le temporall court.
        - Car il appoynt le verse.
        - Il mett fine sur l'ordinary, sil dist, que Lysa, quant ne Lysa.
        - Il allowa clergie in absence del ordinary. Issint le court ne usa l'ordinary forsq; come minister a confirmer lour iudgement, quia est eruditus.
  - 2. Del clerke
    - quis auera ou non
      - per comon ley.
        - Il que ad ascune impediment destre priest, come blinde, mayme, sacrilegus n'auera, sic insidiatores viarum, depopulatores agrorum. Cestuy que tua se defendendo, ou per misadventure n'auera, nec petite laron, car ne sont de prendre iudgmēt de vie, traytor n'aucra: cestuy que confess felony n'auoit tanq; lest. artic. Cleri. Il que auoit semel, auereit rursus per comon ley tanq; lest. 4. H. 7. 13. mes home deins orders videtur exemptus. Bigamus auoyt tanq; lest. de Lyons, et ore lest. 1. E. 6. 12 accorde oue le comon ley in Bigamy.
      - Per lest. vide Stan. 125. vide lest. 1. E. 6. 12. 2. & 3. E. 6. 33: 5. & 6. E. 6. 10. & 9. 1. & 2. P. & M. 4.
    - Quomodo serra use, cap. 48. 49. 50. vbi, de purgation.

H H. Purgation fit per inquest des Clerks 139. ostendit.

- Quel Clerke,
  - Ferra sa purgation:
    - Clerke conuict: et est celuy que pria son Clergy deuant iudgement done sur luy del felony, et ad sa clergy allow: tiel Clerke poet faire sa purgation, si non in speciall cases.
  - Ne ferra
    - Clerke attaynt, et est celuy que pria son clergy apres iudgement, et ad son clergy allow, il ne ferra son purgation, coq; quant il est condemne del felony per iudgement, il ne puit contrary al iudgment estre purge de ceo, le dit iudgmēt remainant en sa force, itaq; vel paret pardon, vel demurrat in prison tout sa vie.
- Ou, non obstant Clergy allow, il ne serra deliuer al ordinary eins remaynera in prison le roy.
  - Si abiuror reuyent sans lycence, et esteant al barre, demaund sa Clergy, et ad ceo allow, uncore il ne serra delyuer al ordinary, eins serra mise a prison le roy tanq; il ad purchace pardon pur son reuenue: car coment q; le Clergy excuse le felony, uncore il ne tolle le contempt de reuenuer in le realme sance lycence.

444. Bien culpable exponit.

- 1. Le nature et forme del cest ple.
  - Car il pledra primùm son ple, et prira allowãce de ceo, et ouster, quant al felony, Bien culpable.
- 2. Les adiuncts.
  - Il est le plus usuall plee sur appele ou Inditement.
  - Quia trench al fayt, il est mult fauour in ley, car il auera cest plee puis que il ad plede in abatement ou barre del appeale ou inditement.
  - Chescune que est arraigne serra enforce a cest plee, si non quil ad matter de Iustification ou matter en ley de pleder, come sil tua le home de necessitie ineuitable pur aduancer Iustice, 13. 14. ou sil tua se defendendo, mes icy le necessitie doyt estre ineuitable. 13. 14. 15. 16.
  - Mes in cest ple de rien culpable, nauera ascune counsayle vers le roy sur inditement (contra in appele) mes pledra in proper person nisi le plee excede son connyng, quià cùm cest plee va al fayt, et le party mesme conust le fayt optimè, il poet mieux responder al ceo, et sil auoyt counsell, ils oue lour sophistry turbarent omnia, ou, si le party mesme parla, son cõscience luy poet stimuler, son gesture et countenaunce poyent declarer le verity, ou son symple parlance &c.

10. 10. 10.
Peruersly, vbi il expounde,

- Quel peruersity ceo doyt estre,
  - Quant cestuy que est arraigne sur felony (car in treason null tiel matter, vide lest. West. 1. cap. 12.) riens responde, eins estoit mute de malice et mal volunte, ou plede tiel matter que nest ascun responce al felony, ou tiel peruerse matter que ne directment respoigne, ou fayt tiel conclusion sur son plee, que il ne peut auer ascune tryall.
- Quomodò il serra vse, per peyne fort et dure:
  - Il serra remaunde al prison dont il vyent, et mise en vne base meason estoppe, et la girra nude sur le nude terre sans ascune littour, strps, ou auter drapes, et sans ascune garnishe enuyron luy, sauant vn chose que couera ses priuy members, et que il girra sur son dorse, et que son teste soit veste, et ses pees estrahees, et que vn brache soit trahe al vn quarter del meason oue vn cord, et lauter brache al auter quarter, et in mesme le maner soit fait de ses iãbes: et q; sur son corps soyt mise fer et pier tant come il poet porter et pluis. et le primer iour ensuant, il auera pane fayt de barly, troys morsells sans ascune boyer, et le second iour il boyera troisfoits, tant sicome il peut del eawe que est prochcine al huise del prison, except eawe currant, sans ascune pane, et ceo serra son dyet tanq; il soyt mort.

7777777.
Confession est le pluis sure respõce: apres confession il poet approuer: approuer aucra sa vie, quia il cõbata pur le peace, mes serra bã-nis le realme.

1. Expo-nit le na-nature del approuer.

briefly per description del etymoligy del nosme.

- Il peut approuer, s. accuser autres qui fueront coadiutors oue luy de fayre felony.
- Hinc dicitur approuor, s. probator, coque il doyt prouer, vel per battail, vel per pais, al election l'appellee, ceo que est cõteigne en son appeale.

Largly per adiuncts.

- De queux offences home approuera, s. de ceux felonies tantùm queux il ad fayt oue auters.
- En queux actions
  - In null action, nisi inditement soyt action, car in appeale il ne approuera, car sic il delayeroit le pl. dauer execution de luy, mes il poet conuster l'inditement, et prier corouer, et sic approuer.
- Deuant queux
  - Ceux que poyent assigner luy Corcner, come Iustices de banks, Eyre, Gaoledeliuery. cõtra de Iust. de peace, Steward & sutors in court Barõ, viscount et sutors in le county court, sans commission.
- coment il serra vse,
  - deuant son apprower.
    - Il doyt confesser et prier le Coroner deuant ascune ple plede. Sil mentu, le court luy tollera de son appele. Il serra iure d'appeller de touts felonies et treasons que il sacha, certen nomber des iours serra a luy appoynt, in chescune de queux, il doyt apprower, ou serra pendus.
    - Il auera gages chescun iour i. d, del roy, quant le corouer est assigne a luy, il serra lesse hors del prison, de appeller sans coertion.
  - Apres
    - Quant il ad fayt son appeale deuant le Coroner il rehercera ceo deuant Iustices, car ils ne voylent leer ceo a luy, et sil fayle in ascun paroll que le Coroner ad record, il serra pendus, come sil dit blanche chyuall pur rouge &c. Car per le repugnancy serra intende que il mentu.

vide, α α α. 2.

A Logicall Analysis of

aux. 2. Dappellee vbi exponit.

1. le proces vers lappellee.

Si lappellee soit in mesme le countie ou lappeale est fayt le Coroner agardera proces tanq; al exigent.

Si in auter county, tunc les Justices devant queux le Coroner record le dit appeale, come Just: de banck, et Vyre per comon ley, et del gaoledeliuery, per lest. de 28. E. 1.

ses exceptions vers l'approuor.

Que il est attaynt de treason ou felony.
Que il est Clerke conuict.
Que il n'est imprison pur felony ou treason, eins pur dette ou trespas.
Que il n'est prisoner, eins alarge.
Que il est deins age, ou ouster l'age de 70. ans, prestre, feme, maime &c.
Si l'appellant apres son appele, est pendus, ou prist soy a son clergy, le roy poet pursuer l'appellee, et auer luy arraigne &c. Imò si soyt destre discharge vers le roy et party, le court poet luy lyer de se bene gerendo.

T. T. Maner

T. I. Maner del Tryall.

- In inditement est vel,
  - Proper al peres del realme, s. per 12. pares al meynes,
    - Vide le order, Stanf. fol. 133. & ceo serra tantùm in Judgements, et nemy in appeles.
  - Comõ as auters, s. per pais, per hões de vicineto ou le felony fuit fait, et serue al Inditement et appeale. exponit,
    - 1. De quel county le pays viendra.
      - Vide lest de 2. et 3. E. 6. cap. 24. quant felony est fayt en un county, et le receipt in auter, le tryall in un, et bon. Vide lest. 22. H. 8. cap. 14. & Stanford. pag. 154.
    - 2. per quel proces, s. venire facias: Habeas corpora: Distingas, hic del,
      - Tales, 155.
      - Nisi prius. 156. 157.
      - Challenge,
        - peremptory sans cause in fauorem vitæ, al nomber de 35. per comon ley, mes per lest: 22. H. 8. cap. 14. tantùm. 20.
        - per cause
          - Come, il fuit son Inditor &c.
          - Et al array, si teuts sont engloys vers estranger.
          - Item pur defaut de franckteneement, Vide lest. de 27. Elis.
      - Euidence, chescune serra admit a doner euidence pur le roy. 163.
      - verdit, estq;
        - vel generall.
        - Speciall, s. alarge, quant ils doubtont an soyt felony.
- In appeale hic triall per battayle est allowe. Si appelle plusers d'un felony, il cõbatera oue teuts, lune apres l'auter: describit,
  - Le order del cõbate ex Britton, 41. Vide Stanf. 117.
  - Les counterplees al battayle, s.
    - Ascune presumption, come sil fuit endite pur ceo, ou prise oue le manor.
    - Que il esteant arrestu, fua, ou debrusa le prison.
    - Imbecilitie in l'appellant, si soyt maime, deins 14. ans: ou ouster 70.
    - Deins order, ou feme.
    - Item privilege del person, come sil soyt arraigne al suite le roy in lappeale. Le def. acquite recouera dammages vers le pl: ou, sil ne soit sufficient, vers les abettors. Vide Stanf. a pag. 168. vsq; ad 117.

A Logicall Analyſis of

X.X. Final iudgement, vbi,

- Exponit les ſeueral iudgmentes, ſ.
  - Del felony, quòd ſuſpendatur per Collum.
  - Treaſon
    - Grande,
      - In home, Il ſerra reameſnue al lieu dont il vient, et ſerra trahe ſur vne hurdle ieſq; al lieu dexecutiō, et la deſtre pendus per le colle, et viue deſtre decoupe, et ſes entrayles et pryuy members deſtre exciſes de ſon corps, et combures deins ſon view, et ſon teſte deſtre abſciſſe, et ſon corps deſtre dyuyde in quater parts a diſponer al volunt le roy.
      - In feme, deſtre trahe et combure tam in grande treaſō quàm petite.
      - Si feme ſoit enſeinte de viue enfant, el ſerra ſemel reſpite del execution, mes le iudgement ſerra done mayntenant.
    - Petite: In home, eſt deſtre trahe et pendus. pur miſpriſion il forfetra ſes biens, mes nemy terres forſq; pur vie, et ſerra in perpetuall priſon. q. Vide Stanf. 37. 38. diuers ſeuerall penalties accordant al offences.
- les penalties, que enſuōt ceſt Judgemēt, & implicantur etſi non exprimuntur,
  - Corruption del ſangue vient per atteinder del felony ou treaſon, iſſintq; les infants ne poyent eſtre heires a luy, ne al aſcune auter aunceſtor. Et ſil fuit noble ou gentleman deuant, il et touts ſes infants ſont deuenus ignobles, et ceſt corruption ne poet eſtre ſalue forſq; per Parlement ſolement.
  - Forfeiture. ωωω.

ωωω. For-

Forfeiture.

- 1. que serra forfet, &c.
  - **Biens pur treason et felony.**
    - Clerke conuict forfetra ses biens, comentq; ad fayt sa purgation, et les issues del terre que il ad in son droyt, ou in droyt sa feme, tanq; il ad fayt sa purgation.
    - Home forfetra son droyt al biens, et chose in action, come obligation &c.
    - Item il forfetra biens in queux il n'ad ascune propriete, come ieo bayle argent hors del bag a rebayler a moy, le baylee est attaynt, le roy auera l'argēt, car ne poet estre conues &c. quia hors de bag.
    - Home forfetra ses Chatteaux sur *fugam fecit* comentq; soyt acquite del mesme le felony, ou ad son charter de pardon pur mesme le felony. cest fuer en fayt.
    - Home forfetra ses biens sur exigent agard, sur vn fuer en ley, comentq; soit acquyte del felony.
    - Home poet forfeter ses biens sans attainter per presentment apres sa mort, Come
      - Felo de se.
      - Home arrestue fua, et est tue in le pursuyte, ou il soit tue deuāt le arrest, *repugnando*, &c.
      - Home que leua guerre, et est tue in ycell.
    - Quant vn est troue culpable del homycide deuant le Coroner, le Coroner seisera ses biens et lyuera al ville. Sur *fugam fecit* troue deuant le Coroner, le vicount ferra in mesme le maner. Mes si vn soyt indite del mesme le felony, ses biens ne serront remoues hors de sa meason tanq; il soyt attaynt, eins serront en garde les vicins, et le felon auera viands de ceo. Le ville serra charge oue le custody des biens, nisi ils poyent monstre, que auter ad eux. Mes le vicount est *semper* chargeable oue les issues del terre.
  - Vide λλλ
- Vide *** 2.

xxx. Terres et droyt del terres serra forfet pur treason ou felony. mes hic l'estate serra consider, car

- Tenant pur vie ou ans ne forfetra forsq; pur son terme, sic pur petite treason ou felony, tenant in tayle ne forfetra forsq; pur sa vie, contra in grand treason, per lest 5. et 6. E. 6. cap. 11. et per mesme lest home ne forfetra terre que il ad in auter droyt, come in droyt sa feme, sa eglise &c. vna cum terre, les charters del terre serront forfets.
- Pur treason del barõ, (grãd et petite) le feme perdra sa dower; mes nemy pur felony, per lest. 1. E. 6. cap. 12. 5. & 6. E. 6. cap. 11.
- In petyte treason ou felony le roy auera l'an, iour, et Waste des terres que sont tenus d'auter que de luy, et donq; le seignior auera lescheate, mes in grand treason, le roy auera lescheate, de quocunq; le terre soit tenus.

xxx. 2. Quant serra forfet, Relation del forfeture.

- In terres il relate al temps del act fayt mayntenant, itaque sil done ou alien apres le fayt, le relation del attaynder defeatera tout.
- Mes in biens nest issint, car le done de eux inter le felony et lattaynder, est bon.

FINIS.